The Rags of Time

A MEMOIR

"Love, all alike, no season knows, nor clyme,
Nor houres, dayes, moneths, which are the rags of time."

John Donne (The Sunne Rising) 1601

The Rags of Time

A MEMOIR

Susanna Jaffe Schwartz

HUDSON
HOUSE

Cover design: Jay Cookingham
Interior design: Jay Cookingham

ISBN: 1-58776-821-6
Library of Congress catalog card number: 2004104834

Manufactured in the United States of America

0 1 2 3 4 5 6 7 8 9 10 NetPub 0 9 8 7 6 5 4 3

HUDSON
HOUSE

675 Dutchess Turnpike, Poughkeepsie, NY 12603
www.hudsonhousepub.com   (800) 724-1100

An Acknowledgement

To my good friend and editor, Emily Mitchell. Editor of redundancies, and the occasional word or phrase; many times bitterly contested, usually over shared coffees; some changes agreed to, others challenged.

Mostly, especially, my deepest gratitude for a friendship which understood she could not edit my life, I give thanks and love.

S.J.S July, 2003

The Rags of Time

Chapter 1

Is this the time?

Do I really want to do this? Relive? Re-life?

I'm not so sure…not even after the vantage point of a life almost ended.

Years ago, twenty perhaps, I imagined I had a book in me. Something I termed "the eternal triangle": my husband, my son, me. With astounding ego I thought it might interest others. I might have called it, "Memoirs of a Revolutionary" since throughout my life, from a very early age, I had done things and acted in ways unusual to my friends but accepted by my family.

I am now the last inhabitant of my universe.

Perhaps I only know myself symbolically since the death of my husband and son. But did I need two deaths to define me?

I was born to Russian, Jewish, parents, cultured intelligentsia, under the signs of water, music, love, art. THAT defined me to myself in childhood. I felt the *signs* as of sweets offered to my hands, but not so close as to touch them, rather as things to acknowledge, to desire, to come to terms with in life-long, bitter-sweet relationships.

So perhaps now **I** can consume, I who was always known as the nurturer, the giver of life, and laughter, and obedient to the demands of reality, and to the current situation…"Die Kleine Dame," my yearnings again pocketed somewhere within.

The Rags of Time

I think I am finally too old to obliterate my own demands on ME.   I cry now, not from physical pain, but from that karma of a life that demanded, yet never satisfied. I have never liked the idea of patience, of sacrifice, of all the artifacts I have loaded my life with, lived my life by.

Forbearance, tolerance…these are not virtues, but are usually hypocritical and denigrating, insulting…not applicable to me at all.   Am I finally truthful? These "virtues" don't bespeak love or acceptance, but are usually second-hand in face of what love demands: honesty, at least to oneself.

My parents met and married in America, each having emigrated from different Russian cities and backgrounds. My mother was a musician, a pianist. My father read extensively, wrote "Dickensian" letters, and declaimed Gogol, Tolstoy, Dostoyevsky. That he became a businessman was the laughable result of Americanism so proudly embraced by my slightly dishonest grandfather.

Father should have been an Edwardian Gentleman, and disported himself as a man who owned land and "souls." Or perhaps had owned an estate under the Tsar! The *declamatia* went over very well at family parties. Gypsy music was played, and sung to, and even danced to, accompanied by my mother on the piano or classical guitar.

Many times police were called by neighbors in our apartment house, as they yelled, "Those damned Russians are at it again!" But the police were kind, the windows shut, and an admonition given. My father gave his thanks together with a glass of vodka, and from my mother, a *nosh*, all gratefully received, and thus ended the Russian nightclub…at least for that Saturday night!

My six years older brother Nathaniel, was a musical wunderkind who at age two and a half, having been taught by my mother, wrote several short piano compositions, which were published. My parents foresaw another Mozart.

As an infant, I suckled to Bach, Beethoven, Mozart, Chopin, all of whom were taken in together with breast milk. I was also weaned from "Malz Bier," which all German-born babies received as formula.

Perhaps the following story is apocryphal, but it was handed down that when I came home from the Berlin Hygeia, I was deposited in the nursery in my wicker basket, as was the custom. Today we use such a one for laundry. When my nurse re-entered the nursery, brother Nat was in the act of tossing me, basket and all, out of the third floor window, saying disgustedly, that I was tiny, red and ugly! I was rescued, Nat reprimanded, but perhaps it presaged his treatment of me in later years!

As my parents were at the time living in Berlin, when he was five, brother Nat was auditioned at the Berlin Conservatory of Music, where mother hoped to enroll her little Mozart. Part of the admission procedure was to station Nat outside a closed door, where he was to identify the various notes played, and it seems that he was pitch and note perfect. Next, he listened to one of the professors play a sonata, and Nat replayed it perfectly, to their astonishment. He was proclaimed a brilliant young pianist, but too young for admission, and given over to one of the instructors until he was some years older.

The following story of my birth is the truth. After a party they attended, my mother asked my father to take her home as she felt queasy, instead of which he took her to the hospital. Mother insisted that she'd just eaten too much, but father was adamant. At the hospital, mother asked to go to the toilet, and my father accompanied her. There I was literally dropped, between her thighs, into the water of the bowl. My father screamed, a nurse ran in, scooped me out of the water, cut the umbilicus, and later the physician who examined mother and me said, "Frau Yoffe, you might have waited!" But it seems I could not wait to enter the world…and take it on!

Is this the time for truth? I'm not certain, nor am I a strong believer in Truth as understood by society. I've always thought it to be a highly over-rated virtue! There are events and feelings I've experienced in my life which I've not shared with anyone.

Shall I then share them with you?

One of my earliest memories of release from the constraints of social custom, of setting myself against what one did or did not do if one were the child of Jewish middle-class intelligentsia, was to rebel inwardly, deep within, against the statement so often expressed to her friends by my mother, a raven-haired beauty, that, "Susie is not pretty, nor even attractive, but oh, so intelligent, so good-natured, so artistic, so witty!"

The Rags of Time

In a creative-writing class in high school, our gentle-voiced, sweet-faced, boyish looking teacher, gave an assignment to write a short, autobiographical sketch. "For instance", said he, "I was born in an apple orchard in France, and…"And", I broke in loudly, "I was born in a toilet bowl in Berlin!" I felt myself no longer able to breathe in the cloying, sentimental air that engulfed the classroom, the sickening adoration of the adoring students!

Amid the laughter that followed, the mood was broken, the teacher (whom I also adored) joined the laughter. He asked to see me after class to discuss the upcoming Rembrandt Exhibition at the Metropolitan Museum, and suggested that since I was an artist, or at least had such pretensions, would I act as guide for the class? It was a flattering and frightening prospect. In puppy love, I agreed!

The first of many truths! I had accepted a "bribe" from another student who imagined I could help her enter the school's honor society, ARISTA, of which I was a member. The bait was a photograph of our teacher. The photograph I placed in the mirror of my dressing table, and I always turned it to face the mirror when I undressed. I was 14 years old, and often rode past my subway stop in Brooklyn, into Manhattan, where he lived, to be able to speak with him one-on-one, listen to his stories, share his space.

Was he always truthful? I never asked!

The Rembrandt Exhibit was another chance to shine. I read, took notes, studied Rembrandt, and carried a small notebook with me to the exhibit. I was prepared, but not for the many erotic etchings exhibited. I used my inner notes, and told the class of the many voyeurs shown in paintings other than by Rembrandt. Rembrandt included voyeurs, as did the Chinese and Japanese artists of the past.

How did I know this? All is open for view in the books of Russian intelligentsia, even in the glass-fronted bookcase, which faced the front door of our apartment. The bookcase was locked, but the key was kept in the lock. At age ten, I had discovered Boccaccio's "Decameron," profusely illustrated with erotic etchings. I pored over these two volumes in our toilet when my parents were out. I had never been told that these books were out-of-bounds, but felt instinctively that it was the better part of wisdom to keep mum about this particular set. Interestingly, the "Decameron" was one of the few books in English in a home which owned books in four languages. I was always being told, "Oh, Susie, if only you could read this in the original language!"

Atop my living room credenza, is a sepia photograph of my attractive six-teen-year-old mother seated at her piano in Russia. She wears a white, sprigged muslin blouse, dark skirt and a gaily-embroidered apron. Her head is turned towards the photographer, her fingers rest atop the piano keys. I have that apron still. It was sewn, embroidered, the lace crocheted by my great-grandmother. The lace is somewhat frayed now, but all the colors are still clear. I used to wear it when my husband and I hosted our annual Zakuska party, a traditional Russian buffet/feast, sometimes of over twenty dishes. I also used my mother's lovely silver Art Nouveau Samovar in which to serve tea, *chai.*

Other memories of my mother are not as beautiful. I realized early on, that a lovely competitive mother was not to be trusted in company of my young men friends with whom she flirted, whom she charmed, and who fell under her spell, so I didn't invite them home, but met them elsewhere. They did not see me, having seen her.

So much for the truth. I loved my parents, trusted them, but not with my life. I was expected to be intelligent but to hide the fact, because as my mother repeatedly told me, "Boys don't like girls who are smarter!" A protective shell was beginning to encase me from an early age. I learned to shield myself from hurt by reading and drawing, and by articulating to adults what they wanted to hear, to judge myself from their approbation of my good sense, good grades, my talents, by things I would have gladly exchanged for acceptance of me, ME, as I was, NOT as a wunderkind!

Truth! I learned to keep my counsel. I yearned to make my parents proud of me, but on my own terms. To make MYSELF proud was the first discipline I self-imposed.

My father was a jealous man. My mother's flirtations, even indiscretions about which I knew, but kept silent, must have given him pain. He adored me. I could do no wrong. One of my realizations of his feelings was when I graduated from high school. My brilliant pianist brother had preceded me in American schools, and as his musical reputation grew, in every grade I entered, I was asked, "Oh, are you Nat Jaffe's sister? Are you also a musician, a pianist?"

I resolved that having great love for, but no particular musical ability, I would find my own way. I had wanted to be a ballet dancer as a small child, but family finances were such, that two talents could not be funded. My mother found a dance school in the neighborhood which charged 25 cents for tap-dance lessons! My hurt, rage really, made me quit after two lessons. My excuse? "I really want to draw, to become an artist!" That seemed a relief to my parents because paper, crayons, watercolors were to be had for pennies, and did not involve an instructor.

At seventeen, after graduating from high school, I longed to be able to attend an out-of-town college, but we couldn't afford it. I shortened my sights to Brooklyn College and the Cooper Union for the Advancement of Art and Science, a prestigious Art school in Manhattan which I could attend for free if I passed two examinations…a full scholarship, IMAGINE! I did pass the tests and out of about seven hundred and fifty applicants from all over the United States and abroad, I was among the two hundred and fifty students accepted! Carfare was 5 cents each way from Brooklyn to Manhattan.

I was so excited that summer.

On one of our daily evening walks, my parents and I played a game of childhood memory. We used to sing operas, concertos, symphonies, and tap the rhythm on another's arm, and we would have to identify the musical selection. It was fun, as we strolled the two or three miles in each direction. One evening my mother was silent, then serious, then said that I should prepare myself to make a living by studying stenography and typing.

I was stunned, and as I shrunk and wept inwardly, my father said angrily, "NO! Susie has been a wonderful student, SHE wants this, has done it on her own, has earned this chance, has never asked us for anything, so she WILL have this chance", he yelled. "We have always given Nat everything, now it is her turn!" My mother was silenced, and I learned what I had not before known, that my father could only be pushed so far!

From that moment my love for my father was unequivocal. Oh, not to say we didn't buck heads, but I felt a security, a love, a strength in my father of which I was unaware.

The Rags of Time

Of course, as intelligent as I am, as quick to learn a new skill, I have NEVER, to this day, been able to take dictation or type with other than two fingers! In the wonderful film made of Michael Ondaatjie's "The English Patient," Katherine says to her lover Almasy, "A woman should never learn to sew, and if she can, she should never admit it!"

What advantage Truth?

And yet I loved my mother, perhaps because I could never give up my need for a perpetual goad to my resistance to conformity; salt in the wound? As a tongue probes an aching tooth? Whatever, it evidently worked. My life seems a series of open wounds, probed, lacerated, worked over! Not happy, but feeling, always feeling something, reacting to the pain, the probe. Lusty, gutsy melancholy! My Slavic Soul!

In my Art School years, which I always called the happiest years of my life, I experienced my first independent Ego trip! Greenwich Village...the Artist Life...HOOHAH!

My munificent five-dollar weekly allowance translated into ten cents daily carfare, about a dollar a week for art supplies, lunch money. Sometimes I was able to treat less affluent friends to lunch consisting of an English Muffin with butter and cream cheese and jam and coffee, for fifteen cents! For more lordly fare, twenty-five cents bought a freshly made, large, chicken or beef pot pie at the Horn and Hardart Automat. Tomato soup could be concocted using the ketchup which was at each table, and adding the boiling water meant for the teabag! When in Greenwich Village, do as the Villagers...

WELL? Is my life to be brick by brick, or prick by prick?

Cooper Union was both these. Here no one knew my mother was a flirt, my father an Edwardian (therefore, unsuccessful) businessman in America where success is measured by the financial scale and ruler and T-Square, not the "Russian Intelligentsia" scale of Intellectual and Artistic Accomplishment. The quotation marks are mine. My life is made up of quotation marks, or divisions between "Culturnye" or "Nieculturnyie" (accompanied by a sneer)! Unparented, my Ego birthed, my umbilicus stretched, and was cut by Cultural Shears!

The Rags of Time

Of course, there were occasional flames of uncertainty, never to be shown, hidden under good-humor and smiles, and eagerness to be worthy of my fellow students' talents. Did I see my own talents? No, I was still my family's "good child", acquiescent, obliging, leaving few ripples of my presence. THAT would take more time. I obviously planned my debut into talent, into wit, into belonging.

But, my name and looks were suddenly introduced, not by me, but by my long, wavy, red-hair, so long I could sit on it, and by my name Susanna, the only redhead and the only Susanna in school. So, despite my desire to blend, I made a mark of sorts! I STOOD OUT, and unbelievably I also became known as the author of original songs, some of which I performed at our Annual Artists Ball, singing them in a not-too-bad baritone. I wrote the words to popular songs of the day. Even the staff and famous guests and Alumni, asked for copies! I shamelessly aped the foibles of instructors and Dean...well I HAD always wanted a reputation of my own!

One of the more popular songs I called, "Ode to Carol Harrison" and I performed it at the Cooper Union Artists Ball of 1944.

"Ode to Carol Harrison"

I am sick of that black, brown, and grey,
I'm tired of artists who paint that way.
My painting's a problem
Xcept Carol's way.
I either make with free space
Or decorate like Klee.
The sunsets ain't for us kids,
Nor is an Autumn day.

The Persians are dears from way back,
Oh Lord, what is it that I lack?

She either shows Picasso, or she
Shows that "dirty" Braque,
And if you don't like Dufy
You can throw away your smock!
Dufresne is mighty,

The Rags of Time

But here's what I say,
I'm sick of that black, brown, and grey!

What's good is in Paree,
What's left will never harm me,
And when I see the Louvre,
I'll be a chef d'oeuvre,
And when I get to Pisa,
I'll kiss the Mona Lisa,
And Rembrandt's chiaroscuro,
Is just a lot of bull-throw!

Oh, Wallace is weighty,
But here's what I say,
I'm sick of that black, brown, and grey!

So, even in Art, I lied…or at least fudged the truth! Only in my somewhat scathing imitations was I, in my mind, truthful…or at least recognizable. I came in each day, and announced that today I would paint a "Picasso" or a "Braque," and I would proceed to paint in THAT style and with the same colors used by "whichever" artist, in his palette! My fellow-students thought me an amusing character, and the instructors put up with me because my "opuses" WERE in style, and had captured the lessons put to the class.

I worked hard, but it was, for me, sheer pleasure, and soon I couldn't get enough, was seen everywhere, attempting everything, begging the Staff to be allowed to take night classes with no instruction, for no credit, "Please, just let me sit in the back and try to do what the night school students and their instructors are working on, PLEASE!" And so of course they agreed. I still don't understand WHY Dean Clark allowed this, but bit by bit I drank in, swallowed, spit out, another set of lessons!

I also received a part-time job through the National Youth Administration program which paid me 50 cents an hour to work in the Art School's Main Library, where my duties were to assist the librarians, and consisted primarily, after putting books in stacks, in evicting the homeless who slept in the wooden chairs, elbows on tables, in an effort to sleep off their alcoholism, and who used the toilets. A very few thought to evade authorities by having an open book as disguise. Of course, I never noticed them until the library closed at 10 PM.

I was also assigned to help out in the wonderful Cooper-Hewitt Museum, which at the time was still housed in the school's Main Building. That assignment gave me my first glimpse into the world of ancient textiles, furniture, and artifacts I might never have come into contact with. It was a heady experience and one which I soaked up, and which led to my interest in antiques of many periods…AND which contributed to my "good eye" for all of my life…and for the many things we collected!

Have I said that I was also, from the age of eight or nine, a political creature? During the Spanish Civil War, some friends and I, or I alone, stood outside our local subway station and collected donations for the Republican cause. We also went often to the many apartment houses in the neighborhood, to collect clothes to be sent to Spain. I felt very safe at the subway station, even at night, because I was known to the owner of a tiny used-book store tucked away into the corner of the building, where, 25 cents allowance in hand, I bought books. You will notice the plural. I bought many treasures for 5 and 10 cents. I no longer remember WHAT I bought from the time I was six or seven, only that the printed page held a drug-like fascination, still with me.

I was a member, at age ten or eleven, of a group called "The American League Against War and Fascism," probably, as I look back, a Communist, or certainly Socialist, organization. We staged plays in the neighborhood, one called "Alice in Nazi-land," in which we youngsters sat around a table, as at a tea party, and each time the Mad Hatter yelled, "Next," we all moved up a seat, and someone was bumped to the floor! I can't recall how successfully this supposed awakening to the evils of Fascism played to the audience, this creative depiction of the take-over of country after country by the Nazis, but we actors enjoyed it.

Were my parents aware of this activity? Oh yes, and if they didn't altogether approve, they knew where I was and that I was safe, and involved in educating myself, or perhaps it was their own social awareness from the time THEY were children in Tsarist Russia, the pogroms they knew of and had spoken to me about, their experiences with bureaucracy and the excesses of the Tsar, the constant awareness that as Jews, no matter their economic status, they were never safe, because that could change at the flick of a Cossak's whip, or a flick of his horse's tail!

When my mother came to America with her parents, it was as a tourist to visit her mother's cousins who lived in Newport, Rhode Island. These relatives, whom my grandmother had visited in the past, owned a hardware store, and for years at "Gymnasium" in Russia, mother had among other courses, studied French and English and was used to translating letters received from them by others, and also wrote letters for them in English to be sent abroad.

Mother was just seventeen and lovely, and in "Nevport Rud Eesland!" After several weeks she complained to my grandparents that she had not come to America to see another small town! "Where do you want to go?" asked her adoring parents. To "NEV YORK" she exclaimed! So they went to New York City and it was shortly thereafter that the Russian Revolution erupted.

There was now no going back as their small hotel for show people had been confiscated, according to information sent by my mother's half-brother, who was an active revolutionary, and who had played his part in the Tsar's overthrow. My grandfather told me when I was in my teens, that his son, Volodya, used to take my mother to "cell" meetings when she was very small, despite his stern warnings.

It seems that because of my grandfather's love affair with the theatre, he had the first Black entertainer, Mr. Cakewalk, as one of his roomers. Also a husband and wife midget couple, and various acrobats and singers, dancers, tragedians, etc…who were rarely accorded space in the more prestigious hotels in Vilna and Minsk. There was a prejudice in those days against "Theatrical Folk." As a child I very much enjoyed hearing about the show-people, and of how the midget-wife physically frightened her slightly smaller husband as they sat at the dining table, elevated by the piles of books or small stools, on the dining-room chairs! He told me that Mr. Cakewalk danced and swaggered in his costume and spats when the troupe paraded in town.

My grandparents had come with gold rubles, and clad in mink-lined caracul coats, and also had much Russian paper currency, so they decided to remain and settle in New York City, in East New York, then a Jewish enclave. My grandmother kept house, my grandfather eventually became a corset salesman, going house to house with his wares, since work was scarce for a foreigner with little English as yet, and one who had been a theatre company's accountant!

All the above is the Truth. Does it make it interesting…or even important to this tale of Love Triangulated? I'm not sure it makes it "beautiful" if "Beauty is Truth, Truth is Beauty," a canard and cliché. Can't imagine that phrase made into our language and lasted this long! Keats should have heeded his own aphorism and become a "foster-child of silence and slow time."

I DO like that "slow-time" bit, however.

As I look back over my life, I cannot ever recall a "slow time." From flame to flame, italic and quotation to italic and quotation, I won't let it be, even now, in my loneliness. Rather would I chafe, burn, rail at fate! My son grins at me in a photo. Better to cry and shout as I do, usually to music! In years past, I remember that when I was unhappy and frustrated, I lit every lamp in the house, as though light could ease me, could search out the shadows of my soul.

Never happened!

My father arrived in America as a fifteen year old, and so hated New York, that he begged to go back to Russia. There, his family had indeed, owned a small estate and employed serfs (whom Gogol termed "Souls"), non-Jews, who worked the farm. My grandfather was a bit of a rake, who sold a "Gold Cure" for syphilis to the gullible. Grandpa Aaron apprenticed my father to Jacob Schiff, who led the senior banking house of Kuhn, Loeb and Company, and who was also the subway-building magnate of his day. My father helped with his office work, and continued at school. The family lived in one of the "better" neighborhoods of the time, in Harlem, in an area of brownstones and middle-class Jews. It was 1905.

My parents met in Manhattan when my mother, looking for a public telephone in East New York, went into an office building, opened the door of an Import/Export company, asked the occupant (my paternal grandfather) if he knew where one was to be found. Fascinated by her accent and striking looks, he was supposed to have said to himself that she must meet his two sons. So the tale was handed down to us, and not disputed by my father.

The Rags of Time

Neither of our families was traditionally religious, but I remember as a child, accompanying my parents to Synagogue during the High Holy Days of Rosh Hashanah, Yom Kippur, Passover, or perhaps to say the Kaddish, the prayer for the dead, for some friend or relative. When I was seven, my brother Nat was a Bar Mitzvah. I remember little of that. Was I even there?

I later learned that my father had been a Hebrew Scholar in his youth. This was revealed to me when our son attended a Hebrew Day School because the public schools would not accept a child in a wheelchair. Although it was not from choice, it added a dimension to our son that he probably would not otherwise have enjoyed, and he became a rather devout youngster. My father became his mentor in that area of his life and education.

My father spun tales to Nat and to me that during his education under the Tsar, he and his brother Sam were "required" to be the best students at Gymnasia, or the privilege of attending with non-Jews would be revoked! My father was always an excellent student, at Cheder and at the Gymnasium, but my darling Uncle Sam was not, and regularly my grandparents paid someone to take exams in his name so that he might remain, and pose as a top student.

Shall this story proceed in real time?

Let us reverse to happiness at Cooper Union, amidst Ego-strikes, mine own that is! Here I was no one's sister. I was now my own italic! I made friends, one of whom I kept and loved my entire life, an upper class student I realized was homosexual, although the word was never spoken between us. Herman was a brilliant student, very talented artist, who wandered through the school, and through my life as a beloved companion, a sharer of my woes, I of his, only I realized later that we had once been in love with the same boy! We cried to each other when neither of us was successful in forming a relationship with him. I found out that this fellow I fantasized about, and cried over, and that I hoped would relieve me of my virginity, thought of me as "exotic" because I was Jewish, he, a Protestant.

In the end, I relinquished the relationship. Did I say Truth? How Herman would have enjoyed that phrase, "in the end"! He would have roared with laughter because, THAT was Herman's fantasy! Indeed, Herman was the most amusing person I have ever known. After a day spent in his company, my stomach ached from laughter.

Herman also introduced me to HIS dearest friend, who would one day become my second husband. They met when they were schoolmates in New Jersey, and each was twelve, and members of a Puppet Club after school. They formed a puppet company, wrote the plays, made the costumes, and performed for neighborhood children at any venue where they might make a few cents. As they got more experience, their shows were more and more sophisticated, and over the years they acquired a reputation, which caught the attention of the well-known Yale Puppeteers, and the Bill Baird Puppet Company.

I didn't know them at that time. My husband always said that he remembered me when I was introduced by Herman while at Cooper Union. He described me as "the long-haired redhead in colorful knee socks, whose smock was always covered with paints."

ALL the Cooper students wore their paint proudly, as a badge of superiority over the cashmere sweater-set, pearl-necklaced, or white shirt pristine-panted students from New York University! WE belonged to that exalted group of artists from Cooper Union who lolled on park benches in Washington Square Park, eating our sandwiches, some of us drinking from beer bottles that the proprietors were kind enough to open for us in their shops, while we scoffed at the more "conventionally" dressed students from "the other school!"

Oh, we had chutzpah!

Besides, I was in "love," tragically, with a, for me, unattainable fellow-student. Or we both were, Herman and I. Oh, the poetry I wrote on the subway at night, going home after classes and my job. Did my "suffering" make me a better artist? I doubt that, but I felt that it made me more sentimentally sensitive to art and artists.

And self-deception is one of the habiliments of immaturity.

Then came the Second World War, and male students were either drafted or volunteered to serve. I say "male" because at the time women were asked if they wanted to serve as nurses or occupational therapists. I was approached and my answer was "No, thanks, I have a job this summer!" Herman was rejected from Military Service, and while mouthing sympathy, I was secretly delighted that my dear friend was still to be with me at school. Those of us with social conscience did our bit by setting up blood drives, making posters, raising money at functions we devised, and joining up as junior members of local USO groups.

When my future husband, Morris, entered the service, I sent my "good wishes" as part of Herman's frequent and impassioned letters. The Cooper fellow we both so doted on went into the Coast Guard and became, in my words, "the cutest 13-button man in that branch of the service." Oh, the relationship was romantic, but not (as I wished) ever "consummated"! I was just his petting and kissing partner, all the passion on my part, and his "exotic" (read Jewish) girlfriend!

I continued busy at school. During one term, I was asked to be responsible for decorating the only ground-floor window Cooper Union boasted at the time. Students were selected, one a month, to take on this job. I was flattered when asked, and was assigned to depict the influence of the Art School Library on its students. I gave it much thought and finally came up with an idea.

The sculpture of the head of Michelangelo's "David" inspired me, and I cut it in reverse outline from a piece of plywood. This I painted black and placed it close to the window glass, and between the head and the glass I attached some library books showing a variety of sculpture, the illustrated pages held open by red ribbon. The interior of the window was all in black, white and red, and on a red-covered plinth I placed the white plaster sculpture done by a fellow-student. It was of an amorphous, twisted shape, rather pretzel-like and of no recognizable subject. The entire window was backlit, and rather striking when seen from the street at night. It drew compliments from my fellow-students and passersby. The window was to remain for a month, when another student would be asked to follow his/her artistic vision.

The day after the window first appeared, I was informed that the Director of the Engineering School wished to see me. I wondered if perhaps it had gotten out that several Engineering students whom I dated, were neglecting their studies! Actually, he told me that he considered the sculpture "obscene and indecent" and should be replaced by another. I refused! I told this Philistine, that nothing in Art is indecent or obscene, that I would not change ANYTHING in the window, but would be pleased to remove the entire window, leaving it empty for the remainder of the month!

I stalked out and went to see MY Dean Clark at the Art School, who listened patiently and agreed with my staunch attitude. I asked, "Who is the Director of the Engineering School to dare to give artistic opinions and do I have to listen to him? Besides, he never explained WHAT he found offensive in the sculpture!" My Dean smiled, patted my hand and told me not to give it another thought.

I didn't! The window remained, and I had struck another blow for Artistic Freedom, thought I.

Does the reader recall Mayor Giuliani who caused a flap when he threatened to close down an exhibit at the Brooklyn Museum over what he deemed as indecent and sacrilegious? And the furor over the photographs of Mapplethorpe involving male nudes? What America needs are bigger and better fig leaves over the nude forms in Art, or over the eyes of viewers who see only indecency in what they don't understand!

I had some further artistic success when I designed a stage set for Marc Blitzstein's "The Cradle Will Rock," which I showed on a miniature stage I had built. It was my contribution for the Annual Art Students Exhibition. The small stage was lit and placed against a black-draped wall in a separate room of the exhibit. I was proud…it was my latest "succès fou."

When a gouache painting I did of "Leda and the Swan" was taken, stolen, off the wall, I complained to long-suffering Dean Clark who kindly pointed out that someone evidently wanted it enough to take it…a compliment, he said!

But more important to a gutsy girl with fragile Ego, was the social success I suddenly discovered, and brazened out, and flirted with! Oh well, thought I, if I can't have my first love, I can capture the many Engineering students who flocked around me with their newly-discovered and ingenuous talk of Life and Ambitions and ME, and helping Humanity, and ME, and "Why are we here" and ME, and Ars Longa, Vita Brevis, and ME! So, successful were they, I retained my Virginity…ME!

I decided I wanted Passion, not Philosophy. THAT seems to have been the running river in my life, the current never diverted to safer streams, to the placid-still-water I imagined most people's lives to be. It must be Waves, Waves, throughout! Water was one of the signs I was born to, what life promised me, and I was going to collect on all the signs and portents promised!

The Rags of Time

Chapter 2

A definite "Wave" was my meeting with Eleanor Roosevelt in the Green Room at the rear of the hallowed stage at Cooper Union, into which never a nail was to be driven by Mortal Stage Hand. The stage where Lincoln and Douglas debated was NEVER to be violated! Eleanor Roosevelt had been invited to speak to the public, come one, come all, and I, as columnist for our school paper, was to interview her before the great event.

What I asked and how she answered, I cannot recall, for I was so nervous and awed, she so kind and obliging, but I remember her voice, high pitched, she smiling at me, waiting politely as I long-hand scrawled her answers to some political question I dared ask. At one point I remember she said she would have to ask the President about some remark I questioned.

As an art student, used to colorful and quirky clothes, I looked beyond her rather terrible non-color dress and hat, and thought her soul had all the color…and quirkiness, and of how much I loved her…and would cheerfully have hammered a nail into the famous stage of The Great Hall had she asked it of me. Heroine Worship had struck and continued all the days of her life. In her later years of "My Day" fame, she lived in Greenwich Village and often I passed her house and looked into its windows hoping to catch a glimpse of buckteeth, ugly clothes, tinny voice, of her Soul. I thought of her passions and of my envy of a wonderful life, withal the Clintonesque behaviour of Franklin! When her son's biography "revealed all" of her life and relationships, I reacted with anger at his (a male) betrayal!

After graduation, the reality: what does one do with a Degree in Fine Arts? Paint? Or prostitute myself by teaching? So, we wonderful, enlightened children thought and discussed our troubling futures over a coffee, or a beer, or a penny-a-cigarette we smoked in sophisticated weltschmertz talk before dispersing to our homes…to be continued as soon as one or another of us had a few dollars to share for Automat food or kaffeklatches. Or had a job, or the hint of an idea in what way we could "prostitute" our art training!

In addition to a few ill-paying stints at department stores, I continued to study painting at night in the private studio run by a then well-known artist, Wallace Harrison, the husband of Carol Harrison, and lover of another Cooper Union instructor, Henriette Schutz. This was my introduction to ménage-à-trois life! Two women sharing one man! It was at his studio that I met a young man from another world: the suburbs.

Herb was blond, beautiful, painted incredibly well…and he fell in love with me, a redhead, dirty-smocked girl who painted outrageous pictures and said outrageous things! But he was unshockable, and smiled at me, and his warmth was impossible to resist, or avoid! Neither of us had any "ready money" after art classes, so we walked or visited people we knew in Greenwich Village, and in a musician-friend's loft on Fifteenth Street, I lost my virginity. What I remember most was the sweetness and the warmth, and my delirious happiness at the knowledge that I was now truly loved and valued in the same way I valued myself.

What greater gift? I did the ordinary things of daily life but always within was the warmth, the ova of passion, enveloping me. I painted my days with his aura, and my nights with the reality of love. Thoughts of him were like his arms enfolding my body, and even now, after long, long years, I remember the childlike bursts of flame, unlike anything since, although I have loved and been loved by others.

The great thing is never to regret a feeling, an experience, an emotion, ANY emotion! It can be recalled at will, its essence as sweet, or impassioned, or painful, as the reality…the Truth?…of the past.

If one believes in a God, I believe that its greatest gift is the gift of memory. THAT is the gift of life. There is none more essential to the human spirit. Can we not, all of us, remember some sight, some smell, some thought, which gives us the entire experience of some past event? None of that is to be coupled with regret, not in MY life, for I have always considered regret as a wasted, negative feeling, teaching nothing but guilt, and we have enough of that, too much, too time-wasting.

"Oh, get on with it!" has always been my prod, whereas regret is a crutch.

When my lover went into the Army, I went into Connecticut!

Cause and effect? Hardly, I decided to "prostitute" my genius into teaching. And so, finally to make a living since jobs in the stage design field were not, at that time in history, an option, certainly not for a woman!

I answered an ad in the Sunday New York Times for a job as art teacher in Connecticut, but the interview was in the Greenwich Village home of the Director, Jess Perlman. I dressed conservatively, for me, and as I entered the home/ office, a rotund, bespectacled man who sat at a desk asked immediately, "Why do you wear glasses?" At my most sophisticated answer, "Because I'm myoptic," he said with a smile, "No, you're myopic." So much for sophistication! It thudded somewhere around my shoes. I was asked other questions which I was able to answer correctly, and was told that if I would travel to the school for a trial weekend, my fare, whether or not I was hired, would be paid by the school. Good thing too, for it was a whopping eleven dollars which I had to borrow from my parents.

I arrived in Madison on a Saturday morning and walked the mile from the Madison Green to the Grove School, then a school for emotionally disturbed children, 27 in all. I immediately responded to the lovely landscape, and over the railroad bridge overpass wafted the smell of water and beach, unseen, but ripe to the nose, as I walked towards a group of Revolutionary and Civil War era buildings set among lawns and woods, and for the first time I felt, suburban, countrified, scared, frightened. Not held in by the frame of a building, a tenement, a small yard, a brick wall.

I was on my own and moving along! Oh, where was the certainty and bravado of yesterday?

The children I met were unknowingly kind and accepting. They ranged in age from five to nineteen. They ignored the fact that I was a stranger, and that I was not much older than the oldest of them. They accepted me at face value and were kind enough not to laugh when I saw their pool table and told them I had never played.

A ten year old then taught me a skill I have always valued. In fact, a skill in, and of, life, that of being able to deal with anything Life served me! I could strategize and plan and "English" a ball, or situation, and if not always win, I at least made a respectable showing! In addition I was able to enjoy tennis, both court and table, and my repartee certainly improved…more to the mark, and if accompanied by a smile, I charmed where necessary, and disarmed the opponent!

The students showed me over the extensive grounds, and I visited the various buildings, one called the "girls house", another the "boys" and the third, the "schoolhouse" where six children lived and wherein all subjects were taught, and which also housed a teacher. All the houses were separated by lawns, and there was a house where meals were prepared and served. A Revolutionary Stone House was the home and office of the Director, Jess Perlman, when he was in residence, and not interviewing "myoptic" would-be staff!

I was interested…and frightened…and terribly vulnerable at this, my first "real" job possibility. At the end of the weekend, the Director told me that my interactions with the students were good, and if I were interested, they would take a chance on me. Would I take a chance on them? Till then I had not made up my mind. Since I could think of no reason to say "no," I said "yes." And so I was hired. The terms were simple, I would receive $100 a month, room and board, laundry, and my time off would be every other weekend from Friday after classes, until breakfast on Monday. On alternate weekends, I was off from Friday after supper until Sunday breakfast.

And that is the way a "nice" Jewish girl leaves home, legitimately, and to be a teacher which was at that time, an honorable profession, spoken of with much pride by my parents to family and friends. "Susie has to leave to return to her job at school, you know. She is head of the Art department."

I WAS the Art department!

I was also remedial teacher of English and math, when the need arose. With math, I, a truly bad math student all my school life, told myself, oh well, no one can excel at EVERYTHING, but I was always one or two lessons ahead of the kids. In English, I was superior, having all my school life won every English and literary award. Not that my skills in either subject were tested...except for writing a report on each student with whom I had contact, and by being given by Jess Perlman three "special" students with whom to form relationships. The art courses were simple. I bought a pottery kiln and flew by the seat of my pants. I presented concepts of art in terms and lessons they could understand, and not one of my kids ever failed at anything! I was able to point out, from whatever they produced, a positive facet of their lives.

Sounds good? Boring!

In reality, TRUTH, I was so unsure of what I was doing, or not doing, that I cried myself to sleep every night for the first month. Finally I went to the little stone house and told Jess of my uncertainty. "No one has said anything to me! I don't know if I can do this, if my reports are accurate in any way. I've had no feedback from you!"

Jess smiled and said that if HE were not sure, I would have been told immediately. But that was not good enough, I said. Uncertainty is not a usual part of my make-up and I wanted more than that. I wanted to learn, to feel part of the staff team, even if I was the youngest, barely 21. My Ego needed stroking! Of course, that last was NOT how I expressed it! Jess put his arms around me and said I must trust to his "psychologically superior" judgment.

Oh well, I DID tell him I wanted to learn!

I remained at the Grove School for two and a half years and loved the freedom, the experience, and found the children fascinating. Their diagnoses ranged from various forms of neuroses to schizoid tendencies, some were called "post-encephalitic," and some were sent to the Grove School by the courts for displaying, "anti-social behaviour." Jess accepted any child who interested him, and fees were cleverly arranged so that wealthy students ended up paying for those of limited means. I applauded this, knowing from personal experience what it meant to be on the short end of finance, and because of my social conscience, my upbringing.

The other staff members, male and female, were friendly and all older...so

The Rags of Time

I was the "baby," which meant being given the less important, and often more distasteful, assignments. Since I didn't know what was expected, I little cared.

I was fascinated by the housekeeping staff, all of whom were Father Divine's Angels, so called by a Harlem Preacher who had gathered those in need of spiritual and physical nourishment, and named them for qualities they possessed, or were to aspire to: we had "Sweet Peace" (anything but, lemony as she was) and "Patience," and "Beautiful Love," truly good and beautiful, and a superb cook.

That we didn't all develop into butterballs attests to the physical demands of our work. We were with the children from the time they awoke until the last of them, depending on in which "House" they lived, were in bed…and then we were often awakened or called upon to calm a child, to settle a dispute. We also held our staff meetings at night to discuss our charges, or to air our philosophies regarding treatments of the children, and discussions of school matters. Our "special relationship" students were discussed privately with Jess at Stone House weekly meetings. It was a full schedule, and I thrived on, and with, my new knowledge…and on the fact that I ate my first lobster while in Connecticut. Oh, not at the school, but on "off" times when some staff and I drove or bused to other towns.

I learned another lesson from Jess: to curb my anger in situations in which anger and reason couldn't hope to win. A nine year old boy had broken into closed and locked cabinets containing art supplies, mainly powdered pigments which, mixed with water, made the paints we used for art projects or the background sets for our semi-annual students' shows. He had spilled and thrown the colorful pigments over the entire room! They were unsalvageable. When I discovered the mess, I ran in tears from the room, and to Jess in the Stone House. He said, calmly, "Forget it. He will be disciplined and his parents will pay for the damage!" I was defused, and although I would have cheerfully wrung the culprit's neck, I was forced to agree that J.P.'s calm conclusion of the incident was the best. In future, faced by other examples of acted-out aggression, I tried to act in a rational, not rattled, manner.

But it was hard…and not nearly so satisfactory!

So I turned to humor, always my style, and wrote satiric poems and skits for the children to perform, and lyrics to songs they knew. In these, the children took everyone on, including me. I realized that what the children lacked was a feeling of power, especially over the world around them. In humor NO ONE was seriously hurt…or insulted.

A wonderful lesson as applied to children, to life in general for everyone, but not so applicable when the world sought to hurt my own child! And NEVER when injustice was the issue. This much I had learned from my life, my family, my parents.

While at the Grove School I learned a difficult personal lesson. My lover had been sent to an Army post in Columbia, South Carolina, and he wrote that he was soon to be posted overseas. Herb had visited me in Connecticut when he was able, and now he sent me a roundtrip ticket to visit him for a week. He had gotten me a room in a boarding house in town, and with great excitement I arranged to go, told my parents, but then I received a phone call from my father, FORBIDDING me to go! The word, "forbid" had never been applied to me, good girl, smart girl, capable girl that I was. My father told me that he had been "through the mill," and knew it was a mistake. I explained that it had been "HIS" mill, and that I would have to have my own experiences. The discussion heated, my father was more insistent, and I said that if was to be his attitude, I would not speak to him again!

I left to go South, and among other things, encountered first-hand what I had only known before and read in newspapers, how Blacks were treated. Everywhere there were signs in public areas: "Drinking Fountain for Coloreds Only," toilets "For Coloreds Only," "Coloreds Not Allowed" on restaurant doors, on bars, and when I expressed dismay, I was told, "Oh, they got their own!" These sights and the public cold dismissal, and the terra-cotta colored soil, were the images I came North with.

I should have known. A very good friend from Cooper Union, who was black, had been drafted into the Army and he wrote often to me so we could exchange news of our doings. Instead of being in Special Services so his talents as an artist and illustrator could be utilized, he was, at first sight, detailed to an all-Black unit that carried supplies and equipment and loaded ships. Dear Ashley Bryan was now a stevedore. I cried when I read his letters and further when I was told that only White officers were detailed to all Black units! This injustice to someone so well liked and respected at Cooper Union, unfortunately was not to change for many, many years.

The Rags of Time

I had collected funds and clothing for Spain when I was young, but how could I begin to address this injustice, this evil, in my own country? The New York newspapers all the time I was growing up in Brooklyn spoke of the lynchings, the Ku Klux Klan, poll-taxes, and the Blacks' inability to register, let alone to vote! What could I do with my fury? My disappointment with my peers? I felt helpless and frustrated. I tried to make speeches, tried to form political action groups, but received little support from most of my fellow-citizens.

Funny how easy it is to find support for anti-war issues, but few wanted to go on record as supporting the second-class citizenry in America! It is not easy or popular to gain support to fight bigotry and injustice in one's own country, when we are so busy and vocal fighting fascism, or now, terrorism, overseas!

So, Susie got on with it! She fought her own battles, although one could not find much humor to fight with, and tried to lead by sheer power of persuasion, satire, sex!

It wasn't easy to stay angry with my father. I had no contact with him for some 4 or 5 months, although I met with my mother in Manhattan from time to time. Then the anger just evaporated. I had made my point, and we just never discussed it.

I heard from Herb, who wrote daily and sent wonderful sketches of his Army life from England, France, Germany, and saved my ration stamps for the salamis and tinned meats and fish and cookies by the score…and daily letters. With so much love traversing the oceans and skies, I was content with my life, and busy learning what Jess could teach me…almost!

One snowy evening when I reported to the little Stone House to discuss with Jess one of my "special" students, he invited me to join him for a glass of wine and some broiled chicken livers prepared by an "Angel," and we sat companionably in front of the fire, after student-talk, discussing poetry. Jess showed me some of his published verse, and suddenly got down on his knees by my chair and put his arms around my waist, and his head in my lap. As I looked down on his balding head, I began to laugh uncontrollably. He turned beet-red, stood up, and I ran gasping from the little Stone House! Oh, it was an hysterically romantic moment!

The Rags of Time

I went for a walk in the snow, and told no one, but understandably the cold winter air seeped into the bones of our relationship! He never addressed me personally after that, hardly spoke in my presence, and replied coldly to any question of mine about work.

I decided finally to apply a bit of his own psychology, and catching him alone, biting my lips in order not to laugh at the remembrance of that evening, apologized, citing my "unfamiliar" glass of wine and the suddenness of the situation, and my total lack of "cool" and lack of maturity…in other words, MY total immaturity. It worked! Jess seemed mollified and again I felt faithful to my realization that TRUTH, in this instance of how ridiculous he seemed to me, was not the answer! The reality was that there could not be anything romantic about the firelight on his balding head, or we sitting amidst the detritus of broiled chicken livers, red wine, and rather limp poetry!

At the beginning of my third year at the Grove School, my brother died of malignant hypertension. At that time, medicine, and treatment of this condition was not as sophisticated as today. Despite his most excellent care under a distinguished physician at Columbia Presbyterian Hospital in Manhattan, the doctor to Madame Chiang Kai-Shek, the only treatment outlined was a spinal tap and surgery, which the doctor told my sister–in-law might save his life, but would certainly leave him blind. This she told my family. She said that taking in consideration my brother's temperament, and what might have been his decision, she refused the operation. Several weeks later, he died.

Nat was twenty-seven years old.

To say that my parents were devastated is an understatement. Indeed, I was in such shock, I couldn't believe he would not be around to tease and argue with me, but most especially that we would not hear his music, the earliest influence on my life. To my parents it was as though Mozart had died again. Nat left a wife, a singer who was known as Shirley Lloyd, and a five year-old daughter.

Nat's life had not developed as my parents had envisioned. Nat had been tall, 6 ft. 3 in., with dark eyes and curly black hair, a "gorgeous hunk," the girls of today would have described him. At 16 he looked 20 and swore his little sister to secrecy: "If anyone asks, I'm 21!" After about five years of my telling this to people who asked, my friends pointed out that he couldn't be 21 for five years!

At 16, Nat had decided to forego classical music for jazz, in order to make money. He was tired of practicing, and so, without our family's knowledge, forayed into Tin Pan Alley, gathered other musicians together and was offered a job to be the orchestra on a cruise ship to South America. Since it was during school vacation, my parents didn't object…indeed, were proud of his enterprise!

Nat returned with some money, a good tan, and a swollen ego. He told my parents he was determined to play jazz, and that he had been asked by then songwriter and musician, Irving Caesar, to compose and play at gigs which he would set up. Caesar firmly believed Nat to be at least 21. This catapulted him into other big names, and big-name bands, and Caesar soon lost Nat to Louis Prima, Charlie Barnett, Lionel Hampton.

At that time Alec Templeton was playing classical music in the style of pop, and Nat was transposing popular music into the style of Mozart, Bach, Chopin. His reputation grew, but he never again studied or played the great classical composers. My parents and his teachers could not change his mind, or alter his direction or aim, to make money, be independent, join the Great American Dream!

Brother Nat met and played with some of the best jazz musicians in the late thirties and early forties such as Charlie Barnett, Jack Teagarden, Coleman Hawkins, and was well known on 52nd Street as a soloist, and as a member of various "combos." He was befriended by Leonard Feather, a musician and critic and loyal supporter of Nat's talent.

When Nat died, his funeral was attended by about 30 to 40 people, almost half of them the most noted Black musicians of the day. Leonard Feather was also Music Critic of Esquire Magazine, and in his "Encyclopedia of Jazz," Nat is listed as "One of the most advanced pianists of his day, combining Earl Hines and modern influences."

Nat made some recordings, now called "collector's items," one of the most famous of which was called the "Fats Waller Memorial Album" in which he and Earl Hines each played four sides. In the album folder, the critic writes that "One of the most brilliant and least recognized of jazz pianists, Nat Jaffe spent most of his childhood in Europe…" In commenting on another selection, he goes on to say, "Nat Jaffe's interpretation of this tune is as great as the tune itself; I'm inclined to regard this personally as the outstanding side of the whole album…this is a truly memorable performance and one that should establish Jaffe as an outstanding modern jazz artist."

What would Beethoven, Chopin, Mozart, have said? Or thought? Well, Martha Raye evidently was impressed, and while my parents were proud, that did not assuage their disappointment over what they called his defection from the world of great classical music. Jazz may have been the music of my youth, but I could not but agree with my parents. Evidently my "revolutions" and fight for personal independence did NOT include my brother's efforts!

Who knows what Nat might have become? At my age of 10 I was busy with my own life. Nat had always treated me with anger and resentment. I was no threat to him or to his musical ability, had always been second to his talent, demands, and temperament. He repaid my early adoration of him, my surface acquiescence to the wishes of the family, by physical abuse. Oh nothing violent, but a punch here, a slap there, a pinch. One day alone together at home, after he slapped me, I grabbed a wooden coat hanger and yelled that if he ever again touched me, I would kill him!

How I would do that, I had no idea. It was a sudden revolt! My brother stopped short, laughed, and walked away, and never again did he physically hurt me. He couldn't hurt me emotionally since I was not competitive, either musically, or for the affection of my parents. I had made peace with that when I discovered my talent for art and writing. I considered myself in all other respects, his intellectual equal.

Okay, perhaps his superior! I hugged that thought to myself.

When finally we became friends, when I was about 14, he used to invite me to see him in some of the more glamorous "gigs" he was involved with, even gave me tickets to those not in night clubs or when he and musician friends had jam sessions. As his "kid" sister I couldn't attend nightclubs, but I remember with special delight his invitation to the Paramount Theatre in Manhattan when Nat was the accompanist and arranger and stage manager for Martha Raye. I sat in the audience as she sashayed on stage, to thunderous applause, dragging her mink coat on the stage floor. She took bows, introduced Nat, and then performed for almost two hours of song, alternating with Nat's solos.

The Rags of Time

I was proud, and then Nat had me go back stage to be introduced to the Grande Dame herself. All I remember of that was of being awestruck at Nat's easy familiarity with her, and her graciousness to Nat's kid sister. It was a matinee and as I went home by subway, I forgot all the grief of second handedness and realized Nat was being as kind as HE could, to an "ugly duckling," my term for myself, secretly. Nat was "on the road" with Martha Raye for 6 months or more, and I suddenly gained fame among my school friends,...and now Nat WAS 21!

When I was nine, my father gave me a Japanese woodcut given to him as a gift by a business customer in the Philippines. My father had long been in the import-export business, and although very traveled, he had no interest in, or knowledge of Oriental Art. Since I was considered by my family as "the artistic child," the woodcut came to me. Something about this woodcut so fascinated me that, as children do, I copied it in crayon and watercolors. I knew nothing else about this art form except that the picture was 10 by 22 inches. I knew not its creator, its history, just that it showed, in an interior, a tall woman holding a fan, and the print colors were shades of blue with rust accents. That is all, except that her costume, the kimono she wore, and her headdress, to me were so beautiful and mysterious.

My parents knew enough to have it framed and hung it in my bedroom. This woodcut eventually sparked a life-long interest in other Japanese woodcuts, or "Ukiyo-é," and I presently have accumulated about forty. Also it developed in me an interest in the Orient, and when I was about ten, I was so taken with life in China and Japan, that I read whatever was available in the library, and urged my parents to help me find and buy books about the Orient. Book-buying was up my parents' alley (if NOT Tin Pan) and this interest, coupled with our strong feelings about injustice of any kind, stayed with me my entire life.

The fact that I was number-two child actually gave me much freedom, something I was not to understand until much later in my life. What I thought of as indifference was really a blessing since I was able to develop at my own pace, with my own talents, into my own Ego. When I was 16, my father gave me a wonderful present. I had told him that the Boston Museum of Fine Arts owned a large collection of Chinese paintings, and that the New York Times had mentioned a folio of sepia reproductions of the Han to Sung periods. He sent for the folio, which I still have, its cover slightly eaten by one of our dogs, who seemed to share my artistic interests! I pored over this volume and learned about Chinese Circles, which resemble nothing so much as squares with rounded edges, and also about some of the marvelous landscapes which undoubtedly influenced modern artists because of their flat planes.

Perspective, as taught by Western artists, is totally different. The fact that I learned by looking, rather than from art classes, added to my artistic and intellectual Ego! It confirmed to me that education comes much more from self-discovery than from dictums handed down at school. I discovered that this was MY way of learning…what I came later to call "experiential intelligence." Learning which came from the gut of the reality to lodge in MY gut, never to be forgotten. Throughout my life, this knowledge has been with me, fortified me, fed my ego. I always felt myself the intellectual equal of anyone I met. It seemed bred in my bones, altered my chromosomes, straightened my spine. If it did not always endear me to others, "tant pis"!

Those for whom I was "too smart" were not smart enough for me! And for my entire life I would rather be alone than in the company of those I consider bores. As Oscar Wilde put it, "To love oneself is the beginning of a life-long romance."

Well, I was, and am, stuck with me. And am again alone. But not bored, never bored. Alone is how we come into this life, is how we leave it.

After my brother's death, my parents begged me to come back to New York. "To do what?" I asked. To work with my father in his import-export business. No, no secretarial duties, just to give him support, to deal with customers, to lend comfort to their grief, to be the good, dutiful, daughter, I told myself. With misgivings I set down rules for my life: I was not to be told what I may or may not do. My private life was to be just that…private!

"Oh yes, oh absolutely," and idiot that I was, I agreed because I was still the good, loving daughter, now their only child. I was needed. I was finally Number-One!

What I was, was a complete idiot, a complete fool to think I was free to make my own life in my parents' home! For a few months I WAS, until my presence empowered them to turn me back into a child, the good child! The puppet-strings in place, they pulled, I jerked, moved, mouthed their words. Oh yes, I was loved, but not for myself, but as part of their needs, dependent. I was to fill an unfillable void. I was to repay their upgrading of me into first place by being entirely malleable. As my brother had never been, as I was not the brilliant musician, surely I would be what they envisaged: a more mature smiling-faced good girl who was pointed out to family, to friends, as amenable and self-sacrificing.

How I hated that! I managed to display my true self to my friends from Cooper, I did not betray my misery to my lover, sure I could handle myself in the reality in which I had placed myself.

If I see one more movie or television program, or read another book, about a "dysfunctional" family, I shall lose it…will vomit between, or into, these lines! What is "dysfunctional"? We all function in one-way or another. More psychobabble to simplify, or obfuscate, what is not clear? In my youth we didn't know the term, felt our families were the norm. Mine, except for the music and art, I thought of as being like every other family. We were not "stressed," we were "aggravated." We never thought in terms of "average," nor were aware of, or interested in Sociological Statistics! Never thought in those terms at all! We were who we were, and if some family members were considered "eccentric," so be it! It was no reflection on the Total Family of Man. We neither consulted Margaret Mead nor Sigmund Freud, but read them as fellow intellectuals!

I believe that psychiatry and sociology are the current religions, as misleading and dangerous to Society as were the zealots of earlier, more established religions. As is the "drug culture" of today, which hypothesizes that, almost every ill can be cured by its proper and particular pill.

This seems to me to be a strange conclusion to embrace, since I went from being an artist, to a psychologist, to a psychotherapist. I evidently molded psychology into my way of thinking, into the manner in which I viewed my "Society." I personalized it, "comme on dit" as I suppose I did every field I encountered along my way. My fellow-therapists and psychiatrists were not dismayed at the way I related to my patients, rather I was viewed as a valuable member of the Psychiatric Team. Perhaps it was my totally non-judgmental approach, another thing I learned during my youth and from my own experiences.

The Rags of Time

Since I had had to build my own Ego within the greater space allowed me as number-two child, I intuitively saw the strengths, rather than the flaws, the weaknesses, in my patients. No one working with me in therapy was ever "wrong," just different, unique, and worthy of respect. At a time when it was very necessary for MY development, I was very successful. Not rich, not ambitions, not greedy, but I thought of myself with warmth. I have never suffered from that peculiarly American capitalist disease, Affluenza.

My twenty-third year found me at home, only now I was to make up to my parents for my brother's death. I was now become a caged and struggling bird, and intelligent as I was, unable to free myself into my own life. Oh, I tried, but in my letters to my lover I said nothing of my inner feelings. Why add to his problems when he was at war? In my silence, I was many things to many people and nothing to myself! It was all a brave front as slowly I sought to find private joy where I could.

I also learned that I was more like my mother than I realized. Or had understood. Maybe my forthrightness was appealing to others, …to men. I looked as always, I told myself, and if men were attracted to me, perhaps I had more power than I gave myself credit for. Did I use that power? I confess I did. It was a heady feeling, but not necessarily really understood by me.

One day I was invited by my lover's family to a Thanksgiving Dinner. I entrained to the suburbs and was met at the station by his father. At his home, and with his siblings and their families, I spent an enjoyable evening, was then driven back to the station. His father and I waited in the car until train time. It was a cold and snowy night. While we waited, we spoke of Herb, of the war's progress, of Herb's role in it. Oh, his father was a charming man. Before I left the car, he suddenly swept me in his arms (I seem destined for clichés in the snows of winter) and kissed me passionately, stroked me, and in my shock I felt unable to move as he spoke of his feelings for me! All I could think of was Herb, and wanting to escape his father, yet hurt no one. I finally got the car door open, and wordless, I ran to the waiting room, and the train.

Oh yes, I was shocked…but may I say gratified, to have had my mother's effect on a man! Well, Mom, here I am: smart, not yet pretty, as you impressed on me…but I MUST be appealing!

The Rags of Time

I spent the ride home thinking and asking myself what message I had inadvertently sent to this charming and kind man whom I genuinely liked. Then I remembered the first time I was taken by Herb to meet his family and spend the weekend at his home. His mother was a plump, sweet woman with several illnesses whom I considered as a typical homemaker. There were several siblings, all on their own by now. The father was a tall, handsome, and very charming man who worked for the entertainment industry as district manager for several theaters around the country, most lately in New York City. We were all outgoing, shared many laughs, and they were amused by my stories of my family, and interested that I was, like Herb, an artist.

At last, I was shown to the guest room, Herb's siblings had left, and because I had lost my virginity too recently to want to be parted from him at any time, I took his hand and led him to his father, having judged his mother as too fragile for my news, and said that I was not used to being so near his son and not sleeping with him, and that I wanted to share his bed, or he, mine. The two men's faces were studies in scarlet. Herb hugged me. His father seemed shocked, not by what I said, but that I had said it, not his son. I also added that we would not "sneak around," as I called it.

This I remembered as the train took me to Manhattan, and I realized that this must have been the beginning of his father's feelings for me. So, maybe I am more like my mother, and yet, "being too smart" was obviously not a turnoff. I have never before told this story, but treasured the warmth as I had my lover's warmth and love throughout these many years. It is said that one's first love is unlike any other. Perhaps my rite of passage began at that time, from the realization that I HAD learned to compete with my mother, albeit unknowingly!

And on her own turf?

I hugged that thought to myself though the years, and I must thank my unwitting mother for having contributed to my development, this time not by struggling against her opinion of me, but once again for allowing me the freedom I had not before then recognized.

So why was I so weak in my attempts to extricate myself from parental strings as yet untied?

As a consequence I did something which hurt me and Herb, and which I remember with pain, regret and a sense of self-dislike. When Herb returned to the United States, to me, with the expectation that I had obviously fostered in us both, and we met one evening at a restaurant, there issued from my mouth a refusal to marry him. Why? After all our loving time together, all the shared memories, and my brave words to my father about needing to "go through my own mill," did I make that decision which I suddenly realized might please my parents since Herb wasn't Jewish? Did I tell Herb this? No. Shamefully, I told him that I did not love him enough. He was stunned, and I in tears. All I felt was hollow, and contempt for myself. No amount of rationalization has ever explained my behaviour to me. It was a case of Jane Austen's "follies and inconsistencies." As much as she is my favorite writer, these follies have never amused or diverted me.

With my gusty melancholy, I got on with my life, which had its own way of punishing me with yet another "folly"!

The Rags of Time

Chapter 3

Throughout the next year at home, I painted, got occasional teaching jobs, worked at commercial art, and even for a fabric-design studio. On a vacation one summer in Lenox, Massachusetts, at Tanglewood to attend the concerts and dance performances, I met a group of musicians which included Leonard Bernstein, and several others from well-known orchestras, and they "adopted" me, and took me with them to tour Lenox, Pittsfield, and the Shaker commune. I went from sitting alone on a blanket under the stars, to a seat under the curtained dome which served as Concert Hall. I watched as Koussevitsky conducted the Boston Symphony Orchestra night after night, heard wonderful soloists, and had the pleasure of watching rehearsals conducted by some of my new friends, one of whom was to become my first husband.

Music had seduced me once again. It began to seem as if I were, from childhood, fated to marry a musician. If I were not a musician myself, I had a deep love of music and enough knowledge and good sense of rhythm to be able to discuss music with any musician.

What better future?

My parents would be pleased, and so, in the way in which I had escaped my parental home by teaching in Connecticut, I could now fulfill my family's desire to be proud of me by marrying a musician. Don't imagine I reasoned all this out and made a decision. Oh no, there had to be something in it for me!

I had the choice of two men, both very good musicians, both performed with major American orchestras: The Philadelphia Symphony and the San Francisco Symphony. My "Philadelphian" was handsome, the other, a better musician, although less physically attractive…and had the good fortune to live

3500 miles away, in San Francisco! Also, he was very passionate, and entreated me to marry him immediately...before the end of the Tanglewood season.

Again in this confluence of misguided and ridiculous circumstances, and because I could think of no good reason to say, "No," against ALL reason, I said, "Yes." I think if I had at the time known the term "masochism," it might have occasioned a red flag, or siren, to put a halt to my less than positive reasons for marriage!

Okay, Susanna, you could have waited!

But visions of me painting as I listened to great music, and attending concerts forever, and seeing my husband perform with other members of the first violin section, of attending rehearsals and operas and ballets, and soloists from around the world, was irresistible.

Within a month, Ervin and I were married at a Rabbi's house in Brooklyn, New York. I met my in-laws the day before the wedding. Rush, rush, rush...and if I was less than enchanted with his parents and felt a first frisson of doubt, I kept it to myself. I wore a long turquoise dress, not really a white virginal confection, my husband dutifully smashed a crystal glass beneath his foot, four friends held a Chupah over us, and so, I was wed!

My family took everyone out to dinner afterwards. Erv and I had reservations at the Plaza Hotel that night, and the next morning we were met by my parents at Grand Central Station, and prepared to entrain for San Francisco.

His parents flew home.

At the station, my father took me aside for a few minutes, pressed $500 into my hand and quietly told me that if I were not happy, that money would see me back to New York.

My mother spoke music and flirted with Erv.

I was too excited by the prospect of the three day trip, the Pullman car, the lounge with rotating seats, the dining car, to think far ahead.

The Rags of Time

Sex in a Pullman car proved very exciting, and when not making love, I watched the marvelous scenery fly by and tried to sketch impressions of it, while Erv studied some orchestral score soon to be performed. It was all exciting, exhilarating, and loverly! My dream scenario of my new life!

If I had scripted the ensuing melodrama, I could not have been more wrong in my self-deception, in my supposed self-knowledge! Oh, I was still the gutsy, independent, mouthing-off young woman in my own mind…but where did the sentimental dreams come in? Was my desire to leave my parents' home responsible for the comedy of errors I indulged in, the fantasy I imagined my life to become? Was this the product of a mature and creative mind?

You wanna bet?

No matter how hard I tried to critique it to myself, I sensed a gnawing in my otherwise, and hitherto, reliable gut, that this was NOT as good as it gets! And I couldn't even blame Erv. His dreams and fantasies of marriage were even more skewed! I found after some five months, that I, the marriage, the daydreams, were falling apart. But does Susanna give up? If Ervin was in the marriage for some scenario of his own, perhaps in order to escape HIS mother, he was not likely to do it in the same San Francisco neighborhood.

I tried the "I'll paint while you play" dialogue to myself, to Erv, but soon found myself as trapped as in my parents' home. But my nature was to try. To fix things.

"Erv, this marriage isn't working. Please let's go to a marriage counselor."

"No, it's fine."

But "fine" was not what was happening to my health at the complete involvement, the daily visits and phone calls, from my mother-in-law. My health deteriorated rapidly. For some time I had been feeling tired, dispirited, weepy. Not my style at all. Finally I went to the Kaiser Permanente Health Center, and I was told by the examining doctor that I was seriously anaemic, and must eat more "blood-enriching foods."

"Would chewing on my mother-in-law's bloody carcass help?" Unfortunately it remained unexpressed. But I must admit that the thought gave me much pleasure and helped me to regain some semblance of humor, now sadly lacking in my marriage. Maybe staying at home to watch him conduct to recordings was part of the problem? Whenever I began a painting, I was called by Erv to the living room to watch him conduct.

I took a part-time job at the City of Paris Department Store.

"What are your skills?" asked the personnel manager.

"As an artist, perhaps I could function in display, or in the gift department. Put me wherever you like. [Good little girl that I am] and I will try to fit in."

"You seem overqualified," she replied.

"Oh no, please, I need this job!"

I became the junior clerk and feather-dusting expert to two senior Ladies! Long-handled duster in hand, every time I began my tour of duties, I flicked lamp-shades, china birds, vases, glassware, silver table-settings, and tried not to see what I dusted: middle-class, tasteless, ugly. Some months later I expressed to the good women in my department my wonderment at anyone's desire to own this terrible stuff!

One of them said wisely, that everything finds its owner! She said it with a twinkle. We were by now colleagues, even friends. I brown-bagged my lunch, and after gulping it down, spent the rest of my lunch hour wandering the departments, when joy of joys, I discovered a dimly-lit Department of Orientalia! Marvelous old Celadon china, Coromandel screens, delicately carved furniture, Scrolls, T'ang horses, and figurines of unglazed pottery! I was so excited that I spent almost every free moment in this completely empty section of the store.

This did not go unnoticed by my colleagues or other personnel of the store, and I was summoned by the personnel manager who asked if I would like to work with the Oriental Antiques? When I told her of my background, she informed me that the store had many inquiries about their very superior collection, and that very often photographs sent in response did not convey the colors or designs of the ware, and would I consider drawing or painting the objects in question? Would I? Even better, she said that for every sale based on my efforts, I would receive a commission!

Hallelujah!

My tenure at the store was now entirely enjoyable and somewhat more remunerative. When I tried to elicit some enthusiasm for my new good fortune, Erv was too embroiled in his vision of what marriage to me should consist: One, to obey his family, Two, to watch him conduct, Three, to hear him play, Four, to attend all concerts (this I truly enjoyed!), Five, to be the wife HE envisioned, whatever the hell that was, and Six, to participate in good sex!

Every evening during our dinner, the phone rang, Erv answered, and I heard him say, "Oh, fish, mashed potatoes" or "steak, noodles." Then, "Yes" and he hung up. Translation of this was that his mother asked first what her little, but soon to be rotund, darling was being served by the little nothing of a daughter-in-law, and the "Yes" was that Erv had had a bowel movement that day!

It varied only in the make-up of the meal.

Naturally, My-Mother-In-Law-From-Hell was a very good cook, and whenever we ate at their home, I always enthusiastically complimented her, in an effort to be thought of a bit kindly, but her entire concern was for her beloved "Apukah's" enjoyment, and I always felt completely "de trop."

But why in hell did I bother? I would never have put up with such behaviour from anyone else. None of my slight achievements were acknowledged, let alone complimented. I may as well have remained at my parents' home where at the very least they valued my artistic skills, while acknowledging (but with love, albeit suffocating) that I was not a cook! Of any sort!

I took refuge in the considerable musical talents of my husband, and the affection and respect of his many friends, in the music world and out, and tried to make this mockery of a marriage work. Many of the other first-chair musicians and their wives were supportive and fond of me. One of the truly memorable aspects of our marriage was the weekly chamber music concerts in our living room. I looked forward to what I called our Coney Island Nights when after the music, I fed the musicians and their wives, New York style: kosher hot dogs with heated sauerkraut, on toasted rolls, followed by a store-bought cake, wine, beer. Laughter and enjoyment, followed afterwards by the sight of my husband wiping down the interior stair-rail and around all light switches, and toilet hardware, with cleaning fluid!

I entreated Erv to see, with me, a psychotherapist. "Why?" he asked. "Because we need help!" "No," was his reply.

The several weeks Erv and I spent in a rented cottage in Carmel, the trips to the monasteries and convents in Monterey, the breathtaking sights of cypress trees which clung precariously to hillsides, my enjoyment of Erv's conducting the annual Bach Festival, the Brandenburg Concerti in which he not only conducted but played…all this kept my marriage going long after it should have ended.

Away from San Francisco, he seemed more like the man I married, freer in spirit, enthusiastic about our lives. Our moods were certainly lighter, and so, on our return to San Francisco, I appealed to my father-in-law, a nice and gentle man, to please, PLEASE speak to his wife to stay out of our marriage. The strange thing is that parents of any man I had dated before, liked me, even encouraged their sons to marry me! My father-in-law tried, but was helpless, in face of the woman who had written to Eleanor Roosevelt and told her that the United States government should GIVE Ervin an orchestra to conduct, that he was too brilliant a musician to have to be a member of ANY orchestra!

In this, she was thwarted.

I realized after two years, that if you can't beat them, it is wisdom to cut and run!

I finally took my own advice and became the sole advocate of my future.

One evening after a concert, I tried again to convince Erv of the difficulties of our marriage; that his mother's excessive interference was impossible, and again begged him to put an end to it.

"You don't understand the love my mother and I have for each other. You've never had anything like it!"

"I'm glad I don't understand it, and were I as suffocated by such a love as you, I would try to convince her that you are now an adult!"

I had already decided that if I were to become pregnant, I would abort myself by any means…"With a fish-hook" were the words I used in my mind. What I actually said was that in the morning, I was going to get a divorce. Erv laughed.

And in the morning I did just that. Embarked on a plan to obtain my freedom…"once again," rang in my mind. One of Erv's and my friends was a lawyer, although not in practice because he had been asked by the state of Oregon to codify its laws. Of this I wasn't aware.

Under a eucalyptus tree in Golden Gate Park, hard by the lovely Japanese Tea House, we met two days later. I told him of my, our, unhappiness and unsuitability. He listened patiently, then when I asked him to refer me to a lawyer, he said I could do it myself, sans lawyer. I was smart, and he would walk me through the process! Of course he pushed all the right buttons with that appeal to my ego…and by the curiosity I suddenly had for ADVENTURE! We went together to buy a notebook, and then he gave me my instructions: to buy legal paper, to go to the library for certain law books, to copy certain forms, to serve my husband by messenger, to send or serve other forms to the courts.

All of the above kept me busy, even entertained, for several days. I was always good at homework. I made only one error (of course.) I served my husband on the same day I had other papers served.

It never does to be too pleased with oneself!

The following day Erv came to me and cried, and begged me not to leave him. I was obdurate and took off my wedding rings and returned them to him. I pleaded, in return, that I wanted NOTHING from him, but my freedom, that I would just take with me the things I had brought: my paintings, books, antiques which my mother had insisted on sending me, and return to New York.

On the day Erv had been "served" I was unaware that he had gone to the judge and cried, told her that he refused to divorce me, that he would commit suicide if I left, and he, being well-known in San Francisco, and I known only to myself…and a few friends, hadn't the chance of a prayer in hell to prevail! Would he go with me to a psychiatrist, I asked one last time. "No," was his reply. "There's no need."

At that time, unfortunately the judge of the District Court was on vacation, and another judge, Theresa Meikle, had been sent from Family Court, to temporarily replace him. This I didn't know, and so the comedy of my errors proceeded. I sat in the courtroom at the stipulated time, other cases were heard and disposed of, and then we were called. Since I had brought the action, I was called first. Ervin sat in another part of the courtroom.

"Susanna Mautner," called the clerk, and I stood. The judge asked my lawyer to stand, and I told her that I did not have a lawyer, that I would represent myself.

"DO YOU KNOW THAT YOU ARE PRACTICING LAW WITHOUT A LICENSE?" bellowed the judge. Where my next words came from, I don't know, as I stiffened my 5 foot 2 inch frame, and said quietly, "Your Honor, I think it within the purview of every American citizen to represent himself!" If I shook inwardly no one would know, I vowed. Again the bellow, "IN MY CHAMBERS, NOW!"

The court clerk kindly pointed the way, and amidst the stunned silence of the spectators, I entered the Gorgon's Chambers. She sat behind a large judicial desk, but I would not be intimidated! Fixing me with a steely and angry stare, she again asked if I was aware that I was practicing law without a license. I remained silent, trying to look as implacable as she, despite my inner quake.

She then described Erv's pain and surprise at my actions, that he threatened suicide if I left, that he was such a brilliant musician, and that he wanted me to return to him, and on and on.

When she paused, I told her of the over two years of his mother's interference, that Ervin had refused to see, with me, a marriage counselor, a psychotherapist, of his fixation of clean stair railings and light switches, of his denial that his mother played any part in our lives, and that he felt I could not understand the deep devotion he and his mother had for each other. I further said that ALL I wanted was to leave with all MY possessions: that I had, unasked returned the wedding rings; and all I wanted was to get out, no publicity was to follow his distinguished career. And that if I didn't leave, *I* would die!

Then I recounted the story, never told to anyone, that at the first of Erv's birthdays during our marriage, I ordered a silver cigarette lighter and asked my mother-in-law how one says "I love you" in Hungarian. The phrase was "tseretlek" and I had it inscribed, with the date and my name. At the surprise party I gave with his and our friends and his parents, I planned that after the catered dinner, he would open his presents, and mine was to be the last. When Erv opened the little box and took out the lighter, and read the inscription, he was delighted, he hugged and kissed me. Then to my, and our guests' shock, his mother presented him with another little box, which when he opened it, contained a gold cigarette lighter with the same inscription!

To this tale of bitchiness, even his loyal supporter, the Judge, could not be entirely indifferent! She merely reiterated through tightly pursed lips, very well, if I insisted on the divorce and pursued it in this manner, since this was a Thursday, I was to appear in court on the following Tuesday. Goodbye, fare-thee-well, and to hell with me, was how I took the dismissal!

When I left I called our so-called-lawyer-friend, although I called him many other things first, and raged and cried, and gave him the low-down on my day in court. He laughed and laughed, said I had done well, but since I could not get into another docket with another judge, he gave me the name of a lawyer friend member of a well-known legal firm in San Francisco. I immediately called the offices of Dreyfus, McTernan, Lubliner, for an appointment early the next morning.

When I arrived at their office the next morning it was to be told that Francis McTernan, to whom I had been referred, was in New York City. The secretary asked if I would speak to a partner. "Yes, please," I answered, whereupon I was ushered into Mr. Lubliner's office. I named the lawyer who had referred me and proceeded to describe the entire sad saga of my attempt to get a divorce. I finished to laughter and applause as I acted out the courtroom scene with gestures and "I saids" and "she bellowed." "I just need someone to stand up for me. If I can't have some lawyer with me, she'll throw me out of court, have me pilloried, maybe even sentence me to life with my mother-in-law!" I concluded.

At that moment, providentially, a man entered the office having been told that a potential client waited to see him. It seemed that Francis McTernan had just deplaned and stopped by his office to pick up his mail before going home. To his partner's question, my soon-to-be knight said that thus far, the case had not gone well. The case? He was on the defense team of lawyers for a group known in the press as "the New York Eleven," who had been accused of being communist conspirators, naughty fellows, and such!

"Aha" thought I. If he was used to dealing with political agendas, bureaucracy, perhaps he was the man to defend this criminal, this woman, who DARED to upset the California Legal System by impersonating a lawyer! His partner asked me to wait in the outer office while he spoke to Mr. McTernan. For the next half-hour there issued laughter, and when I was readmitted into the office, both men were wiping their eyes.

No, not tears of sorrow, but of laughter. Mr. Lubliner asked me to act out my tragic story, and so I regaled them with the saga of a marriage, UNACCOMPANIED by violins which had turned flat, and of my meeting with the judge. I described her punitive attitude, filthy temper and resentment, and that now she allowed me just four days to obtain my degree in JURISPRUDENCE!

I then vented my feelings toward the lawyer-friend who had used me in his experiment to see how a Citizen-Lawyer dealt with the San Francisco courts! Mr. McTernan advised me to go home, relax, and that he would meet with me on the Tuesday morning at the courtroom.

For the next few days I tried for calm, for humor, and told myself that yes, I was doing the right thing. Besides, the die was cast. During that time I received phone calls from orchestral wives. One in particular touched me deeply when she offered to be a witness, had I need of one, since she was at the fateful birthday party and had witnessed Erv's mother's and his neurotic treatment of me. My grateful thanks, but no, I would not take advantage of these friends with whom Erv would socialize, and with whose husbands he would have to work.

On Tuesday, Mr. McTernan, Ace among men, Defender of the Weak, appeared and we entered the courtroom and took seats. Again when the clerk called my name, I stood, and Mr. McTernan with me.

The Rags of Time

Grim-faced, Judge Meikle asked him who he was, and upon hearing his answer BELLOWED, "Do you realize that your client is practicing law without a license?"

Frank put a warning hand on my shoulder, and said, "May I speak to Your Honor in chambers?"

He told me to stay put and that he would fetch me later. I now felt like a recalcitrant puppy, but stayed put as did everyone else in the courtroom, with many a look at me, at this interruption of their cases. Who was this redhead, and what did she want, and, and…Frank finally came for me, Judge Meikle returned to the judge's bench and we left.

In the lobby of the courthouse, My Hero informed me that the judge would see me later that day, and I was cautioned to be polite, politic, and that I was to agree to WHATEVER she requested of me, and that it would be ALL RIGHT, and that he would wait for me!

In the Gorgon's Lair, I agreed to the now slightly mollified, but still disapproving judge, who again had me recount the more lurid tales of my attempts to get Erv into counseling of some sort, to no avail. By this time, I was so upset and unnerved by the past few weeks, that I burst into tears, again saying that I just wanted out of the marriage, no alimony, just with the things I had come into the marriage with.

Whereupon Judge Meikle said, "Well, I'm glad you show SOME human feelings." I then realized that she must humble me in some way in order to seem in control, to save face, whereupon I cried all the harder, groping in my purse for a handkerchief. I left her chamber, sobbing a bit, and was told by my Hero, that an Interlocutory Decree would be issued and that a year later, if Ervin and I had not reconciled (skinny chance) the marriage would be dissolved! What had she required of me was that if Erv wrote to me, I MUST reply, and if he came to see me, I MUST see him.

"Yes, yes, Your Honor, may I be excused now, Your Honor, to go home to stick pins in the voodoo doll I constructed in your image. Oh yes, yes Your Honor, my human feelings have helped me to sculpt your face with devil's horns. Oh yes!"

The Rags of Time

For Frank, "Having gone through the mire with me," I now wiped my eyes and invited him to the divorce party I decided on the spot to throw for myself...and however much he charged, I was prepared to pay, remembering the $500 my father had given me 2 1/2 years before. Father would have been proud and approved the expense, as he had led the way when HE represented himself many years ago in some corporate actions against "the little guy" ...and won! Frank laughed and told me that $100 would amply reward him for the experience and pleasure of working with a Pretender-In-Law! A first for him, a first for me!

Thus ended Day Nine of Susanna's Divorce Agenda, and a great day it was! Free, Free, Free at last! I bought a bottle of champagne, phoned the friends who had been so supportive and loyal even though the only instrument I played was my own Ego, and invited them, even my "legal advisor" and of course Frank McTernan, and that night we were heady with champagne albeit Californian, as I again rehashed, some with laughter, some with tears, a two-year foray into a failed marriage.

Never again, I vowed!

Frank McTernan sipped a glass, then left to, I'm sure, tell and retell the story of the New York female who trialed the System, and won!

I toyed with the idea of remaining in California, even visited some friends in Los Angeles. Above Hollywood I could see the sign, toured the studios, and finally bored with lovely, one-season suburbia, I knew I belonged in New York. I loved the trees and mountains, but hungered for concrete, skyscrapers, the smells of the East River.

When my parents opened the door of their apartment, I cried knowing I had come full-circle, something I could not admit to them. We hugged, kissed, I rehashed the defeat, tried to laugh at the "adventure" of it all, but it was to the melody of inner defeat I moved and recognized that, something else I could not control had taken me over, and no amount of my beloved Mozart and Bach could make it right.

The Rags of Time

Chapter 4

Next was a job! But where? Doing what? My father suggested I work for him again, Thanks, Pop, but NO, never! What did I want to do? I had already phoned some friends, especially my dear Herman with whom I had never lost touch while in San Francisco. We were, through the 2 1/2 years, privy to each other's lives. Herman asked if I were interested in a job at the print and frame shop where he had been employed for some years now, but that held no appeal.

So...I was unemployed, but eminently employable! Two friends from Grove School days, a married couple, whom I called to say I had returned, asked my plans, and I told them that now with my great legal expertise in shedding my husband and MILFH, I might seek a job at the Brooklyn or Manhattan Psychiatric Hospitals.

"No, no, you mustn't do that" the double "E's," as I called them, immediately responded. I had met Ernest and Edith Zierer while I taught at Grove School, as they were friends of Jess Perlman and his wife. "Wait for our call. We'll make a job for you as our assistant at Hillside Hospital."

The Zierer's were head of the Creative Therapy Department at Hillside Hospital on Long Island, where they also oversaw the Occupational Therapy Department. They were Art Therapists, and had evolved a unique theory purporting to show a differential diagnosis between neurosis and psychosis, which involved drawing on a piece of 8 1/2 by 11 paper, using crayons: blue, green, brown. I thought I might be able to handle that! If I got the job, in addition to a modest salary, (nothing new to a Jaffe) I could live at the hospital. THAT clinched it for me!

I was hired, and now gainfully employed, received my meals, and at first shared a room with another employee who helped to show me the ropes, and round the hospital. Hillside was a small, semi-private psychiatric hospital under the aegis of the Jewish Federation, which was entered voluntarily by the patients, and was not for long-term treatment. It was also a training and teaching hospital for the staff of psychologists and psychiatrists, and most of these were of one psychiatric discipline or another. The doctors in chief positions were a Dr. Miller and Dr. Qualwasser, and in the seven years of my association with them, I valued and respected their kindness and abilities. As Hillside was a short-term treatment center, no patient remained longer than six-months.

To say that I was at first overwhelmed by my responsibilities is an understatement. I was being trained by the Zierer's to administer their Test, and also in hospital "etiquette" (read, "chain of command"), and I was definitely at the very lowest level. Below me came the patients, and as low as that I did not wish to go! Everybody had something to teach me, so I thought, but the double "E's" understood my floundering and allowed me to watch them and their techniques with patients, then permitted me to administer the tests, to keep notes and transcribe their notes (long-hand of course) before they let me take over on my own, under their watchful eyes.

Their Diagnostic Test consisted of a piece of paper on which I drew a triangle, or hill, with brown crayon, and then asked the patient, perhaps within a week of his arrival, to draw on both sides of the hill, a house and a tree. I sat and watched, or was at another quiet task, until the patient deemed the drawing complete. Nothing was discussed. Some patients added roadways or paths leading to the houses, while others might add stick figures, or a sun, or flowers. Some amused me as they chattered on while drawing, about matters totally unrelated to the drawings.

In the Occupational Therapy Department, I taught patients to do ceramics, had a potter's wheel installed, and a small kiln in which I fired their work. Patients were free to "create" in whatever medium they chose, I gave "art assignments" to those who asked for them, set up still-life arrangements, played music to release creativity, made supplies available, and as at the Grove School, found some positive aspect in every effort.

After all, there are few if any rules and regulations to creativity, or to life! Everyone was "successful, creative" and there were no "competitive" needs to be met. I DID observe and report to my superiors on the work methods of the patients, or on their approach to a task. I did NOT criticize, or expect from them anything other than their accomplishment. If asked by them, I might explain a way in which an object or figure MIGHT also be worked, but I tried not to influence a result.

There were few if any instances of aggression or unpleasantness in the "studio," but on one occasion, I WAS frightened. As I attempted to explain some pottery technique to a patient, I raised my voice over the hubbub in the room and said, "Please, could you keep it down to a roar?" whereupon a man arose in a menacing manner and started over towards me, when to my surprise and gratitude several of the other men in the room came towards me to protect me from what they thought would be a physical confrontation. The aggressive patient backed off and out of the room. I tried for calm and thanked my would-be rescuers, and the room returned to its noisy, normal state, and I tried to quiet my racing heart. I WAS only 5'2" after all...quite the smallest object in the area.

Whatever diagnostic revelations the "Test" showed, were explained by the Zierer's. Obviously, a house and a tree which slanted as did the "hill," would roll down its sides, and this was considered by them as indicating a lapse in "reality perception" of the patient, therefore showing schizoid tendencies. The houses and trees which conformed to the reality of placement at right angles to the hill, and would obviously remain "on" the hillside, signified to the Zierer's that the patient might be seriously neurotic, but had not lost touch with reality.

The psychiatrists were helped by learning this concept, albeit naïve, in their perceptions of their patients. It was another building block in their estimation of the mental health of their patients and in their approach in dealing with them. Also important were the written reports by the double "E's", and later, by me. I learned about my job by bumbling along, asking questions of everyone, especially those clinical psychologists who dispensed the more orthodox tests.

The psychologist assigned to our Department, a dark-haired and rather handsome man in his late twenties, dispensed a sexual aura I found attractive. Now, out of respect for his twice married status, I will call him simply, ELA, although I would like, in retrospect, to also call him pompous, conservative, even more so now, tri-named as he prefers to call himself...yet I will endeavor to be as circumspect as I have the reputation for being, which is not very!

The Rags of Time

I had been alone for over a year by then, and since I lived, as well as worked, at the Hospital until I could afford a place of my own, he and I embarked on a sexual relationship which progressed from couplings in the Occupational Therapy Department workshop (well, we WERE creative in the venues we chose) where we "fired up" among the soon-to-be fired clay pots. Since my hair was as red as ever, and he was single and had an air of vulnerability I was always, if not wisely, attracted by, we went to hotels, panted a lot in movie-houses, walked in Glen Oaks, frequented bars, and I think were as discreet as our mounting passion dictated. A definite plus was his lack of musical ability!

And you can't keep a good girl down!

Perhaps this last was not the most accurate way to phrase it, but I have never thought of myself as good or bad…just unique and intelligent. See, Mom, intelligence CAN be attractive to men…mature men, I hoped. So why, I asked myself, not see if he was responsive to my, at least outward qualities?

I may have frightened ELA with my openness…but not so much that he withdrew. I may even have fallen a bit in love…while ELA fell in lust! What I had not realized was that he was not brave, just physically needy. The one time in which he ever committed himself in writing, was on a greeting card, brown in color, on which he wrote: "You can see I love you if I send you a card this color!" If I read Freud correctly, I was to ELA, anally retentive!

Conservative in thought and deed, with an image in his mind, from a former era, in which a Virgin was to be deflowered by him, in marriage of course! In short, while he matured in a relationship with me, he remained in all respects, a rather ordinary man. When I realized that MY ideas of a relationship and HIS differed…in all respects except sensuality, and in THAT I would not admit defeat, I took the role of instructor, and far in advance of Viagra, salvaged my ego, and "built up" his, and for as long as I remained in residence at Hillside, kept him on part-time. It does sound ridiculous, but I needed to have the upper hand, not the emotional Missionary Position!

When I returned from San Francisco and the miseries of a failed marriage, I decided that NEVER again would I marry. I had determined my own life, made my own mistakes, made decisions, hoped I had learned from them, and was ready to take on life, …but on my own terms.

The Rags of Time

1- I would have "relationships," not commitments!
2- I would try not to hurt anyone in the above. Especially ME!
3- I would have FUN!
4- I would test the waters of my new-found freedom!
5- I would go it alone! (Except for sex, that is!)

I was ahead of my time. Before Germaine Greer, Ms. Magazine, Gloria Steinem, the Hite Report, Masters and Johnson! In 1950, this was MY Sexual Revolution. But then, I had been a revolutionary all my life!

If I needed validation, ELA told me once that HIS psychiatrist said that, "I was the best thing that ever happened to him; that I must have really loved him!" Of course, the words, "best thing" had a typical male ring, and were hurtful, but evidently that never occurred to ELA with his typical male mindset, and his not having the slightest emotional understanding of WHAT a loving woman can need for herself.

I decided to enlarge the number of my relationships.

All this played out against the background of my increasingly fascinating job. I loved it all, ill paying though it was, and took pleasure in the fact that I was regarded as an important member of the psychiatric team. The Italian psychiatrist, whom I was dating, often said that I had a way of getting to the realistic and psychological crux of a patient's psyche! After my second year I was offered the position as head Art and Occupational Therapist of the Adolescent Girls' Unit, where I soon established the same successful relationships with them as I had done at the Grove School.

It just occurs, is it possible that my success was based on MY being basically still an adolescent?

When I moved from Hillside Hospital to Aaron Burr's Carriage House in Greenwich Village, I was already slightly more affluent. How I was able to afford this historic gem was simple: having Low friends in High places! I had decided to go back to school, perhaps for a degree in Psychology, at New York University, which was, as is everything in Greenwich Village, within walking distance from my new home.

The Rags of Time

As it happened, a friend from Cooper Union days when I was designing and building scenery for a summer theatre in upstate New York, the opera singer, Jack De Merchant, introduced me to Two Boys who lived at 24 Charleton Street. Knowing that I sought an affordable place to live in Manhattan, he thought I might sub-sub-lease their home, which THEY subleased from the noted potter Nancy Wickham, who now lived and "potted" in Maine. The Boys were amenable, if Nancy agreed, with the provision that they would regain possession when they returned from France where one received a scholarship to paint, and the other, "to go with!"

I was introduced to Nancy Wickham who said it was fine with her, and that I might have the Carriage House at the same low rent, if she could continue to store some of her pieces, and would I show them to prospective buyers when necessary? Of course, I would be delighted…and so it was arranged!

Musicians and Gays seem always to have been my Fairy God-parents and Angels, and I cherish them all! Clinton Hill and Alan Tran were my two latest Angels!

How to describe 24 Charleton Street? It was probably the most romantic place in which I have ever lived! And anyone who visited agreed! It was difficult to discourage a man who escorted me home after dinner, or a drink, or the theatre, from staying the night…but I did it gently…and firmly!

Sex was sex, but the Carriage House was above mere Sex! I loved it, loved living in it, and my life was now so exciting and varied…and driven by ME.

The Carriage House was set in among four gardens, and not visible from the street. There was only the bright turquoise front door, with its number, at sidewalk level, to announce its presence. Once opened, the door gave way to a long, narrow, bricked passage, which led to gardens, mine and three others which bordered on either side and the rear. On one side of the entry corridor was a lush Japanese ivy, very broad-leaved, which clung to the brick. I soon learned in spring and summer warmth that the Ivy crept forward and would entangle my arms, face, hair. My solution was to hang a pair of scissors close by the street door so I could cut my way in during the "growing" seasons! The garden itself was about an 8 by 10 foot rectangle, which had within its confines, some "City" flowers. I was not in those days a gardener, but knew a daisy, and a wild rose, a daffodil, amid scrubby grass. I cut away some, and picked others, and used a Wickham vase in the living room/kitchen/toilet-cum-shower, which took up the "living space" as I entered the front door.

The rooms were tiny, having been carved from the small space originally needed to house Aaron Burr's carriage and two horses. None lived in comfort, I decided, but it evidently was enough. The Boys had furnished it with a small couch, a round coffee table, bookshelves, and some stools created from tractor-seats! The walls were whitewashed and sometimes our clothes bore the imprint. Also there were some floor-cushions, and one had to, in company, squeeze oneself around people, furniture, to a small counter in the tiny kitchen which had the only sink in the house, a tiny two-burner stove, and cater-cornered, was a toilet which also held a shower stall partitioned by a curtain. Considering its "intimate" nature, it was enclosed by a bit of wall and a door!

Primitive? Perhaps, but to me, a private haven and heaven, and total joy! Not interested in homemaking, cooking, I installed an electric broiler-oven-toaster, and was in business. Meals at home were rare. Oh yes, there was a tiny refrigerator, but I quickly became European in attitude, and after work would pick up a salad, the two chops and petite dessert daily…or go to one of the marvelous little restaurants and coffee shops on Houston (pronounced HOW-ston) Street.

I also came in possession of Esmeralda, a cat who prowled the garden or came into the house through any window left open. I was under the impression she belonged to the Boys, and so began to feed her. I named her, as the green-leather collar she wore had no name attached, but had a silver bell, which had lost its clapper!

I decided that Esmeralda was an Egyptian cat because her lovely triangulated face and head sat atop a very, very, long neck, as in sculptures I had seen of Egyptian cats in museums. Esmeralda was black with white paws and chest markings, carried herself regally, purred and rubbed up against any quiescent leg, and seated herself without question on any lap, whether offered or not! She was also the first cat with whom I had ever made intimate contact. The Jaffe's were, parents AND grandparents, DOG people.

Esmeralda seemed to share an interest with her Adopted Human. She loved

Male cats, and was sought after by them, especially because in our almost two year relationship, she deposited a litter every sixty-three days! All the kittens resembled, in Mendelian fashion, a large coal-black Tom in the neighborhood. Busy at work, then at school, I left her food and milk and water in a shady spot outdoors in fine weather, otherwise in the kitchen. Where she wandered during the day, I had no idea, but she deposited in the closets, in my shoes, on the beds, under the blankets, evidence of her profligate sex life!

In that regard, we were NOT alike!

I may have lost friends, but I learned how to plead, beg, cajole, people to accept the kittens after they were weaned! If all else failed, I took some to what I called Greenwich Village Cat-House. Actually, it was a quite nice Humane Society! I didn't learn until The Boys returned that Esmeralda belonged to a family around the corner, on King Street, which was where the Tom also resided!

Oh well, another example of a good-hearted Dame with frailties!

My brick Carriage House-turned living quarters was my pride and joy, my nest…for the time being at least. Immediately past the living room, through a door, was what had been Nancy's studio, in which her potter's wheel had been used. The large room ran the length of the house, and at the right, just off the wall, which divided it from the living room, there was a ship's stair which led to the bedrooms above. Upstairs, as one walked off the stair, was a small platform which held shelves filled with Nancy's wares. The stair treads were so shallow, as on a ladder, that one must perforce walk up or down sideways, while clutching a stair rail! To the right was the door leading to the very small bedrooms.

From history books I gleaned only that Aaron Burr had killed Alexander Hamilton in 1804 while he, Burr, was Vice-President to Jefferson, and that he live in New York State in the 1870's and that he kept a carriage and horses! That was as much as I knew. The Carriage House was set among Brownstones, in one of which undoubtedly, Burr resided! The only brownstone I had ever been invited to was the home of my sole supporter and Cat-lover, a dear older gentleman who had retired from his position as Editor of the New Yorker Magazine. In the early mornings I could be seen by anyone in the Brownstones from their rear windows, as I sat in my pajamas or nightgown (or walking naked in my home) sipping my cup of coffee, or sitting on my front stone step in the sunshine, Esmeralda or a book in my lap.

No, not naked, of course!
But not always alone, either!
Esmeralda?
Sometimes with larger Biped!

Well, my third principle was to have fun, and I have ever been a woman who lived up to her principles!

Once, after showing a friend the bedroom, she fell down the stairs. It was insisted she go to St. Vincent's Hospital on Fourteenth Street, and in the emergency room when asked her complaint, she replied, "Doctor, I am a Fallen Woman!" After laughter, the verdict: a cracked rib! She was the only casualty and the story served as a Cautionary Tale to future venturesome and admiring visitors, Male or Female!

Each tiny bedroom boasted a bed, a wooden closet, small chest of drawers, and a squarish tilt-out window showing the back of the brownstones and the gardens. The tilt-out windows were to allow the groom to pitch or fork out the hay for the horses…or to collect the manure to enrich whatever garden then existed. My bedroom had a low half-wall which was curtained off, or not, for privacy. I chose the second of the bedrooms because of its twelve by twelve inch oak beam which was directly over my bed.

The oak beam had its gruesome appeal because a former occupant of the House, the well known, albeit often impoverished sculptor, John Flanagan, had hanged himself from it in 1942. Whether from poverty, illness, or depression, or drug use, who can tell. John Flanagan was considered one of the most gifted of the "direct carving" school of sculpture. He "saw" the finished image he wanted before he set chisel to wood or stone. I was familiar with his work when I attended Cooper Union, and his work was included in most of the great Museums in America. He was just 47 years old when he took his life.

With my gutsy past, and general outlook, I was, I felt, impervious to this ill-fated end, since I would NEVER consider this for myself! Rather, I agreed with Dylan Thomas who wrote:

The Rags of Time

"Do not go gentle in to that good night,
Old age should burn and rave at close of day;
Rage, rage against the dying of the light."

I fully intend to go kicking and screaming all the way!

The whitewashed walls of the House were of brick laid double-depth, horizontally, and were so thick that there was total privacy. The only sounds came from my radio and phonograph, and when I had the time, I painted and drew to my beloved Mozart, which even now, as I write, puts forth concertos with the great Alicia De Larrocha at her keyboard. I imagine that if my neighbors were annoyed they held their collective tongues! I rarely saw them in their Brownstone Mansions. The one friend I made was over Esmeralda. Since he was newly retired from Editorship of the New Yorker, he was free to be called on when I needed advice about the care, feeding, and habits of felines. He even took over her care when I was on vacation for a week, and from him I gathered information about the neighborhood, as we shared a cup of coffee in my garden, or in his living room, very grand by my standards.

It was exciting when he spoke to me of some of the famous cartoonists such as Gluyas Williams, William Steig, Chon Day, Henry Thurber, Helen Hokinson, and told me of some of the policies of the magazine, and I spoke to him of the vagaries of my patients...and of the psychiatrists.

When I attended New York University in pursuit of my M.A., some of the courses proved to be difficult, especially Anatomy, and I became known as the student who handled her body in class in an effort to understand the origins and insertions of muscles, or of nerves and arteries. I also met two male students who were more advanced and into the study of Medicine. They couldn't understand why my Student Advisor had signed me up for this class which was designed for pre-med students, and not the simpler and more basic class for someone NOT slated to become a doctor! The Fellows were helpful, and we sometimes studied together, and NO, they did NOT handle my body in explanation!

They DID invite me to travel with them to Florida during a school break, and as I was able to apply some of my vacation time from my job, I decided I needed a break from routine. We would scrupulously divide into thirds all traveling expenses. I went, leaving Esmeralda to the tender care of my Brownstone Buddy…or to the streets! Lest I be accused of neglect, Esmeralda WAS an outdoor cat, and had survived nicely without my presence. This was before I knew of her hidden past!

We three Fellow Travelers went to many cities in Florida, and stayed in various motels along the way, one being former slave quarters in Virginia. Whenever and wherever I could, I indulged a childhood interest from Brooklyn days, that of collecting seashells, having always considered them some of nature's most beautiful forms…and I still collect them from my shore of the Niantic River, Long Island Sound, especially after a rainstorm, when they and sea glass are to be found in great abundance in the early mornings.

In 1950-51, Florida, now almost synonymous with Miami Beach, was a different and more peaceful and unspoiled place, and much more beautiful, in my opinion. Fort Lauderdale and the Florida Keys were my favorites. In those days, Daytona Beach had horses being ridden into the surf, not NASCAR enthusiasts, or autos of any sort. And the cities were not built up into the ugliness which now infects them. Then, I enjoyed the sight of pink, yellow and blue stucco motels, hotels and rooming houses, some of which hosted us for a night.

The Fellows and I visited the Seminole Indian potters and clothing-makers, and the scene of stilt-houses and often rotted, rotting, and downed trees, were images I drew, and certainly still carry with me. And glimpses of water, water everywhere. I loved all that. The experience of that area of Florida is still, visually, with me, including the unforgettable occasion when I bought a hand-woven basket to hold the art materials I invariably schlepped whenever I traveled. It wasn't until we were on the road back to the motel that I saw stamped on the basket-bottom: MADE IN POLAND! For years I enjoyed showing my friends what the Polish Seminoles had wrought!

One day one of the Fellas expressed a desire to see an Alligator Farm, much touted by tourist guides, spoken or written, because of the Alligator Wrestling! Since they had kindly indulged MY whims in so many ways, once when I led them one-half mile into the water of the Keys in order to see shells beneath crystal-clear waters, and never got deeper into them than my calves, I didn't see how I could refuse ONE touristy sight!

The Rags of Time

Am I not always a good sport?

At the very tourist-crowded Exhibition of Alligator Wrestling, a handsome, half-clad Seminole youth, manfully wrestled the Ferocious Beast (all phrases taken from the colorful posters which were in evidence everywhere). The lissome youth tried to poke the alligator into movement! He attempted to convince the Ferocious Beast to open its jaws, to show his truly fearsome-looking teeth, and then to insert his Seminole head therein. I distinctly saw the alligator yawn in an attempt to go BACK TO SLEEP! The upshot of all this Ferocity (unsuccessful) was that I regaled my Fellow-travelers all the way back to the motel, and continued my imitations of the Seminole Brave and the Ferocious Alligator all the way back to New York!

Neither of them EVER asked me to attend a similar Animal/Human Contest! It made me almost as famous as my imitation of the Frog I "pithed" in my High School Biology Class! But they forgave me my outrageous conduct and helped me to pass the dratted anatomy course as one of them lent me a full-sized skeleton before the final exam so that I might use it and not my own bones…and I wickedly did tend to leave it in full view of my windows and take up slightly suggestive positions while in a state of semi-déshabillé!

By now, all readers are aware of my occasional lapses of maturity!

The required course in sociology I considered stupid and boring in the extreme, and not one student ever spoke up, no matter the bilge spouted. I decided that I had earlier been misplaced by my "ill-adviser" into an anatomy class not designed for my body, but that was finally and successfully, over.

Utter boredom I found unacceptable!

During the next sociology class, I arose and challenged the Professor on some statement he made. I stood in the vast, ill-lit auditorium, and told him that I considered Sociology a "crap" science, and that it was simply a course in statistics of things which already happened, and that people can, and do, bend statistics to fit any theory in need of validation!

The sounds of pen-scratched note-taking and under-breath mutterings came to a complete halt. The silence was complete. I now fully expected to be either tossed out of the class or go to a slower death by boredom, or quit it altogether! I sat primly down, closed my notebook, prepared for whatever, and at the end of class was asked by the Professor to see him in his office.

"Miss Mautner, while I disagree with your opinions, I am aware that today's class WAS being listened to after you spoke, so I ask you to consider the following: Will you act as catalyst to the class, and undertake to defend the opposite of any opinion I advance? I will promise to listen, and hope that other students will be emboldened to get off their backsides and say SOMETHING, ANYTHING!"

This appeal to my intellect I could NOT forego. I decided to remain in the course, and in fact didn't have to stretch to disagree with him, having come from a long-line of revolutionaries, of which he was unaware.

School was more interesting, my life in toto, was more interesting, and I began to vary my social life and "relationships." In short, I was happy. My very dear Herman went with me to gallery openings, to the theatre, to museums, restaurants. Sometimes he brought other friends with him. Life was good.

Herman's closest friend accompanied him to my Carriage House and fell under its spell. Not I, just the house! Once when I invited them to dinner, I burnt the main course, so of course, (as Morris teased me forever, …for 45 years) they took me out for dinner. I noticed Morris really, at about that time, really saw him although I seemed to have known about him for years as Herman's dearest friend. Morris entertained us with stories of his classes at The New School for Social Research in Greenwich Village.

Morris never spoke of his wartime years and experiences in Europe. The G.I. Bill provided him with his first college education, and he told us that the experience was mind-bending for him. Imagine studying a course in Shakespeare with W.H. Auden, psychology with Karen Horney, philosophy with William Kallen! I knew something of the New School which was newly built and established at about the same time I attended Cooper Union. I had audited some classes there, with Irwin Piscator of stage design and lighting fame. I had toyed with the idea of becoming a Stage Designer, but economics took over. Lee Aronson wrote in "Part of a Lifetime" the fact that making a living from designing for the stage was very difficult for a man, and very few ever succeeded. For a woman, it would at that time have been an impossibility. Auditing Piscator's lectures was the closest I ever got to that plan for my future. But, the classes did introduce me to the playwrights and designers from the famous Agitprop theatre movement in Berlin who were then in self-exile from Germany and who lectured about their work from Piscator's class.

Morris and I compared our experiences of those people we both knew about, and his enthusiasm was boundless and infectious. He was an excellent student who drew Auden's interest in him when for an assignment, he presented Auden with a Rhymed Comedy Version of "The Taming of The Shrew." He received the top grade in class, and Auden sought him out in class for Morris to present HIS ideas on literature, poetry, and prose. Morris was truly hooked. His ambition was to become a teacher, despite the fact that he was considered by the Military as an expert in the field of Communication, and he might have gone into that field of engineering at his discharge from service.

Because of their successful boyhood "partnership" with puppets and marionettes, Herman and Morris formed a company to design and build and market window displays which were to be different from the prevailing displays of clothes hung, or draped, on insipid-looking mannequins…and different they were! They displayed accessories in wire bird-cages on the main floor of Macy's Department Store, sculpted wire valises for Bergdorf-Goodman which were filled with cruise clothes, created the backdrop of the New York City Skyline through which were threaded various articles of clothing, and were successful in creating the displays for Lord and Taylor's difficult windows which had proven anathema for other decorators and designers. They were given the distinction of being shown on the cover of "Display" Magazine thee times in one year!

To keep up with the demand, Herman and Morris asked another Cooper graduate, Ethel Bittner, to join them. Now there were two artists AND Morris, who, given their ideas, built the models and sold their ideas to various department stores.

Trouble began when "les deux Artistes" came to work at 10 or 11 AM, broke at 1 PM for lunch, returned at 3, all the time that Morris was at work turning out the ideas which had been discussed. Also it was HIS creativity which transformed the drawn designs ideas into simple, economical, and practical results. Soon Morris grew impatient with the laissez-faire attitude of the two "Artistes" and told them he wanted out of the partnership, but he would work FOR rather than with them…as an hourly "employee." There was friendly friction as Morris made more money than they! The thing which caused Morris to finally part company with them entirely was when Ford Motor Company came to them. Morris suggested a mobile showing Ford automobiles, especially the most famous older models, from the "Model A" to the "Model T" and the most distinctive later models. The Ford company was enthusiastic about that concept, and ordered 100 mobiles which were to be exhibited throughout the United States, in their franchises.

This was to be the largest account Herman and Morris ever received, and Morris suggested a way in which the mobiles could be built, and how they could fill such an order, and set about making a demonstration model. The mobiles, he said, could be powered by fans, to dance gracefully overhead. Then Herman said he was too busy to begin because he had to finish his Christmas shopping! Herman was Jewish, for goodness sake, which excuse caused a collapse, not in the Auto Industry, but in the Goustin-Schwartz business enterprise!

Herman was to continue for the rest of his life to be frightened at the prospect of Fame and Fortune!

But Morris and I loved him for all the rest of his life, and, our lives.

Morris, after finishing at the New School, went to live and work in Massachusetts and it was some years before I saw him again.

By that time I had to leave my beloved Burr Carriage House. The Boys had returned from France and naturally wanted their home again. I HAD promised, but stalled them for several more months. "Fair is Fair," I sobbed, while trying to find another Greenwich Village apartment, but with no luck.

Also, The Boys laid a guilt trip on me! I, who had sidestepped guilt from experts (Jewish Mothers), could not refuse to accept the gift of an original Manuscript page from "The Epic of The Kings," the book of Nahma, which dated from 16th century Persia. Its spidery black and red calligraphy was irresistible to me. I'm a sucker for beauty! It's a treasure, and the world today would be hard-pressed to imitate this art, especially since I believe I earned the page by my sacrifice of Burr Romanticism!

The Rags of Time

Chapter 5

The expression is, "Come-down" but my next quarters and adventure was definitely a "Step-up!" I found an apartment in Little Italy, hard-by Greenwich Village, albeit with a different flavor: more garlic!

I moved to the top floor of a six-story tenement building on Thompson Street, which I immediately "gentrified," ever the revolutionary, by describing it as "Lower Fifth Avenue through the Arch." When one walks through Washington Square Park's Arch, on both sides of which are tenement buildings, one is, (or WAS) transported to another time. The buildings housed "pushcarts" which belonged to the entrepreneurs who also stabled their horses in the same buildings, several stories up. They, on warm nights, had their heads out of the windows, and as I looked up to see them, my sole company, I tried to whistle up to them, as they turned their heads to follow my progress, then nicker at me. We were the only living-things out on the sleeping streets, or so it seemed to me.

The tenement I moved to was of brick and had a marble-floored entry hall and stairway. My apartment and the one immediately next door were the only two in the building NOT occupied by Italians. My next-door neighbor was a handsome, young, Greek architect and wannabe actor, Jim Carlos.

We became friends when I knocked at his door to explain that I was to have a "painting party" the following Saturday, and asked if he would like to attend, and to excuse any untoward noise. I also cemented relations with the tenants on the same floor, and on the floor below by the same ruse, and I offered food and wine, and while none of them ever came, they were pleased to have been asked, and from that day forward, "took care of me" as I was red-haired, Jewish, polite and considerate. The extent of their concern was that whenever a male friend brought me home, there was always a "guard" stationed at the front door who noted the time, and the following day said things such as "You got home late last night!"

Neighbor Jim Carlos and I exchanged amenities: I had no television set, he, no bathtub. When I came home from work or school, I often asked to watch the McCarthy hearings, while Jim went into my flat to have a proper bath since all he had was a granite washtub in his kitchen, in which he would have to stand, or uncomfortably squat, to sponge-bathe.

Neighborliness IS a two-way street!

My old-fashioned claw-foot enamel tub stood against the kitchen wall, and boasted a wooden top which was supposed to serve as a counter when no one lolled in the tub, which as a "tub" was totally exposed to anyone passing through. Next to it was the only sink in the flat, with a small mirror atop. The toilet was grandly housed separately in a tiny room with WINDOW! One backed in and sat down, or if Male, stood with his back against a tiny shelf attached to the door, which held in winter a small heater. When I sat, I had a hot chest and cold feet, since the apartment which rented for $37.50 a month, boasted hot water and no heat. In winter, I invested in a kerosene stove for the living room, but since I had NO experience with such modern conveniences, it was a miracle that I did not set the entire building on fire! I DID manage to turn anything white or light or pale-colored, into a marvelous grey-black, but luckily there was a Chinese laundry which made house calls.

I also had a similar arrangement with a dry-cleaning establishment down the street, my motto being, "What is forgotten is NEVER climbed up for!" I even employed a cleaning lady to come weekly, gave her a key of course, or left it in the Coffee Shop next door, which one of the few men extant in my tenement owned and operated. He also acted as one of my "protectors" and "guards" and was interested in my social life, and when I had a cup of coffee most mornings before I went to work (with or without the bagel which I think he stacked for me), he was like an elder uncle, sweet-tempered and kind, gave me good advice and information about neighborhood events, and introduced me to the famous San Gennaro Festival, put on annually by the local Church and Monastery, just two blocks away. It was a splendid weeklong Festival which had something for everyone, hosted by the brown-robed, sandaled, tonsured, and rope-belted Monks.

The Rags of Time

And I enjoyed it all!

Well, maybe except for the six flights I had to climb. To ward off occasional loneliness, I went to the Greenwich Village Cat House and brought home a Tom I named "Gatto." My having him emasculated must have changed his kittenish personality into a savage because he never forgot or forgave, and now had the habit of pouncing on me from any angle of a room. I had to handle him with oven mitts. He was not to be played with, by ME, in any case. I returned him to the "Cat House" with a gift of money, and the worker there, a male, exclaimed, "Well, what did you expect after what YOU did?"

It was useless to explain that I had never had such a reaction from any of my other men!

The superintendent of the building was a drunk, who, when in his cups, climbed to the top floor and yelled and cursed about his wife who had run off with another man. He was harmless, and if anyone came out of any apartment on my floor, would politely step aside, and then resume his tirade when we were out of sight.

The other tenants rented not one, but sometimes two or three apartments. Whoever rented the apartment at the head of any floor, facing the staircase, kept their front doors open and called a cheery greeting to me. I would glance in and see almost life-size figures of Christ on the Cross, or Mary with Baby Jesus, set against lurid red velvet draperies. The woman on my floor waited always until I was safely home at night, and then closed her door. Evidently the entire building was to keep me safe! I saw very few men, although there were some children. Absent fathers and grown sons, I soon learned, were usually housed at City, State, or Federal expense!

On the one occasion I had a visit from my mother, she brought my grandmother. Bubbe slowly made her way up the stairs, past some open apartment doors and the almost life-sized religious figures, and into my flat, bearing a "care" package of cheese and chicken blintzes she had made. I served them dinner, and at early evening they left. All the time we were together, Bubbe was smiling, interested in my living arrangements and my décor, the neighbors, the neighborhood as I spun anecdote after anecdote. Later that night I received a call from my mother who told me that when they reached the street, my grandmother turned on her, and in a rage accused my mother of forcing me to live that way!

"It's your fault! Susie was never brought up to live this way! What did you do to her? It's your fault!"

Mother and I shared a laugh at Grandma's tact. My mother knew that I found living in the tenement financially useful, since I was now in therapy, and on my modest salary, it was a struggle to pay for my Id and Ego!

In the 1950's the prevailing wisdom mandated that in order to advise others on their problems, deal with their troubled Psyches, one had to understand himself. In this case, herself. Even if I felt I understood myself fairly well, nevertheless, I should be in therapy. I gathered a list of psychotherapists and psychiatrists from the Director of Hillside Hospital, and thus armed, went first to the one geographically closest, a William Marvin, a Sullivanian-influenced psychotherapist who lived and worked out of a brownstone he owned on 10th Street. In years past I had drooled over the building which I remembered from Cooper Union days. I often strolled that block and looked into windows, into tall-ceilinged rooms, glimpsed lamps, bookcases, paintings.

When I entered the house for my "interview" of, and with, the therapist, I was overwhelmed by all the artwork, sculpture, books, and immediately felt at home. I could talk to this man and be understood.

It was Seduction by Premises! If he accepted me, I would throw away the list.

He did, and I did, and thus began a wonderful and painful three and a half year relationship.

I said, "Doctor, I want you to stop me if I begin to spout psychobabble, or come on like a psychologist which I attend school to become." I also told him some bare bones about myself, my job, my failed marriage and divorce.

When I finished, he said to sit, lie down, get comfortable, so I lay on the couch in his office and then for the next six months, soaked it with my tears. Never had a "dry" session since he was of the Harry Stack Sullivan School which dealt with reality and not with the Freudian "You talk and I'll listen," or answering a question with a question:

The Rags of Time

"Doctor, I feel so listless."
"Why do you think you feel listless?"

Who needed THAT!

He also understood my lack of money and so charged me one-third of what he charged his other patients, and often accepted a drawing, or print, or painting of mine, in lieu of cash.

Whenever I made a particularly outrageous remark, he laughed, pointed it out, set me back on the path to reality. I began to keep a notebook by my bed to record my dreams, and some were so interesting to me that I began to draw them...or symbols from them. There was no "symbolism" to be discovered from my dreams...rather my reactions to what my dreams or nightmares envisioned or meant to me.

I remember one of my weepiest sessions. I sobbed that I was "the second best" to my parents, and how fragile was my ego, and how few relationships I had! Sob, Sob, Heartbreak! Bill Marvin burst into laughter and pointed out, quite rightly, that my strengths lay in the fact that what I termed as "neglect" had actually been a blessing, as I was free to develop "IN MY OWN WAY!" Further, what I called my lack of popularity and relationships with men had resulted (and he kept count) in one marriage and nine other involvements which I ended when I wanted them to!

With Bill Marvin, like the proverbial pigeon, I didn't have a Reality Ledge to stand on!

When finally I ended my therapy, I owed him quite a lot of money, in the thousands, and told him that I would, as though I were still seeing him, pay him weekly until my debt was discharged, to which he replied that I owed him nothing. The debt was cancelled because I had given him more pleasure and enjoyment than he had had with any other patient.

And there had been no sex involved!

He was a truly wonderful man from whom I learned to accept and value myself totally as I was. I now felt free, for the first time.

The Rags of Time

I said goodbye to my tenement flat and protective neighbors and moved to Chelsea, to what had been Clement Moore's home on 22nd Street, between 9th and 10th Avenues. I lived on the third floor, over the owner's flat. I must indeed have had the symbol of music ever in my life, as the owner, who retained the bottom two floors, was an Operatic Basso, and also taught students in the room below my bedroom. I now had the pleasure of music at various times of the day and evenings, and when he apologized for any disturbance, I told him that music was NEVER a disturbance…and added something of my own music background, as audience only, and of my love for music.

We soon became great friends and his wife invited me to dinner occasionally, with them and their two small children. The top floor above mine was occupied by a woman who worked as a designer of Haute Couture for Oleg Cassini, one of Jaqueline Kennedy's clothiers.

The house itself was extraordinary. Built of red brick and attached to other houses on both sides, its interior was of vintage wallpaper in the entry and up the staircase. Each of the two rooms of the flats had marble fireplaces, in working order, but I was frightened to use mine lest I cause a conflagration! There was also heat and hot water, a luxury I had not had since I began my Village Odyssey…I mean, both together…at the same time!

The ceilings towered upward of 10 feet, and the two rear windows of my bedroom were almost floor to ceiling height, and looked out over the building and gardens of St. Joseph's Seminary. My latest feline, named "Cat," chose to spend her days in the sunshine of the deep sills. Neither of us got Religion, but it was lovely and peaceful. I furnished the flat. The two large rooms, front and back were separated by a toilet with bath, and led to a wall kitchen in the corridor. Then I set out to explore my new neighborhood. On the corner nearest to 10th Avenue, was a Bodega which sold me the basics and spices and deli meats and cheeses, and wonderful pickled delights. More American fare could be gotten on my way home from work in a small market, and when I detrained at 23rd Street, I was almost opposite the YMCA where they practiced fencing.

How do I know? One of my "relationships" fenced! And sometimes invited me to classes to watch…I also drew them as they "dueled."

Very often on weekday mornings, I would walk a few blocks and then be picked up by one of the psychiatrists who lived with his wife, an opera singer, nearby. He also had a miniature Schnauzer with him in the car, and he leashed the dog at the hospital while he saw patients. He had warned me, as I sat in the front passenger seat beside him, NOT to touch the dog, or attempt to pat his head. I've always regarded warnings as a signal to proceed with caution…but to proceed!

In the mornings before I met the car, I often bought coffee and a doughnut or sweet roll. One day I offered a bit of doughnut, casually, in my open palm. The Schnauzer bit…not me, the doughnut was scarfed down! After that, armed with some pastry offering, the Schnauzer was MINE! …the way to a dog's heart IS through his stomach! Now I could stroke and pet away as long as I liked, and the dog ran to me at the hospital when he could, and sat in my lap in the car.

Another seduction ended my way!

Always among my friends, there was Herman. When I was once in a weepy therapy mode, while at dinner together, I asked him why we didn't marry each other? We were each other's best friend, and we would continue our private lives, privately, no sex, just support each other emotionally. Why not?

"You can do better than me. Eventually we'd make each other miserable," was his reply. Of course he was right. I think I just wanted a "marriage des amis" because it was safe, and I found so many of the men I dated, boring. I would sit and we'd go through the usual dating ritual of:

"Tell me about yourself," I would tell my date.

And he did, and I had to listen to the usual boring account of his work, his hobbies, his meager ideas. Where was the humor, the ambition, the plans for a life other than the ordinary? So, I had a lot of first dates, not seconds. I preferred to go to a movie, read a book, or listen to music by myself.

In the midst of this, Herman's mother invited me to her flat in Jersey City, New Jersey, for Thanksgiving dinner. I had recently bought the most elegant and expensive outfit I had ever owned from a designer/sample shop in Greenwich Village, by paying for it over many weeks. It was a Givenchy original, two-piece with very short skirt and over blouse of Loden wool. I was at the time a size six.

The Rags of Time

When I arrived at Herman's house that afternoon, Herman asked if I would like to visit Morris' home a few blocks away, and then we three would return for the feast. Of course, said I. It was a lovely autumnal day and I wanted to see Morris' three dogs, or was it four? When no one would rent him an apartment since he had five dogs, he naturally bought a house! With a bit of front garden. The dogs were three purebred collies and a mixed-breed, marcelled blond, cocker-spitz named Buttons.

When we returned to Herman's flat, during that family party, I think Morris "saw" me for the first time. I was aware that he kept looking at me, at my very good legs, and saw how much all the Goustins liked me. Before I left that evening, Morris asked, "Can I call you?" "Yes," I answered airily, "I'm in the book."

On that note I walked out.

I thought no more about it, but Morris evidently did, and began calling for dates to dinner, movies, the theatre, ballet. Often it was a threesome: Morris, Herman, me. It was generally a laugh riot as the men related stories of their daily experiences, or I, more seriously of my patients. Morris was at that time the secretary of a labor union, and handled negotiations between workers and employers.

I learned from Morris that often an employee didn't understand the terms of his employment, or would rather have a ten-cent an hour raise than appreciate the situations when he might make more: overtime pay, or on the various holidays which also paid overtime, or that changes in the Union rules would benefit him in other ways. Hell, I didn't know that either! But when he talked about it, I grew a bit more savvy about money matters, and DID apply the lessons learned, in the future.

Sometime between his graduation from the New School and working in Display, Morris attended the University of Wisconsin for special training in, and exchange of ideas in the field of communication. Morris was already adjudged an expert though his work in the Military, as he was responsible for General Patton's Army Tank Corps, where he installed and handled all communication between the tanks and Headquarters, and for the Officers who required special radio hookups.

The Rags of Time

Morris told me that he planned to remain in Europe after the War, but his father wrote to the Army that HE, the father, was ill and needed him at home. It was a lie, but Morris was not to know the truth until his return, and then he rethought his life. With his fine and inventive intelligence and ability, Morris also, once home, designed and created machinery for industry.

Once I was asked to join Herman and Morris for drinks and dinner. Home, after work, I changed and taxied to the American Bar and Grill, the only bar where I would arrange to meet someone, other than in Greenwich Village, where I knew EVERYONE! At the American Bar and Grill, a solitary woman could sit at the bar with an empty stool on either side, unless of course, she preferred "company."

On the ride from Chelsea to 7th Avenue and 45th Street, the driver said or did something which I found amusing, and when I entered the bar, there were my companions, an empty stool between them and I walked over to them saying, "Do you want to hear what happened to me in the cab?" Morris said a swift "No!" THAT got my attention, as my legs had gotten his, because during the 45 years of our marriage, I never told him!

My drink of choice was, at that time, a vodka martini. As we three sat talking, laughing, and sipping, unnoticed my me, each time my glass emptied, the bartender refilled it. I realized this the moment my legs felt strange as we left our stools to walk to the restaurant. I was dizzy, but the two men supported me for the short walk to the Italian restaurant we all knew and often enjoyed.

The first thing I ordered was a black coffee, and I had several of those before I could turn my attention to the menu. When the order was given and I took a taste, I suddenly felt drunk and although I hoped food would help, it didn't!

One has, when tipsy, the idea that when one walks, one has to take especial care to keep the head up, the back straight, the steps even…but with all of this, I had suddenly the impression that I was watching myself from outside my body. THAT will sober "ONE" quickly enough!

The actual occasion for the dinner was a rehearsal of the Ballet of "Hamlet" for which Herman had designed the costumes, and this was to be the "dress rehearsal" of the Ballet. Considering my "out-of-body" experience of a few moments ago, I decided that I was in no condition to attend the theatre, and declined, and Morris said that he would get me out into the fresh air, we'd walk a while, and then he'd see me home. So Herman went on alone, and Morris and I set out on 6th Avenue in the direction of Central Park.

It had snowed the day before, the curbsides were many feet high in shoveled snow, but I was warmly wrapped up in the pale blond fur coat which my grandmother had bought me, since in her opinion NO cloth coat was warm enough for Susie. Arm in Arm, Morris and I walked until 59th Street, the southern end of Central Park. We sat on a bench for several hours, to the amusement of passersby, and spoke of Morris, then of me, and never once was I bored...or aware of being cold. Intrigued yes, bored no! We exchanged recollections of Herman and of how we all met so many years before, and of our hopes and dreams for ourselves, and how this "new woman," Me, intended her life to continue.

When I invited Morris and Herman to my apartment for dinner one Saturday night, I, who had no money for other than a bottle of California wine, was presented with a jeroboam of champagne from Morris and laughter from Herman. I had never seen, or even heard the word "jeroboam." I think today that is called a "magnum." I never had or served liquor to guests for the simple reason that I couldn't afford it!

Then, the Games began!

Every day or so, Morris phoned to invite me out, no more threesomes. Occasionally we dined chéz moi. The theatre was a shared interest, also ballet. I had seen my first ballet performance in honor of my 16th birthday, and at the Metropolitan Opera House on 38th Street...in a BOX! On Sunday evenings, the usual box-ticket holders were dispossessed in order that the bourgeoisie (like us) could have the privilege of riches without money. My birthday present from a fond uncle via his dress factory was a black and turquoise chiffon outfit. My mother had bought me the latest fashion of the day: an Empress Eugènie black-velvet toque with an arching turquoise feather. I wondered if I had suddenly metamorphosed into a Swan. No one could have been more thrilled than I, and thus began a life-long infatuation with ballet. As danced by others!

The Rags of Time

Morris, it seemed, shared this passion, and during the ballet "season," we attended almost every evening and weekend performance we could arrange…and afford. On Saturday or Sunday, we sometimes attended matinee AND evening performances.

In contrast, we both also loved jazz, and went to a Jazz Club held in a small space and performed by mainly middle-aged men, all seemingly well-known to the audience seated at small round tables, and from them would come yells to play certain favorites between the "jamming," such as "Play Butter and Egg Man, Sam. Please play Butter and Egg Man!" And Sam did, to clapping and stomping through cigarette smoke so thick it was hard to see the bandstand!

We often went dancing after the theatre or dinner at Russian restaurants like The Balalaika, which I remember from my youth as a place my parents often went with me in tow! I told Morris what to expect, and some things hadn't changed: Georgian-costumed men performing the famous "Sword Dance" where two swords are crossed at right angles, and the men, dancing ever-faster, stepped between the blades, in breathtaking gyrations. Gypsy singers sang music from the Tsar's era, and now, from the USSR.

Morris and I both knew, from other dates with other people, some wonderful French restaurants, and Morris introduced me to Lebanese and Syrian food. Strange to say, we stayed slim.

Our friendship heated up and I tried to cool it down, but it WAS so much fun, so enjoyable, mainly so laughter-filled, and we had so much in common.

I tried for the "high ground," the airy persiflage, the bullshit! It didn't fly! I spoke with Herman and said I thought Morris was getting serious, but he wasn't impressed. "Its just friendship. Look, we three have known each other for years!"

I tried not to be so available and went on with my other social life, men and women friends. It may not have been as much fun, but it was infinitely safer. But Morris was not to be deflected. He invited me to concerts, operas, ballets, plays, which were not within the tastes and interest of other men I knew. Let's face it, I WAS attracted to him. The proverbial Tall, Dark, Handsome Male…with brains, wit, intellect, yet. How often do we meet someone with all those attributes?

The Rags of Time

I decided to relax…and we went to bed! How much more relaxed could I be? It was no longer just friendship, it was passion…and it was good! Our relationship had a dimension I had avoided since my divorce.

After a play and dinner one night, Morris and I strolled along 5th Avenue and "window-shopped," laughing as we walked, at all the "going out of business" signs in store windows, one of which featured a bargain in dish towels: three for a dollar! For years afterwards, we computed how many dish towels we might have accumulated for whatever large purchase we made!

One night, walking past Harry Winston's Jewelry Store, closed for the night, we saw windows ablaze with diamonds, earrings, necklaces, tiaras, rings, ALL displayed on Steiff animals! I said in passing, "Now THAT'S the kind of stuffed animals I like!" The following week, a package arrived at my flat. It was from Morris. I opened it to find a stuffed cow, with a "Susie" tag in one ear. "Susie" dripped with costume jewelry, earrings, bracelets, a necklace. Among the colorful junk were a few really expensive things. The accompanying note read, "Well, you asked for it!"

Now how could you NOT love a guy like that!

One evening when he came to pick me up, with, as always, a bunch of violets, no matter the season, and was helping me on with my coat, I heard, "There's a large area of seam on one side of your dress which has separated."

"Damn," said I, "Wait till I change."

"No, have you got a needle and thread this color?"

The dress was new, a skin-tight royal-blue wool, trimmed with black monkey fur at wrists and at hem! Trés chic…and separated!

I found a needle and thread, Morris sewed me up, on ME, the dressmaker's DUMMY! And not one stitch showed. It seemed that in the Army, soldiers were forced into these homely chores themselves. And as I discovered over time, there was NOTHING that Morris could not learn to do.

The Rags of Time

During these times together, Morris kept saying he loved me, and then he asked me to marry him.

"NO," was my reply to the proposal each time he repeated it.

"Why?"

"Because I told you early on that I am never going to get married again. I have a job, enough to live on, a flat, I can even afford vacations on my salary. I have independence, relationships when I decide I want them, but marriage, no, no, no! I am my own woman and I don't need a piece of paper to define me! I like my life, and if you can't deal with that, I'm sorry, I'll miss you and all our wonderful times together, but marriage is OUT!"

Boy, give a woman a little power and three-and-a-half years of successful psychotherapy, and she does run on, doesn't she?

"I'm not asking you, I'm telling you, you'll marry me!"

The man refused to take no for an answer! He came at me with every conceivable argument. I kept repeating that we had a marvelous sex life and relationship, many life-affirming laughs, what more did he want? But these Aries, you know their personalities! We butted heads until some 10 months later I felt worn down. Romantically, I said, "Oh, alright! Just leave me alone!" Which contradiction in terms he howled at, swung me up and around, …and Presto, we were engaged! During the next few months I met his father, two brothers and their wives and children. None of them could I feel close to, but with therapy and newly found knowledge and strength, I dealt with them with equanimity and…politeness.

MY parents were less than thrilled, my mother especially, since Morris wasn't musical enough for her tastes and even seemed impervious to her charms. My father adopted a "wait and see" attitude. In any case, no one exerted any influence. Once I decide, I decide!

None of Morris' family had ever expected him to marry, and so for many years had used him for their own ends and needs. His father especially, usually took money from Morris to give to, or buy presents for his brothers and their families. The brothers had very good jobs and more money than Morris, but the habit of taking from him had been long-ingrained.

Once or twice while at the theatre, Morris fell asleep during the performance. I questioned the waste of good seats, not to mention, good money, and he said that he had had to sleep on his couch because a visiting brother was told by his father not to drive home, and so gave him Morris' bed. In a rage I told Morris that if this was how it was going to be, "Don't take me out again! I've had enough of parental interference, and I am certainly NOT going to go through THAT again!" I sent him home. It was the last time it occurred. Morris spoke with his sibling…and father, about such highhandedness!

Susanna, the spine-straightener…and I'm not even a chiropractor!

Another time I learned from an angry Morris that after having loaded his freezer with meats, poultry, etc…, he came home to find that his father had cleaned it out by giving all to his brothers. But that time, with an affection-stiffened backbone, he had handled it himself.

When we discussed where we were to live, it was enough that I would have to leave my beloved New York City and move to Jersey City, which meant giving up my job at Hillside Hospital, but the thought that Morris expected me to share his house was too much! In the early 50's even "liberated" women were expected to follow their husbands. It was when he said, "We'll live on the second floor, above my father, and Max and Rose and the children will live on the top floor!"

That last was when MY spine straightened further, propped additionally by the Sullivanian School of Therapy! "Oh, no," I replied sweetly, "my parents did not raise me to be the filling in a family sandwich! That is not why I escaped my parents' home so many years ago, or an untenable marriage, oh no! I intend to live in my flat and you are invited to join ME, or we can get a flat together in Jersey City, OR we can postpone our marriage but I am certainly NOT going to live in your house!" Memories of my proximity to My-Mother-In-Law-From-Hell flooded my mind, and further strengthened my resolve.

So…Morris sold his house, and thus evicted his family. Oh, nicely, of course. He waited until they found other lodgings…as he finally realized that I would have waited forever…which had been my original plan!

One night Morris called me and said the following: "I've been thinking…I have a good job, a house, insurance, my dogs, money in the bank, so why would I want to change my life and get married."
"You're absolutely right! Let's just continue as we are!"

"There's only one reason," he broke in, "I can't live without you!"

I admit, I melted into droplets of warmth and happiness, as I would never have done, had he not already told me previously that I WOULD marry him, he was not asking! …Just announcing a foregone conclusion!

When I told Herman that we were to be married, he seemed concerned, said Morris was a "loner," was stubborn (to which I could attest), and he seemed to think the marriage "thing," as he called it, would make neither of us happy.

Well, it would not make Herman happy, that was clear, until I pointed out that we would see even more of each other since we were to live in Jersey City…and I also firmly pointed out that he had refused my kind offer of marriage some years ago! But as much as Herman loved me, it was Morris he desired!

Morris and I looked for a flat and found one in a 1920's brick apartment house which looked out over Lincoln Park, and had a lobby resembling nothing so much as a movie-set interior, complete with couches, comfortable chairs, a Persian rug, ashtrays on tall stands, and tables of oak, all of which were "fuming" and everything was chained to the floor surrounding the Persian carpet. All furniture was covered in stunning shades of brown and tan, umber, ochre, beige, which anyone having an anally retentive personality could not help but admire and feel at home with!

For the marriage itself, I opted to go small, since at that time, I would have had to apply to the Chief Rabbi in Israel to obtain a Jewish Divorce, if I were again to be married by a Rabbi. The Jewish divorce proceedings would have taken longer to obtain than my former marriage! With my usual religious bent, I said to Morris, "How about City Hall?" but Morris knew a Judge in Jersey City who would marry us. In the end it was just we two with my parents as witnesses. Afterwards we planned a party in our new flat for family and friends. The following day we were to leave for our honeymoon.

In planning this over dinner at a restaurant in Manhattan, Morris asked where I wanted to honeymoon, and when I returned the question to him, he said, "I thought Bermuda."

"BERMUDA," I yelped, "BERMUDA? I can't think of anywhere more boring!"

"Well, where do YOU want to go?"

"I planned to spend my month's vacation this year in Mexico. I have saved up money for that. I don't know where YOU'RE going for our honeymoon, but I'M going to Mexico!"

So of course we went to Mexico! I have never thought myself unreasonable…and still don't, and although there were many years between honeymoon and our next trip, it was the first of many years of happy and adventurous travels for us, both abroad and in the United States.

We had planned to spend three to four weeks in Mexico, but circumstances extended it to about six weeks. We took traveler's checks, then the usual policy of travelers, and told each other that we would save only the last $20 check for our trip home from Kennedy Airport to our flat in Jersey City.

In Mexico City, a lush, lovely place of Mariachi bands, terrain so elevated it was difficult to breathe, and pickpockets, we decided to acclimatize ourselves slowly, so each day as we left the hotel, we wandered the streets, knew enough not to eat anything from street vendors or drink other than bottled water, or eat any fruit or vegetable not able to be peeled by us, and on the second day had our first adventure, and my experience with the Spanish language: I traveled, as I had always done in America, with a basket/bag slung over a shoulder, which in Mexico held a headscarf in case we wandered into a church. I tried to also wear a sleeved dress for the same reason. If it were too hot, I carried a short-sleeved jacket, and ALWAYS had my sketchpad and pencils and pens, my wallet, a hand-kerchief, and some make-up.

As we waited curbside in a business district for the usual helter-skelter traffic to make it possible for us to safely cross the street, we were soon joined by many others on the same mission, until I felt, then saw, a slim brown hand dip into my basket/purse and come out with my wallet and handkerchief and prepare to insert it into her serape, whereupon in my best Spanish I said, "Oh no you don't" and snatched back my belongings...and Morris grabbed me and we fled into a nearby church, because the other bystanders who had witnessed the exchange thought US to be the culprits!

We had learned a lesson. Morris immediately confiscated ALL my pesos and put them into HIS wallet! He later that day shopped for a pair of Mexican-made pants which not only had pockets which could be buttoned, but also sported a button fly as well!

So much for casual, spontaneous, vacation sex!

I had had visions of being thrown down into a field and ravished! Oh well, the best-laid plans...were not!

The fact which I found to be most annoying was that I now had to ask Morris for every peso! My independence was severely compromised! After a few days at the lovely Hotel Prado in Mexico City, we ventured further and further afoot (no, not afield!) to wonderful museums and plazas and gorgeous, blooming parks and past walled Haciendas. Each morning as we descended in the elevator to the lobby, we were accosted by "guides" who offered to take us to some tourist site or other, but we were firm about going it alone, until we acclimated ourselves to the rarified air which made breathing laborious, and wandered about in areas, upscale or not, but of most which were enclaves of working-class folk.

We saw increasing number of Indians in their colorful *rebozos*, their small shops and homes, and the fascinating street markets where Indian women or children sat or kneeled on the ground, behind their palm-leaf mats on which were placed, oh so beautifully, several pieces of fruit or vegetables, home-made sweets. There were also many vendors with tacos and burritos, all made on the spot, to order, and we watched as they rolled out the flat pancakes then filled them, and the smells were tantalizing, but we had been warned not to sample anything not well-cooked, peeled, or questionable, for fear of "Montezuma's Revenge!"

On one occasion we bought tickets to see the famous "Ballets Folklorica" at the Opera House. The performance was slated to begin at 8:30 PM, and as in New York, we arrived at about 7:45, so that we had to wait another 45 minutes before we were even allowed into the Concert Hall and found that we and about 10 other "touristas" were the only ones in attendance! We chatted together as slowly the seats filled, and by 9:30, even the Mexican audience began to show its displeasure by rhythmically clapping, then catcalling! We were too fascinated by this display of utterly NON-American behaviour, to do other than join in!

When finally the performance began, it was lovely, the costumes gorgeous, the dancing inspired, and we were STARVING, not having eaten since a coffee and small sandwich about 10 hours earlier. By the time we left the theatre about 11PM, we were as tired as though WE had performed! But our adventures continued, Morris and I drifted happily. As it became easier to breathe, after breakfast one morning, we were stopped by a charming, rotund little man who spoke passable English, and who offered to take us wherever we wished. Something about his manner, possibly his humor, appealed to us and we decided it was the time to do the touristy thing. We asked to be taken to the Floating Gardens of Xochimilco.

Julio came with us on the small boat and explained what we were to see, and, as we floated past other boats, all of which offered bouquets of flowers (for a price of course), the colors and scent of the flowers, and the friendly Spanish banter from boat to boat, was enchanting. When Julio returned us to our hotel we asked him to take us to the pyramids, or any "dig," since archeology was another of my passions.

Julio picked us up in his pride and joy, an old and absolutely spotless Cadillac from which, he explained, he made his living, and which provided for his small family, a wife and eight children! He told us he was from Michuacan, and that he had spent some years in Michigan, which accounted for his good English. That day he took us to a current "dig" which had been the home of an Aztec Priest. Thus far, what had been unearthed were a few stone walls and a passage which led down to a chamber in which a mural was being reassembled from shards of color strewn on the ground. Already we could make out some figures, and the colors were as bright as though just painted. It wasn't yet possible to know the subject of the mural, but before we left the site, Julio went back and spoke to a workman. When he returned to us, he handed me a piece of mural. I was grateful for his kindness, but refused it, as I explained to him, that I would not be able to sleep if someday I read of the restored house and mural, of which one piece was missing! And in MY possession!

Perhaps it was that which endeared me to Julio, because when we returned to the hotel he agreed to act as our guide for the next two weeks. Morris and I had mapped out an itinerary which often didn't include the ordinary tourist attractions, but included places and sights of which we had heard, as we asked Julio to make arrangements for us at only Mexican hotels. We learned that we were not expected to pay for Julio's room and board because he told us that the hotel would be delighted that HE had brought us. Also whenever we made any purchases, he always checked the price, what change we had been given, and only once did he allow us to be overcharged, to "teach you a lesson! You must always bargain!"

The day before we flew home from Mexico City, we again walked in some streets not known to us, and came upon a Mexican furniture store. We went in to browse and saw beautiful pieces of furniture, especially chests and tables. I made a drawing of a clothes chest for Morris. I measured the length of his slacks, the width of his jackets, and told them to build it to measure. All the furniture was made from natural mahogany, all the reed woven by Indians. Since we had no money left save the $20 traveler's check which we promised ourselves to come home with, the saleswoman, a beautiful Indian woman, told us we could give her a check. "Yes, but we didn't bring a checkbook."

"Not a problemo," said she. "Just write out a check on a piece of paper, and when you arrive home, you can send another check." She assured us that the furniture would be built and shipped to us in six weeks. So Morris and I did this, and we left for home after our magical honeymoon with sounds of Mariachi bands in our ears…and with the $20 with which we took Herman out to dinner, then borrowed another $20 from him for the cab to New Jersey!

The Rags of Time

Within a day we discovered that the name on the plain paper check we had written was incorrect. It was a composite from the two bank accounts we had, and so we sent a corrected check. When we told our friends of our marvelous Mexican adventures, and of the furniture we bought, they laughed and laughed, and intimated we'd never see the furniture! "Oh ye of little faith," I replied, "We WILL see the furniture! And in six weeks as promised!"

In exactly six weeks, a van arrived at our apartment house and it discharged and brought up to our apartment, four packing cases, in which were suspended our chests and tables and stools, in perfect condition, so "Hah, hah," I chortled to the naysayers, "the Mexican Indian is at least as honest as his counterpart in Los Estados Unidos!"

The Rags of Time

Chapter 6

The other thing I brought back from Mexico was a slight case of pregnancy.

Well, just drop the diaphragm and that will do it for me. Morris and I were delighted, and despite occasional bouts of nausea, I had an unremarkable three months, because that was as long as the pregnancy lasted. In contrast to the excellent bovine example set me by my mother, and after following, scrupulously, all my doctor's advice, and following all the dietary dictums, I miscarried.

We didn't make fun or jokes at the time, but told each other that this child was not meant to be, and that the next pregnancy would go better, would be perfect, as we were perfect, the best possible combination! The following year I was again pregnant. The obstetrician was as before, and because at the time, in 1958, all OBS/GYN doctors held to the principle that the less the mother-to-be gained, the better the result, I had gained a scant fourteen pounds, and was regularly seen, prodded, stroked, by my doctor who complimented me on my flat stomach, my tiny waist, yadda, yadda, YADDA, and in my ninth month, I was hospital-bound to deliver my baby.

Evidently no one told the hospital because I was NOT expected, just expecting. Before leaving home, Morris phoned the doctor who still had not shown up, and I was left in a corridor and "prepped" there…and still the doctor had not shown up.

I reasoned that I was waiting for the baby, NOT the doctor, and there seemed to be many of THEM about! I was given an injection despite my refusal, and my telling the nurses, and anyone else who would listen, that I was really not in as much pain as during my menses, but before I could frame another objection, another protest, I fell asleep.

The Rags of Time

I was awakened by the doctor in an elevator to my room, with Morris holding my hand, and told that I had delivered the baby, a boy, who died during the delivery, a "placenta previa" as it was called. Barely awake, as he explained to me that the umbilicus was wrapped around the baby's neck during delivery. He had been alive in my body during the pre-delivery examination.

The next few days were a blur, my only conscious thought was to spare Morris and my parents and any other visitors the misery of a blubbering, pinch-faced version of myself. Accordingly, I made up my face, wore my prettiest bed-jacket, and tried to build my strength and spirits by getting out of bed and I incessantly walked the hallways, because in my room, my bed-mate was nursing her baby, and I couldn't bear to watch it. Also, I didn't want to depress her by my presence.

What I came home with was a donut cushion and a painful episiotomy. One day I was visited by my father-in-law, who, in Morris' presence made the statement, "It's better to have a living child!", whereupon Morris threw him out of the house, and I hoped out of our lives.

Seeing my depression, Morris stayed home with me as long as he could, although I tried to brazen out my unhappiness by going for walks, seeing friends. The baby was buried in a local cemetery without my knowing it, before I came home from the hospital.

I was told this by one of Morris' friends, Sammy, who visited me at home: Driving home from the hospital one night—having been encouraged by me to go and have a drink, as I knew of Morris' unease at my low spirits,—Morris and Sammy while at a stop light, spotted two nurses waiting for the bus after their shift, and Sam said to Morris, "Why don't we pick up these girls and take them for a drink?"

"No," said Morris.
"Why not?"
"Because Susan will know!"
"HOW will she know?"
"Because I'll tell her!"

The Rags of Time

There had to be a reason to love this man, he so obviously loved me, tried to protect me, and was by this time very concerned by my inertia, depression, and seeming lack of interest in those things which had sparked my imagination and energies before. He asked our friends and my family to keep me busy, planned little surprises and brought me gifts to tempt me out of myself, out of my wounded spirits.

In time I DID work my way out of depression and we resumed our lives. We went again to the theatre, ballet, concerts, and I was able to laugh at, and with, Herman, who more than anyone reawakened in me my usual love of laughter, and my ongoing sense of the ridiculousness of the world in which we live, and of the people therein! I began to paint again, did some woodcuts, even saw a few private patients, and after a time, Morris and I even spoke of my becoming pregnant again.

The major difference in our plans was that we were going to select a different gynecologist, one who specialized in difficult pregnancies and deliveries, so as to assure a different outcome…and for that we were going to find a doctor in Manhattan, where there were, for me, more sophisticated physicians and methods! After my first two disasters, I would not tempt the Fates again with a tardy doctor who obviously loved my tits and ass more than his ability to help me through what might be some difficult times.

Armed with a list from New York friends, I went first to a doctor who, after examining me and hearing my sad history of baby-making, said he would recommend a Caesarian-section instead of a vaginal delivery, making it easier on the child. I was happy and relieved, and threw away the remainder of the list. I went back to Morris with renewed hope. Since the doctor had told me that he would be on vacation in Europe during August, we timed conception and delivery for early Spring.

And the diaphragm dropped.

I DID become pregnant, with a due date in early Spring. The doctor told me my due date was in March, and that I was to visit him every two weeks at his Fifth Avenue office, that I was NOT to fly anywhere, and that I was to keep my weight down, take vitamins and eat sensibly, exercise moderately…all of which I happily and cheerfully complied with, and at my bi-monthly examinations and weigh-ins, I had at the end, gained only eleven pounds!

Indeed, those patients who gained much weight were ridiculed by the doctor who pointed to the rest of us as models of compliance. Stupid, stupid fools that we were, we actually thought of the other women with compassion! My entire pregnancy was uneventful, and the soda-crackers always in my purse as I traveled to the bus and train, then walked through Central Park to the doctor's office (as my daily exercise), grew stale and were left at home, or fed to the birds in the Park.

I was the Model Patient!

Not liking the maternity dresses then in style, I bought lovely fabrics and found the pattern of an A-line dress which I sewed (with a little help from Morris, since he was always better than I at interpreting patterns!). The dresses were so smart, so flattering, so avant-garde, that I was complimented by friends and even strangers, who didn't realize I was pregnant, and that these were my maternity clothes! Not for me was the ugly two-piece, with cut-out skirt hidden by ugly overblouse, the only style then available.

On a Friday visit, Dr. D. told me that I was dilating sufficiently, and that he would induce labor and remove the baby the next day, a Saturday. I was jubilant, Morris was thrilled, it was just two weeks before my due-date, and that night we went to our favorite restaurant, no dietary hold barred! It would, after all, be purged from me the following day. As my karma would have it, that same night I began to feel minor contractions, and Morris decided not to wait until the next day, Saturday, but we would taxi to Mount Sinai that night! The poor cab driver nervously asked if we were in a hurry, was I ready to deliver NOW? Oh no, we airily declared, don't speed, just go at your usual speed through the park, and get us there!

Morris took me into the admitting office, then some nurses took me upstairs. The doctor had given instructions of what was to be done until he arrived. Morris came upstairs after paying the requested $2000 "entry fee," and stayed with me until the doctor arrived. Morris had phoned him from New Jersey to tell him that we were on our way, and as per his instructions, the nurses prepped and purged me. Morris was asked to wait in the lounge, and Dr. D. wanted to give me a pill, which I refused, telling him that my menses had often been worse, my pains were sporadic, intermittent, and that I did NOT need a pill until the surgery. Dr. D. insisted that a dose of Demerol was just like an aspirin, that it would relax me until the birth. Little did he know that the purgatives had already "relaxed" me, and because I had had no sleep for so many hours, I DID fall asleep!

When I awoke, it was to find Morris kissing me and holding my hand, and the doctor was at my other side and told me that I had a "fine boy!" In gratitude I tried to take the doctor's hand and kiss it. When he asked if I wanted anything, I said I was hungry, so food was sent for, but when I saw the spaghetti and meatballs, I promptly fell back asleep.

When I again awakened, I passed my hand over my abdomen, surprised to find it flat and not painful. From the "after-birth-room," I was to be taken to my room, but insisted, despite my grogginess, that I had to see my son. Supported by the nurses, I walked to the nursery, and through the glass window, Morris, who never left my side, and I, saw a lustily crying, completely bald son, up on his elbows inside what I later learned was an isolette. Never having had a living child before, I didn't know what an isolette was, only knew that MY child looked marvelous to me, even in a lucite "cage."

Once in my room and in bed, I expected my son to be brought to me for feeding. I also checked to find that instead of any bandaging, or cloths, or anything I could understand as indicative of surgery, of a Caesarian, there was nothing, but slowly I was made aware of growing pain from an episiotomy. When I asked the nurse for my son to be brought to me for feeding, I was told that Dr. D. had given an order for pills to dry my breasts.

The greater shock was when I found out that rather than a Caesarian section, he had done a forceps and vaginal delivery.

Rather than scream my betrayed feelings, I tried to focus only on my beautiful, purple-eyed son with his barely visible tiny patch of platinum fuzz.

Where was Keats, the infamous Mouther of Truth and Beauty now that I needed him? Where now were my vaunted principles of righteous anger against betrayal and injustice? Instead of screaming the walls down, I concentrated on taking my darling home after the eighth day because I had requested that a circumcision be performed at the hospital. When Morris deemed me well enough and calm enough to accept his news, he told me of the doctor calling him into a private room and informing him that Nat-David during the delivery, once again had the umbilicus around his neck, and that after attempting to extricate him from it, "your son seemed flaccid and slid out of the vagina"! Morris further told me that instead of HIM "taking a knife, or at least a fist, to the bastard's face" he decided to try for calm in order not to excite me! He was worried about me, my health, …and the rest could wait until later.

Once again, our instinct was to protect each other from pain. Before the day of the circumcision, the baby developed "thrush mouth," something else unknown to me. When I tried to give Nat-David a bottle of formula the hospital provided, as Nat-David lay cuddled in my arms, I was told that "he won't suckle unless you hold him with his feet against your abdomen, and his head held in your hands"! Following these instructions, all the time I was at Mt. Sinai, I tried unsuccessfully to get some nourishment into his mouth, and the hospital pediatrician, a Dr. Ginandes, seemed to visit Nat-David daily, gave forth what were meant to be soothing platitudes, and the day Nat-David and I left the hospital, he saw us to the elevator, and as the doors were closing, said, "Give him some extra, tender, loving care!" As the doors closed, I had the uneasy feeling that it was a strange thing to say to a new mother who was so passionately thrilled at having a living child, but I said nothing, for fear of upsetting Morris.

Little did I realize that he was similarly afraid of upsetting me, but for even worse reasons! It was not TRUTH, but a desire not to cause pain for the beloved "other" parent which kept us silent.

Once home, I held Nat as a baby SHOULD be held, against my milkless breasts, and offered him a bottle, which he accepted, nay, guzzled hungrily and lustily! Morris remained at home with us for the first week to keep an eye on us both. An outsized bassinet was Nat-David's domain, and I placed a red scarf where he could see it with his royal-purple eyes.

Nat-David's name was a composite of my brother Nathaniel, whom no one ever called anything but Nat, and my beloved Grandfather, David. Each day Nat took in more and more nourishment and I soon became a Street-Walker, as described by Dr. Spock, (the noted pediatrician whose book on infant and child care was every new mother's bible): to wit, and to viz; take your baby out in all weather; do not feed solids too soon; limit intake of milk except by breast, and so on, and other wonderful advice, no problem for me since I had been dried-up by the hospital, and had been taught how to make formula, and I DID understand what was too hot by burning the inside of my forearm on several occasions!

To this advice, I added constant Mother-Chatter, and was out of the house by 6:30 AM, and on my way to Lincoln Park where I befriended its sole occupant, the Gardener, and while he mowed I read to Nat-David from whatever was my current book, or chatted with Nat about the weather, the color of the sky, the flowers, world affairs! Well, I was NOT going to die of boredom…nor was Nat! When inclement weather prevented outings, I took the gentler interpretation of Dr. Spock, and put Nat-David under comforters in his carriage on the front porch.

By the time of my third pregnancy, Morris and I had rented the top two floors of a private home, complete with large back garden. It had been the home of an oral surgeon who retained the first floor for his surgery and practice. He turned out to be a fine friend, and when we first read his ad, it specified, "No pets, no children!" And I WAS pregnant, and we had our small dog, Buttons. We went anyway because the house was very close to our apartment building and the park, and despite its repellent, exterior color, which I immediately dubbed "Jersey City Green," the apartment itself offered many possibilities: the lower floor consisted of two very large rooms, with fireplace faced by yellow ceramic tiles, and a small room off the living room, which had originally been a sun-porch, now enclosed, a large kitchen, good-sized bathroom, and a large dining/family room. The upper floor had two eaved spaces. One we decided was to be the master bedroom, the smaller eave would become Nat-David's nursery.

As we were shown through the house, Morris and I discussed how WE would transform all this space to suit US. We spoke of tearing out cabinets, redoing the floors, curtaining off certain spaces to create a "summer nursery" and on the main floor, making a curtained-off "winter nursery," and on and on we blathered, as the owner stared at us in amazement. At last, Dr. Joseph Grodjesk said he would let us know in a few days, having promised other applicants that they could view the apartment.

We left, and that very evening received a call from Dr. Grodjesk to say that if we were still interested, we could have the place, "Why?" asked Morris. "What happened to the others who were to see it?" Joe Grodjesk told him that we were the only ones who had plans, who seemed to know what we wanted, and were not put off by the destruction which had been visited upon it by the teenage children of former occupants who had gouged walls and floors and painted over some walls, and graffitied the doors!

By now we had an eagerly-awaited child, AND a dog, and the fun of changing the place completely…which we did…and made it so enchanting that when we invited the Grodjesk's to dinner, she said that if she had known the possibilities, they and their three children would never have moved to the Jersey suburbs!

Days followed each other peacefully and uneventfully and happily. I had, within walking distance, a man recommended to us as the "Best Pediatrician" in Jersey City, and I was so ecstatic to have a living child that I walked the streets with a perpetual and stupid smile, and wanted nothing so much as to shout my joy and pride to all passersby, but of course, I didn't!

Well, all right, only one out of five or six strangers were accosted by a crazy redhead who practically insisted on showing off the Boy Doll in the carriage! At the time there was no leash law, so Buttons was in attendance, and walked properly next to the carriage, leaving only to do her business off the curb, then returning to act her part as Guard Dog. And all 35 pounds of her could be very fierce indeed!

Let us now fast-forward to when Nat-David was five or six months old, and on a visit to the pediatrician, I asked this doctor and father of eight, why Nat-David thrust out his abdomen when I attempted to cuddle or play with him on my lap, and actually cried if put in a sitting position. To this, this supposedly "best of all" pediatricians in our town (certainly the most expensive!), replied, "Oh, you Jewish Mothers are all alike! So he won't play football!"

Said I, "I don't give a damn if he plays ball or not! I just want to know why his body reacts this way!"

"Well, he doesn't hold his head as well as he should, I agree, but let's watch his progress and take it from there!" was his disheartening reply.

I reported this to Morris. Were the Schwartz's going to wait? Like hell they were! Gnawing at us both, Morris and me, was the memory of the hospital pediatrician's parting words as the elevator doors closed on us at Mount Sinai: "Give him some extra, tender, loving care!" We began a hunt for a pediatric neurologist in Jersey City and finally were given the name of a doctor close by, made an appointment, and walked to his office. Inside, the secretary took information, then showed us into a darkened room. The doctor shone a pencil flashlight into Nat-David's eyes as I held him, tut-tutted, put on the room lights, told us there was a great deal of brain damage, and, "Please see my secretary, that will be $75.00, and come back in a year!" And that was the entire examination, which had taken barely ten minutes!

Dazed, Morris and I stumbled into the sunshine with our purple-eyed darling, and spoke not at all. We were both incapable of speech. We walked home, enraged, too angry for tears, just filled with the desire to kick, punch, knee to the groin, ALL of the Holier-Than-Thou-Medics who trampled on our lives by NOT doing what they promised! I told Morris that short of going to see the GYN bastard, and plunging a knife into his lying guts, we'd put all this behind us and do what we did best: take our, and Nat-David's future, into our own hands!

And so we did. And so began an adventure that would become the basic structure of our lives. Of course we could do it!

First, to suss out a GOOD pediatric neurologist, and to do so, not in New Jersey, but to return to MY roots in New York, since I tended to trust that State more. I'm sure there were and are excellent doctors in New Jersey, indeed in all States, but I thought it would make me more confident to begin in New York. We consulted with friends, family physicians, called various hospitals, and were finally given the name of Dr. Richard Reuben, who was connected with the New York University Medical Center in Manhattan.

An appointment was made, not in New York City, but he asked us to come to his practice on Long Island on a Saturday afternoon, so Morris could be with us and not at work. We drove to a ranch house in a suburban section and were met by a young, handsome, smiling man who took us into his office. He asked about Nat-David's birth, medical history until then…not much, since Nat-David was but thirteen months old. Nat-David was examined and his responses carefully watched by Dr. Reuben, who moved a finger to-and-fro in front of him, saw his smiles and speech sounds, checked his hearing, it seemed to me, and watched as Morris and I interacted with Nat-David, and saw that Nat-David's eyes followed Morris around the room, as Dr. Reuben spoke with me, and how Nat-David gurgled and cooed. It was when I attempted to seat Nat on my lap that he strenuously objected with his little body. Also that Nat thrust his abdomen forward. When I let Nat-David rest against my body in a reclining, but not sitting position, he was content and smiling.

Nat-David smiled up at Dr. Reuben when he was placed on his back on an examining table, and allowed himself to be prodded, and picked up, and turned over, always turning his head to see us! By the time the examination was complete, some two hours later, Dr. Reuben told us over a now sleeping child, that his diagnosis was that Nat-David had cerebral palsy, athetoid type!

"What do you think of his intelligence?" I asked.

"What do YOU think?" was his answer.

"We think he is very bright!"

"You're probably right," was his wise reply.

Dr. Reuben then gave us several options as to how to continue during Nat-David's next year or so…and told us to call or see him at his office at New York University Medical Center, or at his Long Island office. Certainly to call him if we had any questions at any time, or needed some additional suggestions in the future.

Morris and I agreed as we left for home, that this was a doctor whom we could trust, and decided to seek out some local center that could work knowledgeably with Nat-David…and with us!

We finally decided that the Cerebral Palsy Unit of Long Island College Hospital was the place to begin, and so, once again Morris adjusted his work schedule so that he could drive us to Brooklyn from New Jersey several times a week. We were supposed to be instructed, together with Nat-David, in various physical therapies.

And so, we began!

The Rags of Time

Chapter 7

"The world will always regard Nat-David as a retarded cripple!" These generous and compassionate words by Dr. Koven, eminent orthopedist and surgeon connected with the Cerebral Palsy Unit at Long Island College Hospital, drew my first public tears. Tears not of pity, or self-pity, nor of sorrow, but of anger and frustration finally undammed. My adult, mature, "moral code" contained my more primitive and immediate desire to lash out verbally, to give a non-verbal slap to the smug mouth that had uttered them! Dr. Koven's remarks, as he held Nat-David stretched out between his hands like a sacrificial offering, were played out to a large group of visiting physicians, and still cause a heart-pounding remembrance of things long past. I still feel the taste of bile in my mouth!

The occasion was one of many on which it had been requested by this treatment center that we bring Nat-David in for evaluation. We had been bringing Nat-David for physical therapy several times weekly since he was some 18 months old. Nat-David was now almost two years old. Dr. K's statement was completely gratuitous, and the more shocking to us, since we had brought him THAT day for a physical, not mental evaluation! His mental capacity could in no way be Dr. K's province. When Nat-David had, at 15 months of age, his first I.Q. examination, the psychologist who administered it, told us that while his physical involvement did not permit an accurate evaluation, his general responsiveness and alertness was good, and that only time and treatment would permit a more accurate assessment.

From the first, his therapists had found him to be responsive and cooperative during treatment, and even, young as he was, to verbal direction. And Morris and I, even with the love that tempers objectivity, had been more prone to lean over backwards NOT to attribute to him capabilities and virtues which he didn't possess.

But that is not the story to be told in this chapter. The above incident served as the goad, the final straw, call it what you will, for the following episode in our lives.

In August 1961, I heard that the Eighth World Congress of the International Society for the Welfare of Cripples was to meet in New York City. What led to my intention to attend this meeting was the fact that the World Commission on Cerebral Palsy was to be held as part of that Congress.

A friend and neighbor, a professor of dental pathology, made it possible for me to attend because I knew that the Congress was for professionals only. John Manhold was delighted to escort me to the Waldorf Astoria Hotel and enroll me as his assistant. Then John left for home and work at Seton Hall, and I, properly gloved and hatted, attended as "Expert Parent," perhaps the ONLY non-professional in this august world-wide gathering. Represented were Israel, England, Canada, South Africa, Belgium, U.S.A., Ireland, Australia, France, Denmark, Scotland, Brazil, Germany, Argentina, Italy, Norway, Singapore, Spain, and Nat-David Schwartz!

I heard many speeches that day, sat in on seminars, saw 8mm movies of the therapeutic techniques, listened to statistics unintelligible to me, and much scientific terminology which, in the copious notes I took, I hoped was spelled correctly, so as to allow me further research within the privacy of my encyclope-dia. Specific diagnoses were discussed, there ensued lively discussions and disagreements on techniques, general agreement about the value of early diagnosis, realistic vocational rehabilitation, education. What I took away from that Congress was more important than notes. It was the comforting realization that all over the world were people concerned with the desire for greater knowl-edge as to the possible causes for, and treatment of, cerebral palsy.

We were not alone!

I remained for the entire day, having been equipped on arrival and registration with an entire plastic valise full of information and printed speeches, as yet to be delivered, from every participant! I left before the cocktail party and dinner.

The Rags of Time

Later that evening, I shared with Morris the notes I had made, the voluminous brochures, and copies of speeches, and my general lay-impressions. I remember saying to Morris, "Doesn't it seem strange that with all their much-publicized interest in neurology, the Soviet Union was not represented?" It seemed strange because not long before this World Congress, there had been shown at New York City's Coliseum, a Soviet Exhibition which together with a display of technological equipment, trade goods and arts and crafts, had included a large exhibit devoted to Russia's achievement in the world of medicine, with special emphasis on neurological research, new orthopedic surgical techniques, and limb, muscle, even nerve grafts.

In the immediacy of problems of daily life, much commuting to Brooklyn for Nat-David's treatments, and the business of life in general, we set aside further discussion and thought of the World Congress.

LIFE, after all, is for the moment, for the daily grinds and triumphs. This was our philosophy. The presence of a child with a physical handicap need not be the focal point of our lives. We were generally content with Nat-David's progress as a little Human Being! He brought us much joy, and if, in the deeper recesses of our minds and spirits there was a well of pain, we loved each other too much, and had too much consideration to be constantly dipping into it.

Years later, when we reached the plateau of REAL emotional adjustment, as different from the intellectual adjustments we made more easily and quickly, and were able to discuss our private feelings, Morris and I laughed at the mutual realization that each regarded the other as a "rock of stability and wisdom," secure in the knowledge, yet never daring to chip at it. Perhaps THAT was our wisdom and our strength!

Now a vein of vulnerability lay exposed, brought to the surface by the callous exhibition of his "personal power" by Dr. Koven! Holding a sleeping Nat-David on my lap in the car, bound for home, I was alternately teary and outraged, muttering! Morris was silent, his face grim, knuckles taut on the steering wheel. It was when we reached home and I busied myself preparing lunch that Morris said, "Do you remember what you said after the World Commission on Cerebral Palsy? Why wasn't the Soviet Union represented? What are THEY doing about Cerebral Palsy? We know that it exists all over the world. Let's find out." We checked the phone book for the number of the Soviet Mission in New York City.

The Rags of Time

The secretary to whom I spoke transferred the call to one of their Attachés. I asked simply whether there was any literature available on the treatment for Cerebral Palsy in the Soviet Union, and could we receive it or purchase it? He asked if we would be willing to come to the USSR, and I remember what Morris said on the phone extension, "That we would go to the Moon if there were a possibility of successfully treating Nat-David by a method unknown to us here!" The Attaché gave us the name and address of the Cultural Attaché at the USSR Embassy in Washington D.C., and told us to forward our request to him. This was in March 1961.

We then called the Embassy in Washington, and were again transferred to its Cultural Attaché, who told us to write to the Ministry of Health in Moscow. Morris drafted a letter which was translated into Russian by my father, then sent off. It read as follows:

Gentlemen:

We would be most appreciative for any information you could give us regarding Medical services in the USSR, specifically about your treatment of Cerebral Palsy.

We are the parents of a two year old boy thus affected, and it occurred to us that perhaps there exists in the Soviet Union some treatment not generally known in this country. We will gladly pay for any brochures or medical papers describing the treatment for Cerebral Palsy, and their being in the Russian language is no deterrent since we will have them translated for us by my parents.

We hope that you will be able to help us. We were so impressed by your Medical Exhibit as shown at the New York Coliseum several years ago.

Thank you for your courtesy, Sincerely, ...

In May 1961 we received a reply, in Russian, from the Ministry of Health-Preservation of the USSR. Since we were living in New Jersey and my Russian-born parents lived in Brooklyn, New York, our impatience to know what was written was boundless. Morris had an inspiration! Why not ask the Priest of the Russian Orthodox Church in Jersey City if he would translate it. A phone call, and his kind agreement, sent the three of us scurrying to the church Parish House, where after modestly disclaiming knowledge of Russian technical terminology, the priest gave us the gist of the letter. It remained for my father, two days later, to translate the letter in its entirety:

Dear Madame:

Your interest in the means and methods of curing childhood paralysis in the USSR was submitted to our specialists and I am conveying their information:

To be able to arrive at an effective cure-treatment, our specialists seek to gain an insight, if feasible, into contributing factors of Spastic Paralysis such as "Birth Trauma," "Contracted Infection," "Toxoplasmosis," etc. Unfortunately your letter is devoid of detailed description of the degree of paralysis, its characteristics, and which parts are chiefly affected. Information about psychical development of your son is most significant in defining a successful treatment-cure.

In the USSR convincing results were obtained by the use of "Galantamin," "Proserpin-Injections," "Sekurenin" and other effective medications. Some helped improve "nerve conductivity" and stimulation of mobile functions. Still other results were brought about by effective training of mobile functions by special means of Medico-Physical Culture, and progressive development of mobile habits.

Various techniques practiced in the USSR in treatment of Child Cerebral Palsy, are to be found in a book written jointly by M.V. Eydinova and E.N. Pravdinoy-Vinarskoy. The book is entitled, "Children's Cerebral Palsy and Means of Combating." It was published by the Academy of Pedagogical Sciences SSR, Moscow, in 1959. All methods of curing Child Cerebral Palsy are detailed comprehensively. You can obtain it by writing to : V/O "Medexport" Ministry of Foreign Trade at the same address, which is in charge of the export of all Medications.

Respectfully Yours,
Dr. P. Chudnovsky
Candidat of Medical Sciences
Chief, Faculty of Consultations

My father added the note to the translation that "Candidat," is the highest University degree given in the USSR.

After some discussion, Morris an I decided that our first course of action was to get the book mentioned in the letter. We tried libraries, Russian bookstores, publishers of medical books in the New York City area, to no avail. We had finally decided to write to the USSR for a copy, but another means unexpectedly presented itself. A cousin of my father's was planning a short trip to Europe within a few weeks, and we asked her to buy the book for us. We had by then realized that mail service between our two countries represented NONE of the technological advances made in other areas.

When she returned, our cousin contacted us and gave us the book, which we, in turn, gave to my father for translation. Knowing our impatience, he gave us first its general outline, then set out to translate it more formally. Throughout this period we had been in contact with Dr. Reuben who listened with great patience (and forbearance and fortitude to our excitement) to our hopes and plans, and expressed an interest in both the book, and the medication called "Galantamin."

My parents, and our, excitement was intense. We pored over the book and its illustrations repeatedly, but were disconcerted to find the terminology used to describe diagnoses and treatment at variance with that which we had heard from all the doctors who had seen and worked with Nat-David, mainly dear Dr. Reuben, our first bulwark, since his initial and correct diagnosis.

At first we ascribed this to the difficulties inherent in any translation, especially since my father was not really medically oriented, despite the fact that he had begun the study of medicine at Georgetown University many, many years before, but had not followed through. And perhaps the way in which the Russian language was used was different since 1905!

I found myself asking, "But where does it say *Athetoid* Cerebral Palsy? The book keeps referring to *Spastic Paralysis,* and describes the drug as a stimulant!" Dr. Reuben also expressed some doubt and said that the drug seemed by description, similar to the drug "Prostigmine" which had been developed here and subsequently found to be of questionable value, as applied to Nat-David's symptoms.

Okay! So now I play doctor! The virtue of a GOOD education!

Withal, Dr. Reuben decided to defer judgment and graciously (and who can deflect a determined redhead and Jaffe/Schwartz from her course?) agreed to cooperate in our attempts to get "Galantamin" to our shores. I realized that parents or no, we had better have some Medical backup! So Dr. Reuben made formal application to the Soviet Ministry of Health by letter, and sent copies of his file of Nat-David's medical history to date. He wrote:

Dear Sirs,

I am writing to you on behalf of infant Nat-David Schwartz, born March 7, 1959, who has "Cerebral Palsy" of the clinical variety classified as "Tension-Athetoid." I understand that the parents of this child have received an offer of help from your Ministry of Health, and I would be very happy to cooperate with you in your generous offer.

Accordingly, I am enclosing copies of the medical reports in my file so that you may have all the information you desire.

If you are of the opinion that medicines will be of value in the treatment of this child, then please indicate which drugs and which dosages are desirable. Further information regarding that mode of action and toxic effects of such drugs would also be desired.

Respectfully Yours…

In addition to the generosity of an American trained and educated physician, as in the case of my San Francisco lawyer/advocate/ experimentalist, it is obvious to us that the Schwartz's MUST prevail! Also, it was one of our amused feelings of confirmation, that "it's a small world after all" and there was now in the Moscow Ministry of Health, a slim folder containing letters, medical data, and pictures of Nat-David Schwartz!

Or perhaps not, after all this time and all governmental changes, but for a while, there WAS a kinder, gentler atmosphere among peoples which transcended government and ideology!

The Rags of Time

Accustomed as we are in this country to the ease of sending and receiving mail, now principally e-mail, and taking for granted its general efficiency and speed, in 1961, our postal exchange with Moscow seemed agonizingly slow. Accordingly, Morris decided to cable our request, and if that failed, to telephone. In 1961, the clerk at the Western Union office refused to accept our cablegram, suspicious that the medical jargon, medical numbers and letters, descriptions of drug and dosage, was actually some sort of "secret code"! We felt very 007-ish, but the more rationally we tried to explain, the more suspiciously were we viewed.

And this was years before 9/11!

Finally, we even took Nat-David out of his stroller in an attempt to prove to the clerk that Nat couldn't sit or stand. Even then, not convinced, the clerk asked for repeat proof of our name, address, phone number, noting everything carefully on various forms, before consenting to accept the cablegram and payment.

This James Bond episode had its side effects. We checked our mail from the Soviet Union very carefully, looking for signs of its having been opened by hands other than ours. If it ever had been, we enjoyed dwelling on the notion, secure in our innocence, that we were the possible objects of secret surveillance!

Finally in November 1961, we received a letter from "Medexport."

Dear Mrs. Schwartz:

We have received your letter of November 3rd. We can dispatch Galantamin, a course of treatment. The cost of 30 ampules 0,25% solution is $24.00 American. We request your remittance to us of the stipulated sum.

Prior to sending us the money, we would like you to contact your Customs House with a view of ascertaining if there will be any difficulty in getting shipment.

Upon receipt of the money, we will forward Galantamin by airmail.

Respectfully…

The Rags of Time

The Customs House assured us there would be no difficulty.

Throughout the over seven months of letter-exchange with the Moscow Ministry of Health, those signed with the names of Soviet Physicians were unfailingly interested and courteous, and usually contained some personal reference to Nat-David plus their, "sincere good wishes for his successful recovery." It was like a small warm blanket offered to us, human to human, parent to parent, within the setting of the "Cold War"!

Our actual receipt of the drug was as inconspicuous, as matter-of-fact, as the correspondence had been exciting. One morning, several weeks later, a mail truck drove up to the house, the driver asked for my signature on a delivery form, and there we were, looking at a small white pine box, unwrapped, covered with several name and address stickers, and sealed by a wire held together by a red-wax seal, imprinted with a medallion-shape. Inside we found, wrapped in cotton wool, several smaller boxes, each filled with ampules of clear liquid.

In great excitement, we called Dr. Reuben who arranged to personally check out the formula, and then administer to Nat-David his first shot, in accordance with the Soviet Physician's recommended dosage. The following week found us all in his office. He had told us to expect to remain for several hours, as he wanted to make certain that there were no unpleasant side-effects from the drug.

Among Nat-David's other virtues was the ability to accept with tranquility the many medical treatments and pills we had to inflict on him. Once again he did us proud. There was no more than a slight shudder as the needle pricked his arm. I maintain that his good-natured submission was due to the fact that we ALWAYS leveled truthfully with him about what he might expect, explaining the need, trying to estimate the amount of pain or discomfort involved, neither dramatizing or playing it down.

In a word, he "trusted" us, and therefore looked with equanimity on most people. He was quite prepared to like anyone, and unless and until, his initial trust was abused!

This is the "legacy" we tried consciously to give him, aware that with this feeling of "initial trust" as a shield and strength, he would later be able to absorb any realities, even if unpleasant, and not within the confines of our comforting presence. In all our dealings with our son, we tried to be as truthful as his understanding and the circumstances permitted.

People who knew and understood this about him, and who dealt with him in a similar manner, who took the tiny trouble to explain what was to happen, what he might expect, all through his thirty-five years of life, reported to us their pleasure at his intelligent and cooperative attitude.

When Dr. Reuben was satisfied that there were no unpleasant side-effects from Galantamin, he instructed our family doctor in Brooklyn, to whose office we could walk, and who knew all our family for many years, Dr. Leo Gottlieb, in how to continue the injections. Thereafter, Nat-David received, three times weekly, injections of Galantamin plus Vitamin B-12, also recommended by the Moscow Ministry of Health, until he received a total of 80 injections.

Also, as I recall, 80 lollipops for good behaviour!

I wish we could have reported some startling change in Nat-David's physical condition, that there had been some dramatic improvement in his ability towards intelligible speech, or a lessening of his physical condition. I'm sorry to say that this was not the case. Before the injections began, Morris and I decided not to tell his physical therapists about them so that we might receive a more objective evaluation of his progress. Instead I kept a little notebook in which I recorded the number of injections, and any gratuitous comments which the staff at the Cerebral Palsy Unit might make.

Coinciding with the third or fourth week of injections, the physiotherapist told us that Nat-David "seems to be holding his head better" and seemed somewhat more stimulated to physical activity. We felt it wiser to say "coincidence" because we had learned that there exist "spontaneous" improvements within Cerebral Palsy, which may have to do only with the general growth and development of a child. I remember that Dr. Meyer Pearlstein of Chicago had amused the members of the World Commission on Cerebral Palsy, by stating that there had been observed such "spontaneous progress," followed by "plateaus" during what he called "young childhood" (5-6 years), adolescence, the "Kinsey Age" (at 21) and in one's forties.

Actually, we received for our $24.00 American, about a five-year supply of Galantamin. I had paid more for a year's supply of pediatric vitamins!

After the completion of the 80 injections, Dr. Reuben agreed that if it were not of any value for Nat-David, (bearing out my initial suspicion that what in America is called "Athetoid" and what the Russians called "Spasticity," was NOT the same) perhaps the medication would benefit some other form of Cerebral Palsy.

For us, it remained a "Noble Experiment" and was a fascinating foray into the realm of medicine and medical treatments in use in other parts of the world. We also had a new appreciation of the limits of language translation and how "a thing" in one language may translate into "another thing" as usage changes, but we were surprised that it might become its opposite!

Concurrently, Morris and I decided to remove Nat-David from the Center he had attended since he was 16 months old, and try to place him at another Center highly recommended by the parents of another Palsied child. This Center, which came to be regarded by Nat-David and by us as a "second home" was the Institute of Rehabilitation Medicine in Manhattan. Its Director was the justly renowned Dr. Howard Rusk, expert in the field of rehabilitation under many Presidents, and I always feel that at the mention of these two names, trumpets should sound!

Morris placed a call to Dr. Chester Swinyard, Director of the Children's Division. His secretary took the call, and when she requested the name of our "referring physician," Morris told her that we had learned of the Center through another parent, and that we were in possession of a drug from the Soviet Union in which the Institute might be interested. Immediately we were granted an appointment with Dr. Swinyard who agreed to evaluate Nat-David's condition, and make recommendations for further treatment.

During our meeting with Dr. Swinyard, he made the generous remark, with an inherent honesty only in those with a true largesse of spirit, that he had heard of Galantamin. When he made inquiry to the USSR for further information, he was not accorded the courtesy of a reply. We speculated that perhaps the Soviets had been intrigued with the idea that two laymen, loving parents, had made the request, or had just responded to a plea on the basis of compassion, person to person! Whatever the psychology involved, we as parents were grateful for interest, wherever found, and immediately Morris offered IRM the remainder of our supply of Galantamin.

The above story, those incidents, don't have earth-shattering value. But in an era notable for its lack of peace-on-earth, and for its large areas of indifference to, and callousness for, the human condition, the responsiveness of faceless strangers across 6,000 miles, makes for a "credit" mark in the ledger of our personal history. A kind of "instant warmth" that requires gracious acceptance, with the feeling that we, its inheritors, have the privilege and obligation, to pass it on to others!

When Nat-David was accepted for admission to IRM, I decided that it would be easier for the staff if he were toilet-trained. On a sheet of cardboard, I drew what looked like a calendar page, divided into about 30 squares, and atop all was the drawing of a toilet seat. Before I attached it to the door of the downstairs toilet, I explained to Nat-David that if he could tell me when he needed to urinate or defecate, and actually did so, we would affix a gold star in a square. I explained that when the chart was full, he would be given a present, whatever he wished!

Nat was pleased with the idea, but first, I told him, I would have to determine what particular sound he would make, and then isolate THAT sound from all the others he made. After he attempted some sounds, I decided that the sound, "ugh" was close enough to "up" as in "up from the wheelchair," and then he and I went to shop for gold stickers in the local Five and Dime. I had already determined that any "accident" was to be ignored, not discussed, but that lavish praise and a gold star would accompany every successful effort. This, I informed Morris and my parents, and daily visitors, was how the toileting and diapers were to be handled.

In our home, no euphemisms were used to describe any bodily functions or body parts, and we always used the proper terminology. There was to be no "siss" or "doodoo" or "peepee" terms used, not in our home.

The first time Nat said "ugh" or "up" and I held his little backside over the toilet bowl, he was successful, and yelled in delight and triumph! At night we still put on diapers, but the control he displayed, and his pleasure at affixing the gold star, was such that he was more times successful than not. For every "miss," I had told him that **I** hadn't responded quickly enough! T'was no matter!

What I hadn't counted on was that his little girl-friend Kathy, and his other friends, were so excited as the number of stars increased, that they ran to see the chart whenever they were in our home! And they were all 1 1/2 to 2 years his senior.

May I brag that within two weeks Nat-David had NO accidents, but insisted on filling in the entire calendar chart before I was able to remove it from the toilet door! And then, he had the joy of helping to put the diapers in my ragbag of dust cloths!

As to Nat's continued toilet-training, before the fateful day that he was to be evaluated for admission to IRM, when he turned three, I said to him at bed-time, "Look Nat-David, wouldn't it be wonderful if one morning you awoke and your diaper was dry and unsoiled, and then we both could throw your diapers away permanently?" The next morning, Nat was dry…and clean…and so we two threw the diapers away forever.

All it took was a suggestion to a "dollink child"!

Now every visiting youngster wondered for what Nat-David would ask as a reward. They even made suggestions, but I was unconcerned, thinking, what could an almost three-year-old child want? Especially THIS child who seemed to have so much…but I WAS curious.

Our neighbor, two doors away, Althea, owned a beautiful Budgiregar (Para-keet, for the unbirdened) and Nat made us understand that THAT was what he wanted.

Morris and I were definitely "dog" people, and I had owned some cats, but neither of us had any experience with birds, so I asked Althea for advice. She often came into her rear garden to show Nat-David and me her Budgie, which was a male, sporting purple-over mauve-over yellow, plumage. AND HE SPOKE!

"Althea, where can we get a Budgie?"

The Rags of Time

"Don't do anything until I can get the information!"

Several days later, Althea told me that the man from whom she had bought her bird was a prize-winning breeder of Budgies, and would undertake to provide Nat-David with a Budgie from Althea's bird family and tell us when one was hatched. The breeder's name was Mr. Tator, and he phoned several weeks later to come and be introduced to Nat-David's Budgiregar!

He showed Nat-David and Morris and me a Parakeet in a room filled with Blue Ribbons, the walls of which were lined with hatching boxes, and told us he was so touched by Nat's request, and the reason behind it, that he had clipped the Budgie's wings so it would not fly, and so would bond with him. He also insisted on supplying us with a cage, some bird-toys, and instructions as to the bird's care and feeding. He asked just that Nat keep him informed about the bird, and how they got on together. Nat was especially pleased because that was a male bird and so would speak, even though HE could not.

Once home, we asked Nat what he was going to name the bird. We made some suggestions, then Morris, the clever one, said, "How about calling him Tator's Chip?" Nat smiled his agreement. The other children soon called him "Potato Chip" but we explained, and we all reverted to his proper name! Mr. Tator was thanked, given Tator's name, and for the next nine years, Tator Chip was a Schwartz!

Morris was, as an "Animal Trainer," very inventive in getting Tator to bond with Nat-David. On a small table before the wheelchair, Morris placed a circular train-track, on which Nat's fire-engine ran at modest speed, with its raised ladder, on which was placed poor Tator, and as it moved, he and I repeated, endlessly, "Tator Chip is David's bird, Tator Chip is David's bird!"

Before long, Tator hopped off the ladder, ran up Nat's arm to his ear, pecking and saying, "Tator Chip is DAVID'S bird!" This and other wise sayings amused us for all his life, until I discovered him one morning at the bottom of his cage, his tiny feet up in the air. "Bye, Bye, Tator...and you never had a sick day in your life!" Tator mimicked whatever was said, whether meant for bird ears or not, and some sayings were definitely NOT meant for ears, tiny or not.

Nat helped bury him in a cigar box in our garden.

The Rags of Time

Chapter 8

Whatever the state of the outside world, we established our own quartet: Morris and I and my parents composed a universe of our own in which we cocooned, nested, with our wonderful son, and grandson. When Nat was born, we "lost" friends and relatives. They fell away when we spoke of his diagnosis. Morris and I said simply, "To hell with them," and while it hurt sometimes to think we were isolated by their ignorance, we shrugged our shoulders, emptied our lives of any who could not, or would not, realize that all we wanted was to be accepted as before: for who we were.

Their loss! And that remained the philosophy of our lives, and if Nat-David had been born without his physical problems, our lives would not only have been different, but the richness our experience gave us, the many adventures we three shared, we would have never known.

While still in New Jersey, I realized that "friends" are a chancey commodity at best, and spent much time thinking about how I might help Nat deal with the problem. I decided that "bribery" was the best course, and when Nat-David had his second birthday, the opportunity presented itself. Armed with a bag of his birthday lollipops, Nat-David and I set out to conquer the world of his peers. Years later, I wrote for *Parents Magazine* an account of that adventure.

The day after the birthday, he and I set out for a walk, lollipops tucked in my pocket. We turned into a street around the corner from our house where children from the ages of 3 to 5 played, or just ran around together, or individually, for at that age children do not so much "play together," as near each other. Nat and I approached a small girl who smiled at us, and I asked if she could accept one of Nat's lollipops from yesterday's birthday party: "But make sure you ask for and get your Mom's permission."

The child sped away and told her mother, and permission was granted. Nat, smiling all the while in seeming delight, was smiled at in return, and the other six or seven children who gathered around his stroller, were not without questions.

"Why isn't he walking around?"
"Nat-David can't walk yet."
"My baby sister is younger than him and SHE can walk!"
"Nat-David's muscles aren't strong enough yet."

The children ran to their mothers and repeated what I had said, the mothers nodded to me, smiled, and Nat-David had friends from that day forth. Each day that we ventured among them, I came equipped with books, or paper and crayons, and some sweet or other and my Grove School training stood me in good stead, as we sat on a stoop, theirs, or ours, around the corner, and the children drew, or told stories, or I read to them, and bit by bit, I curtailed all "treats" until they forgot the bribes for friendship, and often called up to our windows to ask if Nat-David could come out to play. They also devised ways for him to join THEIR active games. For example, when racing up and down the street playing "Train," they would vie to push his stroller as they made him the "Caboose" of their imaginary train.

Since friendship IS a two-way street, I took advantage of their presence, and got permission from more-than-willing mothers to take the children on MY errands to the Post Office, the Bank, my food markets, in each case first giving them a tour and explanation of what they were to see. THEN I left Nat-David in their care, together with our dog Buttons, while I went about my chores secure in the knowledge that Nat-David was safe and happy.

Nat learned lessons about friendship. Friends are NOT always available, not always interested in play, have other things to do, and despite frowns, sulks, tears, on Nat-David's part, the reality of people's personal needs taking precedence over his, taught him the give and take of human relationships. Friends can serve our needs, but we must also take THEIR needs into consideration, as well as the vagaries of their moods.

In this computer age, we hear constantly that to inquire further about anything, we have only to "log on to something or other, dotcom," so if any reader is interested, he/she has only to procure a copy of "Parents Magazine, February, 1969, 50 cents" to read the entire article called, "Can Your Little Boy Come Out To Play?" This title was not my choice. The article I submitted bore a better one, "Friends Come In Different Flavors." I leave it to the reader to decide.

Morris and I had for some time spoken of moving to New York to be closer to Nat's treatment center, as well as to some very enthusiastic baby-sitting by my parents. We were fortunate to find a "Bastard Tudor" town house for sale which had the advantage of being but four streets from their home. On our last day in Jersey City, with the moving van at the door, I held a "moving party." Nat and I made our farewells to the children. I spooned ice-cream into paper-cups, and gave cookies and cakes to what had been my impromptu Kindergarten, together with hugs and kisses all round. The children were not sure what moving to another State meant, and they called out, "So long Nat, Bye, Nat, see you tomorrow!"

Goodbye Bryan, Billy, Theresa, I echoed in my heart, and thank you all very much for your friendship and affection, and fun, and for teaching Nat-David so much about friendship. Nat was similarly unaware what the move meant, was his usual smiling and laughing self with his friends. And I wondered if this ritual would be repeated in New York, and was fully determined and prepared to bribe my, and his, way into other children's hearts.

Our new home had a cement sidewalk which came right up to the front entrance, and was attached on both sides by other such houses, six in all, and in its rear was a small garden which had an ailanthus tree from "A Tree Grows In Brooklyn" fame, several bushes, and the garden was bordered by an ivied concrete wall which overlooked the local subway stop on the Brighton Line. One morning a few days later, Nat-David and I left our new home to explore the neighborhood. Two doors away, a small, night-gowned figure peeked at us from behind her front door. At my "Hello," the door quickly closed.

Later that day I watched from behind my screened kitchen door as Morris and Nat-David were in the rear garden. Two gardens away, concealed by a flowering wisteria, the same little girl watched.

"Hi, come on over," called Morris.
She skirted some flowerbeds and stepped carefully over low dividers.
"What's your name?"

"Kathy"

"I'm Mr. Schwartz, and this is my son Nat-David."

"Can he come out of his chair?"

"No, he can't walk yet."

"How old is he?"

"A little over two."

"I have a cousin who is only one and he is beginning to walk."

"But Nat-David's muscles are weak and so it will take him a little longer to learn to walk."

"Oh."

And so it began, and taking the momentary silence as a cue for action, I fixed a tray with refreshments, came out, and was introduced. Morris and I were grateful for the ease of our new conquest, but Nat-David responded to Kathy in a way which showed he already had some experience with friends, and he appeared to accept his new friend…as if her friendship was his due. He smiled, made sounds, obviously wanted to take part in the games we instantly devised, and was pronounced, "cute."

Kathy was one and a half years older then Nat-David, and she soon became the protector and go-between with other children explaining importantly, why Nat-David could not as yet walk or talk, and soon I had gathered another "kindergarten" group at my front steps. When we went walking, it resembled nothing so much as a parade, with Buttons next to Nat, enduring the pats of the children, and giving licks in her show of affection and attention. As I entered a shop and left Nat-David outside, I said to Kathy, "If anyone approaches Nat, you know what to do." "Oh yes" said she, "I'll scream!"

Since Buttons was an integral member of the group and sat always at Nat-David's side, screams proved unnecessary, but Nat's new friends, over the next few years, also dreamed up ways in which he might join their games. The rules they devised for him to play baseball, were that they positioned a plastic bat in his right hand, and the "pitcher" threw the ball at his bat so that it made contact, while another child ran him, in his wheelchair, to the chalked-off bases on the sidewalk. Talk about bitten-back tears as I watched from the sidelines! I also provided the youngsters with a child-size golf game, complete with mashies, nibliks and putters, all in the miniature golf-bag. Included also were metal "holes"!

With this and other equipment, the children played happily ALL through vacations, after school, and on weekends.

Other mothers were delighted when I led expeditions with their children to Prospect Park, to the ball fields, and to other sites they might enjoy. The children were easier to deal with than their parents, some of whom still withdrew their sons and daughters as though cerebral palsy were catching! When the children went off to school, Nat was unhappy to be at home, so I enrolled him in a United Cerebral Palsy Nursery School to which he was transported three times a week, to his joy. He was now in school, as were all his friends.

That his friends were all older did not now seem to matter as much. Nat was busy with treatments at Long Island College Hospital 3 or 4 times a week, plus mornings at the UCP nursery school, and on weekends, my parents played their inimitable part: my mother offered free piano lessons to any interested child, and many evenings were spent in our home where Morris strung a sheet between two rooms, and put on puppet shows for the children.

Nat-David's life was full…and ours was fuller!

At the UCP Nursery School Center where I attended weekly parents meetings, I heard much complaint about the intransigence of the New York City Department of Education towards the disabled, so I had myself made "recording secretary" and decided to print a survey (no names please!) which I circulated to the parent membership in an effort to establish the experiences of the parents and children. I asked for the age of the child, sex, to which school they had applied for admission, the probable grade level the child might have been in…or if the child WAS in school, what were the child's and parents' experience.

It all seemed very simple to me. But to the United Cerebral Palsy Organization, I evidently overstepped my secretarial limits. See Mom, I was right, I CAN'T do secretarial work! UCP requested the return of my list of names and addresses and I immediately complied.

BUT I HAD THE DATA!

By age 3 1/2, Nat could read, even if unable to verbalize in an understandable manner. I tested his cognition every time I read him a story, by repeating to him what I had read, but in so different a manner, using so many different words and phrases, that invariably he yelled, and stopped me. Also while reading to him, I underlined with my finger the sentences as I read them, and later, I turned to page after page, and holding my finger under one word or another, I asked Nat-David if the word were "thus" or "so," or "so"…at the correct word he whipped his head up to my face and smiled. I asked Morris, and my parents, and even his slightly older friends to do this, and watched their delight as he, unerringly, selected the correct word.

When Nat was five, I read in the New York Post newspaper that two rabbis were to open a school for handicapped children. Excitedly, I networked with some of the other parents, many of whom also had seen the article. We decided to call and go as a group for the interview, the following day, if possible. At an office in East New York, we ten mothers weren't sure if the Rabbi's were interviewing us, or we, them! There were ten of us around a table, together with the two rabbis and a head teacher. One after another of the mothers gave their son or daughter's age, diagnosis, and in each case, it was followed by an avowal of their family's religious practices, of how, were their child admitted, they would do thus and so, and on, and on, ad nauseum!

I left myself for last, stood, and said that I was NOT religious, although proud to be Jewish, and proud of Jewish history and survival through thousands of years, and that I did NOT "bench licht" (light candles to usher in the Sabbath), I was not a member of a synagogue, did not keep a kosher home, and did not intend to change my way of life, but if Nat-David were admitted, would ALWAYS send him properly dressed and hatted, with a kosher lunch, and if he were NOT deemed worthy of admittance, goodbye, and go with GOD!

Then the 5'2" redhead sat down…and guess who was the FIRST child to be admitted?

I imagine that even for rabbis it was refreshing to find someone who was honest, and a child they might imprint with the Orthodox version of Judaism.

Nat's joy at going to a "real" school was evident, and so ten children comprised the first student body, and officially began the following week. Nat was so beautiful and owned an entire wardrobe of hats. With yarmulke in his bookbag, and wearing a beret, he set out. Also he went with ten cookies taken from a larger supply. I read the box labels carefully, and sent a note to Mrs. Kaye, the teacher at the Hebrew Academy for Special Children, that if it were permissible, I thought the children might enjoy the concept of sharing. It evidently WAS feasible, and thereafter Nat always had ten cookies in his bookbag.

The schoolday was divided into typical Public School studies of Math, Science, English language and literature for the first half of the day, and after lunch, the study of the Hebrew language, Jewish customs and rituals began, until 3 PM, when the children were transported home, at private expense to the families.

After the first day in school, Nat showed me the "ditto" pages which outlined the "English" portion of their education. I then decided that "homework" was in order. I questioned Nat-David about the reading, writing, and arithmetic covered in class, and noted both my questions and his answers in a notebook which I sent in with him the following day, together with my note to Mrs. Kaye pointing out that Nat-David made me understand that his neighborhood friends had homework, and where was his? I also pointed out that this gave the children a sense of what school was like. She agreed because henceforth the children were given homework every day.

Whether the other children and their parents were of the same mind did not concern me, since it was Nat-David who was "ours," not the others, and my father who had been a Hebrew Scholar in his youth, was proud and delighted to act as Nat's unofficial "teacher's aide," and solemnly "listened" to Nat-David's answers to questions he devised…and on which he also made notes, to send in to the school.

In Nat-David's view, his school life was now perfect. Some of the other students were not in league with Nat's desire to learn, or had disabilities which involved some retardation, and I soon realized that if the school had only one teacher who bore the burden of instruction for the English portion of the day, we parents would have to lend a hand. I offered to make all the visual aids, another mother acted as secretary, another typed reports, or took dictation of business letters for the rabbis. So it went at the beginning of the school.

Now for the "business" end of the Hebrew School, lest the reader think that altruism and moral ethics were the sole agenda of HASC. What I have not as yet mentioned, is that for the privilege of educating our children, the school charged

$1500 a year, plus we parents had to pledge to raise another $1500 each, in some way. The first year, another mother and I ran a Dinner/Dance to be held in the basement recreation room/social hall of her apartment building, for which we charged a whopping $8.00 per couple.

We asked for, and received, donations of ALL the foodstuffs and goods from a variety of companies, none of whom refused us. We divided the donations of gifts into smaller portions, and several hotels in the "Borscht Circuit," including the prestigious Grossingers and Kutschers Hotels, gave the winners of a raffle, a weekend for two.

We were overwhelmed by the response, and pled guilty to shameless begging!

We ended up with so much stuff that the 100 couples EACH received a gift, raffle or no. How did we do this? Morris and I put our literary heads together and wrote a comic poem that requested donations, emphasizing that it was not for OUR son, but for ALL the children. The poem was clever and must have touched many hearts because we ended raising even more than we had anticipated. The young sons of personal friends acted as waiters and manned the cloakroom, and my dear friend, Margaret, good and faithful Catholic as she was, made centerpieces for all the tables which were to be taken home by the guests at each table.

One of the things I did NOT reveal to the school was that the Hebrew National Company donated a great deal of kosher meat and Deli items…UNSLICED. What to do? I confess that I took the meats to my own butcher who was not familiar with the rules of Kashruth, and he sliced it all on his non-kosher slicing machine! They obliged me because I was such a good customer.

Well Keats, what do you think and say now? To MY eyes, the butcher was GOOD and BEAUTIFUL…and I'm still not a Keats fancier!

But I'm equally sure that Keats doesn't give a damn!

And our lives were still far from "slow time!"

I believe that one of the things which saved our sanity, perhaps even our marriage, is that when everything ran smoothly, Morris and I made our home the centerpiece of our time together. We both collected antiques, according to our individual interests, furnished our home in our fashion of placing one beautiful acquisition with another, no matter the style or period, agreeing with Oscar Wilde that beauty knows neither period nor style!

But when our asses were dragging with one or another physical setback for Nat-David, THEN we had to get away for an evening. Our favorite restaurant was "Luigi's" in Manhattan, on 6th Avenue between 9th and 10th Streets. Morris and I did some of our best crying there. We sat at the bar with our vodkas, and listened to some music duets or trios who played "pop" or jazz, on a small raised platform, and we cried and talked out our anger, sorrow, frustration, over one problem or another. Then we were, with our vodkas in hand, taken to our table by waiters who knew us well, and knew what we would invariably order: boiled lobsters, salads, french-fried onions…and another vodka! When we finally left, we had at least come to a decision of how we were to meet our latest crisis, or disappointment, and could go on in the knowledge that what we couldn't control, we might change.

And this skewed, but personal, approach actually worked. We took on everyone and everything, and in each case, did NOT address underlings, but went "up" as far as we could get…to the person at whose desk the "Buck" stopped!

One morning, just after Nat-David had left for HASC, I received a call which purported to come from Mayor Lindsay's office in City Hall, from a "Mr. Smith" (Yeah, right, thought I!) saying that the Mayor had learned that I was very knowledgeable, an expert, in the educational needs of disabled children in New York City, and he wanted me to "compile a census, never before done, of the numbers of disabled children of school age, and submit a report to him."

No greenhorn, I. I agreed, but directly after the call, I phoned City Hall, requested to speak to "Mr. Smith," the Mayoral aide. To my amazement, I was connected to him. I thought fast, and told him that upon completion of the report, what I wanted was an appointment with Mayor Lindsay. THAT was what I expected, I made very clear. "Yes," said he. I spent about a month compiling and cross checking the figures, and when I completed the 32 page report, sent it off, Return Receipt Requested.

I waited patiently, and after a month, called the Mayor's office and told Mr. Smith that I expected a reply to MY request…and in short order!

I had discussed with Morris the needs of HASC, and we had decided that we had several requests to put to the Mayor…all non-negotiable: transportation for the children, schoolbooks and supplies, and a comparison with the Public School curricula. All of this was meant to relieve the expenses of the families, and give the school some status in our eyes…as well as for the school itself. To that end, Morris and I asked another parent in HASC, who was a lawyer, to accompany us.

Finally, on a Tuesday, we were "granted an audience!" I let Morris do the talking. I would sit by and listen…and take mental notes. Morris told Abe, the lawyer/parent, that he was also to sit and listen, and step in when Morris indicated. This was to be our strategy. At the meeting, Mayor Lindsay heard Morris out, then made the statement, "I'm so sorry, but your children are at the bottom of the barrel!"

Stupid man! That was definitely the wrong thing to say, because Morris then introduced Abe as our lawyer, and told the Mayor that if by Friday, the City hadn't acceded to our demands, Morris would situate 100 children in wheel-chairs at both ends of the Brooklyn Bridge, and if anyone so much as touched a wheelchair (by which he meant the police), he would yell "police brutality" to all the media he meant to assemble, the newspapers, radio, television, so that it was heard around the country!

"Oh please," said the Mayor, "please don't!"

"You have until Friday," said an implacable Morris.

And we left.

On Thursday, the Mayor called to say that he would honor our demands. Big deal! Especially since we were all taxpayers in a City which cared not a whit for our children. But would we please wait until the schoolbus company could make arrangements for our children, perhaps another ten days? The books and supplies would be delivered to HASC forthwith.

The Rags of Time

It DOES pay to get tough, was what we learned, and Morris and I used this experience as a touchstone for many further encounters in our quest for justice for Nat-David. We decided that AFTER Nat-David, anyone could benefit from our actions, and so it was that we also altered the future of the Hebrew Academy for Special Children.

I realized that if the school didn't grow and admit children of other religions and ethnicities, we could never apply to the United States government for grants-in-aid. I wanted to enlarge the school and curriculum. Many friends had already approached me to ask if their children, some of whom were Black, Catholic, Hispanic, and ALL of whom were handicapped, and thus not admitted to the Public Schools, could be admitted to HASC. They understood, as I made clear, that HASC had regulations regarding dress and dietary habits, and all, without exception, said they were prepared to dress their children appropriately, and send them with kosher food, and allow them to study Hebrew, if that were a requirement.

I approached one of the rabbis with the idea of "open enrollment" in order to apply for grants-in-aid. By that time, the school had moved from East New York to the Williamsburg section of Brooklyn, and the parents once again pitched in to help clean and paint, and set up additional classrooms.

During these past few years, Nat-David was already beginning to chafe at the lack of any courses such as advanced science, math, and history, which he felt he would need for any college entrance. I also added my pressure and requested, for history, at least the history of the land of Israel. But nothing changed from the earlier curricula.

During these years, when Nat-David was ten or eleven years old, Morris was busy trying to design and build a machine which would enable Nat to write, to print answers and question. We had already devised a system of spelling, whereby, from the time Nat was six or seven, and could spell, our "alphabet system" enabled him to converse with anyone by using "eye contact."

We supplied his teachers and friends with the system in which another person could "read Nat's eyes." Nat-David faced someone directly and that person would run through the alphabet, and when the letter needed was reached, he looked at the person and made direct eye contact.

The Rags of Time

Since Nat-David rarely discussed Einstein's Theory of Relativity, the person with whom he conversed, through knowledge of how Nat's mind worked, would, after two or three letters, understand what he wanted to say. It was a simple method, sometimes time consuming, but very effective. It certainly would do until something better came along. And my brilliant Morris was always trying for a better system…and finally designed and built it!

Although Nat-David's schooling went well, there were periods in which his emotional needs and frustrations were painful. However, an explosion from Nat, his sulkiness, his whining, did not sit well with his Primary Care-Giver, MOI! One day, after an explosion, I seated him to face me and delivered the following ultimatum, now called, "tough love."

"Look Nat, the worst handicap you can have is a lousy personality! I don't care if you scream, yell at me, spell out that you hate me, but WHINING I WILL NOT ACCEPT! If you whine, I'll simply turn my back on you, and then you won't be able to tell me ANYTHING! Look at me if you understand me!"

Nat looked at me.

He was then seven years old.

Well, in my family, we were always fast learners!

From then on, Nat-David would couch his complaints and frustrations in ways that would permit Morris and me to discuss and to address and sometimes to defuse them. If we could not deal with a specific situation or frustration, ours, as well as his, Nat knew that we would work at it until a solution was reached… sometimes after weeks, months, even years, but he knew that we would not forget, and so he was always able to trust us.

One day after supper, homework finished, Nat saw on television a commercial for the musical "Pippin," which showed Ben Vereen dancing and singing. Nat seemed fascinated by it, and was wreathed in smiles whenever it came on. About the fourth time it was aired, Nat called out, smiling, "I, I, I…" and so his doting Mamma asked, "Nat, are you saying you'd like to see Pippin?"

Nat had already attended, at age 3 and 4, some Children's Theatre performances in Manhattan, and showed his enjoyment by attempting to clap his hands, and once at a performance of "Peter Pan," answered the question posed by Peter, "If you believe in Fairies, say yes!" and he yelled out with all the other children who wanted to believe in "Tinkerbell"!

Fast forward to "Pippin"!

We bought three tickets, explaining to the box-office that we were attending with a family member in a wheelchair. "No problem," we were told. We arrived to pick up our tickets and were shown to 3 seats in the MIDDLE of a row! Morris was in a rage, stormed to the Manager and asked HOW and WHERE Nat was expected to sit! "At least you might have had the decency to seat us at the end of a row, so the wheelchair could sit in the aisle!" he fumed. Some kind patrons offered us their seats for ours, and after the show, which we and Nat loved, Morris made sure to inform the Manager that we had paid for 3 seats, while occupying only two. This taught us a lesson. After this experience, we always asked to see a seating chart, and selected accordingly.

On another occasion when Nat made the same enthusiastic response to a television ad showing an upcoming IceCapades show, we again bought tickets, and this time there were no errors. Through all the years that Nat-David remained an enthusiast for concerts, ballets, plays and movies, we always made very thorough checks with the managements, taking upon ourselves the burden of giving information about our needs, about the wheelchair...but one experience taught us NEVER to assume an interest on Nat's part that he did not share.

After the IceCapades, we knew that the Russian Circus was to be at Madison Square Garden, and felt that Nat would LOVE this. With my parents as our guests, we five were given excellent seats close by ringside, there being only one ring in a Russian Circus, unlike the 3-rings of an American Circus. They regaled Nat with descriptions of the Bear Act, the wonderful Flying Popovs, and more, and added their memories of the Circus in Tsarist Russia. We five sat with huge, expectant grins, and much clapping, as acts were announced by the Ringmaster.

What transpired afterwards was a terrified Nat, his head down, clearly frightened by a chained bear being led around the ring, and cringing while the Popovs flew overhead, followed by horses careening around the ring, "withal Pretty Maids All On Their Backs!"

Morris and I concluded NEVER to take for granted that Nat would like what WE might enjoy, or what my parents remembered as enjoyable, and that unless initiated by Nat-David, we would not foist our tastes on him. And never did.

So much for "Good Parenting"! Through all the years, Nat was the arbiter of his own tastes and desires as far as possible. It also proved a lot less expensive.

I have always believed that a disabled child must be empowered insofar as possible. From the time Nat-David was 1 1/2 years old, when I dressed him, I always held out two shirts and two pairs of pants, and asked, "Nat, what shirt will you wear today? The blue or the orange? What pair of slacks, the red or the brown?" And I always accepted whatever was HIS choice, no matter the hideous combination he sometimes chose. HE made the choice in a world where so much was, had been, and was going to be, the ultimate decision of others! And Morris and I ALWAYS stuck to this precept, trying to imagine OUR world bounded always by the decisions of others.

Morris and I learned to accept Nat's view of things; what the young call, "taking one's lumps," even when we knew that Nat would not always be happy with the results of his decisions. We decided that it would infringe his liberty as a human being to assume that, since we were "able-bodied," we knew best. We gave him as much freedom as he desired, short of allowing him an experience in which his life might be endangered, and let him make the mistakes all able-bodied humans make, and did not expunge from his life those lessons we in 20/20 foresight would have preferred he not make!

I recall my own anger when my father tried to save ME from what HE imagined. His words came back: "Susie, I've been through the mill," and my reply, "but that was YOUR mill!" Along with some hurtful experiences for which HE paid (and WE, secondarily!), Nat-David pretty much ran his own life. While we were not always happy with the outcome of some choices, we could not stand in the way of HIS reality.

The Rags of Time

If we had, it would have been the same as everyone's assumption that the disabled were incapable of determining their own actions, their own goals, their own futures,…of thinking for themselves. I rationalized that President Franklin Roosevelt did quite well. Although he never did break away from his mother's influence, to Eleanor's dismay!

When Nat-David was seven years old, he asked to attend a ballet. There was a so-called Children's Performance at Lincoln Center, which included "Peter And The Wolf," together with two other ballets purported to be of interest for children. We invited Nat's friend Kathy to accompany us since she had never seen a ballet, or even, ever gone to the Theatre to see a play. Morris and I intended to make a day of it with the youngsters, and take them to dinner afterwards.

Our seats were at the end of a row so Nat could sit with us, but in the aisle. Of course, there WAS a pillar almost directly ahead,…BUT…! Unfortunately, the particular theatre we were in had 68 seats all in a row. No center aisle! Anyone lucky enough to sit in the center had to walk past knees, intoning, "excuse me, excuse me," to get IN or OUT of the row. Nat was pleased to be there. He knew the music and score, as we had played the recording with its narration to him many times. Kathy was just thrilled with the set, the curtain, the chandeliers hanging like huge round baubles overhead, the orchestra, all new to her.

WE, Morris and I, were surprised that, oddly, this performance cast Peter as a Dutch boy, in Dutch costume, with a very blond wig, and a background which resembled nothing so much as a lush tropical forest. But the animals were played as amusingly as ever, and applause was deafening at the close.

At the first intermission, Morris who had read ahead in the program, saw that the second ballet concerned itself with a suicide, in Monmartre, in the Seine. We didn't think this suitable fare for the children, so we intended to take them upstairs for sodas, and the toilets, if necessary, but Kathy opted to stay, and I, good hostess, remained, while the "Men" went upstairs by elevator.

The ballet was what I expected, quite dreadful, and watched by Kathy through her fingers before her eyes! When it was over, the men returned, and we were all prepared to be entertained, but instead, witnessed a boring, dreadfully long ballet, called "La Fille Mal Gardée," which dated from 1786. Sometimes it IS better to let sleeping ballets, and dogs, lie!

The Rags of Time

What Kathy and I missed out on, as Nat-David gleefully reported after we left, was their meeting with Jacqueline Kennedy and her son John and daughter, Caroline in the visitor's lounge. As Morris and Nat appeared there, they were stopped by several Secret Service men who attempted to bar their entrance, but were waved away by Jacqueline, who was interested in Nat and his reaction to the ballet. Morris explained why they had left, and Jackie agreed that she took the children out for the same reason. But they would, as the Schwartz men, return for the last ballet.

Within a few minutes, Nat, through Morris' spelling out with him, spoke and answered her questions. Morris reported that during the exchange, Jacqueline took time out to chastise her daughter and threaten her with immediate removal if her behaviour did not improve. Then she asked about Nat's education, his age, and seemed interested when told he was studying in two languages.

It developed that she was seated with the children, and Jean Smith and her children, in the row just in front of ours, but they were in the center, and had to "excuse" themselves to all seat-holders until the end of the row!

Morris, after we left, gushed on and on about how charming and beautiful she was, and Kathy and I were sorry to have missed all that...Kathy admitted she would have forgone the Seine fiasco! This chance meeting was but the first in a long succession of political figures we, and Nat, met through the years.

When Nat was eleven, there came the next important adventure of our lives. One day, before a visit to IRM, we received a call from Liesl Friedman, head occupational therapist, who told Morris that it was important for him to see "something very interesting for Nat-David's communication." For years, Liesl had a sign over her desk on which was printed, "Nat-David, Communication." Liesl had been the evaluating occupational therapist when Nat first entered IRM. She also became a valued friend who occasionally visited our home socially. On her forearm was the tattooed number from a German concentration camp.

In great excitement, we three went immediately to IRM and saw a Communication Machine/Device, which had been slated to be returned to California later that week. The Machine was called the VISTA, an acronym which stood for "Visual Instant Scanning (sonethingsomethingsomething), stood 5 feet tall, and consisted of a letter board which lit up, and which was composed of a grid of letters, and in front of which was an IBM Selectric typewriter. It took Morris about fifteen minutes to understand its workings and application and significance for Nat. It took Nat about ten minutes longer…and I trailed with another fifteen, after Morris explained how it worked.

The method of input was by using a "control," something like today's computer "mouse," or some other remote-control, in order to type. The lights first lit up horizontally row by row, then when halted by a "command," each letter in a row lit separately. The written results could be read on the Selectric's paper.

The letters on the grid or matrix of the VISTA, were arranged in the same way as on a typewriter. You know: "Q W E R T Y, etc…." In other words, STUPIDLY, because SENSIBLY, in the English language the letter "Q" is usually followed by "U," not "W" …and not five letters apart.

Be that as it may, Morris immediately ordered the VISTA from California, but Dr. Swinyard had a better idea. He suggested that we BORROW the VISTA from IRM to see how it would function for Nat, and then we could return it to IRM and order one from California.

There was great excitement on the way home. There were two immediate concerns: one was the manner in which Nat might use it, and the other was the wonderful promise Morris made to Nat on the spot. "Nat, when you know how to use the VISTA, I promise that I will make it small enough to fit in a basket between the rear wheels of your chair so you can take it with you and use it anywhere."

When we returned home that afternoon, Morris set to work to devise a way for Nat to learn to use the VISTA. What he did over several days (after all, he did have a job!) was to install an old-fashioned school bell behind the headrest of his wheelchair. This was to approximate the tapeswitch to be installed when we finally owned the VISTA. I drew a grid showing the letters as they appeared on the VISTA, and armed with a flashlight, I aimed the light on the entire top row, then on one letter after another, until Nat pressed back on the headrest, then I wrote the chosen letter on a sheet of paper, and began the entire process again, until Nat had written a word: "THANKS," and so on and on, every day after school, until he had mastered the technique.

We were referred to a speech pathologist at IRM for consultation about ideas of HOW Nat was to operate the VISTA. She suggested his hand (impossible), his knee, (also impossible), and his "Whatever," (also impossible), but Morris had already told her that the ONLY and best controlled movement Nat possessed, was to use Nat's head pressure against the headrest, and finally Amy said, "Look, I just want Nat to be able to use the VISTA! I'm not wedded to the idea of any of MY suggestions!" One of the training skills was that Nat be able to press his head back against the headrest when he wanted to print a letter, but NOT to press back when he did not want to print.

When our VISTA was finally shipped to us, and Nat transferred his new knowledge to the actual Machine, we realized to our joy, all three of us, that for the first time, Nat could initiate communication with us sans the more laborious method we first established with the spelling-mode.

Now Nat was finally free to pursue his own thoughts...and his own spelling! I soon realized that if a person is unable to reinforce spelling by writing, but uses only how he HEARS another's speech, which may be garbled, or accented, he may spell it incorrectly. For years, we had been in the habit of finishing his words after two or three letters, secure in the knowledge that we knew how he thought...and spelled.

Once when Nat asked to do his homework by himself, I placed his notes before him, and his assignment, in this case, a geography lesson, and when he had finished and I checked his homework, next to one number his answer was printed as "OTION." I puzzled long and mightily over that one, until I remembered that I had told Nat, years before that if he were doubtful over a spelling, he was to spell phonetically. The word was "OCEAN"! I wrote the correct spelling and put it before him, and never again did he repeat the error.

The first communication he initiated was "Mom, I love you." After about two minutes of tears, I hugged and kissed my son.

True to his promise, Morris now spent every free (hah!) moment, designing and creating a portable printer for Nat, because once away from our home, and the 5' Blunderbuss which stood in a corner of the family room, Nat was again back to his spelling mode: he couldn't initiate conversation, and he became more and more frustrated since he now understood the pleasure and benefits of being able to converse freely with anyone. Morris had interested another engineer to work with him to accomplish a portable machine.

Nat and Morris collaborated on improving the letter sequence of the VISTA by reading books on the history of the alphabet, on typography, and scores of books in order to analyze the letter make-up in the English language. They FOUGHT, FOUGHT, over every letter included and its proximity to every other letter, and counted how many I's, E's, B's, etc. were used in a single page of printed material, no matter the subject. By the time, after almost 9 months had passed, they agreed on the placement of each letter, they had invented a Letterboard, copyrighted in Nat's name, which is considered the best of any extant, by the Epsom Computer Company, now sadly defunct, and by Tufts, and the University of Wisconsin's famous department of Communication.

Nat was twelve by the time the machine, called the Portaprinter, made its debut in a basket which Morris slung between the rear wheels of his wheelchair.

In the Schwartz home, a promise made was a promise kept.

The Portaprinter typed on Canon strips, and served other purposes: Morris left several "uncommitted" squares, one of which showed a toilet seat, and when Nat rang the bell on the Printer, it signaled to anyone within earshot what was wanted. Another square turned on a light, another, the television. Nat-David could now slightly more control his environment, and had some power over his life, a power so important to all people, especially to the disabled. Morris and I had long ago committed ourselves to empower Nat-David with the freedom, the personal power, which we of the community of the able-bodied, take for granted.

How did this determined Triumvirate go on? How did our lives continue despite, or outside of, our avowed course?

It would be nice to say, "day by day" …but our lives were often determined by chance, by the crises of the moment, by our collective Karma. The realities of daily life often intruded on our best laid plans, and often shook us out of our "group" life, and despite our love for each other, Morris and I were often waspish, short-tempered, felt imprisoned and unable to escape our mutual imprisonment.

The Rags of Time

Oh, Morris and I got away for an evening, for a day, but a sustained love-life was often impossible. But to whom might we complain? Try as we might, we two consenting adults, parents of a much-loved child, sat down to salvage our relationship, to reorder, if we could, our priorities, coming to the realization that if WE were so dispirited, so frustrated, it could not help but affect our marriage, and impact Nat.

The Rags of Time

Chapter 9

When Nat was nine, a crisis arose which impacted him every day of his entire life: The death of his beloved, and oh so loving, grandfather intruded with a suddenness none of us could have foreseen.

Can death ever be foreseen?

For a child whose universe consisted of a series of concentric circles, with the smallest and innermost being we four: father, mother, grandfather, grandmother, then radiating outward in larger, but consisting always of less important members: from close relatives and friends, to pleasant acquaintances, to lesser relatives, to people who were here today and gone tomorrow, to those who were politically expedient but never in our true confidence, or those whom we never expected to be longlasting, the loss of a member of Nat's Inner Circle was devastating.

From the time Nat-David was an infant, it was his grandfather Leon who first recognized his intelligence. On the day of the Conference of the Crippled and Disabled at the Waldorf-Astoria, when I returned home to New Jersey after a day of seminars, Nat was so hurt by my seeming defection that he would not smile, or even look at me despite my attempts at cooing, and babbling on about my day. All my efforts gained me was a stony exterior, total rejection! Later, my father told me that Nat-David hadn't even cried all that day, had just withdrawn and presented a stony silence, thus proving to my father that only an intelligent child would so behave.

Of course, by the next day, Nat returned to his former smiling demeanor, as I continued to reassure him by my presence that I was NOT going to disappear again.

The Rags of Time

When Nat-David was 2 1/2 and we moved from Jersey City to Brooklyn, New York, to within a few blocks from my parents' apartment, I would leave Nat in their care while I stole a few hours for myself. I might visit with a friend, or shop, or walk to the Brooklyn Museum for an exhibit or concert. When I returned to walk him home, I often found Nat on a small blanket on their living-room rug, my father stretched out beside him, telling him stories of his life in Russia, and of the mischief he and his brother Sam had perpetrated on their friends or the servants. Now it was an ecstatic Nat who was unwilling to leave a doting grandpa and his stories of life under the Tsar, and a loving grandmother who introduced Nat to the delights of Steak Tartare, or copious amounts of red caviar on bread, freshly sliced by her and lovingly fed to him.

Is it any wonder that he developed a taste for expensive and exotic food? Or tastes that are NOW increasingly expensive, since red and black caviar, smoked salmon, white-fish, were considered staples in my parents' home. Of course, in 1961, eight or ten ounce jars of caviar sold for 95 cents to $1.25 a glass jar!

From the time Nat was three years old and in his first wheelchair, my father took Nat-David into his home "office," and as a former import/export expert turned philatelist, he would carefully open his mail, and save the stamps on the envelopes to start an album for Nat. Nat soon had "Geography" lessons based on the stamps. My father reinforced his lessons by pointing out the countries on a small revolving globe I bought for the purpose.

When Nat was with his grandparents, he was their sole guest, no matter who else visited them. Once, a Russian friend, rather a "grande dame" in her own estimation, said in my father's presence, "Why do you pay him so much attention? I have come to speak with you about something important!" Whereupon my father told her that Nat-David was his honored guest, and invited her to leave!

In later years when Nat attended the Hebrew Academy, his grandfather "heard" his Hebrew lessons, or told him of his and his brother Sam's experiences in Cheder, of his Bar Mitzvah, of Sam's less than successful forays into the Talmud and the Torah, and Pentateuch. Nat was a vessel into which all types of knowledge were poured, spilled, absorbed even though it would take until he was ten or eleven for him to be able to eject this digested information to the members of his inner and outer circles.

The Rags of Time

When Nat was eight, he begged to be allowed to attend sleep-away camp for a few weeks, as did his older friends. Morris and I checked with the Staff at IRM, especially with Miss Perfect, who embodied her name! She was quite, quite "Perfect"! She was the social worker to the Children's Unit, and so good at her job, always putting the needs and welfare of the disabled children before those of her Staff, that SHE was their biggest fear…and of course, to reward her, they bumped her up to a position of power: at a desk! Nevertheless, fond of Nat and of us, she inquired and found a Camp which accepted disabled children.

Morris and I met and conferred with the Camp Director and Head Counselor, and set up a most structured program for Nat, giving them all the information they needed regarding his eating, sleeping, toileting, habits. To all this, the Director said, "No problem!"

Why is it that those two little words gave me absolutely NO comfort! Rather, a nagging feeling of unease permeated both Morris and me, and since Nat could not speak with us by phone, or write to us, we and my parents called every day so he could hear our voices, and we had his calendar days supposedly crossed off by the Staff. We comforted ourselves by redoing Nat's room while he was away in exactly the manner he requested: the four sections of wall were to be in his favorite colors: one pegboard section in red, one in blue, one in his favorite color orange, and the last left in its natural brown surface.

Morris added pegboard sliding window-covers for the room's 3 windows, so that if the air-conditioner was on, he could still have light through the holes, or, in winter, even if the windows were open, he would be spared draughts. The pegboard served another purpose. On a shelf which ran the length of a wall, marched Nat's collection of Matchbox automobiles, all of which Morris had equipped with seed-lights.

The day finally arrived when Nat was to return home after three weeks. If there is a question as to why we did not visit, blame his psychologist mother, who had been advised by the Director not to visit, as some children were rendered MORE homesick. We arrived to see horror! Nat was unable to stop whimpering at the sight of us. He had lost weight, was so dehydrated that his lips were parched and seemed almost swollen. Once in my arms, he held on as though I were his life-preserver.

Morris was so outraged he bellowed to see the Camp Director, fists clenched, but the Director was suddenly nowhere to be found. The head counselor bore the brunt of Morris' wrath, and I begged Morris to get us out of there, to go home. My father was so upset and angry, I thought HE might attack someone. When we were in the car, Nat-David still clutching me, my father said to Nat, "Nat-David, don't worry. I will put the Camp in my little black book! You'll see how they will be punished!"

My father had a "little black book" in which, he assured Nat, he wrote the names of Everyone and Anything which was an injustice, and anything listed could expect retribution. The fact that Grandpa Leon had never shown such a book to Nat, did not matter. It was enough that my father had spoken! Nat-David's face at once regained some of its color, and he smiled for the first time.

As a matter of fact, and record, and written of in our newspaper, a fire broke out and destroyed most of the camp. And NAT knew that Grandpa had somehow used his ever-present cigar to effect this result!

From then on, Nat knew that my father could do anything, right any wrong!

Morris and I dealt with the Camp in our "usual way." We reported them to the IRM, to Miss Perfect, to anyone who might want their child to attend this camp, which we renamed "Junior Auschwitz." When we took Nat to our family doctor as soon as we got home, he was equally outraged and shocked, said Nat was seriously dehydrated, and had lost 5 pounds off his skinny little frame.

Thankfully, neither of my parents berated us for allowing Nat-David to attend sleep-away camp, realizing how much, and how bitterly we blamed ourselves. We had had "gut feelings" which we had often heeded in the past, but despite these, hadn't stopped him from having this experience. It remains, after these many years, one of my worst nightmares!

Ever inventive, Morris was responsible for one of Nat's most enjoyable pastimes. With some of his and his friends' input, Morris built for Nat a minia-ture, scaled, version of New York City, complete with 4-lane East-Side highway, bridge, a car-wash, a baseball stadium, a motel with swimming pool, in which tiny dolls seemed to swim. All of these features, and more, were glued to a dining-room table sized piece of plywood, which was hinged, and when folded up, was closed by a slide-lock. It had, on one side, small wheels, so it could easily be moved and stored when not in use. It was extremely ingenious, and the children all had the fun of watching its development and also in suggesting elements, and even buying some of its component parts.

At that time, Nat's friends (the boys) were busily collecting match-box cars, and Morris installed seed lights for them. There were daily gatherings in our home during the winter months, or when inclement weather kept them from outdoor play. Was this another of our "bribes" to insure that Nat would have friends? Probably, but we didn't consciously regard it as such…by now, we just seemed to have one good idea after another, and it became just our way of keeping everyone, including ourselves, interested and amused.

Morris, who could be VERY mischievous at times, also created four controls which activated four cars and sent them spinning along the four lanes. There was one control for each child. What he failed to tell the other three, even Nat, was that Nat's control, when clutched in his small hand, would outrace the others.

Well, we DID try to give Nat all possible control!

Obviously, children were always found who were happy and eager to play with Nat-David, who had such a loving, and terribly clever, Engineer father.

Additionally, every winter, when the demands of homework and inclement weather made it less likely that Nat would always have friends around, I devised projects for us to do when we were alone together. The first winter I bought a very large bar of Ivory soap, and lightly stabilized his hand around a rather dull knife, a butter knife actually, and we carved from it what HE suggested. A bird! The result was not too shabby! Another year, Nat decided to make a linoleum-cut design of a horse standing in a field of earth which had been pawed-over. The design was based on a story told to me by Jess Perlman at the Grove School, and purported to show the difference between an optimist and a pessimist:

Identical twins were separated in early childhood, and placed in adjoining rooms. In one room whose floor was literally covered with every imaginable kind of toy and game, one twin picked through them, tossing them about in disgust, glumly saying, "I know the wheels are going to come off this truck," or "These trains will just crash into each other, or "I'll bet the head falls off this doll," accompanied by pouts and whines and anger!

In the next room could be seen the other twin busily shoveling mounds of manure from one place to another, while saying, "With all this manure, there's got to be a PONY somewhere!"

It was this second, optimistic view of things that Nat-David was trying to carve from the linoleum…as he always tried to carve it from his difficult life.

One winter, watching me as I hooked a small rug, he decided that he, too, would like to try this craft. He chose the design of shells from my collection and I drew and transferred them to canvas. Together we shopped in our neighborhood for the colored yarns he chose. He spent quite happy, snowy, winter, evenings and weekends, clutching the shuttle hook with which he was able to push the colored yarns into the canvas, and then I helped to steady his hand to pull it back towards him after every stitch. The rug hung in his bedroom for years, very bright, and he announced proudly to all admirers that HE had made it!

During the summer when Nat was ninesomething, my father had cataract surgery, developed glaucoma, and was nearly blind, and then within a few weeks after surgery, was diagnosed with prostate problems. Before his eye surgery was performed, we three had planned a short vacation in upstate New York. Nat begged us to wait until his grandfather was out of the hospital, and of course, we did.

When we again planned the trip, my father received a hospital date and because we were again going to cancel THIS trip, my father told Nat that the surgery, as outlined to him, would not be serious, and he insisted that we go. It happened that we left on the very day of his surgery and told my mother that we would call daily for a report on his hospitalization.

We reached New Paltz by noon, went swimming, out to lunch as planned, only to receive my mother's call later that night, that at 9 PM, while in surgery, my father succumbed to a fatal heart attack. We left at once for home, and in the car Nat was inconsolable, sobbing and weeping through the entire trip.

The Rags of Time

Unlike Morris and me and my mother, Nat insisted that he wanted to "see grandpa" in his coffin before the cremation, which had been my father's stated wish. Morris and my mother went to see the Rabbi who would perform the service. The Rabbi was unknown to any of us, since my father, Hebrew scholar though he had been in his youth, did not belong to a synagogue, nor was his faith strengthened through his life. Instead, it was weakened by what he perceived as the injustice of the world towards his grandson.

Morris took charge. He told this young Rabbi, chosen by the funeral home, and who was actually the Rabbi for the Fire Department, that he, Morris, "did not want a generic Service," which might be applicable to anyone, but that he was to say what our family wanted, that the service honored and spoke of my father, as he had been: an imperfect man with a sense of humor, with intelligence, a man who had temperament, vices, and if the Rabbi could not do that, then he, Morris would throw him off the Bimah and give the sermon himself! Mainly he was to depict my father in a way in which Nat recognized his beloved grandfather.

The Rabbi was flabbergasted, but meekly complied…and took notes. Afterwards, friends and family members came to say, with laughter, that they could envision Leon as he was in life. Nat cried quietly throughout the service, especially when the Rabbi spoke of his love for Nat-David, and of his pride in Nat's accomplishments as a human, and as a student.

We were all surprised to see my father in an open casket, in light of his desire for cremation. Nat-David was at first upset when the concept of cremation was explained to him, and Morris and I told him that the philosophy of our family was that underground burial was simply not an option. Tombstones and cemeteries we considered a waste of "living space," and my parents remembered that they had been to my brother's grave just twice, since it was in the Musician's Cemetery in upstate New York and did not permit a gravestone, had just a metal marker with his name and dates. My father did not drive, and it was difficult to get to by rail.

Years later, in High School, Nat wrote a poem about this experience with death, a lovely and poignant poem in which he described his relationship with my father. He called it:

The Rags of Time

THE SURPRISE

Life was forever, I thought
When I was five.
Days and nights followed each other
Like loving grandparents.
(They are not now alive.)

Hebrew School was mystery and magic.
It was Aleph, Bais,
(Grandpa didn't believe in Jews with Peyes.)
Pesach,
(A honeyed Seder with Grandpa at table's head),
Yarmulkes and matzoth.
(It is hard to believe he is dead.)

When I found the Afikoman
The prize was a gorgeous Old Testament.
In gold leaf
The Egyptians repent.
Grandpa said, "A work of art!"
(Published by the Catholic Press).

When I was nine, life was sadder.
Death had entered, much to my surprise.
(When Dad told me, he had tears in his eyes.)
I saw a Pine box.
In it, my cold, waxen Grandpa.
I went into the room
And thought I heard Grandpa say,
(In a voice, lightening the gloom)
"How about a little schnapps?"

The Rabbi spoke little comfort
In a Hebrew drone,
While I remembered our travels,
Grandpa's and mine.
(I never left home.)

The Rags of Time

Through his imagination
(I remember how he used to sing)
He took me to Tsarist Russia,
Berlin, Greece, where
("They put mayonnaise on everything!")

Where are our travels now?
For half a year I cried,
Then, in my mind
Grandpa traveled to Heaven.
("Why did you leave me behind?")

When Nat was ten, I decided to write a book and began to assemble my thoughts, jot down notes…and Nat said to me one day, "Mom, I'd like to write a book. Would you help me?"

What could I say?

So Nat dictated to me, word after laborious word, to fill 13 pages, HIS book about my father and his feelings about him. And when it was finished, I sewed the pages together, and we both made a cover from a linoleum block. Nat asked me to help him draw and cut a picture of an older man seated next to a boy in a wheelchair, and to cut the title, "Eight Years With My Grandpa." After the title page, he dictated: Written and Illustrated by Nat-David Schwartz, Published and Typeset by Schwartz Publishers, First Printing, 1969. All Rights Reserved…$1.25.

On the facing page was the Dedication:

To The Memory of MY Grandpa
LEON JAFFE
I write this book because I
Love him very much and I want
Everybody to know about my
Grandpa.

This book was the story, in Nat's words, about the imaginary travels my father had taken with Nat, based on various stories my father had told him through the years, and his interpretations of them. The title was explained by Nat-David's words that, although he was now almost ten, he didn't see very much of my father for the first two years of his life.

I typed about a dozen copies for relatives and friends, covered them with the blockprint, and sewed each of them together, and we gave them away.

But you noticed that he priced them at $1.25!

Nat insisted that I walk him to a neighborhood bookstore so he could see what was charged for paper-backs. At the time, they ranged in price from 75 cents to $1.25. When I asked why he wanted to sell his book, he told me that since, "Grandpa didn't leave much insurance or money for Grandma," he intended to give her the money. Laudable, to be sure, but how was I to cope with a demand for his literary output?

Help arrived in the guise of a friend who put Morris in touch with a printer, and HE printed up 100 copies. It still remained for me to cover and hand-sew the books, but what the hell, it's just MOM!

First I swore my mother to secrecy about Nat-David's determination to rescue a poor widow, and insisted that she MUST accept his largesse. My mother obliged, of course, and Nat-David never knew that she added the money to a fund my father had left for Nat's Bar Mitzvah, which he so longed to attend.

It is said that no good deed ever goes unpunished. While we were busy, Nat and I, with our literary pursuits, Morris was making Nat a bicycle. On weekends, Nat's friends now went bicycling in Prospect Park, and no matter how fast we pushed his wheelchair, it was impossible to keep up with the scores of young-sters who pedaled for miles along the route which, on weekends, was closed to automobiles.

Morris to the rescue!

He haunted bicycle shops looking for, "The rear end of a girl's bike." The inevitable question was, "What do you need it for?"

"What the hell do you care! Do you have one or not?"

The Rags of Time

"No, I don't!"

On and on, from one shop to another, went my intrepid Engineer, until finally, one day, came the happy reply, "Yeah, I got one, just tell me how you'll use it, and you can buy it." When Morris explained what he intended, the shopkeeper handed him back his money, and intrigued, asked just the pleasure of seeing it when it was completed.

But it seemed that EVERYBODY saw it when it was put together, because some parent in the neighborhood called the Daily News, and a reporter and photographer were dispatched to see this unusual sight of a disabled child and his bike. Of course, in true media and reportorial excess, the headline under the photo read, in bold print:

WHEELPOWER CONQUERS PALSY BOY'S HANDICAP

I added, "From your lousy article to God's ear!"

There ensued a deluge of mail from everywhere in New York City...and other places, and letters of interest about Nat-David, also stories about the writer's experiences with a disabled child, sibling, parent, and questions about Nat's schooling and his physical condition. The reporters had also included in the article mention of Nat-David's book.

Nat was most interested in the money enclosed, either by check or in cash, and the fact that NO ONE sent less than $5, $10, and once even a check for $100 arrived. Nat was thrilled to be able to add this to "Grandma's fund"! I was overwhelmed at the magnitude of people's interest, of their need of me and Nat, of their generosity. Many people after receiving their book, continued to write me for several years.

Life leads us; compels its own course.

And every action had its own fantastic reaction!

A Dr. Ari Klapwyck came to speak at IRM one day, about a village composed of disabled adults in his country of Holland. It is called "Het Dorp," which translates to "The Village," of which he was Medical Director. This village is in the city of Arnhem, and was designed and built because of a need thus far unmet by the Dutch. The people of Holland held a telethon and raised over $7 million dollars, which was matched by the Dutch government. Het Dorp was built to contain individual homes for disabled citizens, single or married, and included also a large building which housed staff, and brilliant in concept, also contained a factory which made and repaired wheelchairs.

All of what was constructed in Het Dorp was placed amidst the gently rolling terrain of Arnhem. Each dwelling was accessible to everyone, inhabitants and visitors, and if it were two-storied had special elevators connecting them all, so even in winter, the covered sidewalks permitted socialization. Each "home" had sleeping quarters, a small living room, wall kitchen, large shower with toilet, and a private garden. The inhabitants could entertain or just relax out-of-doors.

There was a restaurant staffed by the disabled, but open to the public, as was a gas station, an ecumenical Chapel, in which each of the four sides faced in a different direction, so no matter one's religious belief, one could worship with a Priest, Rabbi or Minister!

We three Schwartzes listened with excitement, even awe…and some disbelief that such a place existed! The prevailing wisdom of Het Dorp was the concept of "reverse integration." If the citizens of surrounding Arnhem wanted a food market, a travel agency, or Post Office, they would have to go to Het Dorp to find them. Also there was a fine library and gymnasium where non-disabled athletes came to practice their sport, even to compete with their disabled counterparts.

It was hard to envision, even after Dr. Klapwyck showed us photographs and a short film outlining the building process. Another significant feature was that while help was available for its inhabitants, it was NOT automatically forthcoming. The residents of Het Dorp had to ASK for help. The philosophy that governed the "Dorp" was that every person was expected to be as independent as his/her disability permitted. All of them held jobs, some were in the factory, some were transported out to jobs, and those who were unable to do physical work, or work at the various industries, gave their time as guides, advisers, for tours.

The Rags of Time

It was shock after shock!

After the talk and general discussion and questions, Nat-David presented Dr. Klapwyck with a copy of "Eight Years With My Grandpa." Dr. Klapwyck thanked Nat, and must have read the little book at lunch, because he sought us out, thanked Nat again, and told him that if he were ever to visit Holland, to consider himself invited to see Het Dorp for himself.

For the next few months, between school, physiotherapy at IRM, the development and progress of Nat's first Printer, our lives were busy...also because soon coming up was Nat's Bar Mitzvah. Because of the orthodoxy of HASC which did not permit travel on the Sabbath, it was planned that the ceremony would take place on a Monday. We contacted the caterers who served the Synagogue's social events and ordered a Kiddush for directly after the Bar Mitzvah, and also ordered from them all food to be provided and brought to our home for personal guests later that afternoon.

The regulations applying to a Bar Mitzvah were very strict. We knew that no one from his school, teachers, Rabbis, would travel on a weekend, and that they would not eat food that was not sanctified as "Glatt Kosher," which meant that the vendors and food providers were certified as being closed all the Sabbath. New to me, but I was pleased to comply, even to the purchase of elegant paper goods and plastic cutlery, since mine was NOT a Kosher home.

Nat-David's Hebrew studies were now mainly relevant to the occasion, and he wrote his speech, chose his clothing, sent out invitations to friends and relatives, including one to South Africa where a favorite Hebrew teacher now resided. He didn't expect many men to attend since Monday is a workday, but assumed a Minyan of ten male students and staff would be present at Morning Prayers, and for the Bar Mitzvah itself. Since it was an orthodox Synagogue, women were required to sit in a balcony upstairs.

It had rained for days preceding this Monday, but on that day, the sun shone, the air was washed clean and crisp. When we arrived at the Synagogue (and why are they all built as were Egyptian pyramids?) at about 8 AM, we were surprised and gratified to see that ALL of our male relatives and friends were there. Also, to officiate were not to be one, but TWO Rabbis, who seemed surprised to see a child so disabled and confined to a wheelchair, and who was so loved by his classmates, his family, his relatives and friends.

I had never seen the interior of the Synagogue, and was impressed by its beauty, by its large stained-glass windows through which the sun shone and cast vari-colored refractions over us all. At one point in the ceremony, the Hebrew text of the Torah states that now Nat-David was a Man, and his father was no longer responsible for his actions. THIS, Morris absolutely refused to intone! It was left unsaid.

Because Nat-David had told Morris that he wanted to stand in order to read from the Torah, Morris lifted him from his wheelchair and held him across his body, while the Rabbi traced under the Hebrew Script with a Silver "finger," and Nat attempted to intone the words, which if not comprehensible to those gathered, were accepted by the Rabbis as correct.

I don't think there was a dry eye in the Synagogue. Even the Rabbis at the Bimah were caught wiping their eyes. After the Ceremony, we were all directed to the basement where the Kiddush table was set. Morris carried Nat downstairs, the wheelchair followed, bumped down by a friend. There, Nat made his speech, spoken by him, and at his request, read by me.

I was amused to see, spread out on long tables, various dishes of salads, platters of smoked salmon, chunks of whitefish, tremendous bowls of rolls and breads, varieties of sweet desserts. And towering over all was a swan, sculpted from chopped chicken liver! There was also a table for kosher wines, and a variety of liquors (which are ALWAYS kosher!)

We had ordered food for about 75 people at our home for later that day, but what actually arrived was overwhelming. There was double the food we thought we had bought, perhaps because the Caterers were so amazed by Nat's performance, and the size of the crowd at the Synagogue. They had provided hot-plates...and the only items we needed to provide were glasses and paper goods. There was enough food, easily, for over 100 people, and the turkey was stuffed and displayed resplendently on an enormous platter. When our next-door neighbor, Chinese, and a local restauranteur arrived before our other guests, he asked if he might carve the turkey, then return it sliced, under its skin. I naughtily agreed, besides who would know that NON-kosher hands had touched it. It remained our secret! In addition were bowls of potatoes prepared several different ways, bowls of vegetables, gravies, sauces, and EVERYTHING was Glatt Kosher.

Except James Chin's hands, which were just deft and loving for Nat, and whose three children were Nat's good friends.

All this effort was to ensure that Nat's teachers and Rabbis could eat at our home, and eat and drink and enjoy, they all did.

A friend to Morris who had been in Israel an Underseas Diver and Navy Seal during the Second World War, and who now lived in New Jersey with his family, asked to make Nat's cake as his gift, and aware of the Judaic laws regarding Kashruth, created a "masterpiece" of taste as well as design: an enormous cake filled with fresh fruit, the entire cake encased in Marzipan, and shaped to look like an open Bible on which was inscribed, in Hebrew, Nat's name, and the date, and of course, the occasion.

It was so delicious and impressive, that for days afterwards, neighbors stopped to ask, "Is there a little bit more of the cake?" We had so much food left over due to the generosity of the Caterers, that we sent most of it to HASC where it was refrigerated and fed to students and staff for more than a week.

And no, there was NO more cake left to send!

Generosity does have its limits!

During this time of great joy and excitement, life beckoned once again in guise of a news article in the Sunday New York Times which told of a wheelchair designed by Lord Snowden in London for his friend who had lost the use of his legs in an auto accident. Lord Snowden, then Princess Margaret's husband, had designed it so that the wheelchair served as a bar-stool, as an office chair at his desk, for use in a restaurant…in other words, it served as needed for whatever occasion and could be raised or lowered.

To Engineer Morris, this was an irresistible challenge. He wrote to Lord Snowden, described Nat, and asked if he thought the wheelchair might be suitable for him. In reply, Lord Snowden invited us to come to London to see for ourselves, at an exhibit of equipment for the disabled which was to be held in the Olympia Exhibition Hall, in Earl's Court, a few months hence. He asked us to contact him if we were to be in England.

At that instant, we three resolved that a trip to both Holland and England was a fitting Bar Mitzvah present for Nat. Nat had wanted to go to Israel, but we were told that the cobble-stoned streets, plus the difficulties of traveling with someone in a wheelchair, would prove difficult, and so it was less appealing, even to Nat.

In 1971, the Airlines required that anyone traveling with special needs, such as a wheelchair, have a doctor's letter explaining the disability, and giving his permission, and for the Airline to give theirs. Everything was as properly arranged as we could make it, and we concluded our part of the requirements within a few months.

Our plans were to go to Holland on KLM (Royal Dutch Airline) for two weeks. From there, it was a 45-minute flight to London where we would spend two weeks. To return, we would fly from London via British Air.

My cousin, Bernard Jaffe, who was also our lawyer, drove the three of us, plus my mother, to the KLM terminal. We planned to lunch together at the airport, then board our flight. When we arrived at the KLM terminal, we were told that our plane had developed some technical problem, and that we would have to await a later flight. We were understandably upset that our "best laid plans" had gone aglae!

Morris asked Bernard for his advice. In true lawyerly fashion, he said with amusement, "Sue!"

Morris did better than that. He walked to the KLM departures desk and asked to see someone in charge. The "ground steward" asked the problem with taking a later flight, and Morris explained in no uncertain terms what this flight was intended for, that we happened to be in company of our lawyer, and that a later flight was not an option, and demanded to see someone higher up in the chain of command!

The Rags of Time

The Ground Steward asked us to wait for him in a certain section, and when he returned, he said that we would be put on a flight to leave within 45 minutes. We made our goodbyes to Bernard and my mother, and soon were settled aboard the plane, our luggage having already been stowed aboard. Morris was asked, when we were at the plane's entry door, to lift Nat from the wheelchair and carry him inside to the cabin, the first after the Flight Crew's Cabin, and was told they intended to load Nat's chair last, so it would be returned to us as soon as we deplaned. Made sense to us.

We were impressed to see such elegant surroundings as eight love-seat sized seats, almost couches! We were asked to remain seated and belted until the other passengers were seated, and the entire planeload of passengers went through a curtained doorway, while we sat and waited to be shown to our seats.

The next words we heard were to fasten our seatbelts…and off we flew. We were in their "Royal Section" and were its sole passengers! Our seats, more like love-seats in size when the middle-arm was lowered, were so roomy that we might lie down and sleep during the flight. We also had the services of two stewardesses and a steward, who continuously plied us with food and drink. There were two private toilets. We were urged to taste for the first time, "Early Genever," which was the light Gin.

Nat had his juices and sodas, and was given gift after gift by the crew and staff, all of whom were interested in Nat's upcoming visit to Het Dorp, and they asked myriads of questions of us, also offered advice and told us what not to miss in Amsterdam and other cities in Holland.

During the night, Nat was invited into the cockpit, and with Morris holding him, and I looking on, we saw the lovely, clear, starry sky. He was also presented with a wing-shaped flight pin by one of the pilots, and when the pilots and navigator turned to speak with us, Nat was concerned at how they flew without looking!

Chapter 10

Nat was asleep when we flew over Holland. I think I fell in love with Holland at daybreak when I, who can NEVER sleep on a plane, looked down on what Morris later named a "Mondrian-like" vision of farmland, cubist shapes of color, all separated by blue ribbons of water.

At Schiphol Airport in Amsterdam, the first thing unloaded from the hold was the wheelchair. It was placed next to the cabin door, and we exited, we thanked all the wonderful crew who made the trip such a joy for Nat. This flight proves what air travel could and should be for everyone, but alas, even KLM has not been able to provide such comfort and efficiency on our many subsequent flights, as seats grew narrower, space between rows of seats decreased. Well, we were evidently only Royalty on our initial flight!

As we deplaned and abdicated our Royal positions, we regained our luggage and confidently made our way to the car-rental area where Morris had, from the U.S. arranged to hire a car to drive to our hotel in Amsterdam centrum. Of course, it was Murphy's Law: what CAN go wrong, WILL go wrong. There were no cars to be had which would comfortably hold the three of us, plus all the luggage and Nat's equipment. Morris set off to complain to the Ground Steward and to explain that we needed space for Nat's wheelchair. The attractive blond Ground Stewardess walked us out of the Airpost to a waiting bus.

"And how do we get our son onto a bus with his wheelchair?"

"Like this, Sir. Please be patient!"

To our astonishment, we were positioned in front of the Exit door of the bus, the door opened by the driver, a turnstile removed by the driver, Nat, in his chariot, was lifted on board, we followed and sat while the turnstile was put back in place, and we were off. The bus drove through Amsterdam and dropped us at a park which the driver informed us was just a short walk through the park

The Rags of Time

to our hotel. He reversed Nat's entry at Schiphol, and drove off with our grateful thanks. Morris proffered a tip which the driver refused.

Another first!

We decided that Morris was to taxi to the hotel with our luggage, and Nat and I would walk through the small park, and a further few blocks to the Trianon Hotel. We actually made it there at about the same time as the taxi, even after we lingered from time to time to admire the flowers, which were everywhere. We had been dropped in front of the Rijksmuseum, and Nat and I vowed to return to see all its glories another day.

The Trianon Hotel was small and lovely and in back of the famous Concertgebouw. We were as at Schiphol, hit by breezes, and theorized that THIS is what accounts for the ruddy complexions of the Dutch! The breezes were a constant. Our quarters were on the ground floor, and consisted of a large, ell-shaped room, large toilet with shower, and our own terrace where we might breakfast if we chose…or entertain guests. Not your typical New York City Hotel.

While Morris took a well-deserved nap, Nat and I went to explore our immediate vicinity. We walked to the nearest Canal and fell in love with Holland all over again. We returned to the hotel to find that Morris had discovered the Bar. We joined him, met some other tourists, and soon it was time for dinner. We were assigned to a table, and Nat, bless him, chose from the menu a steak and other goodies. We thoroughly enjoyed our meal, especially Nat, who was introduced to Chocomel, a drink made of sweet cream and melted chocolate, and topped by whipped cream. THAT formed a daily staple of his diet for as long as we were in Holland!

We went to bed soon after, and awoke to another fine day. It was mid-May and we had clear, although rather chilly weather for our entire stay. When we went to the dining room for breakfast, we were informed that the breakfast time was over. A look at my watch confirmed that it was after 10 AM.

We went to find a restaurant for ourselves and as it happened, there was one almost directly across the street, the Keyzer, and we assumed we could get something there, BUT as we saw that the entrance was a revolving door, walked on.

We hadn't gone five feet when a man rushed after us saying, "Madame, Madame, did you want to come in?"

"Yes, but how do we get a wheelchair through a revolving door?"

"I will show you, Madame. It is not a problem."

And he did…and it wasn't!

This was the third or fourth lesson of our trip since its inception: EVERY revolving door has a mechanism which allows it to be folded into a half-pie shape, and it can then be pushed to revolve with the wheelchair inside. The waiter pulled a smiling Nat into the restaurant, and from then on we realized that in the United States we had accepted a lot of nonsense in shops and restaurants which obviously DID NOT want to be troubled, or just did NOT want customers who were disabled.

In the Keyzer, we were amazed and delighted to find each table covered with a Persian carpet, and that the walls were of gilded leather. Also, there were flowers and napery and crystal glasses and silver place-settings, cutlery. Very grand indeed, and there was an etched-glass divider between the restaurant and the Bar.

And all we wanted was breakfast. We opted to forego the usual breakfasts of home and chose from the menu what we imagined were "Dutch" dishes. We ordered something called "Russian Eggs" and got a concoction which was delicious and like nothing we would ever forget. The orders were accompanied by small bowls of tiny potatoes, of tiny carrots, and we gorged ourselves…plus Chocomel for Nat, and the truly great, the BEST coffee, I have ever had. It was addictive and better than Vodka or Genever…for breakfast, that is!

While we awaited the order, we saw that against one wall were stacks of newspapers, all wrapped around tall sticks, which were for the perusal of customers while they ate. It not being very crowded at this hour, the obliging waiter gave us a list of things and events in the neighborhood which might interest us. He was equally interested in how America cared for and treated the needs of its disabled citizens.

The Dutch, it appears, all speak three or four or more languages since, he explained, tourists don't want to learn to speak their guttural language. I said that since I knew German, and that my father had so loved Holland, and had spoken some Dutch phrases to us, that perhaps I might have some idea of what was printed in their newspapers. I then proceeded to read (to hell with the guttural sounds) to the waiter who was kind, and only smiled at my efforts.

We three were thoroughly smitten with this kind and friendly man and went back many times. Especially we loved and valued the lesson about the revolving door he taught and which, believe me, we applied and taught to the City of New York.

Not the least of what we learned while taking the time to sightsee for the week before our appointment in Het Dorp, was that the Dutch people are the most progressive in the social aspects of disability. When we visited the Rijksmuseum across the Park, we discovered that the entrance led to a flight of stairs inside the door, and was blocked at its top by a turnstile. The moment we opened the door, a museum guard came racing down the stairs, and he and Morris carried Nat in his chair to the top, where the turnstile was removed, we paid our admissions, the turnstile was replaced…and then Nat happened to see two enormous stained-glass windows, floor to ceiling in height, and he was so entranced, that he insisted on looking at them for about 15 minutes!

Morris and I were anxious to see the Rembrandt paintings which we had not seen at the Metropolitan Museum, or at the National Gallery, but usually only in Art books. We took the elevator to an upper floor where were these treasures of chiaroscuro, such as "The Night Watch," and the many portraits of his wives, and self-portraits. Nat was particularly taken with his paintings of himself and of a Rabbi. We spent hours there, having seen just a fraction of this marvelous Museum, with its Hals and Breughels, then tore ourselves away. When we descended in the elevator to the first floor, the helpfulness of the guards reversed our entry, and we left, our appetites artistically whetted.

Another time we walked from the Hotel to the Van Gogh Museum in another part of the City. While Nat enjoyed and appreciated the artistry, HIS passion was the canals, and we went on as many canal trips as we could, including a night trip devoted to wine sampling. While Nat did not imbibe, we did, and perhaps our Wine-Host and Guide was a bit tipsy, Nat suggested, as the boat kept scraping the sides and stone walls of the bridges over our heads. We three loved ALL the canal trips, and eventually boated on all the canals from the Prinsengract, the Herrengracht, the Keizersgracht, to the Singelgracht…and more.

Oh, *Gracht* means Canal!

We also went to wonderful and plentiful bookstores on Kalverstraat in Amsterdam Centrum, and through the red-light district which surrounded the main avenues and cross streets, in which the prostitutes were displayed behind beaded curtains, in rooms which were brightly lit in the dark streets. In alleyways there were posters and notices on which one could read, "Mariana" or "Carlotta" resides here…in Dutch of course. Even Nat could understand THAT much Dutch!

Everywhere were marvelous sights and restaurants and outdoor *Terrasses*, and Sex, Sex, Sex!

The parks at night were so safe that we often walked quite late through Vondelpark, about 10 PM, and NEVER did we witness unpleasantness or violence, or have other than a feeling of complete safety. What we did see, and come to expect as a daily sight, was the freedom of drug-taking and selling. There were shops and restaurants with painted, or otherwise depicted, Marihuana leaves and Hashish advertising. I was once emboldened to ask if the police ever intervened in this overt practice:

"And where ARE the police?"
"There are very few police!"
"Why?"
"No one wants the job!" was the reply.

But what we did see were the hundreds of bicycles, perhaps thousands of people on them and on *Brommers*. When I asked again what happened if someone parked his bicycle, and these were never parked and chained, and it was stolen?

"Then that person takes someone else's bicycle, and so on, and again EVERYONE has a bicycle!" was the reply.

We also saw disabled people on bicycles, even those whose disability did not permit them to sit erect, but were on litters, face down, and propelling themselves along with their hands on large wheels, or with joysticks.

What kind of society had we entered?

We asked ourselves this every day!

On one occasion we were at a Railroad Station, and noticed that there were travelers in wheelchairs, or on motorized litters, in lines at the ticket windows, and while no one got ahead of them, neither were they given any preferential treatment. In Holland, it seemed, everyone was, and is, equal!

We decided to take a tour bus to Delft, the great pottery city, and to Den Hague, the Capitol, and some other towns along the way. Nat's chair was loaded under the bus, we were given three seats, Nat was seated next to Morris, who also carried with him a small rucksack of tools and an air pump, if the wheelchair tires developed a leak, and at every stop, whenever we alighted, his chair was automatically unloaded and set up for him! When we returned to the bus, the process was reversed. The driver and two guides, usually law students, repeated in three and four languages all information given, and any questions were answered the same way.

It reminded me of "Cabaret", when the German M.C. says:

> *"Meine Dame und Herren"*
> *"Mesdames et Monsieurs"*
> *"Ladies and Gentlemen"*
> *"Wilkommen"*
> *"Bienvienue"*
> *"Welcome!"*

The guides saw to it, together with the employees of the Delft Potteries, that Nat was ALWAYS able to see the wares and the artists as they painted the glazes, or when we visited a Cheese Farm, that he was provided with samples of cheeses and crackers or bread, and he insisted we buy large wax-encrusted rounds of cheeses we particularly enjoyed, and as always, "Some for Grandma." We bought Delft tiles, and at a Chocolatier, many Droste goodies such as "*Hopjes*" that his grandfather had loved and often sent to Holland for when I was young.

Each tour led to another. We couldn't get enough of the wonderful treatment and courtesy, of the sights of the Art! Once, at a Railroad Station, Nat needed the toilet, and I spoke to a guard, and he escorted us to an elevator, sent us up a floor. We found this large, spotless series of toilets, some with the symbol for the disabled, and when we left, the matron in charge made sure we were comfortable and had everything we needed, and she escorted us back to the elevator, in which we went down and rejoined Morris.

An incident occurred on one tour which absolutely endeared the Dutch to us: before leaving our home in New York, Morris designed and had made a ring for Nat. It was of gold, and set with a ruby from my mother's ring, and a sapphire surrounded by tiny diamonds from my father's stickpin. It was unique, and Morris wore it while we traveled because it might have fallen off Nat's slim fingers. We planned to buy a gold chain in Amsterdam, reported as a great jewelry center, so Nat could wear it around his neck.

After about an hour's travel on the bus, I heard what I thought was the sound of metal striking the bus floor across from where I sat, while Morris and Nat sat on the other side, back a row. Morris said it was the clink of the tools in his rucksack. At the end of the tour, we were the last passengers to be returned to our hotel.

We were hungry and travel-messy, so washed, changed our clothes, and went first to the bar where Morris and I had a drink, Nat, his usual Chocomel. All our stay at the Trianon, the bartender saw to it that whenever we entered, Nat and we had our pre-prandial drinks. While drinking his vodka, Morris absently fingered his ring, and turned pale when he realized that he no longer HAD the ring! He checked our room, and when unable to locate it, immediately called the Tour company, describing the ring, and they said they would check and call us back.

Morris was so upset he felt ill, couldn't eat, even said he wanted to go home. He then remembered the sound I had heard and which he dismissed, realizing that it must have been the sound of the ring hitting the bus floor. I then vowed inwardly that I would buy Nat another ring. We sat in near silence as I fed

Nat, but at 11 PM, Morris was called to the phone. The tour company had found the ring, it had bounced into a corner of a step, and they would send it around to the hotel that night.

At this news, we revived, but shuddered to realize that any departing passenger might have knocked it to the street. It was returned to Morris who gave a hefty tip to the Bearer of Gold Rings and Good Tidings. We realized that its return would probably not have occurred in America. We surmised that it probably would have beringed the finder's finger. The following day we bought a gold chain and Nat proudly wore HIS ring!

We rented a station wagon for the drive to Arnhem, Het Dorp, and our hotel. Morris felt secure driving in Holland because they drive on the same side of the road as in America, and he commented on the clarity of the marked highway signs. When we arrived at the American-styled motel, we found that they had provided a small wooden ramp for the wheelchair along one side of the few steps, where it remained for the rest of our stay.

At Het Dorp, we were guided by a young woman who propelled herself along as she lay on a litter. One of the regulations of life at Het Dorp was that no resident be in an "acute" stage of his/her condition. The residents must already be in a "chronic" stage, over the age of 18 and all must be Dutch citizens and able to interact socially with others. Those who cherished their privacy might have it, those who desired socialization were free to indulge their wishes. One might eat alone in one's home, or join with others in groups, or eat in the restaurant.

Dr. Klapwyck met with us, and was so taken with Nat and his reaction to Het Dorp, that he might have overlooked the age and citizenship requirements…but this was what Nat feared, that we might leave him there.

"Are you insane?" we yelled!
"How would WE manage without you?"
"And don't forget our appointment with Lord Snowden!"

But unbeknownst to Nat, Morris and I DID wonder if we could move to Holland, if Morris could find work there, and then when Nat was 18, he could be admitted to a wonderful life in a country which revered and respected the lives of ALL its citizens.

Again and again we were told by Dutch friends, that the reason the Dutch were so sensitive to the needs of those ill, or those requiring special environments, or the elderly, to the many ethnic peoples within their borders, including the Jews they had harbored so lovingly all through the war years, was that they had personally witnessed the horrors of the Nazis, the bombings, and the forced assimilation of the many cultures that had fled to Holland.

The term, "reverse integration," as well as the concept of Het Dorp, fascinated Nat. The idea that if a resident of Arnhem wanted groceries, gas for his automobile, the library, a travel agency, he had to go to Het Dorp. Soon, the children of Arnhem who bicycled its gentle hills, looked on the residents and disabled citizens of the Dorp, as people who were, to quote Morris whenever anyone spoke of Nat's physical condition, "inconvenienced," as are those "inconvenienced by asthma or a broken limb, or a mental illness."

Nat-David was "inconvenienced" his entire life.

But since we did not permit self-pity, or whining, HIS take on his condition was to treat himself with humor, with using what he called, "the only thing I have going for me, my good head, my good mind!" And he used that "good mind" his entire life, to create a book, articles, a play, much poetry, and to teach his peers, handicapped or able-bodied, and any adult around him, to use theirs.

When Nat was in high school, he was asked to act as a "human resource" by the New York City Planning Commission. He was regularly interviewed at our home, or at the Commission offices, by officials who opined that if Nat could benefit from a service, so could other disabled people. A young woman who had Muscular Dystrophy was employed there, and Nat hoped that eventually HE might be similarly employed.

But back to Holland. After absorbing as much of its environment and philosophy as possible, we visited surrounding tourist sites such as the Windmill Museum, where now, paper was made, and the Doll Museum, toured the beautiful countryside and parks where we were enjoined and cautioned NOT to stop the car, or depart from it, because there were, among other wild animals, Wild Boars.

The Rags of Time

We had occasion to do just this, because we had to rearrange our bodies and Nat's wheelchair. As Morris got out to give us a hand, a large tusked Boar trotted towards us from the woods. Morris gave one look, and in his most imperious tone of voice, pointed his finger at it, and said sternly, "Boar, GO, Turn and go!" At which the Boar halted, turned, and trotted off! Morris became known as our "Big White Hunter!" …after we stopped laughing.

Oh, how often in our social lives, I had wished for him to say sternly, "GO, Bore, GO!" And how often we were trapped by the social constraints of TACT (mine), followed by sounds of annoyance from Nat…and the disappearance of Morris from the room!

We visited one site where, to my initial surprise, Nat was very and visibly upset: Madurodam in Den Haag. I had thought he would love this square block-sized miniaturization of buildings, canals, various cities in Holland, but he positively hated it and asked to leave. When I questioned his reaction, he replied that it "made fun of little people," meaning those born with Dwarfism, or Midgets. Now that was something that I had not thought of. When much later I mentioned this to a fellow psychologist, he said that Nat's response was not unusual…also I reminded myself of our earlier injunction NOT to take for granted that what WE found visually or artistically enchanting, Nat would also appreciate.

Of course, Morris and I could physically "look down" on the buildings of Madurodam. Oh yes, Nat taught everyone within the radius of his presence a great deal.

When we visited Den Haag in order to explore the Mondrian Museum, Mondrian being Morris' favorite artist, we were surprised to find that his early work, was not a precursor of what his mature Art would become. Morris decided that Mondrian gave a bird's-eye or plane's-eye view of Holland in his later work, and when we returned to Amsterdam, he haunted the offices of Dutch architects while advancing his theory. They were delighted by his interest, gravely heard him out, and said that they might agree if Mondrian's style had not been influenced by the early French Impressionists. They did consider him, however, an artist who was influenced by architecture, and in turn, influenced IT, and when he died in 1945, and until the present, Mondrian does not have a large following.

156

The Rags of Time

He did, in the Schwartz household. Morris was faithful to Mondrian until his last day! But then, I know something of Morris' faithfulness.

We were all sorry to leave Holland, and commiserated with each other during the 45 minute plane connection to Heathrow Airport in London, and thereafter discovered other, and as noteworthy ideas, concepts, and acts of kindness on the part of "Strangers on whom we Depended", to paraphrase Blanche Dubois.

Doei, Doei, Holland!

The Cumberland Hotel into which our travel agent had booked us, proved a disaster. It was clearly a businessman's hotel with what seemed like one-half mile of corridor which boasted but two elevators, both at one end of the corridor, which took us 3 to 5 minutes to traverse. Our quarters were lordly. We three had a large room set up as an army barrack, a bed, a night stand, a bed, a night stand, a bed, a night stand! Facing these were a couch, two over-stuffed chairs, and in the center, an enormous television set. The barracks led to a large entry-hall, leading to an enormous toilet with a tub (no shower). The tub was so long and narrow and deep, that the three of us might have bathed together, were we so inclined. Indeed, Morris climbed in, and I handed Nat to him, and they DID bathe together. The toilet was the only piece of ordinary-sized equipment. The floor was tiled, and so large, we might have played hop-scotch!

We decided not to unpack, but to look for another hotel immediately. Luckily, before leaving home, friends had given us the name and phone number of a relative, so Morris called, found them in, introduced ourselves, explained our problem, and they gave us the name of a hotel in another part of London.

The first of many lessons the British taught the Colonists was their very civilized custom of NOT using a euphemism in describing toilet requirements.

A thing, is still a thing, is a thing, no matter the descriptive adjective.

Morris called the Prince Hotel and requested a "room for three people. Do you have an elevator? Good! We need a room and bath. Thank you. We'll arrive tomorrow about noon!"

The Rags of Time

The Cumberland Hotel was given notice. We were especially glad to leave because, as was his Dutch wont, Nat asked for a Chocomel, which translated from the Dutch into a chocolate milkshake, and while it tasted almost as good, said Nat, cost a whopping 5 pounds, instead of the 5 guilder we were used to paying in Holland. Also, at our evening meal at a Steakhouse down the road, Nat ordered his usual, a steak, which when it arrived, could literally not be cut sans a hacksaw.

In 1971, food in England was very bad indeed! We were not as yet acquainted with Pub food, but dieted and ate as we had in Holland or in the United States. Nat became mainly a vegetarian in those days, or would have, had he craved grey Brussels sprouts, grey string beans, mushy peas, and overcooked everything, except Fish and Chips. We found and went often to Tea Shoppes run by English women in Reduced Circumstances, for excellent Roast Beef. What passed for a "salad" was an education…and consisted of pickled everything…but no lettuce or tomatoes.

But the Schwartz's were made of sterner stuff, and in coming days we learned to think, to hell with the food! The people were fantastic, marvelous, considerate, kind, and we fell in love all over again.

The Prince Hotel on Spring Street was small. The elevator was tiny and held just Nat's chair, with me sitting almost in his lap. Morris came up alone with the luggage stacked behind him. The room was small but adequate, and just as Morris had specified over the phone, had a shower, but NO toilet! THAT was down the other end of the corridor from us!

While this mattered not a whit to Morris or me, Nat was definitely discommoded!

We decided to put up with all the difficulties and Morris said that within the next few days, we three would walk, explore, until we found a more suitable hotel. Besides, the other guests who were from everywhere, were friendly, the staff was helpful and charming when we three weren't laughing at their ideas of hostelry! The Prince Hotel was but three streets from Paddington Station, and Nat told us that the FIRST thing he wanted to do was to take a train ride, having never been on a train in the United States.

The Rags of Time

Accordingly, we walked to the Station, and were directed to the Station Master's office.

"Sir, may we ride on your train? My son has never had the pleasure of a train ride in the United States."
"Of course, Madame. Where does your son wish to go?"
"What do you suggest, Sir?"
"How far will you travel?"
"We thought perhaps an hour's trip and back."

The Station Master arranged for our tickets to Reading and escorted us to the proper train platform, where he asked us to wait and someone would see us on the train.

And that was that!

All English Railway System trains have a Postal Van which is in use for wheel chair passengers, or any other disabled travelers needing extra space, which may not be available in what we refer to as the "rush hour," but since we were traveling on a Sunday, the cars were fairly empty. We boarded a car, one of many linked together into a long string of cars. This was not a "corridor" train as often seen in British films such as "The Lady Vanishes," or the early Agatha Christie films featuring Hercule Poirot, pompous sleuth. For all movie background and film trivia, we had Morris to thank. He must have spent his entire early life in a movie-house, and I often teased him that he must never have attended school. But he was full of such irrelevant information…and usually correct.

The car we were escorted into had plush seats, about the size of love-seats, facing each other, and between the "couches" and under the window, was a drop-down table affixed to the wall. We seated ourselves on the couches and Nat at the table-end, facing outside so he might see the view as we passed. Above the couches were metal racks to hold parcels, luggage.

When the door opened at the next stop, a look of sheer delight and surprise came over his face as a couple entered. They were middle-aged and dressed for Sunday. She wore a print dress and jacket, gloves, a hat, but the MAN, the man was dressed in pleated Clan kilt, complete with tam-o-shanter, a fur trimmed sporran, knee socks, and a pair of tasseled brogans on his feet!

The Rags of Time

"Are they Scotch?" Nat spelled out?

"No, they are Scottish," his Schoolmarm Mother corrected. Nat asked to be turned to face them, smiling. They smiled in response and asked about Nat. We explained that this was Nat's first train ride EVER, and that other than in pictures, he had never seen the Scottish National dress. A lively conversation ensued, and they seemed charmed by Nat, and by the way we conversed with him, and for the next 20 minutes or so, there was mutual admiration. I felt that when they reached their destination, they described the meeting, as did we on our return to the hotel.

When we got out at Reading, we were directed to the platform on the far side of the station. It looked as though the only way we could get up the stairs at the platform's end, to walk to the other side and down again, was to carry Nat's chair up, one step at a time. But we were approached by the Reading Station guard who escorted us to an elevator, we went up, walked over a short overpass, then to another elevator, and down. There we were. And we congratulated ourselves on having found another country with heart, consideration, and good sense, not only for the disabled, but for mothers with prams, anyone using crutches or a walker.

The following day was our Anniversary, and Nat planned to take us out to dinner, having borrowed $25.00 of HIS from an obliging grandmother before we left home. At the end of our block was a pub/restaurant, and because Nat was too young to enter the pub, we went to the dining room where Morris asked and was given permission to bring Nat into the pub and show him its mysteries. Nat saw the darts corner and the billiard tables, and then they rejoined me in the attached restaurant. The dining area was set up to look like Paddington Station coaches, and there were murals of the scenery outside the coaches, and separated by booths. Additionally there were freestanding tables, one of which we chose, because of the wheelchair.

Near the entrance was a large counter, atop which was a great haunch of ham, a saddle of roast beef, salamis, sausages, and all manner of meats and salads, large bowls of pickles, cheeses, loaves of bread, and another smaller counter that held great vats of soup. Behind all this display stood a tall man wearing a very tall Chef's hat, and an apron which covered his clothes, as he surveyed has domain.

The Rags of Time

When we were seated, he removed his Chef's hat and his apron, and putting a small towel over an arm, he advanced and asked:

"How may I serve you?"

"We will have one large Lager, one-half Lager, and our son will have a Shirley Temple," said Morris.

For those not privy to this 1970's delight for children, or non-imbibers, a Shirley Temple is a rather sweet drink consisting of a quantity of Maraschino Cherry syrup poured over some club soda, and topped by a Maraschino Cherry.

Our Chef, now a waiter, went to the Pub door and called to the Bartender with our drinks order. When it arrived, it was delivered by the Chef/Waiter who then took our dinner order. I don't remember what we ordered, probably Roast Beef, and Nat was again fascinated that day, at the sight of the Chef/Waiter who first shed the towel, donned his apron and tall Chef's hat, then sliced from the giant slab of beef, made thick sandwiches, and again, before serving us, took off the Chef's hat, the apron, and with the small towel draped over his arm, brought our plates heaped with salads and pickles.

It was almost as good as a Shakespearean production to see his grave demeanor and respectful attention to his guests!

The food was excellent. We three tucked in, and when we were asked if we wanted dessert, we pleaded fullness. We asked that the check be presented to Nat, the waiter nodded, and did just that. Nat asked that his money be removed from his wheelchair bag, and when Morris suggested that HE be allowed to pay the tip, Nat declined.

At Heathrow, on our arrival, Morris had explained and shown Nat how American currency is exchanged into English pounds. Now Nat inspected the bill, and figured the tip. I think he used 10% as a guide, but Morris surreptitiously slipped in a few additional pounds. When the waiter returned to the table, he gravely took the check and Nat's money, smiled for the first time, and amidst his profuse thanks, bowed us out!

The Rags of Time

Back at the hotel, Nat told of our outing to the two young women we had met who were from Newfoundland, and figuring that he had enough pounds remaining, invited them to join us for dinner at the same Pub, the following evening.

After breakfast, we three took a long walk and explored various neighborhoods, looked into store windows, then decided to taxi to see Big Ben and Parliament. The London cabs were a sheer delight and a novelty, were high-ceilinged, and Nat's chair was tipped back, and he was placed inside, between the rear seat and the front jump-seats, which could be put up or pulled down, to suit the passenger's needs. Nat faced the direction in which we rode, and soon we were at the Embankment of the Thames River, from which we walked to Parliament building, which on this day had long, long lines of tourists and visitors waiting to enter. We queued up with the others, and immediately a Bobby appeared to ask if we intended to enter.

"Yes," said Morris, whereupon the Bobby asked us to follow him and led us to a small door which he opened, then called to a guard who helped Morris carry Nat in his chair up a few steps. He told us that when we were ready to leave, he would be happy to reverse the process.

We walked the marble halls, peering into rooms, then went into the doorway of the House of Commons, Morris doing Tour Guide duty, and we saw a scene reminiscent of our Senate and House of Representatives: men up on their feet or seated, arguing issues, as we watched from the open doorway. As we walked the halls, Nat told us that he needed to use the toilet, so I stopped a guard to ask if there was someplace Nat might use. The guard asked us to follow him, we came to a sawhorse outside a closed entrance, which the guard removed, opened the door, and we were in the Lounge of The House of Lords! The guard asked me to please wait there, and led Morris and Nat to another door, and in addition to pointing the way, told Morris, who related this to me afterwards, that each cubicle had within a button which lit red in the Lounge, to show that the cubicle was occupied, and was also used to alert a guard that someone needed help.

In the Lounge in which I waited, and which was nearly empty, save for the ever-present guards, one gentleman spoke with me, and having seen Morris and Nat enter, told me that HE was himself disabled, and was responsible for setting up this special facility. We seem to have made all the right moves while in England within just a few days of our arrival. We three went on with our sightseeing, and looked into the beautiful and impressive House of Lords' chamber, not in session at the moment, so we could enter and look more closely at the furnishings, and look up to what was formerly the women's and visitor's balcony.

We made our exit finally, full of gratitude, and in awe of the kindness of the English…and their courtesy. Outside, armed with our good map, we decided to visit Westminster Abbey, not far, and also in Parliament Square.

It was what the kids today call "Awesome!" We entered this gorgeous building and wandered through the Great Church, through various Chapels dedicated to this or that Marble-sculpted Lord or Lady, resting on their sarcophagi, and read of the occupant's birth, rank, death, accomplishments, as etched on marble plaques. From one to another spot we wandered, marveling at the great literary and artistic figures buried there, and saw beneath our feet, many gravestones, etched with the names of poets and writers, now ensconced under their gravestones…and our feet!

We were overwhelmed, but realized that three hours had sped by, and that we were hungry, and left, resolving to pay many more visits. I think Nat loved this place beyond all he visited in England and through the many years we three traveled there, he NEVER missed an opportunity to revisit, to look, to marvel, to dream!

When we returned to the Prince Hotel, the two Newfoundlanders were waiting, and we all went back to Nat's favorite Pub.

Well, alright! The ONLY pub Nat had ever visited!

When we arrived, we seated ourselves in the restaurant, and our Chef/Waiter approached, be-towelled, and asked what drinks we wanted, then before Morris could answer, he turned to Nat and asked, "Your usual, Sir?" From then on, the young ladies watched as the Comedy/Play was reenacted, realizing that Nat's description had been accurate. They were totally enchanted by our Host, and said that they would probably have a more enjoyable time sight-seeing if they were to accompany Nat.

Sorry ladies, it was not to be!

The Rags of Time

By walking around London, we finally came upon a hotel facing Leicester Square which suited our needs, and we bid a sad goodbye to staff, new friends, and the corridor toilet, and moved once again. This hotel, the Royal Angus, gave us a room facing the Square. It had tall French doors leading to a tiny, elegantly-gated balcony, and we could open the doors to morning sunlight, to evening lights from street lamps and from the Penny Arcades and movie houses which lined the edges of Leicester Square.

At the time, in 1971, London seemed nothing so much as a friendly small town. At night we wandered the streets and Nat asked to go to an Arcade, where for 50 pence, we played, gambled really, at one-arm bandits. Nat was fascinated, and he could grab and push the levers down. One evening he actually hit a jackpot and won 10 pounds! Our gambler was wheeled happily across the street, and when we were in the Lounge, announced through us that he offered, "Drinks for everyone, on me!" There were smiles and laughter from the half-dozen customers, and the bartender who made the announcement joined in the applause for this generous gesture!

The following day, Morris called Lord Snowden's office and we were told that he was not in, but there were three tickets being held for us at the Earls Court Exhibition Center box-office, and would we please afterwards, one day, call Lord Snowden to give our opinion of the wheelchair he had designed. On entry, we were supplied with a small "briefcase" full of literature concerning all of the inventions on display, which represented many countries. We went first to see "the chair," and found that while Lord Snowden's friend might be elevated or lowered to sit at a dining table, or lifted to the height of a Pub's bar, it was NOT usable for Nat, because it had none of the features such as a headrest, side arms which embraced his body and belted in front, or a footrest, nor could it recline, if necessary.

As Nat commented, "It is just an ordinary chair and perhaps anyone who can use his hands and has good head control, can use it, but any disabled person who needs specific adaptations doesn't need a kitchen chair that goes up and down!" Also, he wanted to know what, except friendship and convenience for a single and particular individual, would cause this to be reported on in the New York Times.

The Rags of Time

Smart son! He did indeed have a "good brain," and used it always. We were more tactful however, and Morris phoned Lord Snowden to thank him for his kindness, and said that it was an interesting concept, but regretfully, would not function for Nat.

In addition to a "good brain," Nat also had a good ego which was encouraged and nurtured by us during his childhood, and he spent his life "clubbing us with it," as we ruefully admitted!

I miss my son. I miss his humor, his grace while in pain, his total love and commitment to those he admired, his unfailing recall of, and gratitude for, acts of understanding and kindness. His smile and love might have melted and changed our harsh, mean-spirited world into one of compassion, and all during his too-short life, he tried to create the world he was fortunate enough to see as he traveled.

In a movie house across Leicester Square, they were showing "Fiddler On The Roof" which we had not as yet seen in New York, and when we inquired if it were possible to seat Nat, we were met by the unfailing, "Of course, Madame," and shown to a box, where we three sat, in lordly fashion. We watched the film, and learned yet another delightful and civilized British custom, that of ordering and paying for, in advance of the "interval" or intermission, a glass of sherry, or a soft drink, or a dish of ice-cream.

My beloved grandmother was not so wrong when she took me, at age 5 or 6, to the movies, ALWAYS armed with a bag containing sandwiches, some fruit, and other goodies. In those days, going to the movies was an almost all-day affair: a movie was not just ONE movie, but always a double-feature, Pathe News, a cliff-hanger, the March of Time, and music might be played on an organ under the screen, and a body could die of hunger after some five hours of filmdom! Also, there was the constant traveling: my grandmother might start out in the tenth row, but was always apt to decide that the fifth or fifteenth row was better, so we two schlepped from seat to seat, carrying our outerwear, our supply of food, sometimes a thermos of cold tea ("a person shouldn't die of thirst!")

I think sometimes that had we had been criminals, the authorities would NEVER have caught us!

The Rags of Time

But let's leave The Bronx and return to London.

We discovered that there were many canals in London, and since Nat always wanted to go somewhere, anywhere, by water, we went again to the Embankment on the Thames, and spoke with a boatman.

As I approached the boat, he leaned out saying, "Yes, luv?" When I put our usual request to him saying we wanted to travel to Hampton Court, he smiled, pointed to the small boarding ramp, and helped Morris by gripping the front wheels of the chair, and eased it into the boat. On board were two women from Australia…we were the only five passengers. Nat stared all about him as he faced the front of the boat, and as we rode up the Thames, he saw the Queen's Black Swans and the lovely and lush green banks of many Manor Houses, and the boatman obliged by giving us a running commentary to explain what we saw. Soon we came to the Locks System which either raised the boat, or the level of the water. I'm obviously NOT an expert on matters nautical, but I know what I like! After a snack on board, we reached Hampton Court in three hours.

Hampton Court, we learned, was the residence of Cardinal Wolsey who served under King Henry VIII, and splendid it was, until he had to turn it over to the King. Even in 1527, politics were to make it impossible for poor Wolsey to do other than bribe his King with its splendors, and as always in politics, Tom lost to Henry, and in short time, lost his head as well! Oh well, even in the 1500's treason was punishable by death, and what is one man's treason may be another man's gain!

It was but a short walk through the gates, and past hundreds of tourists, till we three were brought up short at the sight of a magnificent stone building, the marvelous King's Beasts on the Moat Bridge, and everywhere we were visually halted to lick our artistic chops.

Queen Mary's Maze is triangular, with six-foot tall hedge walls which are two feet thick. That is where Morris and Nat tried to lose me, and if it were not for my superior sense of direction, and being a woman, with a woman's superior brain, I might STILL be wandering!

We decided, at the end of trying to see through the backs of other visitors, to go back to London, but by train. It was just 45 minutes later that we reached the outskirts of London, and decided to leave the train at Waterloo Station, and perhaps walk over the Waterloo Bridge. A train guard told us that the other side of the very, very long bridge would bring us to a Tube Station to return to our hotel.

It was a glorious, sunny, blue-skied, cloudless day, as we sauntered to the other side...to find ourselves about 6 stair-flights up in the air! Well, Morris said he had no intention of going back to kill the guard for his mistake, and blued that air even more with oaths. Thin-lipped, he told me to back down the first flight of stairs while holding Nat's footrest, while he held on to the handlebars of the chair and guided me down, the eyes in the back of my head, normally New York functional, not working that day!

We had not gotten to the middle of the first "flight," when we were hailed by two men at the bottom, who yelled, "Stop, and wait!" We looked down and saw two men wearing bowlers, business suits, and carrying "brollies," who dropped their umbrellas and briefcases, but still in their Derbies, rushed up the stairs to us, apologizing to us, TO US, for not having spotted us sooner! One grabbed the handlebars from Morris and the other, the footrest from me, and carried the chair down the remainder of stairs, to terra firma.

I may not be my mother's kind of flirt, but I DO know my duty! I soundly bussed each man, while Morris rescued their briefcases and brollies, and shook their hands. Nat smiled, laughed, and thanked them the only way he could...with unintelligible sounds, all heartfelt!

Another never-to-be-forgotten incident, and another reason for our love-affair with England. When we fall in love, we are faithful to the end, and for the next 25 years, whenever we traveled overseas, no matter our final destination, we always spent part of our vacation in England.

It was impossible for us to walk directly from one place to another in London. Instead we meandered as sights and our curiosity led us from one street to another, and always we caught peeks of this or that, which we couldn't resist exploring, and some of which led us to memorable adventures. One Sunday morning we discovered the Inns of Court, a building, or group of connected buildings, which housed the Barristers and Counselors and Judiciary of the English Legal System.

The Rags of Time

Through an archway opening, we saw a little park, and as we walked through it, I heard Bach being played and sung as the sounds issued forth from a low stone Church building. As Morris pushed Nat on ahead, I went back to the Church and peeked through the door and saw a string ensemble and some soloists who seemed to be in rehearsal for the upcoming service. I ran after Morris and told him we simply HAD to enter the Church because here were SUCH sights to be seen as would astonish Nat…all three of us.

We tip-toed in and were not stopped, don't even think we were noticed, and we wandered about to see that in the stone floor of the Round Church, were set stone sculptures of Knights Templar who had been in the Holy Land, and who occupied Chambers in the Middle or Inner Temple, from about 1580.

They were depicted in stone as wearing a Knight's or Military Uniform with helmut, sword in one hand, and at their feet, was sculpted a small dog or a lamb. On the walls surrounding these slightly eerie sculptures in the ground, were stone tablets, inscribed with English or Latin Maxims, and sometimes there were lighted areas of breaks in the walls. All the time we were quietly walking around in awe and admiration of what we were seeing, the Church itself was filling with ladies and gentlemen, very formally dressed, the men in suits, the women in elegant, usually print, dresses, begloved and wearing large-brimmed hats, very like those depicted as worn at the Queen's Lawn Parties.

The music rehearsal had finished, and as we tried quietly to exit the Church before the Church service, a woman ran over to us and said, "Oh please, won't you join us?" I quietly explained that we had originally been drawn to the music, and then to the sight of the Knights Templar, all new to us, and that we would not for the world intrude on the Church service. She continued, "Oh, please stay for the music. You can sit at the edge of the pews!"

She was so English-charming, so quietly insistent, that we decided to stay for a while. At least, I whispered to Morris, until the Minister appeared. The entire place, its enchantment, its welcome bespoke a movie with the wonderful Joyce Grenfell, whose looks and slightly awkward manner were always such a delight to us…and now to Nat. So we remained through the Bach Chorale and small Chamber Ensemble, whose members were now dressed to fit the occasion.

The Rags of Time

When the Minister appeared, I smiled a "farewell" to our "Joyce" and we exited. Nat always called this experience another "first" and never forgot it. Once outside we explained to him who the Knights Templar were, and who Joyce Grenfell was, and when we returned to the U.S., we had him watch a movie in which she played a Games-Mistress at a school for girls, and he laughed, and agreed that the lady in the Church was indeed our "Joyce."

Since we were unable to tear ourselves away from England, we arranged to stay another week. Morris decided to take Nat for a visit to the Morris Automobile factory which made those wonderful taxis, and I was to have a vacation from them both for the day. Nothing loth, I went to the Tate Gallery to see the Turners, Whistlers, Constables, et all, and treated myself to lunch at the Museum, AND a glass of wine, and to top off my hedonism, after my Bangers and Mash, eat a "Trifle," which consisted of some pound cake topped by jello and whipped cream. I felt terribly British that day!

When Nat and Morris joined me at the hotel they related THEIR adventures: they had gone to the factory by taxi, and later, before they left, the weather had turned into a steady drizzle. Unfortunately, when they arrived, the taxi discharged them at a roadway from which they walked up a winding path through the lawns to the factory building. When they exited, in the rain, Morris left Nat under a tree while he went up to the roadway for a taxi. He hadn't gotten more than a few steps, when seeing a taxi in the distance, he waved, and the driver, seeing Nat under the tree, rode up on the lawn and parked next to him. When they reached our hotel, Morris tried to pay and handsomely tip this very considerate driver, who refused both, and with a smile to Nat, said to Morris, "This one's on me, Guv" as he drove off!

Of course, this happened to us everywhere in New York.

"Not!"

We compared over Lagers and Shirley Temples, how our day had gone, and Morris told me that to ship a Morris Car to us, wonderful as that would be, would actually cost us as much as a new American car, so he decided against the purchase. Unfortunately, that was NOT the best decision he ever made.

The Rags of Time

We were comforted by the experience on British Airways of sitting, business class, directly in front of Philip Nolan, the American actor, who spent much of the trip being interested in us and Nat, having never seen a disabled passenger on an airplane before. Unfortunately, when we deplaned at Kennedy Airport, we had to wait rather a long time in our seats for the wheelchair to be brought to the plane door, the Staff not being as smart as the Dutch who loaded it last, to be retrieved first.

Oh well, you can't have everything!

But we sure as hell had had a lot, and enough happy experiences to last a long while!

My Mother, Judith Borst, at the piano in Russia

Maternal grandparents arrive in America.
Golde and Tevya (David) Borst

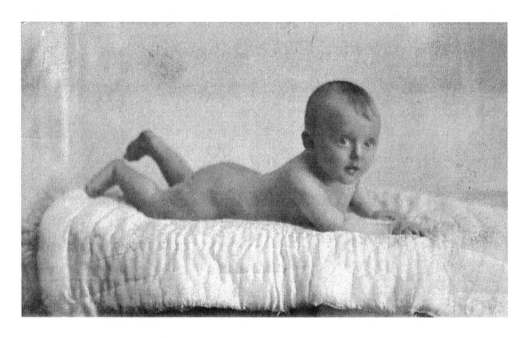

Susanna, age 3 months,..out of the toilet bowl....

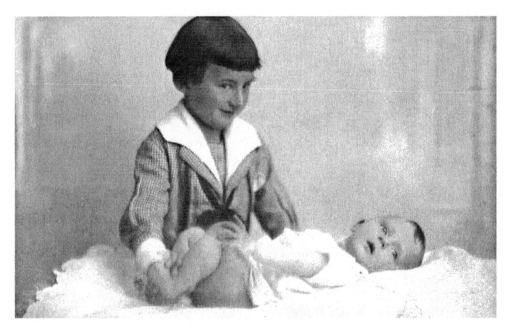

Brother Nathaniel and Susanna, ages 6 yrs...I, at 3 mos.
in Berlin, Germany

My stage and its set at the Cooper Union:
"The Cradle Will Rock" of Marc Blitzstein

My controversial window at Cooper Union, N.Y.C.

Susanna at the Grove School in Madison, CT

Herb Mears and Susanna at the Grove School

Morris and Susan (and Buttons) in early days of our marriage

Here's a great page from the legendary scrapbooks of Bob Inman.

Mr. Inman kept meticulous notes regarding his musical adventures during the 1930s - and collected some fabulous autographs as well.

The front of this page tells of Mr. Inman's experience attending a "Saturday Night Swing Broadcast" for WABC radio on January 2nd, 1937 - at 6:45PM. He also managed to get a few autographs while he was there - which he cut out and pasted to the page.

Although Mr. Inman misspelled a few of the names in his notes, those who have signed are:

Glenn Miller - trombone
Claude Hopkins - piano
Nat Jaffe - piano
Cliff Natalie - trumpet
Joe Sodja - guitar
Ben Chaney - bass
Jules Jacob - saxophone

There are some great rare autpgraphs here - most obviously the Glenn Miller and Claude Hopkins signatures - but the one that really stands out for me is the inclusion of Nat Jaffe.

Pianist Nat Jaffe was a musical prodigy who was only 19 years old at the time that he gave this autograph. Before his 23rd birthday he had recording dates with such legends as Louis Armstrong, Sarah Vaughan, Jack Teagarden and Charlie Barnet. Tragically, this promising career was cut short in 1945 when, at the age of 27, Jaffe died from complications arising from a high blood pressure condition.

For those jazz collectors who look for the true autograph rarities - this is it.

There are no autographs on the verso, but there are some more notes regarding other jazz broadcasts that Mr. Inman attended in 1937.

About my brother Nat Jaffe, in the words of a Jazz collector

The Rags of Time

158 JAN 2
1937

Show
26

Glenn Miller
trombone

Saturday Night Swing Broadcast (26th) Sat. Jan. 2, 1937 WABC-6:45

Hughie and I went in by subway to see this weeks broadcast. We met
Reddy Snow, H. Pinger, Morningstar, and Mortimer there. Claude Hopkins,
famous negro pianist who leads his own band, and Joe Sodja a
swell, young new guitar player, and his accompanist on the piano, Nat
Shifes. Got their autographs and Cliff Natolie (trumpet), Ben Chorny
(bass), Glenn Miller (trombone), and Jules Jacob (sax).

I Can't Get Started (theme featuring Benny Berrigan on trumpet)
Pick Yourself Up (CBS Band playing swell brass, sax, Moffie's guitar)
I Never Knew
Three Little Words (Claude Hopkins on p's
Vampin' A Coed (
Organ Grinders swing (one of their best arrangements - BALLSY)
Love Me Or Leave Me (Doris Kerr singing - Great)
Down By The Old Mill Stream (Berrigan trumpet solo)
China Boy (Joe Sodja on guitar with Nat Shife on piano)
Sheik of Araby ("
Who's Sorry Now
Hand In Glove (CBS Band playing some fi

Best Wishes
Claude Hopkins

Nat Jaffe
piano

Jules Jacob
sax

Best Wishes
Cliff Natolie
trumpet

Joe Sodja
guitar

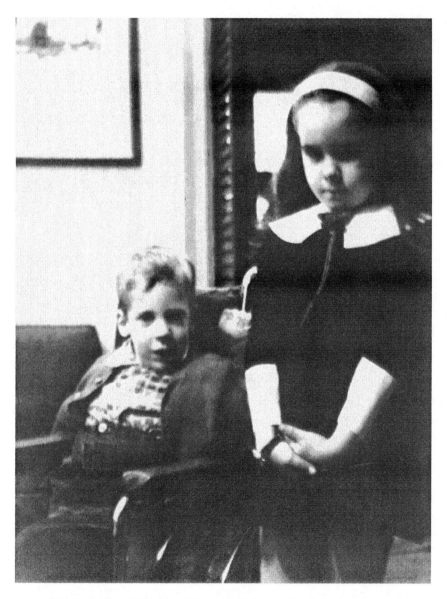

Nat-David and Kathy. Nat in his first wheelchair at age 3

The Rags of Time

NEW YORK UNIVERSITY MEDICAL CENTER
Department of Rehabilitation Medicine

CO-SPONSORED BY THE AMERICAN ACADEMY
OF PHYSICAL MEDICINE & REHABILITATION

fifth annual short course in

PEDIATRIC REHABILITATION

NOVEMBER 12-13-14-15-16, 1973

FACULTY
HOWARD A. RUSK, M.D., *Department Chairman*
CHESTER A. SWINYARD, M.D., Ph.D., *Program Chairman*
LEON GREENSPAN, M.D., *Clinical Director*

REHABILITATION MEDICINE
Angeles Badell-Ribera, M.D.
Edward H. Bergofsky, M.D.
Gisela L. Brady, R.P.T.
Julian L. Brower, Ed.D.
Leonard Diller, Ph.D.
Michele K. Dorf, R.N.
Boguslav H. Fischer, M.D.
Lawrence W. Friedmann, M.D.
Liesl Friedmann, O.T.R.
Phyllis Gillette, P.H.N.
Joseph Goodgold, M.D.
Ronnie Gordon, M.S.
Selene Jaramillo, M.D.
H. Richard Lehneis, C.P.O.
Irene K. Rush, R.N.
Martha Taylor-Sarno, M.S.
Judith Silverstein, M.S.W.
John Whelan, R.N.

NEUROSURGERY
Joseph Ransohoff, M.D.
Fred J. Epstein, M.D.

NEUROLOGY
Richard N. Reuben, M.D.

OPHTHALMOLOGY
Newton B. Chin, M.D.

ORTHOPEDIC SURGERY
Nicholas A. Tzimas, M.D.

PEDIATRICS
Leon Greenspan, M.D.

UROLOGY
Pablo A. Morales, M.D.

VISITING FACULTY
Clare Baker, M.S.
Educator

Ira Belmont, Ph.D.
Psychologist

Stephen A. Richardson, Ph.D.
Pediatrics & Community Health

COMMUNICATION DEVICES
MORRIS SCHWARTZ
Nat David SCHWARTZ

Nat-David's life-long hero

184

The Rags of Time

EMBASSY OF THE
UNION OF SOVIET SOCIALIST REPUBLICS
WASHINGTON 6, D. C.

March 20, 1961

Mrs. Morris Schwartz
650 Bergen Avenue
Jersey City, New Jersey

Dear Mrs. Schwartz,

In reference to your letter of March 11, we advise you
to apply for the information you have mentioned directly to
the Ministry of Health of the USSR at the following address:

Ministry of Health, Moscow, USSR.

Sincerely,

A. Izvekov
Third Secretary

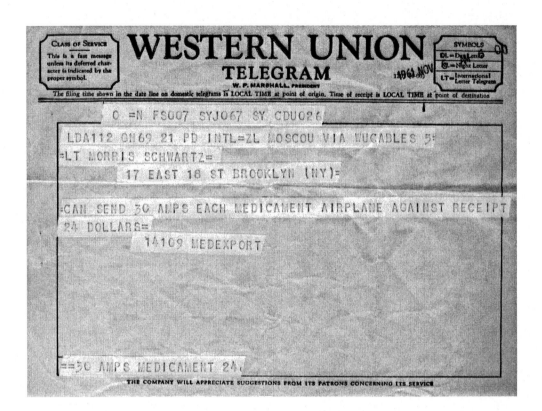

ВСЕСОЮЗНОЕ ЭКСПОРТНО-ИМПОРТНОЕ ОБЪЕДИНЕНИЕ
МЕДЭКСПОРТ

Москва Г-200, Смоленская-Сенная, 32/34	Moscow G-200, Smolenskaja-Sennaja, 32/34
В/О „Медэкспорт"	V/O „Medexport"
Телегр. адрес: МОСКВА МЕДЭКСПОРТ	Cables: MEDEXPORT MOSCOW
Телефон: Г 4-28-05	Telephone: Г 4-28-05

№ 391-22/ *4429*   *14* ноября 196*I* г.

Уважаемый г-н Морис Шварц!

Мы получили Ваше письмо от 3 ноября с.г.

Мы можем выслать Вам галантамин на курс лече-
ния. Стоимость 30 ампул 0,25%-ного раствора
18 ам.долларов. Просим перевести в наш адрес
вышеуказанную сумму.

Прежде чем переводить деньги, просим выяснить
в таможне не будет ли у Вас затруднений при
получении посылки.

По получении денег мы вышлем Вам галантамин
авиапочтой.

С уважением,

В/О "Медэкспорт"

Our 9 month Soviet adventure during the cold-war!

C O P Y

Richard Reuben,M.D.
17 Dogleg Lane
Roslyn Heights, N.Y.

July 26,1961

MiNistry of Health - Preservation
Moscow, E - 51
Rachmanovsky per.d.3.

Dear Sirs:

     I am writing to you on behalf of infant
Nat D. Schwartz, born MARCH 7,1959 who has "Cerebral Palsy"
of the clinical variety classified as "Tension Athetoid".
I understand that the parents of this child have received an
offer of help from your ministry and I would be very happy
to cooperate with you in your generous offer.

     Accordingly, I am enclosing copies of the medical
reports in my file so that you may have all the information
you desire.

     If you are of the opinion that medecines will be
of value in the treatment of this child, then please indicate
which drugs and in which dosage are desirable. Further information regarding the mode of action and toxic effects of such
drugs would also be desired.

               Respectfully yours,

               Richard N. Reuben, M.D.

Nat-David's book

Ask first, "Is it a statement?" or "A question?" For the
correct reply, Nat will look at you (meet your eyes) for a "yes"
affirmative response or look away for a "no" response.

If Nat indicates he has a question, ask the following:

Is it "W"? (for the what,where,who,why,when questions.
If Nat says yes, ask: Wha, e, o, y, etc. He will stop you at correct
letter by a look.

If it is NOT a "W" quwstion, ask:
"Is it H? (How, have,has,etc)
C? (can, could,etc)
D? (Does, do, did,etc)
A? (are)
I? (is, if,etc)

If Nat indicates he is making a statement, ask: "Is it I?"
(meaning Nat) and if not, procedd as follows: For both statement
and question the alphabet is divided into:
First half : A - L
2nd half : M - Z

When you have determined which half, run thru those letters
of the alphabet & Nat will stop you with a look. More often than not
you will have guessed the word by the first, 2nd or 3rd letter. With
a pad & pencil (for you) and 15 minutes to practice, you'll have it!

Nat-David's spelling-mode

190

"CAN YOUR LITTLE BOY COME OUT TO PLAY?"

by Susan Schwartz

An all too familiar question in most households, but to the mother of a handicapped child, these words have a very special meaning.

■ I grabbed a handful of lollipops and tossed them into the wicker basket on Nat David's stroller. Then we set off to make friends. The lollipops had been given to Nat David by a fond relative; the idea of using them as an encouragement to friendship was mine. It had been born of necessity, and I was trying it out for the first time.

I stopped at the little park near our house where I viewed a familiar scene—children playing near the trees, their mothers sitting and talking on benches. I smiled a greeting to the adults, whom I didn't know, and then deliberately stopped the stroller near the group of children. After a time of watching and being watched, as Nat David, slightly slumped in his stroller, stared gravely at

S. PERL

the other children, one little girl spoke to me:

"How old is he?"

"Nat David was two years old last Saturday. Do you think your mother would let you have one of his birthday lollipops?"

The three children scattered, and returning with permission granted, sucked slowly and pleasurably, silently surveying us. Then:

"Can't he come out of his stroller?"

"No, Nat David doesn't walk yet."

"My brother's a year old and he walks a little."

"Yes, but Nat David's muscles are still very weak and it will take him longer to learn to walk."

"Oh."

"Mommy," one little girl called to the group of women nearby, "he can't walk yet. His muscles are weak."

And so it began—the first overtures on my part to help Nat David, our cerebral palsied child, enter the normal world of children's play and friendship.

I had thought a lot before that day about how to approach other children, and how much to say to them about my son's handicap. It certainly wouldn't do to let Nat David become an object of pity. I spent many days rehearsing the way I could account for his differences so that toddlers would be able to understand and accept them.

My husband and I knew that the sooner we could adopt, and act (Continued on page 75)

43

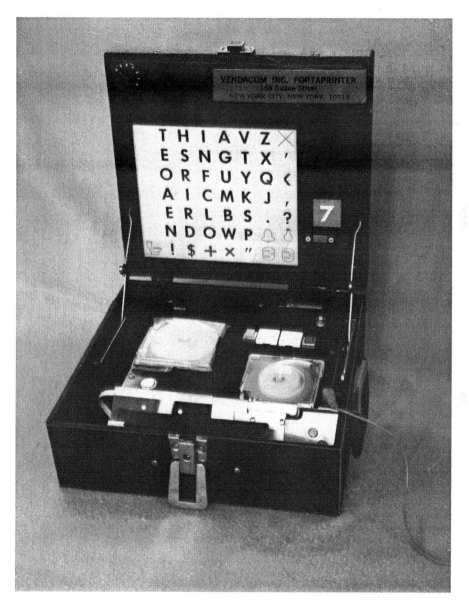

The Portaprinter, that Morris' genius contrived for Nat using the still-best letter-board extant, every letter and placement, bitterly fought over by Nat and Dad!

I TRIED TO WRITE THE STORYE ABOYKUT MYSELF.

I NEED INFO INFORMATION WHAT WENT WRONT WITH ME?
UMBILICAL CORN<D ITS WRONG.

WHER IS MY BELL? I GOT FROM ANIQKY.

        THANKS D DAD .>
   LOOK GRANDMA ITS TOO HOT FOR YOR YOU TO G GO
                        WH EN YOU COME ST AY
   I M NEED THE KEY.

   JOE IS STARTED TO GIVE FOR SCHOOL.   FORGET IT.

   WE HAVE TO TALK YET.

ELECTRODE
   * TO HE I DONT K CARE!

   CALL RAB BI KAHN.

      NO I AM NOT HAPPY TO GO BACK.ARE W WE T GOIN G AWAY?

   DONT YOU CALL DADD AT HOM E! OWHEN IS T THE MEETING?

WHAT DID JA CK. SAY? P I WANT TO FIGHT! - GIVE ME DAD CASS. E

Portaprinter tapes during early trials by Nat-David

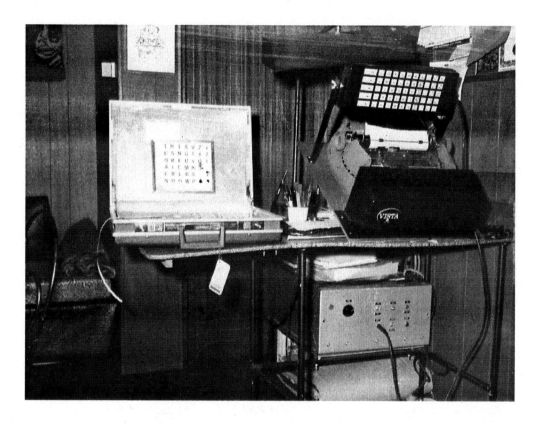

The VISTA,

PORTAPRINTER - 4

THAT YOUR BEEN VERY WITH FROM GOOD WHEN HAVE THEY COME THIS KNOW
SOME HERE WILL WANT TIME JUST MUCH

This final letterboard gave the greatest ease to spell out the commonly used words and the most commonly used groups of letters forming most other words.

Credit for this letterboard must be given to Nat David who spent months researching the best possible placement of letters. Testing, re-testing and revising, he was able to establish a letterboard which created the easiest and fastest method of creating words to facilitate communication.

Incorporated in the display panel is a bell to summon assistance or to signal the completion of a communication; there is also a light to illuminate the printed message. Included in the printed characters are numbers, punctuation marks and mathematical symbols, giving a total of 50 characters.

In contrast to existing electro-mechanical communication devices, we offer the following data:

WEIGHT & SIZE	SELF-CONTAINED POWER	PORTABILITY	NOISE LEVEL	DISPLAY PANEL
VISTA - approx. 3 cu.ft plus 1½ cu.ft. for electric typewriter. in excess of 120 lbs.	NONE	NONE	highly audible clicking	detached
POSM - size & weight same as above	NONE	NONE	audible clicking	detached
CYBERTYPE - size & weight same as above	NONE	NONE	highly audible clicking	detached
PORTAPRINTER - 1/3 cu. ft. 12 lbs.	YES	COMPLETE	SILENT	SELF - CONTAINED

* The PORTAPRINTER is smaller in size than the display panel of the POSM or CYBERTYPE

Referring to the first sentence of this article, tests made on the above - mentioned devices, shows that the phrase, "man's need to communicate has always existed" require the following full machine periods:

VISTA : 237   POSM : 241 PORTAPRINTER : 130

Nat's favorite pub in London, near Paddington Square Station
on his first trip overseas, 1971

Niantic News

POSTAL PATRON

Volume 33 — Number 27   June 3, 1980   Serving Niantic/East Lyme/Waterford/Quaker Hill   20¢

SEAT super service in full swing

"If someone doesn't use it, we're going to lose it," Harland Daman stated succinctly as he boarded one of the SEAT passenger buses in Niantic.

"I've been hoping to see a bus come along here for many years," he went on to say. "I'm just taking a ride into New London," he added as he took a seat in the nearly empty bus.

David Harris of Niantic was the only other passenger on the 9:30 Thursday morning run.

"I'm going to be a regular rider," he said. "I work in Norwich and I used to have to take a taxi into New London to catch the Norwich bus. This saves me money, its convenient and it cuts down on commuting time."

Along the entire route from Niantic to the Groton Shopping Center on Fort Hill Road, and back again, genial boarding the bus waved their approval at driver, Bernard Fitzoy, stopped wherever a potential passenger waited along the route.

At one point on the Boston Post Road Bernard stopped the bus to pick up Joan Carroll of Waterford.

"This is wonderful", she told him with a smile as she mounted the steps which had been automatically lowered for ease in boarding. "My car broke down this

morning and the bus solved the problem of how to get to work!"

It is hoped that more and more Electric Boat and Pfizer employees will feel that way, too. The EB commuter bus, at present, leaves in front of the Morton House in Niantic at 6 a.m. and arrives at EB 45 minutes later. During that run, Bernard says that he goes to the commuter parking lot at the East Lyme High School where he picks up workers headed for Groton jobs at that early hour. The afternoon return trip is geared to the EB shifts.

Bernard asked that everyone be patient.

"Like any new organization," he said jovially, "our service will have to go through growing pains. Schedules and the times involved may have to be adjusted as passenger service increases.

"There's no need for anyone to worry," he added. "We will not run ahead of schedule and, in fact, we may even be a few minutes late. But, I guarantee we will make connections with all the other buses.

As he said that, he drove the sleek new bus away from the New London Railroad Station and continued on to make the loop back to Captain's Walk where other buses were converging from Norwich and

(Continued on Page 8)

It was a 'first' for Nat Schwartz of Lakeview Dr., Niantic, who had never been able to use public transportation before the SEAT bus service started. Nat was also the first to try out the hydraulic lift provided for the handicapped. His mother, Susanna, accompanied him.

RESUME

Nat David Schwartz
17 Lakeview Drive
Niantic, Ct. 06357
Tel. 739 - 4181

Education :

1981 - 1983   Mohegan Community College.
                      Studied: Literature, Creative Writing, Sociology,
                              Psychology, Ecology, World History.

1978 - 1980   New Jersey Institute of Technology (Engineering School
                      of Rutgers University)
                      Studied: Adaptive Engineering

Activities: Worked in Macro Lab for 2 years, with the blind, to
                      adapt equipment for their use. (Pub. in Nexus Magazine)

                      Presented idea and information relating to the necessity
                      of the development and adaptation of equipment used in
                      the living and working environment of the disabled.

1977   Attended Long Island University prior to Hight School
                      graduation.
                      Studied: Political Science and American History.

1978   Graduated from Edward R. Murrow High School for Communi-
                      cation Arts in New York City. Was awarded citation as
                      New York City's Student of the Year.

Activities: Held position as liaison between disabled students and
                      school officials.
                      Representative for disabled students to the Student Gov-
                      ernment for three years.
                      Created "buddy-system" for disabled students with non-
                      disabled students.

                      Wrote syllabus and established course with science
                      teacher on "Sex and the disabled."

                      Edited book on typing in Hebrew for typing teacher.

                      Introduced disability-awareness sessions in Edward R.
                      Murrow.

Accomplishments: Contributed input as a "human resource" to New York
1975 - 1980   City's Planning Commission concerning issues relating
                      to the disabled.

                      Fought for the rights of the disabled in New York.
                      Was responsible for retaining services of personal care
                      attendants at schools during N.Y.C.'s financial crunch
                      when jobs were frozen.

RESUME (·cont'd)

Nat David Schwartz

Accomplishments:

1983 - 1984   Formed ADAPT, a social group for the physically
               disabled.

1986 - 1988   Charter member; helped to establish D.N.E.C.
               (Disability Network of Eastern Ct.) Acted as
               Public Relations officer.

               In Niantic, Ct., Proposed and succeeeded in having
               sidewalks repaired and replaced and haviing side-
               walks cuts made to accommodate not only wheelchairs
               but baby carriages and making it easier for the
               elderly to walk.

Biographical data: Born March 7,1959. Male.

Physical Disability: Cerebral Palsy, athetoid type, quadriplegic.

Personal: Foreign Languages: Hebrew - read, comprehend,speak
               Russian - read, speak, comprehend; Dutch - compre-
               hend, speak; German - comprehend, speak.

               Foreign Travel: Canada, England, Holland, France,
                               Belgium.

               Travel through entire continental United States.

Volume 35 — Number 15   March 16, 1982   Serving Niantic/East Lyme/Waterford/Quaker Hill   2 Sections   20¢

He hopes physically disabled will form group

By CAROLYN BATTISTA

Nat David Schwartz of Niantic wants to get out of the house and be with friends. That's normal for any 23 year old man, but for Nat and other physically disabled people, it's difficult.

Nat, who has cerebral palsy, has scheduled a meeting at East Lyme Town Hall March 19 at 7:30 p.m. for physically handicapped adults who want to form a group to socialize, discuss problems and plan programs.

The sons of Susanna and Morris Schwartz of Niantic, Nat must live in a specially designed wheelchair. He cannot sit up by himself or speak. But he has attended college at Mitchell, writes plays and poetry, and has plenty to say. He can communicate alphabet letters to his parents with eye signals, or use a special machine built by his father. Present sensors in his wheelchair pillow with the back of his head, Nat selects letters to send his messages. Letters and other symbols light up on a board (which he designed) and messages can be printed on the machine's tape.

"My brainstorm" is a message he sends to describe his idea for the March 19 meeting. He has several suggestions for a group of disabled people, and he's looking forward to hearing what others attending would like to do.

The main purpose, says Nat, would be social — getting together, enjoying, rapping.

The group could also discuss problems disabled people face, like access to buildings and facilities. The Schwartzes, who have traveled in Europe with Nat, say European facilities for the handicapped are much better in general than American ones. But they praise "the attitude of people in Connecticut." "Why not," people reply when they ask whether they can arrange for a wheelchair person at various places. The Schwartzes note the accessibility of East Lyme Town Hall, where the meeting will be conducted, and of Niantic restaurants and movies. But such convenience is not widespread, they point out.

Nat would also like to see the group plan weekends together — maybe at some place like Camp Harkness (for the handicapped) in Waterford. When he was much younger, his parents recall, they happened to stay in a small motel that was especially convenient for a wheelchair member, with a pool and a nearby restaurant.

"Wouldn't it be great if we could get together with other handicapped kids and their families, and just take over this place for a weekend?," Nat thought then. Camp Harkness "would be perfect" for group weekend vacations, the Schwartzes observe.

Nat will be attending a regular two week camp session at Harkness this summer, and he hopes to interest staff and other campers in his plans for a group.

Nat and his parents note belonging to such a group wouldn't cost anything, and the group would be run by the participants themselves. "No members," Mr. Schwartz says firmly. "They'd plan their own programs.

"So far as we know, there is no socialization group for physically handicapped people in this area," says James February, executive director of United Cerebral Palsy in New London County. The Schwartzes are seeking participants — a meeting than Southeastern Connecticut. The group could rotate meeting places for the convenience of members.

Formation of such a group would also help the families of the disabled to form a support group. "Parents really need a group, like this," Mrs. Schwartz said. "Often other parents are the most help to you, even more than professionals (like counselors and therapists)."

While Nat looks forward to socializing, he's also hoping for a further step — some group members might like to live together on their own. "It's not that Nat doesn't love us," his father grins. But most young adults, he notes, can leave home when they're ready simply by walking out the door. Nat doesn't want more than other people, his father says, "but he doesn't want any less."

In his poem "TO A WHEELCHAIR..." Nat acknowledges the frustration of being handicapped, but he isn't giving in to those frustrations. Nat just thinks, his mother points out, "the disabled must get off their duffs and make things happen." The March 19 meeting is to be a start.

To a wheelchair

How do I hate you? Let me count the ways.
My body rusts with your metallic pipes.
You make me feel the anger of two me's.
When fingers catch you wheels. You bang my knees
And scratch my toes and complicate my life.
Why can't you be my friend and let me go.
To walk through life as other people do.
Your powwad blinks me like a crazy horse,
And I am always sore and black and blue.
I feel your armrests right around my chest.
Sometimes I feel that I will suffocate.
All in all, you really are a pest.
If I could, I would break your pipes apart.
There you may sway, before you break my heart.

— Nat David Schwartz

DEP issues report on coves

Tapping a New Source of Scientific Manpower: the Handicapped

Until little more than a year ago, the lives of Nat David Schwartz and Bill Kappler were extremely different and seemingly unrelated. But subtle flaws in nature's engineering caused the lives of the two young men to intersect in a large room called the Macro Lab at New Jersey Institute of Technology in Newark. It is a place where human engineering strives to compensate for the effects of nature's system gone wrong.

It is very quiet in the lab as Nat and Bill attempt for the first time to do something which most people take blissfully for granted: to simply communicate with each other.

Nat's Story

Nat Schwartz has been struggling all his 20 years — against doctors, school administrators, an ignorant and prejudiced society and, most of all, the physical disorder which he has never let control his life. Nat has cerebral palsy of the type known as athetoid, which means that he has almost constant, involuntary, uncontrolled motion.

Cerebral palsy is actually a single term for a group of disorders with a variety of symptoms, all having in common impairment of motor function due to brain damage sustained during fetal development, birth or early infancy. Although a number of conditions have been implicated as factors causing cerebral palsy — from lack of oxygen to infection in the mother during pregnancy — the exact causes are still unclear in most cases. Symptoms may be slight or severe; intellectual capacity may or may not be impaired. Drugs, physical therapy, braces and, sometimes, orthopedic surgery are used to give a measure of control in some victims. At present, however, there is no cure.

Nat Schwartz is confined to a wheelchair which looks rather jaunty with a denim bag slung over its handle. He has virtually no use of his arms or legs and he cannot talk. He does, however, have control of his neck muscles which enables him to operate a switch by pushing against it with his head.

It is this one controllable function which is the key to communication for Nat. Another key is this young man from Brooklyn's strong, gutsy personality, which reveals itself even in small ways like sporting a beard. His mother recalls him "saying" angrily to his therapists and doctors when he was younger: "Don't talk down to me!"

A remarkable young man, Nat attended private schools most of his life until he and his family fought his way into public high

school, Edward R. Murrow High School in New York City, where he studied social studies, mathematics, chemistry and other sciences. He wrote term papers, took tests and graduated with honors, accomplishing all this with the aid of a machine, the Porta Printer, designed by his father. By pressing the switch behind his head, Nat spells out words by stopping a light when it shines on the desired letter on a letter board in front of him. At the end of a day in high school, he spelled out to his family: "Every day I have to fight for my education."

Last year, Nat's mother was put in touch with Dr. Harry Herman, professor of mechanical engineering at New Jersey Institute of Technology. Dr. Herman directs the program officially called "Physically Handicapped in Science" in the Macro Lab at the technological university. Nat was immediately accepted into the program.

Enter Bill Kappler

Also about a year ago, a young mechanical engineer from Toms River, N.J., went blind as a result of diabetes, the leading cause of new cases of blindness in the United States. Bill Kappler has juvenile diabetes, which develops before the age of 15. This type of diabetes is often more severe than adult-onset diabetes, the more common form,

---

(L. to r.) Bill Kappler, Nat Schwartz and Prof. Herman work in NJIT's Macro Lab with Handi Voice, a computer communications device which produces speech.

which occurs after the age of 35. The disturbances in body chemistry which cause excessive sugar — glucose — in the diabetic's blood can result in damage to the organs, particularly the kidneys and eyes, and to the blood vessels in the form of hardening of the arteries. These complications usually result when diabetes is severe over a long period of time.

Bill had conventional rehabilitation for blindness which greatly increased his ability to function but did not prepare him to return to work as an engineer. Then he heard about the work being done at the New Jersey Institute of Technology, and joined the program. "It's allowed me to continue in the engineering field," he says. "And it's given me a chance to get back to work. After this semester I hope to return to my job. I've also been helped a lot by Dr. Cochin (who is blind) and others who have gone through it, just by asking them questions."

A Day in the Macro Lab

Nat's mother wheels him into the large room known as the Macro Lab. It is the first time that Bill and Nat are working together. But it is not the first time Nat has faced the challenge of communicating with a blind person. "When Nat first came here," Dr. Herman recalls, he tried to assist a blind student using an instrument that was not designed for use with the blind. Ever since, he's wanted to specialize in technologies which will help rehabilitate the blind."

(please turn to page 5)

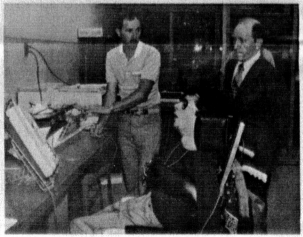

Monastery of Sint-Sixtusabdij, in Westvleteren, Belgium....
Bruder Daniel at the organ...

The Brewery at Sint-Sixtusabdij

The Portuguese Synagogue in Amsterdam

Sept. 8,1992

Jerry Lewis
M.D.A.
3300 East Sunrise Drive
Tucson, AZ 85718-3208

Dear Jerry,

I have Cerebral Palsy but you are my idol.
I want to give MDA a check for $5,000 because when
my organization, Inlife, Inc. (Independent Living Is
For Everyone) was formed 5 years ago, I had written
into its By-Laws that if it was not successful in
its aim to build affordable, accessible homes for
the disabled, the corporation would dissolve, and its
assets would be turned over to M.D.A.

I have not been able to get a government
or private grant to finance my dream. I am now 33
years old, and since 1967 I have supported MDA, at
first with a few dollars, and now this amount that
that was raised by InLife of which I was President.

I realize that medical research is the
best hope for people with M.D. and C.P.. Like you,
I didn't want to give up, but people who are disabled
are no more intelligent or militant or compassionate
than any other segment of society. The only bright
spot about giving up on housing for the disabled is
being able to support M.D.A. Several of my friends
have already died of the disease.

I hope you will personally acknowledge
this contribution as you did when I was a little boy.
I still have your note.

L'Shana Tova,

Nat Schwartz

The Rays of Time

Jerry Lewis

National Chairman
MUSCULAR DYSTROPHY ASSOCIATION
3300 East Sunrise Drive
Tucson, Arizona 85718

September 17, 1992

Mr. Nat David Schwartz
17 Lake View Drive
Niantic, Connecticut 06357

Dear Nat,

I was deeply moved by your recent letter, and thank you from the bottom of my heart for your generous donation to MDA. Although I'm saddened that your quest to finance low-cost housing for the disabled has yet to be fulfilled, I can assure you that MDA will put your donation to good use by providing research and patient services to benefit individuals with muscular dystrophy and related disorders.

Your unselfish gift to MDA will help our dedicated researchers come closer to finding treatments and cures for neuromuscular diseases so you and I will no longer lose friends to these devastating disorders.

You're a very special person, Nat, and I'm proud to know you.

God Bless you...

Love,

Jerry Lewis

3/9/94

Elizabeth (Betty) and Peter Nazarko East Lyme, CT.

My Connecticut "family," The Lloyd Bayreuthers
In order of appearance: Peter, Lloyd, Heidi, Jonathan

State of Connecticut

QUI TRANSTULIT SUSTINET

GENERAL ASSEMBLY

In Memoriam

Be it hereby known to all that:

The Connecticut General Assembly

extends its sincerest condolences

and expressions of sympathy to:

THE SCHWARTZ FAMILY

on the passing of

NAT DAVID SCHWARTZ

Introduced by   REPRESENTATIVE GARY OREFICE, 37TH DISTRICT
SENATOR MELODIE PETERS, 20TH DISTRICT

Given this 21ST day of MAY 19 94

John B. Larson
President Pro Tempore

Thomas D. Ritter
Speaker of the House

Of your charity
Pray for the repose of the soul of
THOMAS STEARNS ELIOT O.M.
Born St. Louis Missouri
26th September 1888
Died London 4th January 1965
A churchwarden of
this parish for 25 years
He worshipped here until his death

"We must be still and still moving
Into another intensity
For a further union a deeper communion"

Part of our "religious odyssey" following Nat's death - 1994

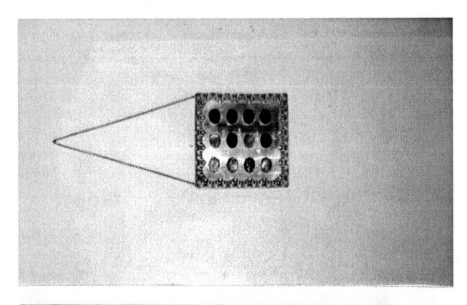

Aaron's breastplate...out from under my lingerie in the United States!

Morris and Susanna at his last birthday party

IN GOOD
KING CHARLES'S
GOLDEN DAYS

a history lesson by

BERNARD SHAW

illustrated by Feliks Topolski

CONSTABLE & CO LTD LONDON

Chapter 11

When we picked up our lives, and Nat's treatment at IRM, there emerged another crisis, this one instituted by Nat. He began to complain, via his Portaprinter which went with him daily to HASC, that he was not receiving the science and history courses he required if he were to attend college. THIS, he fully expected to do, he informed us. I spoke with the Rabbi, with the head teacher, and passed on Nat's statement to us, to support what he had already told them. They did nothing to remedy the situation, and I suggested that they at least give Nat the history of Israel. This was likewise ignored. Finally, when Nat came home from school one day and the Canon strip on the Printer read: "Every day I have to fight for my education!" I decided that enough was enough and sprang into action.

At that time, within New York City's Board of Education, there existed an archaic and obsolete, even in my opinion, sadistic practice known as a "screening procedure" for admission to any of the pitifully few Intermediary and High Schools that MIGHT accept a disabled student. When Nat was five, he had undergone this "procedure," but after he was accepted at HASC, we let continuation of our battle with the Board of Education slide. We had fought that battle, we thought, and NOW we had to help Nat leave HASC and get him into high school. I told Nat not to worry. I would begin the process the very next day.

The following morning after Nat left for school, I went to Manhattan to see the Head of Education for Disabled Students at the Board of Education. When I met Dr. Helen Feulner, I told her of Nat's and our desire to see Nat in the Public School System for the education to which he was legally entitled.

Dr. Feulner told me that there were really NO such schools which accepted children in wheelchairs. I was adamant and said that Nat WOULD have a public school education, no matter what the Board's position was, or hers, and further, that I would take it up with the New York Governor and ALL elected officials! At that, we got down to business. She recognized my steely resolve, and interpreting my remarks as a threat, asked, "Where does your son want to go?"

"Intermediate School 303," I answered, having already discussed this with Nat. He wanted to know WHAT the courses would be like, and although it was now late February, he went into that school, where happily, our dear friend and a former HASC teacher, Les Grussgott, now taught.

It took a week for transportation to be available, and Nat entered I.S. 303 after that. He was placed in a class with students who studied subjects with which he was familiar, plus science and history, and physics. Nat was now not only at the level of his peers, but insisted on going back, in the texts provided him, to what he had missed since the beginning of the school year.

The subject of physics was unfamiliar to any of us. I suggested that we read the glossary at the back of the text to see if ANY of it made sense to Nat, or if he might already be familiar with any of it. Well, we knew about Isaac Newton and the apple…and a bit more…but what amazed Nat was that he had already covered quite a bit of the course just in being present on some Saturdays, and listening, and watching, as Morris built a wheelchair ramp in our back garden, to go from the kitchen door, and he heard, as Morris in his customary mode, spoke aloud while mathematically figuring the ramp's dimension and direction: "Let's see now, the ramp's slope is measured at 1 inch to a foot…and the concrete rest before its turn, is approximately 3 feet…then to the forward down-slope again!" …and so on, for several weeks.

When Nat took the physics exam, he brought back the test paper with a grade of 98, having gotten just two of the 100 short answers wrong. Of course, we knew his intelligence and almost total recall of ANYTHING he heard or read, and his ability to retrieve or figure out a combination of information…rather like the retrieval of information one stored in a computer. Now everyone was convinced of what Morris and I always referred to as Nat's "experiential intelligence."

In his other classes, he was just as fast a study, and in addition, he learned valuable lessons NOT in the curriculum. He came home from school one day and wrote on his Canon strip tape, "She gave it to me."

The Rags of Time

"What did she give you?" I asked, checking his bookbag.

"No," he wrote again, "She gave it to me!"

Knowing my kid, I repeated the phrase to myself, with all possible inflections, which inflections, sadly, could not be entered into this marvelous invention of my husband's. "SHE gave it to me." Nat looked away, or down, as was his wont when his response was negative. Then, "She GAVE it to me!"

Jackpot!

Nat then explained that when he left a classroom, he forgot his text for the next class. His teacher sternly admonished him, telling him that his books were HIS responsibility, and he was expected to look around and make sure that ALL proper books accompanied him to classes. The "She GAVE it to me!" meant she gave him HELL!

When I told Morris this at night, *WE* laughed like HELL! But never again did Nat forget a text. And four months later, he graduated from I.S. 303 in the top ten percentile.

Now began a search for a high school, not an easy task at a time when any and all education for the disabled was difficult. Again I contacted Dr. Feulner, told her of Nat's success in intermediate school, and asked her help in placing him in a suitable school. There was ONE high school, Sheepshead Bay H.S., near that body of water, in Brooklyn, and so we enrolled him, confident that his past success would enable him to compete with his peers in this school.

I accompanied him the first day, to explain Nat and his Portaprinter, and I met with his home-room teacher and the aide who was to take him to classes, and up or down the elevator, and explained the use of the Printer, and how to plug it into a wall outlet. I was sure that the information I gave would be passed on.

I came home by subway, pleased that I had prepared the way for Nat and when he came home that afternoon, eagerly quizzed him about his experiences. What I received were troubled looks and terse replies. When Morris came home and was told, he asked me to call the school and tell them, "Dr. Schwartz wanted to see the Dean of Students and the Principal." We sent Nat off the next morning, told him just to go through the day, and things WOULD be better. The next day, instead of going to work, but as "Dr. Schwartz," Morris drove with me to what Nat on his Printer called, "Sheepheads Bay," and while I waited in Nat's home room, Morris met with the staff and found out that the Aide flatly refused to transport the Portaprinter or connect it! She reported that the teachers were "upset, didn't know what Nat was doing in their classes, and were," as she put it, "hysterical!"

At first Morris was tactful (always MY first approach), and again reiterated information about Nat, about the Printer, about his fine record as a student, how both IT and NAT performed, that no one had to carry the Printer, and that all that was required was that it be placed before him on his desk, opened, plugged into the electrical outlet, the attachment from the Printer to the connection at the back of his headrest set up, and VOILA, Nat would do the rest; that even another student might be entrusted to connect and disconnect the machine, and take the cord out of the wall socket.

"No, not possible!"

"Then Nat will wait for the Aide to do it."

The following day was no better: the Aide flatly refused to take or connect the Printer. Nat came home and cried his frustration. Now he was able to communicate, but kept from it by stupidity.

That was definitely NOT that, we assured Nat. WE and HE would prevail!

The next day Morris and I drove to Sheepshead Bay High School and demanded a meeting with the Principal and the Dean. When we were all assembled, and Morris reported that the Aide had refused to perform her duties, and we were charging her with incompetence, the Principal said, "She is very well liked by me, and for as long as I have been here and known her, she has ALWAYS performed very well!"

Said Morris, "How can you say that? I have done MY homework, and found that YOU, Sir, have only been at this school for 2 1/2 weeks and came from a school on Staten Island!"

The Rags of Time

Came the reply, "Well, harrumph, harrumph…"

"I am withdrawing my son from this factory of over three thousand students, and while YOU have won this battle, I will win this war!"

That night I wrote a letter to the Board of Education, citing all the facts, and also sent copies to the entire legislative body of New York City and New York State. I was in no mood for any more of this nonsense, and raged and fumed to family and friends. I was ready to sue the entire State and ALL the incompetents on the Board of Education!

My phone kept ringing off the hook, and I received daily mail from Senators and Congressmen, expressing regret at the situation, "promising not to let the matter drop, but I will investigate further," and asking what WE wanted, and "How can we help?"

To all inquiries, I said we wanted our son in a public high school and "right now!"

Dr. Feulner called to say that a new high school was presently being built in Brooklyn and that it was mandated that 10% of the student body be disabled: vision or hearing impaired, educably retarded, plus students in wheelchairs…BUT the school would not be completed for another two or three months, and would Nat consider this?

This was a far cry from the intransigence we had encountered in the past, yes, Nat would consider it, but what was he to do in the meantime? She told me that the other incoming students and teachers were to form classes in another school building, and that Nat would also be transported there.

On the incoming staff there was to be a Mr. Alan Zelon, who would be the coordinator and trouble-shooter between the disabled and non-disabled students. The school was to have a policy of integrating and mainstreaming all students, insofar as was possible, and every teacher hired for this, The Edward R. Murrow High School of Communication Arts, was to understand and agree to this before being hired. Thus, no instructor could complain about his class and its students.

The Rags of Time

On the first day at the make-shift, provisional school, I also attended to make sure everyone understood about Nat, his Portaprinter, and his other mode of communication, the spelling-mode. I provided printed sheets of instruction, and examples, for every teacher and interested student. Then I sat down with a "cuppa" to wait out the day…or to run interference. After about three hours, Mr. Zelon came to where I sat and told me he had gotten several phone calls from Senators and Congressmen, and from the "Board," wanting to know how Nat was doing.

"Mrs. Schwartz, how do these people know about Nat, and what did you write to them about his past experiences at Sheepshead Bay High School?"

"Mr. Zelon, I will NOT tell you, but if Nat's experience here is anything like the past, I'll write another letter…and you'll be the first to know!"

Needless to say, Mr. Zelon became Nat's greatest booster, though NEVER knew what I had written, and Nat made some wonderful friends and had four positive years at E.R. Murrow. When word reached the various Department heads of his superior scholastic abilities, they requested him for their classes in order to check him out for themselves. The two aides, one male, one female, were very efficient and extremely nice and cooperative, asked all the right questions, got all the explanations from Nat or from us, and Nat's years at Murrow were a daily joy.

The school was somewhat based on the Dewey School which had five terms a semester, but Murrow divided each school semester into quarters, so that if a student chose a class, from the second year on, and was not successful or did not do well enough to desire another, or did not enjoy the subject, he or she could ask to be put in another, or not be "stuck" in it for more than 8 weeks. If a student did poorly in more than one subject, he was transferred to another school because there was a large waiting list of potential students.

In his or her first year, a student was assigned to fundamental classes in Math, Science, English, Social Studies, and Foreign Language, and on his success depended his ability to progress into other and elective subjects. Because of Nat's physical and speech limitations, he decided not to take French, but continue his Hebrew studies. Also Nat doubled in English classes and Social Studies, to make sure he garnered enough credits for college admission.

The Rags of Time

THAT was always his goal, and the possibilities in this unique school made it entirely credible.

Amidst his happy days, days of triumph, and days of frustrations, Nat always made us proud by his ability to make and hold friends. Especially there were two, a fellow and a girl, who went up to Morris one day and asked if they might befriend Nat, and how would they communicate with him if he were unable to use his Printer? Morris explained about "reading his eyes" to get a fast response, and by spelling out his words, letter by letter until they knew him well enough to understand his response within a few letters. Rachel Rubin was a pretty brunette, intelligent, and from a very religious Jewish family. The boy, Jonathan Pazer, was equally bright, and the three not only became best friends, but were referred to as "the unholy trinity," for their mischief, and for always banding together, and when they were in the same classes, on several occasions, the teachers who thought Rachel and Jonathan "carried" Nat academically were shocked to find, and admitted to us, that Nat was the most gifted and innovative one, when he was in classes sans the other two!

When any disabled student came to Nat for help or advice in his role as Student Representative for Disabled Students, he often pled their case with the Principal, who, we were told, when he saw Nat coming, often buried his head in his hands. Once when Jonathan who was very dyslexic told Nat he had failed a written exam because he had great difficulty in reading the questions, Nat went to the Principal and said, "Why not give Jonathan an oral exam? After all it doesn't have to be the same one as written. Have the aide read him the questions, have him answer them, THEN grade him. It's only fair!"

Sol Bruckner, Principal, spoke with the instructor, it was done, and Jon received a grade in the 90's! Jon told us this later, at a party in our home. The trio also met at parties at their homes, since Rachel knew how to feed Nat, and Jon, how to toilet him.

Since there was no problem in these two important areas, Morris and I were able to take the trio to one of Nat's favorite places, Greenwich Village, drop them off, give them some money for the day, and turn them loose to wreak their magic, havoc and trickery, on unsuspecting Villagers. Then Morris and I got away together for a few hours, and when we picked them up later for the ride home, they regaled us with an account of their adventures. Nat was familiar with the Village from the time he was very young, and he guided the unholy trinity to many streets not usually on a tourist's map…also he found some really out-of-the-way restaurants and "gay" bars! They were too young to enter of course, but often sat at an outdoor café with sodas to, as they put it, "check out the action!"

Like Mother, like Son!

On several occasions, Nat fought his own battles of discrimination as some teachers tended to overlook his obvious ability, and we would not step in to help "unless your back is to the wall," and fight them he did, and with great success…and won tremendous respect and affection from his peers and instructors.

He came home one day with a sad face and told me that his social studies teacher had not allowed him a role in the Congress Game he presented to the class.

"Why not," queries Mom.
"Because I don't speak intelligibly!"
"What will you do about it?"
"I don't know."

"Look, Nat, let me put it this way. If you can't solve it, I won't get you any material from the library, or type up any of the information you present, nor will I intercede."

When Morris came home, Nat told him privately of his problem with the teacher who was assigning to each student the fictitious name of a Senator or Congressman from a particular State. They were supposed to vote on certain bills in Congress. Each student but Nat was assigned.

"What are you going to do about it?" queries Dad.
"I don't know. I'm stuck…and angry!"
"Listen kiddo, I'm not going to get involved unless your back is against the wall, you KNOW how we feel about justice in this house."

Nuff said!

The Rags of Time

The following day Nat came home, his face aglow. "Well," said I, "What happened?" "I told Mr. M. that since he wouldn't let me participate in the Game, I expected an 'A' for the course!"

"AND?"

"And he said reluctantly, well, okay, you can try. I think he expects me to fall flat on my face! You know who he assigned me to? Some Republican Senator from Mankato, Minnesota. Where the hell is that? Better get me a map!"

So, my very politically liberal-minded son was now a VERY conservative Senator. When Morris came home, I signaled that the "problem" was solved.

For Nat's first General Science course, the teacher assigned the class a term paper to be on any subject of their choice, and to be dealt with also as they chose. Nat? Well, he chose the subject of "Sex and the Disabled" because he was determined to share what he had learned in Het Dorp, and he sent away to various groups, Veterans Organizations, organizations which dealt with spinal cord injuries, United Cerebral Palsy, Muscular Dystrophy victims, and many pamphlets arrived, some with explicit photos, and written explanations regarding the sex act between disabled adults.

Nat was a teenager now himself, and when he was about 10 years old, had asked Morris to take him away for a weekend, just the two of them. He had things to discuss with Dad, he said, questions to ask. I was delighted to send them on their way, and while they were in upstate New York, I enjoyed the freedom of two plays, a musical, and ate out all the time, Hedonist and Sybarite that I was!

I welcomed them home, refreshed, and after Nat had gone to bed, Morris told me that Nat questioned him about sex between adults. As in everything, Morris and I never used euphemisms with Nat while discussing bodily functions. Morris was certainly not going to start now, when Nat was 15! Nat wrote his paper, even citing written sources, and providing illustrations from the pamphlets, and the report was handed in as written.

When Parent-Teacher conferences were scheduled, it was at night, and always, for us, a pleasure.

Morris asked the science teacher what the other students thought of Nat's paper, and she said that she couldn't read it to the class because none of them were "sophisticated enough to understand it!" Morris then asked what SHE thought of the report. "It is absolutely marvelous!" and she learned facts of which she was not aware…in fact she passed the report to colleagues, so impressed was she. He received an "A" as grade, and some very flattering comments.

On our drive to E.R. Murrow, I asked Morris to PLEASE let **me** at the social studies teacher. We were the only parents remaining in the classroom, and Mr. M. gushed, "I must tell you that Nat is my best student! He was the only one to research and defend his position as a very conservative Republican…and with knowledge and humor. No other student even came close to the excellence of his paper," he smiled, thinking we would be delighted.

Instead, I attacked, ever my way with injustice! "Mr. M., in that case, why did you disenfranchise my son? Why did you send a message to the class that if one is not able to speak, walk, write, in the same way as the able-bodied, they are not to be counted as citizens, indeed, are to be discarded as functioning members of our society? Nat, and we, have fought too hard, and for too long, to EVER accept such a dictum!"

After Mr. M. had recovered his composure, and apologized, and his face had regained its former color, I relented with, "I think you should know that Nat thoroughly enjoys your course, and told us that he rarely enjoyed any research as much as this, despite his diametrically opposed opinions as a liberal. We just wanted you to learn from this, and NEVER to repeat or send such a message to any other student!" We smiled, shook hands and left.

Nat had the good fortune to be in several English classes which were for him a joy. In one, he discovered he had a gift for writing poetry. We knew nothing of this until the instructor told us, and showed us his work, and with great amusement related an assignment of Nat's which dealt with the following: the class was to select a fairy tale, and update it. When he gave out the idea, Mr. Oster told us, Nat got very excited, "verbal," even raucous, rang the bell on his Printer for attention, and wrote that he wanted to be first.

Nat's idea was that Cinderella's mother was a woman of easy-virtue, a prostitute! Her daughters were ladies of the brothel run by the mother, and contrived to ensnare "Johns" such as Prince Charming, and on and on...the class was by now in hysterical laughter. All agreed that Nat's idea was excellent, and all added their own embellishments. Mr. Oster asked if Nat had reported any of this to us. No, we replied, Nat did not always share everything with us. He was loved in English classes, and whether or not the other two of the trinity were in class with him, he was always regarded with affection and respect by his peers.

In later years, Nat wrote some term papers and poetry into which, in one way or another, he wove himself and his life, and his views of life, and his personal philosophy. Some were afterwards read by me, with tears of recognition.

He had a course with a much-loved English teacher, Mr. Levitsky, who had a great influence on him, on his writing, and for whom Nat wrote so movingly, and/or with such humor, that he had the option of remaining in his class for an entire year. It was not a class one could request, rather the students were chosen by Mr. Levitsky, and of about 40 students at the beginning of a year, by the end of the 4th quarter, Nat remained as one of less than a dozen still in the class, and he was the highest regarded, and received the highest grade.

One paper which Nat wrote was so moving, and so involved his beliefs, that I feel compelled to share a portion of it.

Nat called it: THE OVERWHELMING QUESTION

Hamlet, Raskolnikov and J. Alfred Prufrock are intellectual heroes, preoccupied with thoughts of "Who am I? Why am I here? What is man?" and are represented basically as men who react to society more successfully than they act. The question, "Who am I?" is difficult to answer. I will try, by comparing Hamlet, Raskolnikov, Prufrock and myself, since I can only understand them, if I understand myself.

Early, primitive man was only concerned with his day-to-day survival. His life consisted of trying to find enough food for the day's needs, and shelter from his enemies and the elements. He didn't think about his situation in relation to the universe. He met it head-on by doing what came naturally. Early man was on the level of any other animal, and then man grew, and developed, and thought, and so we have "history."

From that point, his intellect was as important to him as food and shelter. At some point in this continuing process, Shakespeare, Dostoyevsky, and Eliot wrote.

And I write.

A character in the Broadway musical, "A Chorus Line" sings,

"Who am I anyway?
Am I my resume?
That is a picture of a person I don't know."

In every place, at any time, whether he realizes it or not, man asks, in his gut, what the song asks in "Mahagony,"

"Do you know where you're going,
And what you're hoping for?"

It takes the genius of writers and poets like Shakespeare, Dostoyevsky, Eliot, to put into beautiful words and images what not everyone can say, but all can recognize in themselves.

Who is Hamlet? Is he his public image of the young intellectual Hero-Prince that the Danes love? Or is he the boy-man who anguishes and reflects endlessly?

Hamlet expresses feelings of guilt because he cannot act on what he knows about his father's murder. All he can do is wring his hands and soliloquize:

"To be, or not to be, that is the question."

To act or not to act: that is REALLY the question. Hamlet is not a man of action. He is obsessed with the idea of his father's death, as Raskolnikov is obsessed with the idea of his mother's and sister's spiritual death if he allows their sacrifice for him. But ideas don't take revenge; ideas don't plunge knives, shoot arrows or guns. Ideas don't necessarily drive Hamlet to revenge. Ideas drive Hamlet towards more ideas. Hamlet is a man of reaction and he uses subtle, intellectual and philosophical ways, which accidentally lead to violence on his part. In a sense, he is a "premeditated" killer, yet all the violence is unpremeditated. Poor blundering Polonious is caught "behind the arras" by Hamlet and killed by mistake. Hamlet had hoped to kill Claudius, but he must have known, intellectually, that the King was elsewhere because he had just passed Claudius at his prayers, and while he "thought" of killing him, he reflected:

"Now might I do it pat, now he is praying;
And now I'll do it: and so he goes to heaven:
And so I am avenged. That would be scann'd:
A villain kills my father; and for that,
I, his sole son, do this same villain send to heaven.
O, this is hire and salary, not revenge…"

So again, the time is past and his purpose blunted. When his father's ghost appears to him in Gertrude's room, Hamlet sums up his own feelings of guilt:

"Do you not come your tardy son to chide,
That, lapsed in time and passion, lets go by
The important acting of your dread command?
Oh, say!"

Does Hamlet need goading to keep his purpose? Evidently he thinks he does. While he is busy exploring his ideas and thoughts, and "Shall I?" and "Is the moment right?" I think he must have been upset to be forced to take a stand and go into action by the demands of his father's ghost. Now he is expected to DO something! He might have happily spent a whole lifetime, since suicide was out of the question on religious grounds, in planning revenge and setting up elaborate schemes, like having the Players perform the murder from "Gonzago" to trap Claudius into a confession. Hamlet certainly enjoyed and took the time to instruct the Players in their art. Hamlet is a witty hero and enjoyed all the intellectual games this tragedy called for; it called for his best intelligence and for the best in him as a man, according to his view of himself. He sees himself as Claudius and Gertrude see him, in grief, but tells them:

"I have that within which passeth show;
These but the trappings and the suits of woe."

But what did Hamlet mean? Did he mean grief, or action, or all of these were within him? E.K. Chambers writes in "Shakespeare: A Survey":

"The tragedy of Hamlet lies…not in the content of the soliloquies, but in the fact that the soliloquies come to be uttered. It is the tragedy of the intellectual, of the impotence of the over-cultivated imagination and the over-subtilized reasoning powers to meet the call of everyday life for practical efficiency."

This applies just as well to "The Love Song of J. Alfred Prufrock." The very name, "J. Alfred Prufrock" is an odd one. It has a pompous ring, is a little ridiculous for an intelligent, carefully dressed man who is concerned with an "Overwhelming Question." Prufrock, who leads us to this overwhelming question, follows always with, "Oh, do not ask what is it?" Is our J. Alfred afraid of an absolute answer, as Hamlet is afraid to force the moment to its crisis? Or is it that Eliot means that there are no answers to life, just more clever, or complicated or stupid answers, or ways of dealing with life's problems? Prufrock doesn't compare himself with Hamlet. He says:

"No, I am not Prince Hamlet, nor was meant to be.
Am an attendant lord, one that will do
To swell a progress, start a scene or two…"

I wonder if Prufrock is saying that he, as an intellectual, can start something, but is too insecure, too reflective, like Hamlet, to follow through or make a definitive statement. Prufrock IS like Hamlet though, because Hamlet is also:

"Full of high sentence, but a bit obtuse
At times, indeed, almost ridiculous,
Almost at times, the Fool."

As in his relations with Ophelia, as in his talks with Polonius, Rosenkrantz, Guildenstern, mocking and witty. Hamlet is a wit, but he uses wit to prick, not to stab. Prufrock asks:

The Rags of Time

"And should I then presume?
And how should I begin?"

As Hamlet is a certain person or image to his people, Prufrock also has a public face. He says:

"Do I dare disturb the universe?
In a minute there is time
For decisions and revisions which a minute will reverse."

Prufrock breaks through the monotony of his life in drawing rooms and over coffee cups, over the cultured conversations, with threads of Hamlet-like reflections, little bits of soliloquies, yearnings, but with the unhappy, defeated feeling of frustration, and that he might be thought ridiculous. Hamlet thought grandly and largely, and ended in somewhat the same way. Both men are disappointed in themselves. Prufrock always brings you back to earth from intellectual wanderings by bringing back the humdrums of life. Even the rhythms are repeated and monotonous:

"In the room the women come and go
Talking of Michelangelo."

And sadly, Prufrock realizes that there will be:

"Time to prepare a face to meet the faces that you meet,
There will be time to murder and create,
(but only in his mind!)
And time for all the works and hands
That lift and drop a question on your plate;
Time for you and time for me,
Before the taking of a toast and tea."

Prufrock thinks he has seen his own death and he is afraid because he has "seen the moment of my greatness flicker," and all three protagonists, Prufrock, Hamlet, Raskolnikov, are concerned with their short passage through life and worry about its meaning, agonize, question. At the end, Eliot has a woman say:

"That is not what I meant at all
That is not it, at all."

Each time Prufrock might get an answer, or come up with it himself,
Eliot pulls him back from the knowledge, the way Hamlet pulls back
from action.

What does Eliot mean? What does Prufrock mean? Are we really supposed to know, ever? Or as in Hamlet, is it the pleasure and pain of
exploring the possibilities of life, not in finding the answers, in performing the act? Hamlet says:

"Had I but time…as this fell sergeant, death
Is strict in his arrest – O, I could tell you…
But let it be."

Dostoyevsky's Raskolnikov is a Russian with a true Slavic Soul: he is
passionate, never indifferent. Everything means something to
Raskolnikov. Nothing is meaningless; people and relationships are divided into schizophrenic patterns of joy and sorrow; anger and mad-
ness; happiness and religious fervor. I think that in "Crime and Punishment," you always know where every character stands and what he
stands for.

Raskolnikov is a schizophrenic hero who has within him both intellect
and emotionalism. They are at war within him, and that war is the
basic theme of "Crime and Punishment." Raskolnikov commits a
crime and his constant suffering and anguish is his true punishment,
not Siberia.

He desperately wants to be thought of as "extraordinary" and not be
lumped with the ordinary people of his time. He even tests out his
theory of crime by murdering the pawn-broker and Lizaveta. He
rationalizes that he murdered for money, for his sister and mother's
sacrifices, because the pawn-broker is a miserable wretch who deserves
to die; because he is sick and often out of his mind; but deep inside he
knows that he murdered for intellectual reasons, and to prove his "extraordinary" nature. Raskolnikov's theory is that society is made up of
"ordinary" and "extraordinary" men. The "ordinary" accept their lot

passively and have no right to sin. The "extraordinary," because they are chance-takers, the seekers of truth, the movers of Society, THEY have a right to sin. If they have to murder a few, it is for the good of society as a whole.

As much as Raskolnikov tries to convince himself that this is so, he cannot, and so he is punished by his guilt and suffering. In his guilt and anguish he is somewhat like Hamlet, but less like Prufrock because Prufrock's life is not lived on the same plane of emotion as Raskolnikov or Hamlet.

Raskolnikov refers to Kepler, Newton, Lycurgus, Solon, Mahomet, Napoleon, and would dearly love to be of their company in the opinion of Society. He says, "In short, I maintain that all great men or even men a little out of the common, that is to say, capable of giving some "new word," must from their natures be criminals, more or less, of course. Otherwise it is hard for them to get out of the common rut; and to remain in the common rut is what they can't submit to, from their very nature again, and to my mind, they ought not indeed submit to it…the first preserve the world and people it, and the second move the world and lead it to its goal…" "The new word," the new Jerusalem! Oh, his ego is marvelous! The new morality; he sees himself in the company of men who changed Society by their ideas, and he ended up being changed by an "ordinary" prostitute who believes in Christ and by accepting Society's rules and punishment. He hasn't risen above ordinary man after all. Raskolnikov is human, not super-human, and with a humanity people identify with, after 100 years, as they still identify with Hamlet and his humanness after 400 years.

Who am I?

To a group of disabled people, my image is that of a rock, a leader, a wise-guy who ALWAYS has an opinion, and has a fantastic ego. I probably annoy people. I act as an irritant because I can't stand injustice and I am surrounded by it. But I have to appear in this role to give myself strength, as well as others. I have my "Public Face."

How do I really feel in my gut? I feel anger and resentment and I am afraid of the future. Many nights I lie awake and scream inside me.

Some people don't look at me as they look at others. They just see a wheelchair. Earlier this year I wrote:

"Don't take away my private thoughts and dreams,
My ego cries. Oh serpent set me free.
And like a bird is eaten by a cat,
My ego tears my chains and eats at me.
This dream I've had. A bloodless Civil War.
My body is in chains. My spirits soar."

Reading these books has taught me that you have to get beneath the surface, the public image of people, to understand them, to see what motivates them. I would like the world to realize that this also applies to me.

Nat-David Schwartz January, 1977

Mr. Levitsky, the instructor, hand wrote the following on Nat's paper:

Nat,

This is more than a project. It stands as a testament almost, to striving against odds.
It is a wonder how a novel, a play, a poem can be "lived" by a reader, not just understood or analyzed, but taken as part of a world-awareness, as part of growth.
Beautifully done!

A – College
4+- Advanced Grade Level
E – Murrow

Nat was happy with his school, his friends, and with his growing reputations as a student, as a leader in the recommendations he made for the disabled, and as their ombudsman. His grades were generally excellent, and while he still smarted under the attitude of the occasional teacher who saw the wheelchair, rather than the occupant, he managed with little or no help from us. We afforded him as much freedom as possible, while remaining his safety net.

The Rags of Time

When Nat was sixteen, my mother died in our home…just died in her sleep. Morris and I had, just nine days earlier, asked her to give up her apartment and move in with us. We realized that, despite her successful recovery from two cancer surgeries, her desire not to go on was more and more apparent. She remained as always, attractive, well-dressed, vivacious, even flirtatious, but when not in a "social" mode, she was increasingly depressed.

Since my father's death, she and a lively coterie of friends, now all widowed, spent a great deal of time together, and when she was not with them, I insisted she eat dinners with us, in an effort to make sure she was eating well. She had totally given up cooking, and Morris who suggested she come live with us, asked her to cook some favorite dishes. He said he wanted to learn her recipes for "special" dishes, and I asked her to continue to give Nat "Russian lessons."

We became aware that she kept things from us, the fact that she had a bad flu and would not go to the doctor. We insisted, accompanied her to the doctor, and when she exacted from me the promise that I would never "put" her in a convalescent, or retirement home, we packed her things and brought her to us. Before we could arrange for her removal from the apartment, nine days later, she died.

Nat had already left for school, Morris picked him up, told him what had happened, and then we three arranged for her funeral. Since my mother had also, as my father, wanted cremation, we acceded to her wishes. Nat requested the same Rabbi who had officiated for my father, and we three briefed him on WHO my mother was. Nat also asked that as with my father, the Rabbi NOT put a halo on her image, that her casket be closed, and he was more truthful, I must confess, than either of us.

He told the Rabbi that, "While I didn't love my grandma as much as my grandpa, she did do some wonderful things for me, and I loved her humor and her music, and if sometimes she made me mad as hell, I will miss her!"

I couldn't have put it better myself!

While Nat continued to excel at school, if the bus company went on strike, or if he were too ill to attend, he carried on and insisted that I call the school for his homework assignments.

233

Nat's education in the realm of injustice and how one fought it, was brought to our notice in one of the more ridiculous attempts of the City and Board of Education to bridge the budget gap. They sent down the ruling that any school position from which "for any reason" someone was fired, or left of his own accord, was to be "frozen" and not refilled. Well, the female aide for the girl students had just left to move out of the City!

When Nat came home and told us, we were outraged. But worse, Murrow was utterly without any way to reverse this stupidity. Nat and I, with our VAST experience, sprung into action. We had read a few days earlier in our newspaper, that there was to be a Street Fair on the upcoming Saturday, and I told Nat that, "Dollars to Doughnuts," there were sure to be politicians in attendance because elections were in the offing, and ALL politicians were sensitive to "Photo-Ops." He and I made a plan: since the fair was within walking distance, we would arrive by 10 AM. When we set off, I told Nat that if he saw a group of people gathered in one spot, and saw Newsmen and Cameramen, he was to alert me, even if he didn't spot a politician, because Mayor Beame, who was barely 5 feet tall, was also up for re-election.

And so it proved to be!

Within half an hour, Nat let out a "Nat-yell," and we charged! I said, "Excuse me, excuse me" to many people until I reached the inner circle, and there was the Mayor, a bit startled to see a redhead pushing a wheelchair in his direction! He immediately recognized the photo-opportunity, ruffled Nat's hair, mouthed, "And how are you young man?" while I, speaking as quickly as ever I had in my life, told him of how the Board of Education's policy impacted Nat, other disabled students, and his school. I concluded with, "Sir, how would you react if your DISABLED daughter, had you one, were to be toileted by a young man?"

At this Mayor Beame, waving aside the photographers and reporters, turned and said to his Aide, "Get the information from this woman and her son, and give it to me after the Fair!" Nat and I retreated to the edge of the crowd, with our heartfelt thanks, and hopes for his re-election! Never let it be said that Susanna and Nat lost an opportunity to show respect, gratitude…or failed to take advantage of a photo-op for ourselves!

The Rags of Time

I gave the Mayor's Aide all pertinent information, and after buying some gee-gaws and ice-cream cones, we made our way home.

On Monday, I received a phone call from Mr. Zelon: "Mrs. Schwartz, what did you do and say to Mayor Beame? This morning, I heard from City Hall that the previous order has been rescinded, and the position of female aide can be filled!"

"If you have any other problems, Mr. Zelon, just tell Nat, he'll tell me, and Presto, we'll work it out!"

I was of course surprised and delighted at the Mayor's quick response…and okay, was childishly boastful! And Nat was hailed as a Hero by his fellow-students!

At the end of his third year at Murrow, Nat was proposed for, and accepted into, an Advance Placement Program at Long Island University, and for six weeks was driven there daily. He chose a course in American History and acquitted himself well, but the handwriting was on the wall, as far as college was concerned, because there was no elevator at LIU, and getting him to the class on the second floor was a problem.

In Nat's second year at Murrow, he had elected to take what Murrow called a "pre-law" course. He was eager and excited because he had considered a career in law in order to help other disabled people in receiving their "due," and also because our cousin, Bernard Jaffe, who was our lawyer, was one of his favorite people in the entire world. Of course, Bernard was someone I had loved and adored since the age of five, since he treated me with the attention and affection not accorded me by my own brother.

Nat's Law Course? After the second class, he came home and wrote, "Mom, I have never been so bored in my life! If this is what it means to be a lawyer, I'll have to think hard about some other field!" I pointed out that perhaps the teacher, a sweet young woman, was not a very good one…or perhaps this was not her subject. And, I concluded, he had just seven more weeks of boredom! Give it a shot!

The Rags of Time

Later that year, Nat opted to take a psychology course, and when he found that this same young woman was to give it, he feared the worst. When he came home from school the first day, to my "Well" he wrote, smiling, "I just loved it!" After his first term paper, Nat told his teacher of his misgivings at first, and then of his enjoyment of her class, adding, "I guess THIS is your subject, not LAW!" and she laughed and agreed. "How did you know?"

At graduation which was held at Brooklyn College, our tickets were distributed among us and the Grussgotts, and we all sat together while Nat, capped and gowned, sat with his graduating class. At the first mention of Nat's name to receive his diploma, he insisted on going onto the stage to receive it, and with the aide and Morris to help him, was placed on stage, at which time he received a thunderous, standing ovation, from his classmates, his instructors, and soon everyone in the auditorium stood, while clapping and cheering.

Nat went onstage to receive a total of five other academic awards, and one was from the New York City Chapter of the New York State Association of Teachers of the Handicapped. It seems that Nat's name was forwarded, with a letter of recommendation, from Mr. Bruckner, the Principal, plus many of his instructors, and he was presented with a certificate as 1978's Student of The Year!

There wasn't a dry eye in the house…at least not in our row!

Chapter 12

After High School graduation, what?

THAT was Nat's problem.

College and the usual academic life was not at that time an easy or predictable transition. There were few opportunities for physically disabled students at any college. We could not envision Nat at an out-of-town college, since even middle and high school had been a challenge, sometimes after great struggles on our part. Few colleges included such amenities as elevators, or had aides on hand, all of which Murrow had been so fortunate as to possess. Could Nat find a college which would offer him such fine instructors and experiences? We three thought that we might pray and strive and fight and STILL not be able to effect such a scenario.

In actuality, the past five years had taken its toll on the three of us, and Morris and I were not so young as to undertake a move to yet another State, resettle Morris in work, have the easy transportation facilities which allowed me, a non-driver, to do the ordinary things which I had as a New Yorker always taken for granted: visits to museums, libraries, theatres, not to mention caring for our small family, or entertaining large circles of friends.

Month after month, day after day, we three tried, as creatively as possible to come up with some, ANY, situation which would satisfy and feed Nat's intellectual and emotional needs. We recognized, with pain, his increasing frustration, impatience, and unhappiness, as he daily said goodbye to school friends as they left for various colleges around the country.

Many of these youngsters were not Nat's intellectual equal, and Morris and I privately asked ourselves if we had indeed done Nat a service, by making him, despite such odds, such an intellectual misfit. While we agonized, Nat wrote some wonderful, and to us painful poetry and prose, kept journals, in which he described his inner yearnings, angers, fears and disappointments.

One he called, "Speaking of Speaking," and he wrote:

When I was a baby, I gurgled, cooed, laughed, cried, and made other sounds. Now, at 18, I still gurgle, laugh, cry, and make other sounds because I have Cerebral Palsy and my speech is mainly unintelligible. How have I communicated with my parents, friends, classmates, teachers, all these years? Dear reader, let me count the ways:

My earliest memory of communication is of my parents and grandparents, "reading my eyes and sounds." Don't all parents do this with their infant children? Mine had it down to a fine Art; when they asked me a question or made a statement, if I looked in their direction, or smiled, it meant an affirmative response, or that I liked or agreed with what was said to me. A sad look, an outthrust lower lip, or tears, said only one thing to my world: "I am frustrated, unhappy, defiant, defeated or in pain," and there were plenty of replies like that!

I still have these feelings and these responses, except for one small change: I can now write them! These feelings of frustration and rage are usually based on the difficulty in making myself understood easily and quickly enough in a world that still tries to fit me, a square peg, into its round hole of what it thinks I should do, namely speak clearly and easily in the same way IT does!

I am told that I am a good listener. I have had to be, because I try to remember what is said to me, and to give back information. I remember feeling ready to explode with what I have wanted to say, witty sayings, scathing remarks, curses, almost all of my life. Even now! People think I am retarded because I am in a wheelchair and make odd sounds. I hear people ask my parents, "Does Nat understand what I am saying?" I think of wearing a sandwich board on which is printed:

I am NOT retarded
I am a high school graduate
I already have 3 college credits

Instead I hear my parents quickly run through a checklist of my accomplishments to forestall the hurt! Inside I laugh and cry. I am so sick of having people speak to me through my parents, as though I were invisible, instead of facing me directly.

(Then Nat writes of the VISTA, of the Portaprinter which Morris created for him, and which allowed him to enter public school) and to attend social gatherings with my friends, and it is with me at home. It is my "voice" that writes out my wishes, hopes, despair, anger, curses. There are my 'for my eyes only' messages that I ask to have removed from my Printer, unread. After all, everyone has to get things off his chest now and again. Would you believe I "yell" at my dog with it? Too bad Dolly can't read!

Now I'm told that this method is "too slow and inefficient" for society!

My feelings at this verdict are rage and self-doubt and real aggression towards a system that would reward me for trying so damn hard, and then reject me when I had almost reached my goal! I felt as though I had been "playing school" and had not been taken seriously, and that I had been lied to and deceived all along!

My senior year at Murrow was a chore and a trial. I no longer knew what to do, where to go, how to find a program I could fit into. Even the Vocational Center of U.C.P. refused to see me because I was "too disabled"!

What the hell does the world want?

A month ago, my mother heard of a possibility which we investigated: a new program offered by the New Jersey Institute of Technology in Newark. What I saw there slowly pushed open the door society was slamming shut in my face! Not hoping for much, I met with three professors and an assortment of engineering students some of whom were blind. One professor was blind, another is physically disabled, others were able-bodied.

They explained their humanistic concept of teams of students, the able and the disabled together, who work on, and develop special aids and models to permit disabled students to study and work in the mainstream of science and engineering! It's a new and exciting idea, and has got to be the way to go! They are going to include me in their program, and try to come up with a way for me to plug into the computerized, sophisticated, electronic R2D2 technology of the twentieth century.

I, in turn, will assist blind students by my good eyes, to inform them of the readings of certain of their instruments, also my Portaprinter will, through its bell, give them answers for the use of their scientific instruments, not "brailed"!

World, keep your wires crossed for me…I hope I'm on my way!

(Nat Schwartz, 1978)

The State of New York evidently felt that Nat deserved to be financially supported in light of his academic successes in the Edward R. Murrow High School of Communication Arts, and willingly paid his tuition fees, PLUS they picked him up and transported him to New Jersey daily. I went along to act as aide, taking books to read, a small sketch pad, and my curiosity to see and understand how this intelligent, European-sounding curricula worked. I also felt it important to show Nat that his independence WAS important and appreciated.

I was "on call" when Nat changed classrooms, or required toileting, or when I fed him the lunch I daily brown-bagged for us. I was also on tap if there were questions about Nat's academic past, while he was busy dealing with his future! For two years I watched as groups of students undertook to satisfy Nat's need for a "good" and effective page turner, which after years of searching for, had led Morris, brilliant engineer that he was, to the conclusion that none existed. It could not be bought, "not even for ready money" as Oscar Wilde put it in his greatest play (in OUR opinion), "The Importance of Being Ernest." Why did not Morris take the time to invent one? Simply, there was NO time which was not allotted to the more important task of his making a living.

I watched as students made blueprints from their sketches, and used ordinary chewing gum, Velcro-like substances of thin metal, cord, paper clips, all meant to move across the page just read, and "grab" the next page, and so on. Problems arose, just ONE page, please, not two or three! Also the structure, easel really, to hold the magazine, book, newspaper, or whatever, page of text, upright and balanced, just never seemed to serve its purpose! Remember, these were engineering students, and their grades were also based on their "inventions," successful or not. They had to show effort, ingenuity, and an understanding of the project.

Nat was very complimentary, grateful, and hid his amusement at some of the more Rube Goldberg-ian results!

Meanwhile, Nat was busy adapting his Printer and its special features, mainly the bell, for use by the legally blind students some of whom had been professionals in the field of engineering. In several instances, he "read" or informed the other student after he had been taught how to read their equipment, on when a certain number or "level" on a gauge was reached. All this he did readily and was delighted to be helpful…and correct!

The Institute of Technology put out a monthly publication called "NEXUS," and in volume 6, No.2, January, 1980, an article appeared, with a photo, showing Nat, Professor Herman, and Bill Kappler, an unsighted mechanical engineer, and which discussed their work together.

In the article it said that, "Nat Schwartz is confined to a wheelchair which looks rather jaunty with a denim bag slung under its handle. He has virtually no use of his arms and legs and he cannot talk. He does however have control of his neck muscles which enable him to operate a switch by pushing against it with his head."

"It is this one controllable function which is the key to communication for Nat. Another key is this young man from Brooklyn's strong, gutsy personality, which reveals itself even in small ways like sporting a beard. His mother recalls him saying angrily to his therapists and doctors when he was younger, "Don't talk down to me."

Then this page-long article goes on to speak of Nat's education, and of his meeting with Dr. Harry Herman, Professor of Mechanical Engineering at the Institute, and of Bill Kappler who lost his vision due to juvenile diabetes. Dr. Herman directs the program, officially called "Physically Handicapped in Science," in the Macro-Lab at the Technological University, connected with Rutgers University, into which Nat was immediately accepted.

Nat stayed with this program, worked with other students, and then one day was told that in order to "come into the twentieth century," he needed to be hooked up to a computer. "Great," said Nat and we! "How do I go about this?" asked Nat.

Good question! We were informed that the Mechanical Engineering students would put their collective brains together, their collective minds to the problem, and enlist Nat's good brain in order to ascertain in what manner, and how, the computer device might work. They decided to apply for a Grant-in-Aid. Nat enthusiastically worked on the wording, made suggestions, having gone through much similar thought when Morris worked on the Portaprinter. At that time, whenever Morris hit a snag, he enlisted the help of two electronic engineers, whom he had hired, for advice. Nat was similarly involved when the engineers turned to him for his "input" on a reality level.

Problems arose when Nat was told that because he was a sophomore and the others juniors, HE among all would not be entitled to a piece of the financial pie! Nat felt that this injustice perpetuated all the other injustices he had endured. He suggested that if ALL the other students pooled a small amount of their possible grant money, it might make Nat's work equally monetarily worthy. Next, Nat, who smarted under their lack of understanding, informed the other students that if he were not to be considered on an equal footing with them, well, okay, then what he already had written was to be deleted, together with his name…they were on their own, could continue sans his help!

Nat, a true Jaffe-Schwartz, hated injustice and realized that yet again lip service might be paid to the appreciation of, and to the value of the disabled, but that was as far as it went. Nat insisted on recognition in the same vein as his peers, and although it might appear as though he were cutting off his nose to spite his face, the students had not as yet invented anything remotely useful for him and other disabled folk, and Nat had progressed much further with his family and other "professionals."

Professor Herman, kind man that he was, tried to dissuade Nat from his defection, but Nat asked him when might HE receive a computer? Would it be in the twenty-first century?

The Rags of Time

Unfortunately, before the Professor could get back with an answer, Morris suffered a heart attack, and everything, including Nat's schooling, was no longer as important as the saving of his father's life, and getting him home from the hospital.

It was fortunate that our next-door neighbor was a nurse, and responded at once when I rang her bell at night, examined Morris, and when I called the physician son of my best friend Dorothy Ross, he said, "don't waste time waiting for me, just have an ambulance rush him to Kings County Hospital, and I'll meet you there with a cardiologist!" Kings County was part of Downstate Medical Center, a teaching hospital, and when we arrived, Jonathan Ross met us and introduced us to Dr. Alan Lieberman who swept me aside, confirmed the diagnosis, and took over Morris' care. Morris kept repeating over and over, in complete denial, "I can't be having a heart attack! We're going to Connecticut! I CAN'T be having a heart attack!"

They sent me home in a taxi, with the assurance that they would be in constant touch with me. Nat had been so frightened when I went with Morris in the ambulance that our neighbors stayed with him until I came home with personal reassurance. I HAD to be sure, because it was our "group" intention that Morris would NOT die! Our will would not permit it! I intoned my Atheist prayer, whatever that was, and was awake all night, and at daybreak, began calling friends and family, anywhere, everywhere, and set up my personal calendar for people to drive Nat's van to the hospital in order for Nat to be able to see for himself that Morris was alive, and also lined up people to stay with Nat while I made taxis my life every night when I visited the hospital.

At this pace, I discovered after several days, that Nat and I might die before Morris, because the immediate cessation of caffeine and cigarettes had turned him into a smoke-free maniac! Morris, who was used to 3 or 4 packs a day, plus about 10 cups of coffee, was a termagant, and I called Dr. Lieberman to ask if I could vent my anger at his behaviour, or must I curb my tongue, and I promised him ANOTHER patient…ME! He told me that I was free to tell Morris anything I might have said before his heart attack. Having his permission made it a bit more possible for me to relax, and curb the worst of my temper. You know, there is no one more impossible to live with than an ex-smoker.

The Rags of Time

I had, some years earlier, quit my maybe one-pack-a-day oral habit, cold turkey, by convincing myself that I couldn't breathe! I simply awoke one morning, and as was my wont, lit a cigarette, a small cigar really, before I took my first cup of coffee, and before I woke Nat to get him ready for school. At that habitual move on my part, I suddenly realized that I, I, was a slave to this filthy, smelly habit, put out the cigarette, and after Nat left, broke all the cigarettes in the carton except for one pack, and threw them into the toilet, and divided the remaining pack, leaving one cigarette in each ashtray in the house, while the rest followed its mates into the toilet. I told myself that if I became desperate, I had a cigarette! After some weeks you can imagine the condition of these "smokes"! I never smoked again, and although I must have driven Nat and Morris crazy by my mood swings and generally maniacal withdrawal behaviour, we three survived. I have never been tempted to smoke at any time since.

I just came across some Canon strips used by Nat on the Portaprinter on which he wrote, "So help me, if I could, I would run away. Since Mom gave up smoking, she is impossible!"

I'm sure I was!

My present theory is a better one, and occurred to me as usual, unreasoned, and on the spur of the moment. It came to me when I was introduced to the young, perhaps 22 year old, son of a friend while Morris and I were in Mystic. We met by chance and while speaking together in front of a clothing shop, he lit a cigarette. To his and his mother's, also a smoker, and Morris' surprise, I burst out with, "You are so young and handsome, instead of smoking, why don't you masturbate? It's better for your lungs, keeps your hands occupied, is more pleasurable, and to my knowledge, no one has ever died of it!"

Well, his mother never forgot it! How the son, after surprise and shocked laughter, reacted, and if he quit smoking, I'm not sure, but if they repeated my outrageous remark to others as an anecdote, perhaps SOMEONE quit! Of course, I have yet to figure out how public smokers act on this advice!

About a year before Morris' heart attack, he and I had decided to look for a house in Connecticut because New York was becoming for us well-nigh unlivable. The filthy streets, the mounds of refuse piled each night in front of restaurants, the neglect of middle and low income neighborhoods, was increasingly evident. People formed neighborhood watch groups to change conditions and "take on" the politicians and the police department, in order to try to halt the increase in crime and burglaries and also the noise of sanitation trucks and the men on them, as in the middle of the night, perhaps at 3 or 4 AM, they yelled gaily to each other and slung empty cans on sidewalks, and kept other hard-working citizenry awake five nights a week.

My neighbors, especially those from surrounding apartment houses, finally elected me as "block captain" as they gathered in my living room to voice their complaints and discuss what course to pursue. They knew something of our experience with Nat's educational woes, and of our activism. I explained that we needed more than letters or phone calls of complaint.

Accordingly, I both taped the sounds of trash collection and photographed evidence of filth left on the streets AFTER they had been cleaned, and sent both pieces of evidence to the Head of the Sanitation Department in our borough by registered mail. Within the week, there appeared on my doorstep, a Captain, wearing his gold-braided uniform and hat. Holding my letter and tape and photos, and his identification badge, he very nicely apologized, and told me it would not happen again.

And it did not, for as long as we lived on the street!

What remained to accomplish was to protect the residents of the apartment houses from thefts of brass and copper pipes, and of porcelain sinks and toilets from any empty apartment. This equipment was sold by the thieves to supply their drug habits. There were also nights when we were awakened by women's yells or screams, and Morris, in his robe over pajamas, often went out to investigate.

I drafted a letter to the Chief of Police, outlining the situation, and said the worst "crime" would be if the police failed to respond to the complaints of our neighbors because of their color or economic status, and if there were no resolution to this problem, I would take these complaints to our Congressmen and Senators as a "first step!"

Needless to say, I received letters and phone calls expressing "earnest willingness and determination" to redress the situation. I wish I could say that all criminal activity ceased, but alas, 'twas not so! Indeed, our own home was burglarized three times, the thief never discovered, although Morris and I suspected the culprit and barred entrance to one family with whom we met, and chalked it up to our inability to recognize the changing times.

Morris kept warning me to keep my tongue behind my teeth! However I insisted on confronting the kids who rode their bicycles at break-neck speed on sidewalks. I simply stood there, with my arms outstretched, to DARE them to knock me over! None did, but soon, I, who always felt secure while pushing Nat in his wheelchair anywhere in our neighborhood, now began to remove all my jewelry, including my wedding rings, because these bikers were now in the habit of speeding past women wearing necklaces, earrings, carrying purses, and pulling the jewelry from their necks, ears, grabbing purses, and speeding off.

I had always thought and voiced, "Surely no one would attack a mother pushing a wheelchair!" Now sadly, I realized that I was a target, simply BECAUSE I would not leave the wheelchair to give chase! I now removed all jewelry as I walked out, put in only a handkerchief, wallet, comb, pencil, pad, and anything Nat might require for his comfort. I certainly did NOT take his Portaprinter!

It reached the point that Nat, hearing my "behind my lips" grumbled anger and resentment, was quick to spell out, "dammit, don't take me out if you're going to be angry all the time!"

We two, accustomed to rambling and walking the streets of Brooklyn, going to Prospect Park to attend free concerts, or watch tennis matches, or to find books at the Brooklyn Main Library, and going to the Brooklyn Museum, or to have a picnic of bagel and cream cheese in the Park's Rose or Botanical Gardens, were now virtual prisoners of our more immediate environment.

The above was made worse by Mayor Wagner's opening of a Methadone Center a few blocks from our home. You can imagine how the area emptied of the middle-class, as they sold their homes and moved to the safer "suburbs," and how this little redhead LOATHED the idea! I didn't want to leave my beautiful home, didn't want to leave the City's musical, artistic, theatrical, treasures to move to a state I somewhat knew, but also knew was bounded by strangers! After all, we knew no one personally in Connecticut. Morris' family from Moodus were almost all dispersed, his much-loved Aunt Lena and Uncle Philip both deceased.

In the past, Morris and I thought that perhaps when he retired, we might look for a home in either Manhattan or Connecticut. Nat was never very enthusiastic about moving from New York and those disabled and able-bodied friends with whom he attended school, socialized, and visited in the company of friends or paid companions. He had attended several "special" camps in upstate New York or in Connecticut, and had made friends with other campers and staff, and enjoyed the experience and was well-liked. His leadership ability asserted itself, and he was termed an "idea" man. And he did enjoy going with us to various restaurants, and despite his "kosher" childhood, soon became, as were we, a lobster-lover, able to devour two, if Morris removed the meat from the shell.

But that is definitely not all of life!

We always called Connecticut our "why not" State, because whenever we entered a movie house or restaurant there, or any type of amusement area, Morris always explained that, "we travel with someone in a wheelchair, and can we be accommodated?"

"Why not?" was the inevitable answer.

An artist friend since Cooper Union days, Rosie Entman, now lived with her husband and two children in East Haven, and she became my advisor and mentor on life in Connecticut. "Don't move here," she said, "unless you have a circle of friends, because Connecticut folk are NOT friendly, are suspicious of any newcomer who hasn't lived here for 40 years!" She then told us of many instances when she was only accepted as the "wife" to the man who was almost the first administrator of an adult-living center. Today this experimental center is known as an "Assisted Living Center," and her husband was an early geriatric specialist.

I suggested to Rosie that she behave in a flamboyant manner, and pass herself off as a neurotic New York Artist who had no time for the vagaries of small-town life! She tried this approach and it did work for a while…until she divorced and moved on…or back…to her New York roots.

What finally decided our move was a visit that Morris had scheduled with people at M.I.T. and which was planned as part of our summer vacation one summer. They were to meet Nat and see the Portaprinter which had so changed his life by giving him the ability to communicate and be educated in the main-stream of public school life in New York. Surely, Nat was the best advertisement for this wondrous machine and its intelligent letter-board.

I say, "what decided us," but it would be more accurate to have said, "what deterred us" from our appointed course…or, "stayed us!"

We could not enter Boston…not get anywhere near it, from any direction, because a "Big Dig" was in progress, and the miles-long, parking lot conditions, caused Morris to exit the highway in ANY direction as soon as possible. From a public phone, Morris called to explain and cancel that meeting, and we spent the night at a motel in Rhode Island. The next day, Morris told Nat that we might try a "You CAN go home again" tour of Connecticut. Would he like that?

We went first to Moodus, the town in which Morris spent three happy years with his uncle, aunt, and their eight children. None of them were in residence of course, but as we drove up to the old frame farmhouse, the present occupant came out of her front door, and when Morris explained who we were, she gasped, yelled, "Wait a minute please!" and disappeared into the house. She emerged a few minutes later with a post card showing Morris' beloved Aunt Lena standing in front of the house. The postcard had served as advertising when the farm was also run as a "kochalein," which is Yiddish for "cook yourself," and meant, he explained to Nat, that each of the small cottages bordering the main house had facilities in which the Jewish families who rented them for some weeks, or the entire summer, could provide meals for themselves.

These "boarders" also had the option of eating in the main house where Aunt Lena cooked their meals, helped by the small army of children whose chores consisted of peeling carrots, snapping beans, or gathering fresh eggs from the chicken house, of feeding the livestock, like cows, and running errands.

Uncle Philip was spared these tasks, except as general, (and "General") overseer, and stern rule-and-task-assignment-giver on weekends when he returned from New York City, where he was employed as a baker. All the children, including Morris, had chores, which meant getting up between four and five in the morning, then after chores, washing up, eating breakfast, to be ready for the 7:30 AM bus, or hike, to school.

For all the 45 years Morris and I were married, he spoke with great love, and with humor, of these two good people. Uncle Philip was Morris' mother's brother. Morris told of once when he helped with the haying, Uncle Philip strode over to him, yelling, "Why aren't you in school?" accompanied by a slap to his face. When Morris explained that this was a school break, Philip said, "Well, that's for any time you DO cut school!"

Morris loved to explain to Nat the ritual of weekend mealtimes. They all sat around a groaning board of foods of all sorts. Philip sat at the table's head, all plates before him. He always asked as he filled a plate, "Is this enough?" If the answer was affirmative, the plate was passed to the child, and so on, until all the children had plates of food. A negative reply, and Philip added food a bit at a time, until the child was satisfied.

Woe to the child who asked for more and did not eat all on his plate. He might have to sit there until the next mealtime! Harsh? Not really. There was a lot of talk about how blessed these children were. One could always have more, but they also had the lesson of greed, and its result given them!

Aunt Lena? She never ate with the rest of the family. She prepared, then served the food, and retired for mealtime, to eat in peaceful seclusion, away from a husband and from eight or ten demanding children.

Oh yes, and in the dining room, NO talking was permitted at mealtime. It was not that Philip was so strict, but it emphasized that eating was serious business. Afterwards, one went to one's chores, or if none, went out to play.

During school nights, Lena was in charge, and homework was done around the kitchen table, while Lena went to each child in turn, checking their work. She, who could scarcely read or write English, told the teachers during parent-teacher's conferences, that "the children don't get enough homework!"

How Morris came to live with them, the youngest charge of Philip and Lena's family, was that when he was eight, he ran away from home and hitch-hiked from New Jersey to Moodus. He had $1.00 plus change when he left, and told whopping tales to people in cars or truck-drivers, who questioned his solitary presence, "My uncle in Moodus is expecting me. He will meet me in New Haven." …or whatever! And he did get as far as Moodus, and walked to the Auster Farm, where Lena's questioning elicited the reason: he was desperately unhappy!

Morris' mother had died during the influenza epidemic of 1928, and he and his two older brothers were farmed out to strangers, or sent to orphanages, so their father could go to work. Morris was 18 months old at the time he was orphaned, and except for one photo, had little recollection of her. His two brothers fared a bit better, because they, by now, were more independent.

When his father remarried, the family was reunited once more. Problems arose when this beautiful woman supposedly cared for them. Actually, she tried to kill each of the boys in turn. The oldest brother was almost poisoned, when she, "by mistake, oh, so sorry" put some cleaning substance in his food. Sometime later, she hit Morris' middle brother with a brick, as he slept. When the boys told their father of her mistreatment, he didn't believe them. When Morris was eight, he had a tonsillectomy at a doctor's office, and afterwards at home, she turned the gas on in the stove, and left the house, leaving him home alone. Smart boy that he was, he opened the window and ran to a neighbor, and while his voice was barely a croak, they ran in and shut off the pilot-light.

"Oh, so sorry, what a terrible mistake to have made. I was preparing some tea for myself, was going to put on the kettle, forgot to light the burner, and went out for some ice-cream for Morris."

Even then, after hearing from the neighbors, his father refused to believe that any of these attempts were more than "mischance"! Morris in telling these tales said, "Well, he slept with her, not with us!" Goldie resembled the famous "IT" girl, Clara Bow, of silent films and early talkies, and was thought a beauty by all who met her…and his father was smitten.

Morris loved his life with the Auster family, and they were devoted to him. Whenever his father visited the farm, the children hid him in the barn and cautioned Aunt Lena, "Don't let them take him!" However, there came the day when his father tricked him by returning after he had supposedly driven off, and insisted that Morris move home. Morris often said that although he did, he was able to survive because he met Herman and his mother and Aunt Cora, and like his Aunt Lena, they loved him and protected him and gave him the affection and sense of "family" that his own kin denied him.

From my personal knowledge of the Goustin family, and of the Schwartzes, I must agree with Morris' reiteration that his friendship with Herman kept him from becoming, as he often said, "an utter bum!" In this case, in psychological terms, it was more "nurture" than "nature"!

Back to Connecticut…this trip introduced Nat to the Grove School which had by this time gone from being a school for emotionally disturbed youngsters, to a school for addicted boys. It was no longer Jess Perlman's domain. The present Director, after I introduced us, was very welcoming, told us to look around and invited us to lunch. Nat was familiar with something of the school as, through the years, I wove anecdote after anecdote of the children and my life there (selectively of course!) and we spent a pleasant afternoon.

We wanted to spend a few days in a motel on the Shoreline in Old Saybrook, but when we arrived, the only accommodations were on the upper floor…patently impossible! We drove around a bit in that lovely town, and Morris asked the owner in an antiques shop where we three might stay. She referred us to a motel in East Lyme, "The Starlight Motel." It was some 13 miles north of Old Saybrook, and just off exit 74. It had a pool, the buildings were accessible, and there was a restaurant on the premises.

Mr. Miller who ran the motel was friendly, charming, and when he met Nat, he gave us the largest of available rooms. It had an "ell" with a third bed, and a small sink and refrigerator, and two-burner hot-plate. All the amenities, but only the pool and restaurant seduced me. I was certainly NOT going to cook while on vacation!

For Nat the swimming pool was all-important, and he and Morris shed their clothes, put on swimsuits, and we all headed for the pool. Nat was put into his double swim-rings. Two, because if one broke, he had a back-up! Nat was a fish! He absolutely loved water, was fearless if dunked under, came up spluttering and laughing, and true to their past history in pools, Morris went onto the diving board, dove in, and came up under Nat, between his legs.

The Rags of Time

Oh, they were a pair!

I, never a strong swimmer, or so foolhardy as to essay a dive, swam a bit at the lower end and acted as ballast for Nat while Morris did some serious diving and swimming. We so enjoyed our stay at the Starlight that in the future, Morris had just to phone Mr. Miller, and he reserved the most convenient room for us, and let us bring our dog Dolly who was always, in Mr. Miller's words, "the model guest. Dolly doesn't smoke and burn holes in furniture or get drunk or make loud noises at night. She is welcome ANY time."

A few trips into the town itself, some three miles away, convinced us that a town whose Main Street bordered Long Island Sound was our kind of town. That end of town was called Niantic and had more attractions, and all my life I have lived fairly close to water…whether seen or not.

But as you recall, water IS one of my birth signs!

When first we decided to employ a real estate agent, we came across an attractive young woman who seemed not to realize that a Levittown type of house or one which was too far for a walk into town, was NOT what we wanted, and despite all the descriptions we gave, and explanations we made, because she was "new" to the territory, just having married the boss' son, she explored Connecticut with us in tow, as her guinea pigs.

When we managed to extricate ourselves from her clutches, we did better, and followed a lead to a house not too far from the center of town, but rather too far to walk. What thrilled Nat was that the property had both a running brook AND an above ground pool! Morris envisioned building a ramp to the deck around the pool for Nat's convenience. The house itself was the cleanest I had ever seen. My own home, while neat and organized, was not as clean. The owner who lived in it alone, was charming and helpful and so several days later, before returning to New York, we put down money as security until we could see to a mortgage at a local bank, and set about to sell OUR home.

It was at this time that Morris had his heart attack, and why he went into denial.

The Rags of Time

When I called the owner and asked her to release us from the contract, she was upset and disappointed, and said she'd hold the house for us as long as necessary. "I'm sorry, but I can't commit to a time frame. I don't know if Morris will survive this, or how long his convalescence will be, if he does. At this time I can't have this hanging over me! Please, keep the money, I don't care about the money!"

I was distraught. Here was a situation even a gutsy redhead couldn't control. I was terrified! I couldn't imagine the loss of Morris. At home, as far from Nat's room as I could get, with my fist shoved in my mouth, I wept, and silently screamed my rage at heaven, at any Deity in whom I could not believe, but who might in some sort of greater-than-belief, take pity not on ME, but on Nat, to whom enough had been done…despite HIS belief in the greatness and goodness of a God figure!

Surely, THAT was enough to tip the skewed scales which condemned a pure spirit, Nat's, to the disappointment of a completely empty spiritual life! Why blame or lump Nat with his parents, who had never asked God for anything, and who had always averred that a world in which God was worshipped, if indeed there WAS a God, surely He, She, It, did not punish such a one as Nat for something in no way his fault.

I kept asking how one could believe in a vengeful God! People were vengeful, not the God prayed to by all peoples, everywhere on earth, no matter the Name they conferred. If God were not good and just, and we ascribed to HIM, HER, IT, human virtues and vices, who the hell needed HIM, HER, IT! But the God Man created was always in Man's Image. This I have ALWAYS believed! No hypocrite, I!

Every morning I made all the rational decisions, prepared my schedule of transportation, unashamedly relied on, and asked others for help, which they freely gave. Those days I used to say, despite all our struggles to give Nat a good, productive, independent life, that I believed in the Human Spirit. I hoped that there were enough compassionate beings who, during our lives, had NOT turned their backs on us, on Nat, to tilt the scales of my disbelief…or Unbelief.

I remember what my father had said to Nat once, when Nat complained that an injustice had been done him, that someone else had been credited for an accomplishment of Nat's: "Nat," said he, "Pray to ME, not God, because I love you, and you cannot always rely on God's justice! So pray to ME, and say, 'My grandpa loves and blesses me!' I bless you!"

This, from a former Yeshiva-Bocher, to whom Nat looked up, as one looks to perfection. Nat believed his grandpa was in Heaven, and that he could bargain with God for his father's survival. I've always liked that aspect of Judaism, that Jews speak directly with God.

There is no middle-man! Jews feel free to rail at, yell at, curse, question God, and not worry about retribution! On Yom Kippur, the Day of Atonement, man is supposed to forgive his enemies, ask to be forgiven by them in turn, repay debts, or hope they will be expunged for the New Year.

Morris survived.

In fear that he might not survive if we remained in New York City, daily, when home from the hospital, I packed books, rolled carpets, newspapered china in cartons, put clothes in valises. In my "magical thought" process, I reasoned that if Morris could see that we WERE going to move to Connecticut, that I was making preparations, even though we had not as yet sold our home or had anywhere to go, specifically, then EMOTIONALLY, we were on our way!

Dr. Lieberman had told me that if one suffered a heart attack, and Morris had suffered two more episodes in the hospital, the least damage might happen to the upper left ventricle. While in the hospital, in tobacco and caffeine withdrawal, Morris phoned me daily and begged me to bring him cookies, candy, fruits. I obliged, and the problem now swung in the opposite direction. My slim, V-man-figured husband could not get enough sweets, even the low-caloried goodies I looked for, and sometimes consumed them so quickly, that before I exited the hospital, they were already eaten.

His rationale was that until he stopped smoking, he never really appreciated the taste of food! By the time Morris was discharged, he had gained 20 pounds, and the doctors cautioned him against gluttony.

But I was right! The day Morris came home and saw the packing boxes, cartons, rolled rugs, and read the ads I put into newspapers offering our home for sale, he WAS encouraged, and didn't dwell on his illness. But I awoke many times during the night to convince myself that yes, Morris WAS breathing. A neighbor who visited told Morris that she always considered our home, "a home of love," and offered to buy it, wanted it desperately, she said, told us it was the only house that so appealed to her, her husband and teenage son. So, Morris was "Heartened" and we were again on the path of activity.

We three never thought of it, or considered it a difficulty. Indeed it went along with our professed lack of prejudice, but since the potential buyers were Black, the bank to which they applied for a mortgage, evidently DID think it was a problem. The buyers called, the wife in tears, to say that they were refused a mortgage, that the bank told them the refusal was based on our neighborhood's being "red-lined!"

I had never heard that term before and learned that New York City, in its wisdom, and in cahoots with banks in the area, now considered certain neighborhoods not worthy taking a chance on! And they drew on the map of the borough, a red-line encircling the neighborhood…and the red-line included our beautiful street, and the beautiful homes therein. I was sure that Vincent Price was NOT amused, his home being just a few blocks from ours.

I told the buyer's wife to dry her tears, that I would see to THAT! Not to worry! I went into action as in the past. I wrote a letter to then-Mayor Koch, the first line of which, after the formal salutation read, "You're always asking, 'How am I doing?' Well, Mr. Mayor, you are doing badly indeed!"

I explained that this family, Black, both adults gainfully employed, with two adult children, likewise employed, and a teenage son who was a top student at his high school were ideal homeowners, and "are you against upward mobility for people who just want what we all want, a good future for themselves and their children? I'm ashamed of a democratic system which preaches upward mobility and then denies it to decent, hardworking people, and which aligns itself with corporations and banks which desire a safe-guard for themselves, and NOT for the people who trust them to safe-guard THEIR interests! They are not aware of people, but the profit-motive that has them turning handstands to appease the upper echelon which has no concept of what is 'The greater good!'"

The Rags of Time

"Yes, Mayor Koch, in my book you are doing very badly indeed!"

The letter went off "express mail, return receipt requested" and within the week I received a joyous, albeit teary call from the couple's wife who so craved our "home of love." She told me that the letter had ended up in the hands of the Mayor's Department of Human Development. It seems that the Mayor told them to investigate the matter, and to "speedily resolve it." So the Schwartz/Jaffe principles of justice had again prevailed.

The price of our house proved a temporary glitch to a speedy conclusion, so we took back a second-mortgage, deciding if it were not repaid, we'd simply put it down to experience. Actually, it was repaid in full, when the Minister-husband died a short time later, and the widow repaid it out of the insurance she received. Sometimes a kind act brings out the best in others, and we felt that our trust and lack of prejudice was once again rewarded.

Shall I say that a worthy principle is its own reward? Probably not…too soppy!

Within a couple of months, when the cardiologist gave his permission, we drove to Connecticut, but Morris was not allowed to drive our van, so an engineer friend drove up with us. Before we left, my cousin/lawyer expressed his dismay that we were driving up without a house to move into. How did we know we would find a suitable house? But we three had the feeling that we would be lucky! "Oh, we'll find one…or stay until we do," was my "tough it out, and I feel lucky in my gut" reply.

My reliable "gut" hadn't yet let me down.

We pulled in to "our" motel in East Lyme, we three explorers, and friend, and dog Dolly. We contacted a real estate agent listed in the local newspaper, and set out to locate our new home.

Chapter 13

We told the real estate agent that we would like to find a house on water, some water, any water! There were no houses available on Long Island Sound which were within Morris' "magic circle." He had drawn on a local map, and from a point of the protractor which he positioned at a corner of Main St. and Pennsylvania Avenue, he circled the distance of a mile within the radius. He told the agent that since I did not drive, this is as far as he would expect me to walk, especially since I would often be pushing my son in a wheelchair.

The second house she took us to see was the one we bought. It was on a fresh water pond, and the marsh bordering it was a bird sanctuary, or so it appeared to us.

For a city-bred girl from Brooklyn and Manhattan who recognized a sparrow and a robin and not much else, I was in shock to see an assortment of waterfowl, large and small, none of which we could identify, but a hastily purchased bird book by Roger Tory Peterson soon solved that problem, plus the pair of binoculars which soon resided permanently on a window sill. Once in our new home, we spent many happy hours and identified large and small heron, all manner of ducks and drakes, and visually "owned" a pair of mute swans.

Even before we bought our house, we knew at first sight, that we were "fated" to live in it! There were two reasons that this house HAD to belong to us. The first was that on a prior visit to Niantic, as we drove street by street, and saw all the cul-de-sacs, and twists and turns, we actually drove down what turned out NOT to be a through-road, but the driveway to a house on the corner. We immediately turned out of it and Morris turned to the agent, saying, "My wife doesn't drive but is a great walker."

Thank you, Darling, for that vote of confidence!

257

The Rags of Time

An equally compelling reason was that the small, unstylish ranch house had, in its kitchen, totally empty except for a sink under the window, in direct proximity, two colors I most loathed. The half wall to the ceiling was of a repellant apple-green, and it sat atop plastic tiles of an equally repellant pink. This gorgeousness ended at the floor which was covered by linoleum patterned in a spatter-design which looked as if "someone vomited over it."

When Morris saw this combination of ugliness, he whispered to Peter, our engineer consultant and traveling companion who checked for copper pipes, "This has **got** to be Susan's house, with colors like this!" And right he was! This house with the view that I always refer to as "the second most beautiful! I don't know who has the first, so I call it modestly, the SECOND" just had to belong to us!

And the Birds!

All ownership of nature is visual. I don't believe we can "own" nature. We can just attempt to organize it a bit, and as in the Hippocratic Oath, "First Do No Harm!"

We were fortunate that our new, undistinguished, but overpriced ranch house was bordered by a pond, State-owned, and by woods which yielded owls, peregrine, and other falcons, and both great blue and smaller black-backed heron, which made their homes in its trees.

One season, a glossy-ibis paid a visit, and each year we see the American heron, white and lovely, and snow geese, and Canada geese, and in the pond and above, are swooping kingfishers, osprey, and at our feeders gorge cardinals, hummingbirds, chickadees, tufted titmice, orioles, and on and on! We plant to attract many birds and butterflies, and dragonflies, and they visit and eat us out of much money!

We were also fortunate that the land we own slopes so steeply to the woods and the pond that the Town refuses to permit any home to be built there, since no fire-truck could negotiate it.

Oh, Glory and Hallelujah!

The Rags of Time

I write of nature as my neighbor because it is much safer and more friendly…and soul-satisfying. The one-third acre which is our land, was completely devoid of anything more than tall, unmown grass, one scrubby bush which may or may not have been an azalea, and bordered by scrub willows, marsh maples, but when the grass was mown, and we set out a round table and chairs, we had what Morris called, "our back 40" and began the slow process of acclimatizing ourselves to our new environment.

We were now "in the country" and soon friends and family angled for invitations. When they came, I was chief cook and bottlewasher, and resented it not a little! We had, within the first week of our move, had the 3 front steps to the front door removed and replaced by a ramp, and had a short wall removed because a wheelchair is not able to turn a sharp 90° angle, then the walls were painted white until we decided on what furniture we wanted, and where.

On the day we moved in, we went to buy a stove, refrigerator and a clothes dryer, because we now lived in a state where electricity ruled. The thing Morris insisted on was that the appliances we purchased must ALL be delivered the next day, "or don't bring them at all!" was my Hero's directive! We could, 22 years ago, buy them on our Main Street, which was our intention, because I believe, if possible, one should help the economy of one's town. We, of course, received them the next day.

There was an amusing clause in our house deed which states, "if a member of the Smith family wants to walk on your beach, this must be allowed."

Of course! Since the "beach" referred to was under water, any Smith would be accommodated! For a long while as I looked out of our rear window, I wanted to see if another Saintly Figure walked on water. I also kept binoculars and a camera at the ready on window-sills, in hopes that they would capture this miracle!

Never happened!

But we three, plus guests, very often had "High Tea" on our back 40, and each time I walked into town, alone, about 8 minutes on foot, I sang to myself, and anyone else within earshot, "My kind of town, Niantic is," and felt happy to be here. I rarely saw another person on what passed for a sidewalk on one side of the road, and since I walked always next to the Union Cemetery, only the gravestones heard my birdsong. I was once again a "street walker," and loved every bit of it.

Connecticut was, and remains, "Car Country." No one ever walked at that time in the 80's. A car was driven to purchase a loaf of bread, or pack of cigarettes, or to stop for a cup of coffee, all of which might be had within an 8 to 10 minute stroll! Often Dolly, a city dog belonging to city-folk, accompanied me, or us, and grew to be loved by children and dog-lovers, who transported their pets in autos.

On our second or third day, I pushed Nat into town, and while I was passing a sage-green house several streets away, a woman emerged from her side door, greeted us, smiled and asked who we were. I told her of our recent move from New York, and she introduced herself, "Hi, I'm Athena Cone…that's spelled C-O-N-E, I'm not Jewish!" To this, I replied, "I'm Susanna Schwartz, this is my son Nat, and we are!" The beginning of a friendship, still ongoing. Soon the townspeople got used to seeing us…and our lovely dog, Dolly. I pushed Nat, Morris was leashed to Dolly, obedient to the law of the town.

Another wonderful "first" for Nat was our Town Hall with its ramp, and our meeting with the Town Clerk, Esther Williams, who registered us as voters, and as self-proclaimed "Democrats," and then irrevocably won Nat's heart when she turned to him and said, "Mr. Schwartz, would you like to vote at a school building, or would you prefer an absentee ballot?"

As Esther remembers it, "the joy on Nat's face I will never forget!" Nat did absolutely want to enter a voting booth for the first time, as an independent voter, because in New York, votes are cast "up" or "downstairs," and from the time he was a babe-in-my-arms, whenever I cast a vote, I carried him into the booth with me. As he grew, and I could still physically manage it, I showed and explained to him the voting ritual, how the voting machines operated, how the opening and closing of the booth curtains registered a "private" vote.

While we were settling in, Nat was trying to find a routine and pattern for HIS life! He missed New York, his friends, our relatives, but since we returned to New York for doctor's visits, he was able to call ahead and see them, or came with us to visit the few relatives we still had in New York City. Sometimes we stayed at a hotel in Manhattan for the weekend. Especially he missed the man on whom he looked as an "older brother," Les Grussgott, who had been his teacher at the Hebrew Academy, and later at I.S. 303. We had all, his family and ours, remained close, and when his first child, Jordana, was born, Nat called himself her "godfather." He adored them all. They seemed equally devoted to Nat, to us, and we treated them as our children, and Jordana, or Jordi, as a "grandchild."

Of course, Les' parents were alive and well, but we had never met. When Jordi was about 2 months old, we gave her her first "party" at our home in Brooklyn, always thought of her whenever we came across something we thought she might like. Mainly, though, we allowed Nat the personal freedom to forge his relationship with Les, sans us.

Les and his family had moved from their Brooklyn apartment to a home in Merrick, Long Island, and often invited Nat to spend a weekend with them. Morris and I brought him there, then we enjoyed a weekend alone, full of romance and with the freedom to enjoy our interests. We haunted antique shops, went to the theatre or ballet, dancing, to jazz clubs. We did all those things we were now too busy to indulge in, being too busy with work, with Nat's life, to recapture our formerly carefree lives.

We exchanged a lot of, "Remember this?" and "Remember the time...?"

Actually, in the last year of Morris' life, we did the same things and talked the same talk, seated on our Niantic deck facing the water, watching "our" birds, speaking of our favorite books, music, art, reading poetry to each other, discussing future plans, trips we might take, all while sipping our preprandial vodkas. And sometimes wondering how many other discussions of a similar nature were taking place in this, our "tight-assed" state!

These New York weekends that Les allowed us revived us, and made it possible to bear with equanimity the intervening weeks which were usually fraught with one or another battle for justice. While in New York, when Nat was sixteen, he began to speak of finding a trustee or legal guardian, to help in his care, if we pre-deceased him.

Not an easy matter for a VERY physically limited boy who possessed an active and enormous EGO, with which he clubbed us continuously, ironically, an ego which we "Pygmalions" had given him! He also had a very superior intellect, what I termed "experiential intelligence" and a brain which functioned like a human computer, into which all knowledge, overheard, read, or witnessed, was forever stamped, entered, and which he was able to retrieve as needed, and used intelligently, all made possible by a devoted and brilliant father.

When Nat was quite young, and both my parents were still living, we had discussed a legal guardian, but considered this eventuality a future problem. Morris and I thought that my parents, while loving and totally devoted to Nat, were not possible candidates because we didn't imagine they would outlive us. We cast about for someone younger, or someone who would be willing to undertake this difficult role. What we finally resolved was that, in time, Nat would be part of the solution.

His decision would eventually depend on his willingness to make his life under the stewardship of another…and not a loving parent or grandparent, but someone closer to him in age, and so, after speaking with Bernard, devoted cousin/loving friend/lawyer, to advise us, we now kept our eyes open for a possible candidate.

We knew that this was not going to be solely Nat's choice, but would have to be equally the choice of the Chosen! After explaining this to Nat, he began to assess if this or that cousin or companion might do. He went away for a long weekend with two young men who were to care for him physically, as well as for his entertainment. Nat had met them at the Cerebral Palsy Social Center he attended in Manhattan every Saturday. Nat asked another friend, also disabled, to join him. We paid all expenses, Nat's van was to be used, and we provided money for its use, as well as prepaid the fellows' salaries, and allowed them money for any unforeseen expenses, and told them that any out-of-pocket expenses would be reimbursed by us.

We had met these fellows on previous occasions when we picked Nat up on Saturdays after his fun and games at the UCP Center. Nat thought highly of them and enjoyed their company while they served as companions and aides to his group of friends. We had, in the past, invited one of them to accompany us to a restaurant after the social group disbanded. He was bright, charming, a fun companion who lived in one of Nat's favorite places, Greenwich Village. To Nat's 16 years of age, this chap was about 21 or 22, and studying for a career in Social Work, so he said. He invited us to his small Village apartment where he and I exchanged, from our two different eras, Village gossip, anecdotes and experiences.

Oh, we four had high old times…while Morris and I watched him and his relationship with Nat, very carefully. And Nat thought he had found his man!

Bernard, bless his smart advice, at Nat's enthusiasm over the next few years, for one or another possible trustee, always told us privately, that he was deliberately taking "a lot of time over the paperwork" to complete the official nature of the contract.

When Nat and his friend returned after their 4 or 5 day trip, Nat looked absolutely exhausted and explained to our anxious questions, that both he and his wheelchair-bound friend were forced to keep to their companions' private social schedule and agenda!

What happened? The fellows were in the habit of imbibing and socializing with THEIR peers, fellows and girls closer to them in age, and then when Nat and his friend were finally put to bed, they were forced to wait until the bleary-eyed fellows awoke to toilet them, dress them, feed them their breakfast!

No, this was definitely NOT what Nat envisioned when they all set out! When we confronted them, they were upset at Nat's report, but didn't deny it. "But we thought that this was to be OUR vacation!" I, not so gently pointed out that this trip was to be for Nat and his friend's enjoyment, and that THEY, supposedly mature and responsible, were being paid to do a job, and that this was not a vacation for four.

Thus ended THAT definition of "paid vacation"!

Bless you, Bernard!

Bernard kept doing what he deemed HIS job to be, to protect Nat…and us, through years of mistaken possibilities. One involved his own nephew, Jonathan Klate, the charming son of his sister Charlotte and her husband Ruby, with whom we often socialized…sometimes with Nat in tow, as they all loved him and treated him with the same respect and affection as did Bernard.

The Rags of Time

I have earlier written that I loved Bernard from the time I arrived in America, at about age 5, when Bernard was about 13, a handsome, blond, athletic, tennis-playing, brilliant academic.

So what's not to love about such a combination?

My cousin Charlotte was younger than Bernard, and my memories of her attention to me while I was at Cooper Union, were warm, and she had an endearing wit and talent as an actress with a small theatrical troupe in Manhattan. She used to invite me, at times, to the theatre or the ballet, both of which she knew I loved. It was from her that I learned the technique of folding a dollar bill into a rectangle and presenting it to the ticket-taker at the entry, in place of a ticket.

Together with this enriching bit of wisdom, was also included the pleasure of a performance, and wonderful memories. I also loved Bernard and Charlotte's wonderful parents, Katie and Louis, their hospitality, the music, much Gilbert and Sullivan, as I remember, and the wit and laughter of their home, so much like my own "Russian Nightclub," and after Bernard was to be married, (when I was 16) I cried secret tears of jealousy and disappointment, but dressed up and went, with the humiliation of disappointed affection, to the wedding. Oh, the bride was pretty, I granted, but I admit to unexpressed and "womanly" feelings, not too far from death wishes!

Oh, not for me!

I do remember how I felt when Bernard kissed me goodbye, or good-night, or did I kiss him? It remained for years, a tender memory. Through the years, through his two later marriages (the first was annulled), we all remained close friends and often a foursome at social gatherings.

While I worked at the Grove School, and my lover was in Europe, often Bernard would arrange to meet me at Grand Central Station, and then we would go to the Algonquin Hotel for drinks and conversation. The Algonquin was a favorite spot of ours because of its notoriety as the home of the Round Table, dubbed by Dorothy Parker as the home of her "Vicious Circle," and it remained a lovely setting as we sat at our square table and unviciously downed our drinks in the setting of comfortable furniture, soft lighting, and quiet!

The Rags of Time

I retain memories of the color "brown" in its drapes, woodpanelling, but my heart sang as I enjoyed the thought that my companion was as warmly attentive to, and as interested in, my tales of my students, their mischief, especially as I began to realize that Bernard was as affectionate, even loving, as when we had first met, so long ago.

My grown-up fantasies are unrelatable!

But Bernard obviously enjoyed my company as much as I loved being with him…and soon I did not divulge to friends, or my family, my feelings, as we continued to see each other every two weeks for dinner, dancing. There were no expectations, just pleasure in his company and in our warm friendship.

At this present lonely time in my life, it is hard to relinquish warm, achingly warm, memories, and return to the colder reality. So, Bernard went back…or forward…to his own life, and I went forward to mine!

Back to Nat and his quest to replace us with someone he could equally trust. His cousin, Jonathan Klate, was older than Nat, and seemed to enjoy being with us, with Nat, and when we visited his parents, asked us many questions about Nat, his friends, his relationships, his interests, and was impressed. When Nat finally asked him, after some time, if he would serve as his trustee, he agreed. But later, he came to Nat and told him that while he was ever Nat's friend, he didn't feel as though he could deal with the responsibility it involved. At the time, Jon was seeing the woman he eventually married, Carlotta.

Interesting that: his mother was Charlotte, his wife, Carlotta…but since I am NOT a Freudian, I think it better not to speculate!

Nat said to us, "Well, I guess I'm single again!"

When our "singleton" was 16-plus, and on an occasion when Les and his wife and little Jordie visited, Nat asked Les if he could speak with him in our garden. Privately, not having confided to us his reasons, he asked Les if HE would serve as his trustee. Les replied, "Well, I wondered how long it would take you to ask me, to ask us, and of course I'll be your trustee!"

And so it was, till the end of Nat's life, he looked to, and confided in Les, and asked his advice on many things, and Les NEVER let him down, and remained always a loving "elder brother" to Nat. And our dear, dear friend.

We and Nat traveled many times in Europe, and while we went over together and returned together, often Nat, and whoever acted as his companion, made their own itinerary, and sometimes traveled to other countries, to Holland, to France. From time to time, if Nat was in England, we met for dinner...and just to check how Nat fared under the protection of his aide/companion.

On one trip overseas, we were asked to provide Nat and his aide with a van which they were then to drive to Paris...or Dieppe...from wherever the Channel boat deposited them. Unfortunately, France was not as welcoming to Nat, and on one occasion when they needed help on the road, no one stopped. This experience served as a wake-up call for Nat, who by now expected the same kind of kindness and courtesy he had been accorded in Holland and the United Kingdom. When they were finally rescued, and drove on to Paris, they found, as Morris had warned them, one set of prices for the French, another for non-French-speaking visitors. When they returned to England, it seems that the charge for the van was doubled from what they had been led to expect. We vowed at that time to never set foot in that most inhospitable land.

This was part our stand against injustice of any kind, especially towards Nat, who might understand French, but was incapable of defending himself against injustice by "speaking up" which he might have done if his computer "voice" was at hand. And so, France joined Germany as one other country which was NEVER to see a cent of American Coin of The Realm from the Schwartzes.

Cousin Bernard's daughter Cynthia resided in Holland for some years, teaching English while learning Dutch, and when we decided to return yet another time to Holland, Morris called her and asked her to recommend a man to act as companion/aide for Nat.

Several weeks later, Cynthia phoned to say she had found a young man, a nurse, and did Morris want to meet him via the phone? Morris did, and gave him some idea of what was expected, that Nat did not require a nurse, but that was fine, and how much would he expect to be paid for his services? He named a figure which was tantamount to a year's salary in Holland, but he impressed

The Rags of Time

Morris, who hired him on the spot. He was to meet our plane at Schiphol Airport, and rent a van for Nat's convenience.

This was our first meeting with Henk Erkens, who became a friend, and with whom we three had a multitude of adventures. To imply that there was an instantaneous bonding with the three Schwartzes would not be accurate! Suffice it to say that we were met by Cynthia and Henk and the van, and driven to our hotel in Amsterdam. Morris arranged for Henk to take the van home with him and meet us the next morning at 10 AM.

We three were outside the hotel about 45 minutes earlier in order to walk a bit and acquaint ourselves with the area, which as in New York, was busy with pedestrians, shops, art galleries, charming little side streets, cobblestoned, and of course, close by a *Gracht*.

By 10, Henk had not arrived, and not by 10:15 or 10:30, and at almost 11 AM Henk drove up to a fuming Mr. and Mrs. Schwartz, and a visibly upset Nat. Oh, there followed a quantity of non-Dutch curses bluing the Amsterdam air over the hotel! Henk sensed our grim displeasure, and at Morris' angry questioning, Henk made some airy excuse. "After all, what is 45 minutes or an hour's delay?"

Morris told him in no uncertain terms, that to Nat, out-of-sight meant that he had been deserted, Henk might never be seen again, and that this was unforgivable, and if he wanted to work for Nat, one prerequisite was punctuality, give or take a few minutes, and if Henk couldn't adhere to this, or didn't understand it, he would be replaced! Henk apologized and was forgiven by my two men.

Me? I was unsmiling, but my attitude was clear to Henk: I would wait and see if I approved of him. His subsequent behaviour was to be my guide. And so it was that for the next six weeks, Nat and Henk bonded, and in addition to being a superb driver and guide, Henk proved to be witty, intelligent, fun to be with, and we all very much enjoyed ourselves.

Originally, we had intended to spend 2 or 3 weeks in Holland, then to take Henk with us to the U.K. for another 2 weeks, but there occurred a very unforeseen circumstance. Within the first week of our stay in Amsterdam, Nat awoke one night with a high fever, chills, and difficulty in breathing. We called Henk who came and drove us immediately to a hospital, the Academisch Medisch, where the physician told us that Nat had a flu, perhaps pneumonia, and would have to remain for at least a week until his lungs cleared.

Nat was given a room, and I went into my New York mother mode of spending the nights, since no one could as yet communicate with him since we had not brought his Printer. Also I served as interpreter to the physicians and the nurses who made up the second bed in this very large, grand room, with private shower and toilet.

During the day, Morris and Henk stayed with Nat while I went back to our hotel by subway, where I bathed, rested, changed clothes. Sometimes Morris arranged to take me out to dinner, and on one occasion, spent the night at the hospital to see the routine, and look around.

Once I had the pleasure of eating alone at a very good restaurant nearby. I became especially adept at deboning Tong, a very large and flat fish, rather like our flounder. I had never heard of it before, but Henk had described it to us. It arrived on an enormous oblong plate which it overhung! The waiter also brought small bowls of tiny potatoes, tiny whole carrots, and other vegetables, and stood over me, asking solicitously if he might debone my Tong?

"Thank you, but no, I am quite used to deboning fish for my son," and while he continued to stand, fascinated, I expertly slid a knife into the center of the fish, just above the long center bone, and turned the half over, then slid the knife under the long bone and lifted it neatly off, and out, of the Tong. The waiter actually applauded, and I "bowed" in my seat!

"That'll show them!"

I was pleased in my usual "mature" girlish heart, and in my former "gutsy" style! After my feast, I street-walked in the lovely starry night, amid throngs of tourists and Amsterdammers.

My come-down, and squishy it was, was when I stepped into dog-droppings! The Dutch, ever-touted for their constant and superior cleanliness, had one never-addressed habit: they never legalized the enforcement of Doggy Etiquette, and dogs were lovingly allowed to "poop" anywhere. I have in my possession a post-card showing a large deposit of dog manure, enclosed artistically in an outline of a red, nose-wrinkling person, beneath it it says, "AMSTERDAM HEBBUT." Morris suggested that THAT was the reason the Dutch wore boots or wooden shoes!

Chapter 14

During Nat's stay at the Academisch Medisch, the last built and a training hospital for physicians from everywhere in Europe, he was seen by many doctors, including a woman physician who gave Nat a test of some sort and decided he needed to have a tube inserted in his mouth which ran down his throat, through which medication and other fluids were administered. In addition, Nat had an I.V. in an arm. As good and cooperative a patient as Nat had always been, he protested vigorously! He wanted no part of the intubation, but the doctor told him it would only be in place for a few days, and finally persuaded him to allow the procedure.

Everyone, Morris, Henk, all visitors like his cousin Cynthia, encouraged him, and in order to keep his mind off the tube, I took Nat to every floor of this beautiful hospital, which had, among other architectural features, vari-colored metal structured pipes enclosing glass elevators. We rode from floor to floor and into hallways where were exhibits of paintings, sculptures, ceramics, blown-glass in wonderful designs and colors…and everything exhibited was of museum quality. These works of art were created by students of the many Art Schools supported by the Dutch government, and which were asked to lend their creations to various government buildings.

Nat and I were enchanted. We had never seen a hospital in the U.S. which had such a proliferation of art displayed, except for the occasional print or original painting on corridor walls, usually on the lower or entrance floor. The freedom with which Nat and I strolled the many floors was a testament to the entire philosophy and freedom of movement permitted by this hospital!

But then, art was to Holland, what literature was to England, what music was to the Germans! I have always believed each people, every country, has some proclivity to a particular art or science.

The Rags of Time

Every day, Nat begged anyone within earshot to have his throat tube removed, and after some 3 or 4 days of this torture, I told the good doctor that enough was enough, and that she was to remove the tube immediately. Nat was an adult, and we had always respected his sound judgment about his physical needs.

The tube was removed.

I cannot say enough for the kindness and interest shown by the entire nursing staff. They went out of their way to see to Nat's and my comfort, and invited me to their board or card games, or to chat in their lounge when Nat finally went to sleep. They also provided comfort, and tried to understand how Nat communicated, asked many questions about his education, his travels, his life in general.

After the tube was removed, we continued to explore Academisch Medisch life. On the ground floor we discovered the Hospital of Another World. Imagine the sight of a completely stone-tiled "*terrasse*" as was in front of the many restaurants in Amsterdam. There were areas of umbrella'd tables, a bookstore, a bank, two restaurants, a small convenience store which sold drug store items, perfumes, small gift packages of cosmetics, a flower shop, an ecumenical chapel, a post office!

There was a street sign bearing the name of this crowded and varied ground floor: "*Vogelgesang Plaats*" or "Birdsong Place."

More astounding was the sight of patients on litters, in hospital beds, some with limbs elevated in a splint raised by a pulley, patients in wheelchairs, as was Nat, and most with breathing apparatus, with I.V.'s, some intubated. And these patients were surrounded by friends, family members, companions, their children, all enjoying this respite from the usual hospital routine. There were others, more ambulatory, who queued up for trays of food, or were buying, together with visitors and doctors and other staff, some treat not provided upstairs.

Especially, the marvelous desserts and cakes heaped high "*met slagroom,*" and the magnificent Dutch *koffie*.

The Rags of Time

When Nat and I asked about this very civilized concept of a hospital, we were told that the hospital found recovery was both helped and speeded-up, and was certainly more psychologically beneficial in this atmosphere! In fact, where and when possible, patients were allowed to be taken home for the weekend, on the understanding they return by Sunday evening.

It literally blew our minds…and in directions that even, WE, enlightened Schwartzes, never foresaw!

One further surprise awaited Nat during his hospitalization. When Nat and I saw the chapel, we saw ministers, priests, on "OUR" daily rounds. Nat asked Henk whether there was also a rabbi on call? Asked Henk, "Do you want to see a rabbi?" "Yes," was Nat's reply. Two days after that, as Nat and I sat talking in our room, a handsome, hatted gentleman stood in the doorway, smiled at us and said, "Mr. Schwartz, I am Rabbi Nager." We invited him in, and he explained that he came from his position in Den Haag, where he was Official Chaplain to the Military, in response to Nat's request, which had just reached him.

Oh yes, refreshments were always served to include visitors, refreshments such as yogurt, *koffie*, *gebak met slagroom*, and not just the paper cup of juice one invariably sees given to our patients…and NOT offered to visitors.

Score up another one for Henk!

The discussion which followed between Nat and the rabbi was very illuminating: the rabbi was interested in hearing about Nat, about his Hebrew studies, about his schooling in America…and I helped translate some of Nat's questions to the rabbi. When Nat asked, "What kind of rabbi are you? Are you Orthodox, Conservative, Reform?" Rabbi Nager replied, "My dear young man, since the war, we make no such distinctions. A Jew is a Jew is a Jew! Don't you think so? We have no time for such thinking. The war taught us that!"

To which Nat agreed, satisfied and impressed with this gentle, sweet man, who then added that when Nat was discharged from the hospital, would we please visit him at his home in Amsterdam and he would introduce us to his wife and three of his five children and they would all be delighted if we could have dinner with them. He gave Nat his address and phone number. It was one of those things Nat was determined to do.

The Rags of Time

Morris and I had already decided that since Nat had spent over a week at the hospital, we would not go on to England, but would remain all the next month in Holland. Since Henk had relatives ALL over Holland, we let him guide us. In retrospect, there may be two or three small towns in Holland which we did NOT see, but I would be hard put to give you their names!

We traveled to Middleberg where we met Henk's parents, also to his own home where his wife and three children lived, in Purmerend, outside of Amsterdam Centrum, hard by a canal…to his wife Els' family in surrounding towns…anywhere which interested us. I established a custom when visiting, to always bring fresh flowers and a cake to our hosts, and so, since there are flower-stands and flower markets at almost every corner, and pastry shops almost as common, we were always to find gifts to bestow…everywhere.

I realized before we visited Rabbi Nager's home in Amsterdam, that I could bring flowers, but didn't know of a bakery which sold kosher cake, and so the bouquet I bought was so large as to completely hide my upper body!

When we arrived and at our ring at his door, Rabbi Nager came downstairs to greet us and insisted on helping Morris up the flight of stairs with the wheel-chair, while Henk carried Nat, and the bouquet carried me. Once inside and Nat reseated, the scene was one of domesticity. Mrs. Nager, the Rebbetzin, was up to her elbows in flour, as she kneaded the dough for the Sabbath challahs.

She greeted us warmly, introduced Nat and us to her three children still at home, explaining that one son was studying for the Rabbinate in Switzerland, the other son was at work in an Israeli kibbutz. She was also baby-sitting a small child who appeared to have Down's Syndrome, the son of a working mother. All the children were friendly, smiling, seemed happy, and were interested in the young man in the wheelchair.

The introductions over, I asked Rabbi Nager if I might see his garden and he took me down to the rear of the house…and I saw that I had, unwittingly, carried coals to Newcastle! I explained the size of the bouquet, and he was amused at the story…and the fact that three vases were necessary to contain the garden I had brought. He took the opportunity to question me further about Nat, and seemed genuinely moved when I told him of how grateful Nat was to have been invited, a circumstance not always readily forthcoming in the United States, not even by members of our own families.

Once again upstairs, we found that Morris, who was a very good baker, especially of challahs, asked for, and received permission from Mrs. Nager to demonstrate how quickly he made the egg-twists and round challahs with his large hands. He had around him an audience, amazed at the speed with which he fashioned the breads.

Nat loved the visit, the luncheon, the entire atmosphere and kindness of the Rabbi and his family. The Rabbi presented him with a calendar of Jewish holidays and events to take home with him, plus the promise to keep up a correspondence with Nat, which in fact he did, for years.

But, from one "sublime" moment to another!

One of Henk's uncles was a Catholic Trappist Monk in a monastery in Belgium, known as Sint-Sixtusabdij, which was located in Westvleterein. When Henk asked if we would like to meet Brüder Andreas, his uncle, whom he had not seen for several years, he was met by a resounding "YES!"

We drove up one day at about 11 AM and saw a large enclave of buildings surrounded by high brick walls. We parked the van and followed Henk through an opening in the wall, and went to the front door of the main building. We waited while Henk rang the bell which summoned a tall monk, later introduced as Brüder Daniel, the official "welcomer" and "greeter" to visitors. Henk spoke to him in Flemish, and then in English, after being told that his uncle was unwell and could not see us. Henk told him that we, American friends, wanted to enter, that we had come all this way, and Henk did not want to disappoint us, and, and, and then Brüder Daniel broke into smiles…and English…and told us that they rarely had American visitors, and the monks would be very happy to converse with us in English!

In we went, and were led by Brüder Daniel to a visitors' room and seated around a large table. Immediately we were seated, *koffie*, *bier*, tea, milk and cakes were brought in and offered to us. On the walls of the room were large paintings of past abbots, and crucifixion scenes, and in between these, were hung large silver crucifixes.

The Rags of Time

To a Jewish girl, the prospect of eating in a Trappist Monastery was irresistible! Morris and Henk, even I, tasted the *bier*, of course. The Trappist were a working/order, and supported themselves and the Monastery with their brewery. They explained that they only produced and sold enough for their annual needs, and that, plus the chickens and pigs they raised, the fruits and vegetables they grew in their gardens, the breads they baked, sustained them. All of this kept them busy...plus taking time out for lots of laughter, interspersed with their Rule of Prayer! OH, it seemed to us a relaxed and jolly place, and one or another monk came to see us, to serve us, to converse in English. I admit to the devilish thought, unvoiced, that the *bier* may have added to the merriment!

By about 12:30 or 1 PM, Nat asked to be shown around the gardens, and while we were outside, Nat said he was hungry, as breakfast at 8 AM seemed a long fast, for a non-monk!

When he and I returned to the visitor's room, I suggested to Morris that we leave, and reported what Nat told me, whereupon Brüder Daniel exclaimed, "What? You haven't had your lunch? Please, will you allow us to feed you. It would be our pleasure, but before that, will you join us at a "Celebration" which will take just half an hour?"

Of course we all agreed, and Nat was taken by Brüder Daniel through the Monastery cells, while the rest of us were led by another monk through various rooms, to the chapel. I say we walked, but the monk floated along before us, a beautiful young man, who actually floated along...I would say...about three inches off the ground, his flowing robe propelled through the air, his sandals not touching the floor! First, we were taken through a room where the brothers donned special overgarments, surplices, suitable to the occasion. The brothers were all smiles and friendliness, and those who spoke better English tried to converse with us. Soon, we reached the chapel, a lovely brick-walled room, streaming light through the overhead glass-ceiling.

At both sides of the chapel walls were chairs and small lecterns, one for each brother, and at the chapel's rear, was an organ, at which Brüder Daniel seated himself. He was the official musician; also he was the Monastery Librarian, and when we were seated in the visitors' chairs, he handed us hymnals...in Flemish. I told him that it was a language we didn't know, and he excused himself, and brought from the library, two hymnals in which one side of the page was printed in Flemish…and on the facing page, in English, the "Celebratory Psalm" for the day. I held one in my hand for Nat to read with me, Morris got the other, and I was pleased that I could follow the text which was the 23rd Psalm. THAT one I knew, and my fingers traced the words for Nat as we listened to one monk's song, while the other monks recited the lesson for the day.

Now, THAT was memorable!

After the "Celebration," we retraced our steps to the visitors' room and found that during our absence, there was set a groaning board of ham, breads, cheeses, milk for Nat, cake, salad, and we all ate voraciously. The food, together with the hospitality and courtesy shown us, and the attention to Nat, charmed us. What we had not experienced, or I, as a woman, was that Nat was the only one of us favored with the sight of the monks' personal cells, which gave him some inkling of the life these men led. He was delighted to hold that over Henk, Morris and me!

Before we left the Monastery, Henk and Morris asked if we might buy a case of the beer. We were told that there was probably none left, but if we liked, we could follow him to the brewery. We inspected the gleaming steel vats, while the Brewer-Brother finally found a single case, as yet unsold. After inspecting the spotless brewery, and with grateful thanks to all the kind brethren for this truly heart-warming and unexpected hospitality to three Jewish-Americans…as warm in their reception as were Rabbi Nager and his family, we left.

A most fantastic trip this had turned out to be! Nat described the monastic cells to us, the breeze-swung curtains which separated the tiny cubicles which contained beds, chairs, robes hung on hooks, crucifixes, small chests of drawers, Bibles atop, and sparse individual belongings of each monk…at least that was Nat's description. He hugged to himself the knowledge that only HE had been permitted this peek into Trappist Monasticism!

As for the other two "more mature" male adults, both Nat and I had a good laugh as Hank swung over to the side of the road, and he and Morris promptly opened two bottles of *bier*, and each took a swig! Morris spat his mouthful out immediately, while Henk drank his, unconcernedly. Morris asked me just to taste, just a swallow, which I also spat out. The bottles were full of what I can describe only as very dark, sweet malt…probably the same as had been my formula as an infant…but I guess I enjoyed it then!

The Rags of Time

During our travels with Henk, we were taken to the Portuguese Synagogue in Amsterdam. Henk tried in every way to accommodate Nat's interest in the Jews of Holland. The Synagogue stood across from the Jewish Museum. The Ashkenazic Community of Amsterdam erected this amazing Synagogue some hundreds of years ago. It was built of wood, there was no electricity or heat in the building and very tall candelabrum held tall candles for the services. The stained-glass windows and the carved details in the pews and bible-rests in each row of benches and the stained wooden walls and raised pulpit, the Bimah, and the balcony above, which held seating for women, all this was overwhelming to Nat, who had never before seen such a place of Jewish worship in the United States.

We went just to see the interior one morning after breakfast, and I went upstairs to sit and look down over the lower floor, and to admire the candelabrum and carved pews, and realized that we were unexpectedly to witness some boy's Bar Mitzvah! The pews below were filling with men, very elegantly suited and hatted, or yarmulked, and Henk had provided Morris, Nat and himself with the paper yarmulkes the Synagogue provided. I watched from above. Luckily I had in my purse a scarf, and soon, one after another women arrived, most with mink stoles, or fur jackets, or woolen coats. I soon realized that what I had thought of as "fancy-schmancy," questioning furs in late summer, was actually very prudent as I clutched the lapels of my linen jacket, over my light-weight dress, in an effort to keep warm…or just not to freeze!

I quietly went to the end of the row, and looked over the balcony to see Morris looking up. I motioned that I was leaving, and made a show of being cold, and Morris signaled that he and Nat were also on their way out. It was before the actual ceremony, but when the rabbi appeared, I HAD to stay a further few minutes. He wore black satin knickers over white silk hose, black, shiny heeled pumps, a lovely embroidered jacket, and had on a "shtramel," a wide-brimmed fur-trimmed hat. I recognized what I thought of as Polish-Jewish clothes of the Orthodoxy of the 16th or 17th century.

Thus ended our religious experiences in Holland. Considering my personal lack of faith in organized religion, although my views were NEVER imposed on Nat, I mused that perhaps this last experience was sufficient for one year…or one trip!

The Rags of Time

Nat and we were taken to many, if not all, *Polders*, canals, windmills, museums, which we may have missed on previous trips to Holland.

May I mention the nude or half-nude beaches, where the Dutch, sun-lovers that they are, dig trenches for themselves to lie in, to capture the sun, since the winds never stop blowing…and there was, for Nat, always, water, water, water, to the left of us, to the right of us, and when we drove the highways, water-bordered, he was always turning his head from side to delighted side. We sometimes saw flocks of birds swoop in heart-stopping acrobatics.

For me, the most fascinating discovery was when Henk drove us and introduced us to his slim and beautiful wife, Els…

And then introduced us to his slim, lovely, model-like Surinamese girl-friend, Els!

Well, thought I, if Henk talks in his sleep, he need never utter a "wrong" name to his current bed-mate!

Henk spent four days a week with his wife and children in Purmerend, and three days with his girlfriend in Amsterdam. They all knew each other and were "friends" of a sort, and the extra day with his wife was in order to be more with his children, with whom he seemed to be very close.

Els ONE, Els TWO, and Henk, were all three, nurses!

I never discussed this singular, or should I say, pluralized, life style with any of the principle players, much as I was tempted. Indeed Morris and Nat liked them all, and they were all very hospitable and friendly and interested in Nat, and in us as a family. I thought much about their intertwined relationship. The two women were both beautiful, …and Henk could, by no long stretch of the imagination, be thought of as handsome, being shorter than either woman, with a slight paunch, and thinning hair, so I decided on what I should have realized from the beginning: that the Dutch give not a fig for the usual "Western" concepts of what physical attributes deem a person "beautiful" or "attractive," or "desirable."

The Rags of Time

Talent, good-heartedness, kindness, courage, lack of prejudice, THESE are what is considered true beauty. In our travels in Holland, we were many times aware of couples, hand-in-hand, or enwrapped in each other, who did not conform to our Hollywood images of the handsome man, the beautiful woman.

The influence that Nat had on Henk was very marked. After we left Holland, Henk, ever-enterprising, decided that since Nat and we were so pleased with his plans and "tour" for us, he would interest the Dutch Medical Establishment in setting up "tours" for disabled people, and organized a company with other nurses, male and female, and sent out brochures and business cards. He surmised that if he could satisfy Nat's tastes in certain sites, and if anyone as disabled as Nat enjoyed himself so thoroughly, certainly so would others! When he told us of his new enterprise, we thought it a fine idea, and said we would recommend his "services" to others.

By the time we were ready to leave Holland, Henk, evidently mindful of the adage that "the female of the species is more deadly than the male," had made it up with me...not only by his exemplary behaviour...and promptness, ...but by proffering a "bribe" of his own!

We were invited to the apartment of Els Two, for a Saté dinner, prepared by Henk. It was an Indonesian *rijstafel* feast. To bowls of boiled rice on a table, one added pieces of chicken, beef, and one was supposed to add from bowls of curry sauce, soy sauces, coconut milk, peanut sauce, yogurts, hot sambal sauce, whatever one wished to dip pieces of the chicken or beef and vegetables in, pausing only to pant...or to drink cooling beers...or wines! All truly delicious, and Nat very much enjoyed sampling till his eyes teared.

Morris and Nat had, during our tour with him, bought Henk some gifts, trying to find something to symbolize his description of himself as Leo, the Lion! They looked for a gold pendant, a chain, whatever.

Henk countered by saying that he didn't know what Nat or Morris might like, still looking, he said!

At the end of the *rijstafel*, Henk presented me with a gilt-wrapped box, which when I opened it, seemed to contain an inordinate amount of tissue paper! When I finally dug into its center, I found a tiny box of tortoise shell which had on top a small, painted enamel miniature of a woman's head, set in a silver frame, which looked as one imagines a portrait from the time of Jane Austen. That sight alone, even before opening this box, cut from a single piece of tortoise, held me in such thrall, I could scarcely open it, I could scarcely breathe! It is one of my most treasured possessions! I opened it to find an 18th century ladies écritoire!

All the fittings from this tiny box are of silver, and consist of a silver handle which, as desired, will pick up a silver paper cutter, 3 silver pen-points, a silver-topped glass jar for ink, another such for sand, to blot the ink message. And, when the paper is folded for sending, and a bit of sealing wax is melted over the two edges, it can be inscribed by a crystal rose carved into a seal. All the units of this exquisite box are set in red velvet, with a tiny mirror inside the lid.

What could I say? Only the truth, that it was the loveliest thing I'd ever seen…then followed by my question of, did Henk steal it? …or was it from his family estate? …whatever, any animus I had felt toward him…was completely demolished!

On the occasion when Henk visited us in Connecticut, he took pictures of Nat as he went through an entire day, and these photos so impressed and interested people he knew in Holland, that he became a video producer! His reputation spread, and he told us on another of our trips to Holland, that Queen Beatrix requested that he do a video for the Anniversary of the Tulip, soon approaching, and he received permission to film paintings, prints, fabrics, and anything else pertinent to the importation of the tulip from Turkey, in the 16th century. Henk's offices in Amsterdam held many photographs of him with Royalty!

Nat may have made a difference in Henk's life, but Henk made an equally great contribution to Nat's life, and one for which I will always be grateful. Morris and I had often spoken to each other of Nat's frustration at not having a girlfriend, a marriage, children of his own…nor indeed a sex life. In light of our, and perhaps, especially **my**, sexual relationships and pleasure therein, I was made aware that Henk saw to it that Nat's needs were met!

The Dutch, they ARE a civilized people!

The Rags of Time

Nat never discussed this with me or Morris, and I respected his desire for privacy, but it occurred to me that I was now helpless to help Nat in this aspect of his life. I remembered what a child-psychologist/psychotherapist friend of mine from Grove School days told me when we three visited him and his family at their "camp" or homestead on Lake Champlain in Vermont.

Privately, we discussed Nat and his diagnosis, and as he was just six years old, we were not yet discouraged by his physical limitations. We truly expected him to progress in speech, to eventually walk, to be able to sit unaided in other than his wheelchair.

Morty Schiffer and I discussed these things at length, because Nat was wholly dependent on me for his physical care, toileting, bathing, feeding, although Morris could do equally well with Nat if the need arose. I always maintained that Morris could do everything but breast feed! Ironic, since the doctor had eliminated that possibility without asking me. I seem to have been, in the fifties, an adjunct to men's decisions, as much as I fought this most of my adult life!

Morty said he understood, merely stressed that I treat Nat's physical needs casually, especially when bathing and toileting him.

But Nat grew to manhood...and I was STILL doing this. I grew aware that while Nat never discussed his sexuality with me, he had made a study of disabled male sexuality...and it was a subject I could no longer ignore.

Nat had an intercom system which led from his bedroom to ours, and I could hear his every breath and movement, and call to me, even when both air-conditioners were on, because with his degree of disability, he needed to be turned during the night, sometimes, several times. His special bed was equipped with motors that raised its back, or elevated his legs, or folded him like a sandwich, I used to joke, and when he lay face-down, the top was almost flat. This, every one of his companions, whether at home or in his own apartment or his home, was made aware of. When he was hospitalized, I, or a companion, informed the nursing staff about what must be done to change his position, or make him more comfortable. It was one of the stipulations for anyone he hired.

I soon realized that almost every night that Nat was in our home, he asked to be put on his stomach in bed, and that the sounds I heard, were of Nat masturbating. I tried to shut my ears at the recognition of his breathing, and as he sought release in orgasm, and I often arose and wept to think that my child had even to share this aspect of his sexual nature and fulfillment with me.

It was not an easy thing to hear, and even more difficult to write.

Love may not be easy to share, or to write, but if the sharing IS love, it is reality! And still, in my child's maturity, how could I deny him those sensual feelings which I had so long enjoyed? Morris did not aid him at night, because his loving father no longer had the acuity of hearing I still enjoyed…although "enjoyed" is not the word I would have chosen!

Chapter 15

Perhaps it would have been easier for Nat to live apart from us, and that was what he attempted, again and again, and since we were convinced that we had prepared him for an independent life, he now took over his own quest for the final cutting of his umbilicus. With our blessing!

His first attempt was when he learned of a hotel-turned-apartment complex for the elderly and disabled. For no apparent reason that the three of us could ever suss out, Connecticut seems to lump the needs and lifestyles of these two quite disparate groups of people together. Despite what we learned in Europe, Connecticut operates on a philosophy from another time and place…and planet!

We obtained an appointment with the woman manager of the apartment building, who took all the information about Nat, and informed us that there was not at present a two-bedroom apartment available. We had gone to the interview at the behest of the Department of Social Services, who seemed to, as did we, support his bid to live independently, with a companion of course. Nat was told that as soon as a two-bedroom flat became available, we would be informed.

Nat was delighted to be on a "list" and began to make grand plans for his foray into "life on his own!" He immediately made lists of furniture and linens and expenses, and planned for the shopping of his food, and looked at shops, happily, and had Morris help him with possible housekeeping expenses, and what he needed to do, and how to make sure that he had utilities and phone service installed, and, and, and! His enthusiasm caught everyone up. Friends offered advice, tables, chairs, and other items he might need…and time passed in excitement and pleasure.

In advance of his move, he felt he should be advertising for a live-in companion. After a number of interviews with those people who were patently NOT suitable, he finally met a young, attractive woman who had recently relocated from Iowa, and whose aunt saw the ad I had posted in ALL church and synagogue bulletin boards…and Nat was always partial to a female companion!

Diana was pretty, young, well-spoken, and when interviewed by Nat, they seemed to hit it off. She was anxious to have the job. Morris gave her HIS driving test to make sure she could handle Nat's van, the ramp, that she followed all our State rules and regulations, that she kept to the designated speeds, made turns correctly, did NOT go Up the Down ramp, and could read a map.

She passed his test!

The Manager of the Mohegan Apartments who had promised to call Nat when an apartment became available, was not heard from for 5 or 6 months, and Nat asked me to call and find out the status of his request.

What she told me was that, yes, there had been a two-bedroom apartment available months before, but that she had been told by the Department of Social Services which monitored requests for housing for the disabled, NOT to inform him, or to give it to him! To my shocked, "Why?" she said that they told her that Nat was too disabled to live there. THIS, after she had approved his tenancy, reassured by Nat that he would ALWAYS have a live-in companion.

When I relayed this to Nat, after his initial shock and anger, he decided to do as our ex-Governor Lowell Weiker had advised in a frequently-aired television promotion for the Connecticut Department of Protection and Advocacy, to seek legal redress.

Nat had me call this agency, which sent a case-worker to our home. She interviewed Nat through various modes of communication: his Printer, the spelling mode, eye contact for easy "yes and no" answers. She wanted to experience first hand in what way he "spoke." She told us that she felt sure that Nat would absolutely benefit from the Agency's services. She went to make her report, and told Nat that they would further investigate his claims of injustice and get back to him.

The social worker was as good as her word, and kept in telephonic touch, and within about six weeks, called to say that she had retained, on Nat's behalf, the services of their lawyer, at no expense to Nat, and that we were to have a hearing before a judge within 10 days! Mr. Berliner, the lawyer, would meet Nat at the appointed time and place.

And so it was that Nat had his day in court!

It was as good as a play! There we all were, in a tiny room, long and narrow, with the judge seated at one end of a conference table. Nat's lawyer and advocates sat along one side, and representatives from the Department of Social Services, sat opposite. Because there was so little room, Morris suggested that I accompany Nat while he waited outside the office/turned courtroom.

Inside, the judge introduced himself, placed a tape-recorder on the table in front of him, and announced that as we were called upon to speak, we were to identify ourselves each time. When it was my turn, I introduced Nat and myself, and our relationship to each other. I gave them a rapid, simplified explanation of the way in which Nat would ask or answer questions, and said I was in no way going to speak FOR him. Unfortunately, Nat did not have access to his Printer because the electric outlet was at the other end of the room. Nat in his wheelchair, and I barely made it into the room, and the closed door was at his left hand.

I added that both the advocates and Mr. Berliner understood how Nat communicated. I carefully kept my hands away from Nat, from the wheelchair, so it would not appear that he was being "coached" by me, or that I was influencing his replies. I explained how one could elicit a quick and accurate affirmative or negative response from Nat through eye-contact. If an affirmative response was given, he would meet the eyes of the judge; he would avert his eyes in case of a negative reply. In the event that an explanation was needed, the advocate, Mr. Berliner, or I, would assist.

First the Department of Social Services had their say, then Nat, then I, then the Office of Protection and Advocacy. The lawyer, who had met with Nat for a few minutes before the "court" was convened, got some additional information from Nat, practiced speaking with him, and he was a very quick study. He was impressed with how clearly Nat expressed himself. When all the "evidence" had been given, the judge gave his thanks, and told us that he would issue a written decision and verdict.

Within two weeks, the decision came in a letter to Nat, which indicated that copies had been sent to the Department of Social Services. The judge stated that, "The Department of Social Services had treated Mr. Nat Schwartz in an unconscionable manner, and directions must be given to the Mohegan Apartments that the next available two-bedroom apartment was to be his, and in view of their treatment, he was awarding Mr. Schwartz, a money judgment of $..."

This was something Mr. Nat Schwartz had NOT sued for, had not even thought of! But this was clearly Nat's victory...and he used the money to buy some furnishings for his apartment, when he finally got one.

When Nat and Diana were finally settled in their flat, Nat took great pride and pleasure in its roominess, its furnishings, and they went together to buy those things which he, or we, could not supply, such as the furniture for Diana's room.

When Morris had given Diana her "driver's test," she passed, but what she did NOT pass was the requirement that she answer Nat's interview questions truthfully when he asked if she smoked, drank, or took drugs.

The "business" arrangements were left to Morris, who gave to Nat each month, in advance, monies for his rent, Diana's salary, money for van expenses, groceries, clothing items, plus extra money should we be unavailable at any time, and I arranged with our wonderful pharmacist, John Birmingham, in Niantic, to refill his prescriptions, introduced him to Diana, and told him to charge us for any drug-bills incurred. She had, in the past, while Nat still lived with us, often gone to refill his prescriptions.

What we did NOT know was that Diana refilled, for herself, Nat's prescriptions for the controlled substance he had been on, from the age of five or six, which was prescribed originally by Dr. Reuben, and which was always being evaluated and reassessed by his present doctor in Niantic. It was by now a very low dosage, just enough to curb or make more comfortable his athetoid tendencies.

We were also not aware, since her salary and all Nat's monthly expenses were paid by us in advance, that she regularly stole Nat's money to supply her drug addiction, after she had depleted Nat's stock of prescribed drugs.

The Rags of Time

How we discovered this was a horror we would rather forget, but served, we decided, as a wake-up call to us and other parents in our, and their, quest for their child's independence.

During the first six months of Nat's sojourn in his flat, we visited, but only when invited. Nat hosted a housewarming within the first month of his stay, to which he invited friends, and whatever family might like to travel from New York to see him revel in his hard-won freedom to live alone. He and Diana shopped, and provided canapés, wine, buffet food, coffee and desserts. We were all a merry group as we witnessed his joy, and as he led "tours" through his domain!

On the occasion of a Jewish Holiday, Nat had Diana walk him to New London's only kosher meat market where he ordered the foods he had seen served at our home, or at friends'. They bought brisket of beef, chicken livers, and the proprietor was so interested to see how Diana and Nat communicated, that he told her he would deliver the order himself, where did they live? The day before the holiday dinner, to which we were invited, the shopkeeper not only delivered the meats, but he brought them a bottle of Kosher wine, a challah, and a honey-cake, telling Diana of the part they played in a Jewish Holiday. An example of kindness not forgotten! We had intended to supply the items ourselves, we told Mr. Soltz, when we stopped by to thank him for his interest. He remained Nat's friend.

Nat and Diana and we planned a Thanksgiving dinner at our home. I think Diana was to bring the turkey, cooked, under Nat's tutelage, and we were to provide the "befores" and "afters."

The night before Thanksgiving, we received a call from the New London police that Diana was found on the living-room couch, upon which she had overdosed, and Nat was found in his bed, totally unaware of what had happened. The scenario in my head, one I have never forgotten, was that if Nat had awakened the next morning, or called out at night to be turned, but went unanswered, he would have tried to throw himself to the floor and crawl to find her, and then scream, or call, as well as he might, to summon help from someone, anyone…!

It was fortunate that Thanksgiving was the next day, because WE would have called to check if anything was wanted, and receiving no response, would have gone over to investigate. Why the police were alerted was that Diana had called a former boyfriend in Iowa, and during a rambling discourse, had threatened suicide. The boyfriend called her mother who called the aunt in our town who alerted the police, and by the time the aunt arrived, the police had taken Diana to Pond House, the psychiatric unit of Lawrence and Memorial Hospital. Her aunt and a policeman remained until we arrived.

Diana, unconscious on arrival at the hospital, survived…and I am NOT ashamed to say, within my rage, I almost wished she had not!

Morris and I, as we searched through Diana's room, came upon drugs, hypodermic needles, and marihuana cigarettes. I then understood the sweetish odor I had often remarked on, but attributed to spray deodorants. We also discovered that Nat's money had disappeared…evidently to feed her habit. I found out later that her mother came to collect her from Pond House and took her back to Iowa.

Nat was worse than devastated. He was outraged at her betrayal. And realized the danger she had almost put him in! He could now understand OUR feelings of betrayal through many years of interaction with supposedly "compassionate" and "understanding" persons in power, who through stupidity or cupidity, tried to grind our lives and spirits into dust beneath their feet.

I stayed at Nat's flat while we tried to replace Diana, to find another companion. There was the occasional ex-companion who sincerely wanted to help, but who now had fashioned their own lives and were not available.

We finally moved Nat's belongings home, and tried to buoy his spirits with travels, with as much enjoyment as we could dredge up, as we attempted to help Nat move on with his life.

Since Nat was clearly not employable in our "Why not?" State, he decided to start some organizations which might better the lives of handicapped people. The first was to put together a Social Club. He received permission and encouragement from Niantic's First Selectman to use our Town Hall for weekly meetings. The Town Hall, when built, was equipped with an entry-ramp for wheelchairs, or for anyone with mobility problems. Nat sought members from our town and surrounding areas, had us make phone calls, advertised on bulletin boards, and at places of worship, for anyone who was, or who knew someone disabled and in need of socialization.

When calls came in from interested people, he went to local supermarkets where friendly and sympathetic managers honored his requests for donations of chips, dips, sodas, cookies. He bought some paper goods, and was allowed to use the coffee-maker in Town Hall, and was even given the services of the maintenance staff, if needed. This positive response did much to raise his spirits.

The first meeting had about eight or ten attendees, some in wheelchairs, or with waking aides, one blind woman accompanied by her husband. I was later told by Nat and his companion, that this first get-together concerned itself with pitching ideas for social events, how to increase membership, how the members, who paid no fees to attend, could incorporate their town events to include the "Social Group."

In the beginning, the club, called ADAPT (All Disabled Are People, Too), was successful and attracted a larger membership, and even marched in the East Lyme Appreciation Day parades, carrying a banner to announce themselves. They gained recognition and support from onlookers, and on several parades, State Senator Richard Schneller, an early friend to Nat, left his parade vehicle to shake Nat's hand. Senator Schneller is a wonderful man, warm, supportive, encouraging, and Nat was proud of their friendship.

In these early days of our life in Niantic, in the small shoreline community of East Lyme, while he and ADAPT were partying, going to bowling alleys, to local fairs, Nat was also "enriching" his life by attending Mohegan Community College. This he sometimes enjoyed, but many times was embroiled in the same battles for recognition which he had encountered during most of his educational "history."

And why not? Changes in geography do not necessarily equate with a change in societal, or bureaucratic attitudes, or personal attitudes and bigotries. So, our "Why not?" State became often a "State of Confusion" instead.

The breakup of Nat's Social Club came, of course, when he advanced the shocking and unheard-of proposition, that the other members of this totally free, non-dues-paying group, for which NAT had done all the planning, found all the venues, arranged all the details, might now, in turn, plan and arrange social possibilities in THEIR towns!

WHAT? Was he mad?

Was Nat stupid or perhaps insane (certainly he was naïve), to expect the others in ADAPT to exert some initiative, to plan some outings, to use their energies on behalf of the total membership? Within six weeks, the group dwindled by half, then again by a few members, and finally it was entirely abandoned by Nat who suddenly realized what WE, as mature adults in our Society understand, that in any organization, it is always the same one, or two, or three people, who are relied upon to do ALL the work!

The next "*crise de nerfs*" for our family occurred when we decided that Nat might do better with a house of his own, and we three set out to find one for him. Morris and I would have preferred a house in Niantic or East Lyme, but there were none that were suitable, that might be ramped, and at this point Nat thought he'd love one that had enough property for an in-ground pool. He said it would be easier than going to our very Nat-friendly beaches in Niantic, while schlepping all his tubes, towels, umbrella, special beach chair.

While our search went on, Nat advertised for another companion. He had moved home since the near tragedy of the "Addicted Aide," and felt that perhaps if he employed more than one person, perhaps a family in residence, it would prove safer.

At the time of the advertising, Nat okayed a house set on an acre of land in a neighboring town. It was a two-story Colonial with two bedrooms and a bathroom on the upper floor, and the lower floor had all the possibilities of providing a large bedroom and private bath, and also a third, fully equipped bathroom, in addition to two bedrooms, living-room, kitchen, dining area already there. Also a two-car garage, attached, some outbuildings, and a small but adult-sized playhouse, which was charming, and could serve some purpose. The property boasted a stand of lovely trees at one end, and a vegetable garden, and fields.

Nat's marvelously creative father redesigned the garage by having a ramp built leading from the middle van doors, up to a mud-room/laundry area, leading into the house, and to the kitchen.

The Rags of Time

After advertising and interviewing for some weeks, Morris was contacted by a young man recently arrived from Ireland to visit his brother, who headed an alcohol/rehab program and who had saved our ad to show his brother when he arrived. Nat thought that Kevin was pleasant and seemed adequate for the job. Kevin spoke of his wife and two very young children who were at home in County Cork. Morris administered his "driving test" which Kevin passed, and Nat thought ahead that if Kevin got his "green card," we might be able to sponsor his family as well. The family would fill his upper floor, and he posited to us, that an entire family would prove safer than a single person.

At least, that was his reasoning!

Nat contacted our good Senator Dodd in Hartford who agreed to help with the green card, after we explained that IMPORTING help was not our aim, that the wages paid would be the same as for a United States citizen, but that, given Nat's severe physical disability, and that after interviewing some 35 Americans of varying ethnicity, we had not been successful.

Kevin was hired and lived with us in our home during the reconstruction of Nat's house, the time needed to provide furniture for an entire family to come. The family arrived, and they all moved in, with Nat, to his new home.

AND the trouble began!

We, good-intentioned three, arranged for Kevin and his family to have a car at their disposal. In addition, there would also be someone, or we, to care for Nat on Kevin's day off. Kevin seemed disappointed that we had not as yet hired someone. Actually, he was not thrilled when his wife and two children arrived.

Stupid Susanna! It was MY push that got them here! What Kevin's fantasies of "life in American" were, I was not intelligent or perceptive enough to discover early on. The fact that he might not have ever wanted to see them again, was to an incurable romantic like me, impossible to conceive. In that, I was as stupid as we discovered Kevin to be!

We had explained to Kevin, from the beginning, that whatever Nat ate, would also be provided to the family: Nat could no longer chew the texture of chopped meat, so steak was offered as substitute. There were other foods Nat could not eat, such as nuts, green peas, corn kernels, olives, raw fruits. If Kevin wanted these foods, he would have to provide them for himself from his very good salary. Also, whenever or wherever Nat wanted to go, to a play, to a concert, to take a trip, Nat always bought and paid for the tickets, and for all traveling expenses.

These were the ground rules, and Kevin agreed.

While in our home, Kevin shared in whatever foods we parents and Nat ate…and we were considered good cooks.

Because of our previous experiences with aides, we worked out a "code" with Nat, which proved successful…as successful as the Navaho "Windtalkers" of W.W.II fame. Since we always owned one or more dogs at our home, all of whom loved Nat and were very protective, we told Nat that since he could not dial a phone, or speak intelligibly, that if Kevin ever brought up a dog's name in phone conversation from Nat, for example: "How is Pepper?" or "I thought Dolly didn't look well when I saw her last" or "Give Sam a pat for me," what that meant was, "Get over here. I need to speak to you privately!"

If such a call was received, Morris and I paid an "unexpected visit," and while one of us engaged the family in conversation, the other spoke with Nat. Once Nat told us that he often felt as though HE were living in their home, rather than THEY living in HIS! Another time he complained that the children were walking on the furniture, and were undisciplined by either parent.

The final horror occurred when Nat told Kevin that he wanted to go out to a very good Italian restaurant in Niantic. That night, about 9:30 we received a call telling us that Nat was in the hospital! When we dashed there, Kevin was unable to provide a coherent explanation of what had happened, just that Nat, while being fed, began choking on some food, was turning blue, the restaurant owner called for an ambulance, and Nat was seen in the emergency room by the doctor in charge, who told us that Nat was "passing air," was out of danger, but would have to remain for tests and observation. I remained as well, as was always my wont, and as Nat didn't have his Printer, I served as translator to the nurses and other medical staff. After spending time with him, Nat spelled out to me that Kevin had pushed an olive into his mouth, and reflexively he had swallowed it!

The Rags of Time

Nat had never before in his entire life eaten an olive. When I told Morris, he confronted Kevin, who insisted that Nat imagined this, that he had NEVER fed him an olive. Since Nat was kept in Intensive Care and monitored by nurses, I suggested that Morris and Kevin go home, I would remain the night. The nurses were kind and gave me linens and a pillow so I could bed down in the empty waiting room on that floor. I couldn't sleep, so after telling and showing the nurses how to elicit a "yes" and "no" response from Nat, went to my lonely couch, read some magazines, paced the floor, put the television on low...

Every hour or so, a phone called me into the ICU as Nat complained of pain in his esophagus, which the staff told me had already been x-rayed from his mouth through his throat. The following day, a probe would be inserted to check the source of his continued discomfort.

But Nat, whom I always trusted to be accurate in describing his physical being, kept insisting to me that he felt pain. When I suggested to him that perhaps what he had eaten had scratched his throat, he told me to have the nurses suction his throat. I relayed his request, and went back to the waiting room, but within 15 minutes, a nurse called me to say that Nat was extremely agitated, and would I please come back. When I did, Nat spelled out to me, "Open my mouth!" I did so, and screamed, and all the nurses came running, and when they did, I told them to scoop out what was in Nat's mouth...and out came a very large, untoothmarked, Sicilian olive!

Then everyone came, including the doctors, to see what Nat had given birth to! And again I marveled at my son's intelligence. He knew what we did not, that frequent suctioning would lift whatever was still in his esophagus, and which had been missed in the x-rays.

I immediately called Morris with the news, and he called Kevin and told him in no uncertain terms, that he was a liar and very nearly a murderer, and that if he and his entire family were not out of Nat's home by 9 AM the next morning, HE would come down and punch him out, and personally boot them all out of the house!

And see to it that Kevin's green card was revoked!

And when Nat came home he was accompanied by the enormous olive in a bottle of sterile water, which we kept for years as a testament to our brilliant son's ability, if given the opportunity, to be responsible for his own life. The fact that I was sickened by the image of what might have occurred if the probe was pushed into his throat, I kept hidden.

This difficult time was compounded by the fact that I moved into Nat's home until another aide could be hired. In discussions with Nat and Morris, I told them that **I** would NOT survive another such incident! I told Nat that we would have to move him back to our home, and that we would give him every freedom. He was to use whichever of our two living rooms he pleased, and in the event of his having guests, or a party, Morris and I would leave the house for the evening, or overnight, or whatever…so that he might make any social plans he pleased. And he knew us well enough, and could have faith in our pronounce-ments and promises, BUT, we could at least speak with him sans a code, and intervene at his request, in any situation he felt unable to control.

Sadly, we sold his house to the second person to see it, and took no profit, just recouped the money laid out for its renovations. Whenever before its sale, I walked its grounds, and saw how lovingly Nat had furnished "HIS" home, I was filled with loathing for the way his, and our, trust had again been violated; there were times I wept with rage…and the desire for revenge.

I am NOT a perfect person!

After a while, I had the idea for a book to be called "The Tragedy of Aides!" But as I began to recall the over 70 persons we had, over the years, interviewed, I called it quits. Some were funny, some shocking, some unbelievable, some potentially lethal, but there are examples which cannot be left unwritten!

Nat had interviewed so many people, male, female, cross-gendered, through advertising in newspapers from Boston, Providence, Long Island, New York City, all the Connecticut cities and towns, that I decided to list them, and began again, thinking to write for magazines, newspapers…also I began to think the examples would help other hapless employers.

1 – The young Black woman named "Roxanne," who under the guise of helping Nat pack the contents of his desk, disappeared with his entire collection of old silver dollars, and other antique American and foreign currency. She had

been sent by an Agency in New York City. Nat had been so delighted to be able to "help with my packing!"

Ah, Roxanne, we will never forget you…and thanks! Nat was just 20 years old, and a trusting soul, but as we said, tempus fugit…or tempus fuck it!

2 – Who can forget "Margaret," who when she was told we intended to hire, not one, but two aides to spell each other in his first apartment, or in his house, said, unforgettably, "Oh, I can't work in a house or an apartment with another man, or woman, or child, or pets!"

Sorry to let you go dear, but will rehire if we come up with a species not yet named!

3 – "Missy" from New York, pretty, anorexic, witty, intelligent, who actually cried when she discovered she could not lift more than his arm from the wheelchair, as she struggled into her woolen overcoat on this fine July day. She and Nat wept on each other's faces as she kissed him goodbye!

Oh yes, after eating three grapes…a cracker, a turkey slice for lunch, she disappeared into the toilet to regurgitate her enormous meal!

4 – "Kevin" from "Down South" who was VERY bleached blond, who wore VERY short shorts over no undies whatever. He was however funny, smart, a good driver, and hired in full knowledge that he was tres gay. We routinely had physicals done on any sexually doubtful employees, which included a test for Aids. There we were lucky, and Kevin came to work for Nat, and daily they set out happily for one or another non-sexual adventure, after Morris laid down some rules for him:

Kevin was to dress more conservatively, deep-six the short shorts, wear underpants, and NEVER be caught in flagrante in a car, or gay bar, and after his day off, be at work by 8 AM!

Alas, Alack, dear Kevin was in the pokey after a policeman found him in a car with two men! Nat was upset when he was late one morning, thinking he might be in a hospital (he wasn't…I called) but Morris would not let me call police, saying it would give solace to the bigots who had already referred to them as "the cripple with the queer!"

The Rags of Time

When Kevin resurfaced in the afternoon, Nat fired him, albeit with reluctance, asking first why he hadn't used his ONE phone call to notify us? So dear "Kevin the Cruiser," as we referred to him, disappeared from our lives, leaving behind three gallon-sized bottles of Hair-bleach, shampoo, skin-softener, and a booklet, found under his bed, which listed in the contiguous United States, every gay bar, restaurant, movie-house, and the web-sites of clues re the type one preferred in gays: skin-color preference, sizes (and I don't mean height and weight), and "signals" such as colors or stripes in headbands, and wristbands, and other such pertinent information! I have this informative booklet still, which is called, "Bob Damron's Address Book," with the addendum on the cover "includes Mexico" '86!

5 – Then there was the lovely Black mother and daughter combo who drove up from New York City, and when Nat's interview included the question, "Why do you want to work for ME?" the mother said, matter-of-factly, "Oh, we don't!" Then why did you drive up from New York?" asked a disconcerted Nat. "We just thought it would be a nice day in the country," she replied!

Nat, the true, if misguided gentleman asked to see what they paid to rent the car, and for the gasoline, asked me to pay them, and threw them out of the house!

Then the Schwartzes laughed like hell! Another lesson learned. We were about $47.00 poorer, but decided laughter always enriched!

6 – We had another such chuckle when a man "in his cups," came to be interviewed, and then when rejected, called from another town (probably a bar) to ask, indignantly, how did Nat have the nerve to reject him, HIM?

7 – I must admit that our all-time favorite among the rejectees was, when one day, at the front door bell's ring, Morris admitted a very tall, lanky, woman, dressed in a long, ill-fitting tweed skirt, long-sleeved blouse, her scraggly hair dangling to her shoulders. Since it doesn't behoove us to be critical of a person's looks and clothing, even Nat, who gave this apparition a disapproving look, began the interview. She was almost ingenuously sincere in why she wanted, nay, almost begged Nat to give her a chance. "I need to have this job," she quietly pleaded, while I cast about in my mind for a way to effect a "make-over" of her appearance.

The Rags of Time

"Why do you need this job?" asked Nat, now interested despite his obvious reluctance to give her the opportunity. Her explanation, "I am a Nun in Society, and am a member of…Parish, …Church," in another town.

To Nat's questions, no matter how pointed, and dispite his obvious disinclination to hire her, she replied calmly, and he finally fell back on, "I will have to be taken to my Synagogue." "Oh, I'd welcome the opportunity to see the Jewish service and rituals," and then Nat, in desperation said, "I masturbate!" "Well, we all do!" was her reply.

And so Joanne came for a paid 3-day trial, which we always imposed. The interview ended and I told Joanne to bring pajamas, slippers, and a robe, explaining that I must know if she would hear and respond to Nat's call during the night, to be turned. Morris gave up his twin bed next to mine, and slept in the guest room, and Joanne and I went to bed.

When Nat called, I immediately awakened to find that Joanne was up, put on her robe and slippers, and went to him. All went well and good, thought I.

The next morning, I fixed us all breakfast, explained to her how Nat was to be fed, what he could and couldn't eat. Afterwards, Joanne bathed and dressed Nat satisfactorily, and they went out somewhere or other. Morris and I went to some yard sales to find Nat a lamp he still needed, and came home some 3 or 4 hours later. During the trip, Morris asked, "Why do I feel as though she's a man in drag?"

Morris and I came home to find Joanne in the kitchen, looking dejected, and Nat in his bed.

"I have to tell you something," she said.

"Is it that you decided you don't want the job?"

"No, it's just that you've all been so kind, and…" her voice trailed off. "I just can't say it!"

I handed her a sheet of paper and a pencil, saying, "Then write it!"

Instead, she said, "I am in transition!"

"I beg your pardon," said I, "What the hell does that mean?"

"I'm in transition means that I am taking medication, but I haven't had the surgery yet!"

I now knew EXACTLY what she meant! I had never heard this latest psychobabble for transexuality! "Why didn't you tell us before?"

"I knew that if I told you, you wouldn't have hired me!"

Now I realized what her hints had meant when she spoke of her family history of hirsutism, and that her voice was peculiarly monotoned, and that she seemed, despite her intelligence, to have trouble in conversing with Nat. Of course! Her mind was preoccupied in her role-playing!

"We won't be able to hire you," said I.

"I never lied to you," she responded.

"Perhaps not, but I have always considered the sin of omission as great as that of commission! Please pack your things and leave," as Morris handed her a check for the 3 days.

She cried and left, and I went in to Nat and asked him what had gone on. He told me that Joanne had told him the same thing, whereupon he asked to be put down in his bed, giving the excuse that his back felt fragile. He added that he asked to lie down because he felt safer, citing the manner in which a friend with Muscular Dystrophy handled his alcoholic aide, knowing that his next-shift aide would find him. He also added, "I really didn't want to discuss this with her!"

Very smart was our darling…and the Reader will note, please, that we three ALWAYS referred to Joanne as "SHE."

A few weeks later, a letter arrived from the Connecticut Department of Labor, Unemployment Division, informing us that Joanne had applied to them for unemployment compensation, but they didn't understand the circumstances surrounding her "dismissal." They asked us to come to their office to clarify them.

The Rags of Time

We drove to Norwich. Here Morris took over, and explained that whenever we advertised for a companion/aide for Nat, we were not permitted by law to specify male or female, or non-smoker, also that no religious or racial preference could be asked for.

"When I put in the Ad, M/F, I did not expect them to be embodied in the same person!"

"What do you mean, Mr. Schwartz?"

"Joanne told us that she was 'in transition.'"
"WHAT?"

To this second "what?" Morris explained that we wanted ONE or the OTHER, not both!

I regret to say that after the social worker picked herself out of the chair in which she collapsed in laughter, we were excused, and we were all rather sorry for Joanne, who, if she had first called us to say what she intended to do, we would have supported her claim!

Perhaps it wouldn't have been honest...or legal...but we had a rather more compassionate feeling towards her, especially after we received a letter from her priest, the opening sentence of which read, "When I first met Joanna, and she told me, I was revolted!"

Oh yes, and Morris and Nat "compassionately" did not ever remind me of the night Joanne and I spent together!

We lost track of Joanne for years, but during the second day after Nat's death, the doorbell rang, but I felt I couldn't see anyone, or hear any more words of condolence, so I went into another room. Morris came to me afterwards and told me it was Joanne, whom he did not immediately recognize as she was dressed in a modish frock, her hair-styled, still soft-spoken, and who, with tears in her eyes, expressed her sorrow, and left.

Obviously, Joanne was no longer "in transition!"

Thus ended the Tragedy of Nat's Aides!

The Rags of Time

Chapter 16

In 1986, Nat met with some friends, disabled and able-bodied, and thus was born the idea for the Disability Network of Eastern Connecticut. We even suggested the name by which it is still known. The original purpose of this group was to be an all-encompassing organization to help the disabled in areas of education, to find them living quarters, to establish group homes which THEY ran, to provide for social needs, to help them find employment.

The group hoped to expand the horizons for those for whom "disability" was synonymous with loneliness, lack of opportunity, and whose entire horizons were confined by their family's lack of knowledge, or ability to "utilize" their environment.

In Nat's words: "To get political!"

In the beginning, meetings were held at members' homes. On several occasions, Mohegan College, now known as Three Rivers Community College, kindly lent space for the endeavor. Soon the membership expanded until a permanent home for the organization was necessary. Many venues were explored, and Nat plumped for one which was close to places of interest, or where there were restaurants, movie houses, shops, …anywhere which was, as he expressed it, "not in the boondocks!"

Nat actually located such a place in Niantic, not for any self-serving interest, but because the store was large, the rent affordable, and parking was unlimited.

I guess the road to hell IS paved with…etc.

D.N.E.C. wound up in Franklin, Connecticut, where it was close to nothing, not even to a member's home…just a confluence of roadways and filling stations.

It was not long after this that Nat decided to part company with this organization, as it grew to be managed and headed by the able-bodied, NOT the disabled. He felt that this was another example of "paternalism" by the able-bodied over the disabled. Nat, though a charter member, was totally ignored. Perhaps the other disabled members were not as aware of societal discriminations against the disabled. Decisions over the lives of the disabled were STILL made by the able-bodied! What example, asked Nat, did this send to Society, and/or to the disabled, who were supposedly fighting for recognition and independence? True independence, said he, lies within the spirit of the person, and is NOT based on mobility.

No answer was, or is, forthcoming, and the struggle continues!

But Nat did not give up on his long-cherished dream of creating another "Het Dorp" in the United States, and began to outline a plan for an organization which would have, as its main thrust, the locating of affordable and accessible housing for the disabled and their families. To this end, he tried to interest other disabled people to join him. He and his aide, Donna, set up a corporation and its guidelines with our lawyer's cooperation. It was named "Independent Living Is For Everyone," and used the acronym "INLIFE" on stationary and cards, and Nat had it imprinted on the special license plate he sported on his van.

And having, for many years, absorbed sufficient lessons from his, and our, dealings and experiences with governmental bureaucracy, and from what he thought of as errors of the other organizations, he felt that the only path to independence and survival for INLIFE was MONEY!

The Corporation listed Nat as its President, Donna Valente as his Executive Director, and all other positions such as Vice-President, Secretary/Treasurer, and Board Chairman, were held by disabled members. He was NOT going to have a group advocating for the rights of the disabled handed over to the able-bodied, no matter how well-intentioned!

The Rags of Time

Nat and the membership explored various ideas. Remembering that as a family, we had always supported Habitat for Humanity, both for its own sake, its philosophy, and because we sincerely liked and admired President Jimmy Carter and his commitment to it, Nat felt that this organization might be sympathetic to INLIFE's aims.

Nat dictated a letter to be sent to its office in our State, and received a reply saying they were certainly sympathetic, and that this was the first time they had been so approached. They would see what they could do, and what was it that INLIFE required of them? Nat replied that if there were buildings being renovated for sale, could one be found which would be both accessible and affordable for its members? Not as a group home, but there were several members of INLIFE who desired to share their lives, and also there were members with one or more persons suffering from Muscular Dystrophy, Cerebral Palsy, or other genetic conditions. Habitat said that they would keep INLIFE in mind.

Donna had an aunt who was a contractor/builder with a women's group, and tried to enlist their help. Other members concentrated on fund-raising by asking (and sometimes leaning on) people for donations of money, or goods which they might turn into money by running tag and garage sales. Morris helped at one such, by baking two dozen loaves of bread, which he priced so reasonably that they sold out quickly, and the following day, people rang our doorbell asking if there were more.

There were picnics and parties and cook-outs and boat-rides, carried out by the group, and generally people were responsive and generous…but Nat knew that unless some part of our government, whether local, state, federal, became involved, there would never be enough money for an American Het Dorp.

Nat haunted the library for books on grant-writing, and together with the membership, made proposals and sent them out. The mails may have flown, but the money did NOT flow in! Nor did any government agency hold out hope. Oh, they mouthed and wrote sympathy, but as any adult knows, they "Spoke with forked tongues!" Not for any politicians to go against whatever was the "prevailing custom."

The Rags of Time

I told Nat that he was like Don Quixote. Tilting at American windmills was not as successful as in Holland! But Nat was not to be deflected from his aim, his dream, and even when the membership became discouraged, this true Jaffe/Schwartz pepped them up and told grand tales of what he had seen in Het Dorp.

After five years of fund–raisers had amassed only $50,000, and every plan had foundered, Nat finally decided, together with the membership, that this was evidently not yet the time for this sensible and reasonable way for the disabled to enter the housing market. The heart-breaking realization came to haunt Nat when people called, referred to INLIFE by Infoline, and other established organizations for the disabled, and he felt powerless to help. He DID find housing for three or four individuals, but that was far from what he yearned to achieve.

"Het Dorp, USA," had been his dream!

During its fifth year, Nat decided to, as the by-laws dictated, abandon INLIFE, and donate all monies raised to other organizations which concerned themselves with health issues. Among the bequests was $5,000 to Jerry Lewis' Muscular Dystrophy Association, United Cerebral Palsy, Lawrence and Memorial Hospital, every AIDS foundation listed at the time, ambulance and visiting nurses' funds, until every penny in the bank account had found a more successful home.

Nat decided, with us, that for the time being, we would concentrate on his, and our, travels…and other pleasures!

Throughout the remaining years of his life, Nat lost the ability to swallow and chew easily, and we bought three Petite Moulis grinders. One traveled with him everywhere in his van, and also accompanied us to Europe, and one remained at home as a spare. Both in the United States and Europe, NO restaurant ever refused its use. Not every food required it, however when Nat desired some meat or vegetable which could not be fork-mashed, or cut small enough, he sent the Mouli with the waiter, and his food when served looked and tasted the same as his companions', although different in texture.

It grew more and more difficult for Nat to swallow many foods he formerly enjoyed, and his hospitalizations grew more and more frequent, as he aspirated these foods into his lungs, this often resulting in pneumonia.

The Rags of Time

One of Nat's doctors recommended that Nat have a permanent catheter placed through an opening in his stomach, through which foods, mainly liquid, could be fed to him several times a day. This recommendation **I** refused and so I told the sweet and kind Indian endocrinologist, Dr. Gautam, who Nat decided had saved his life on the occasion when his breathing grew labored, and his pallor frightened us.

Dr. Gautam, in the Emergency Room, asked Nat what he had ingested, and Nat spelled, "chicken," and the doctor sent down a probe which Nat dutifully swallowed, and Dr. Gautam saw it, removed the offending piece of food, complimented Nat on his fortitude, his good grasp of the procedure, and his cooperation. After this, Dr. Gautam was as Vishnu, the Hindu protector, and Nat asked to see him privately for a consultation.

He saw Nat alone at his office, while Morris and I waited, and afterwards called us into his office, and outlined his plan to place an opening into Nat's stomach. He explained the use of the tube, and about its care and cleansing.

As he spoke, I attempted to unclench my stomach muscles, and to keep my tears in check, as I delivered, as calmly as I could, my refusal to care for, or have anything to do with this tube. Quietly, I explained my reasons: Nat enjoyed the taste of food, and to dine out with friends, and that travels within and outside the country would be more difficult, and ended by saying, that if Nat chose to have this procedure, that I would NOT have anything to do with his feeding, or with the care for the tube; that his companion/aide would be totally responsible! That I wanted no part of it!

But the decision was Nat's.

He was in his early thirties, and had always made his own choices in, and for, his life…from an early age, CERTAINLY since his first Bar Mitzvah, which "turned him into a man."

Within, I felt as though the noose was tightening once again, about my own throat! Was I selfish? Perhaps I was, but my life flashed before me, increasingly fragmented, and Nat's, and STILL I had not one of my own…I was still in thrall to circumstances caused not by me! I felt sick at the realization that if I were being selfish, I must save my own life!

Morris sat quietly, not saying a word.

Morris and I knew, from the beginning, had been told by physicians when Nat was an infant, that his life span, considering the severity of his "inconvenience," that we fought, struggled, cried, and laughed over, to salvage whatever life we had, despite the pain, was not to be but 35 or so, years. I also knew that I could NOT go on much longer.

Oh, not that I was ill, or thought I would die, which I increasingly longed for, in the desperation I felt, when once, attempting to lift him from his chair, or bed, to his commode, I slipped beneath his weight, light as he was, and we both landed on the floor, the air knocked out of us both. I called, tersely, "Morris, Morris, come quickly!" He did, and picked us up...and I never forgot the tears, Nat's from pained surprise, mine from the knowledge that I could no longer count on my good health, and that age was overtaking me and Morris.

I couldn't ask Morris to undertake Nat's physical care, since his heart and lungs were not responding as they had in years gone by...and I was always afraid for him.

Dr. Gautam said he could reverse the intubation if Nat wished it. I left the decision to Nat, who refused it.

So, for years, Nat had his Mouli, and we continued to travel, with or without Nat, as he made independent plans for travel in the United States, or he went to France, while we went to the United Kingdom, to Wales, to search out books, or London or Ireland.

When Nat felt especially depressed, he went to see his very dear "older brother," Les, who listened to his fears and anguish over his decreasing ability to eat, or his despair that, much as he wished it, he could not marry and have children of his own. He considered Les' three children as "his," called himself their Godparent as each was born. His relationship with Les and his family gradually became one of the most important in his life, and always he tried to enjoy their triumphs, and was always on the lookout for some gift or pleasure he could bestow on them.

The Rags of Time

When Nat decided that perhaps he was become too much of a physical burden on us, he privately enlisted Les' help and support for a contract he worked out, so that if WE became incapacitated, or if he predeceased us, Les would take care of us! A pretzeled concept indeed, since Les was to be HIS guardian in the event of our demise! Les told us afterwards that Nat even enlisted the help of a lawyer to legalize the "contract!"

It had always been difficult to find a gift for Nat's birthdays because he always had all the clothes, books, recordings, trips, or anything else he might express a wish for, so when his 32nd birthday drew near, in reply to my annual, "What do you want for your birthday?" we were surprised and delighted when his response was, "May I have a second Bar Mitzvah?"

That was a request we had not expected, but it seems that he had discussed the possibility with his rabbi, who was very supportive. Nat asked me to call him, and we planned the date, invitations and food for the Kiddush, the celebratory buffet at the Synagogue. I enlisted the aid and advice of the rabbi's wife, a lovely, intelligent, and warm-hearted woman, who was very enthusiastic, and offered to prepare some special dishes we enjoyed at other Synagogue events, and she suggested certain wines, amounts of food we would need, and daily, Nat grew more and more excited…and very happy!

For Nat's first Bar Mitzvah, Morris and I had also catered a luncheon party at our home, and we contacted a caterer in Niantic who kindly sent special chafing dishes and trays, as Nat was very much a favorite in our town of Niantic, and people were interested in the entire project.

Nat wrote another speech, and I regret that I don't have a copy as they were all distributed…but I do remember that he quoted Maimonides: "If not now, When?…If not I, then Who?" …and as in all his other writings, he wove himself, his ideas, and ideals and spirit, into the speech. He was happiest when Les and the children attended, and read portions of the Torah. It was for all, a memorable day!

A surprise awaited us during the party at our home: there appeared a reporter and photographer from our newspaper, The Day, to interview Nat. Either the rabbi or his wife, or someone from the Synagogue, made mention of

The Rags of Time

the Bar Mitzvah of a disabled congregant, and since Nat was known to the newspaper from countless past articles, Nat felt it to be rather his due!

Modesty was NOT a trait to be applied to Nat! A great day, a great article, for a very great human soul!

Nat's aide, Donna, lived with her husband and two young sons in a neighboring town, and Nat went often to swim in their in-ground pool. Donna posed Nat on the pool-deck, and he "sat" in a wicker chair and smiled at us. When he gave it to us in its gold-metal frame, inscribed, "Mom and Dad, From your loving son, June 6, 1991," which was our anniversary, Morris and I kissed him…then I wept, because he had never before sat in a chair. This sudden transformation was due to the fact that while her husband took the photo, Donna kneeled behind him, and through the wicker of the chair, had hold of his shirt, and so kept him from sliding to the ground.

Time is inexorable. We may not feel its passage, but it flows like a river, no matter our conscious or unconscious denial of its existence. Despite our, and Nat's attempt to bridge, to dam it, Nat was on his way to death.

How can I write this?

Nat went to our lawyer, Kenneth McKeever, in Niantic, who drew up his will, also a "Living Will," in which he insisted that other than to keep him pain-free, no resuscitation was to be performed if he fell into oblivion. We honored his wishes, and distributed copies to our doctor, the lawyer kept one, and gave a copy to our local hospital, and of course, we added this to our other papers regarding Nat. Nat had stated in his will the wish to be cremated as were his grandparents, and what we, his parents, wished for ourselves. All was legally written, witnessed, for him and for us.

Don't imagine that the Schwartzes dwelled on thoughts of death! No, we went about our daily duties, pursued our various interests, traveled, entertained, as always.

We laughed, loved, and lived!

310

The Rags of Time

One night Nat awakened me from sleep and complained of feeling ill. "It's hard to breathe, Mom" and when I took his temperature, it was very elevated. I woke Morris who drove us to the hospital. There, the doctors confirmed another pneumonia, and admitted Nat to the ICU. I, of course, stayed with Nat, while Morris went home to alert the aide, and to see to our Wolf/Dane's welfare, and then to call Les, who arrived the next day, as Nat's condition steadily worsened. I remained with Nat all the day, as well as the nights, which I spent either in a chair, or on the couch of the small ICU waiting room.

I was not the only one in vigil, as the loved ones of other ICU patients spoke among ourselves, but mostly I withdrew into a book. Morris came daily, and together we sat at Nat's bedside to converse with him, if he were alert enough. Mostly we sat.

Les and his children, and many other friends of his and of ours visited, had to wait for hours, away from him, until one or another medical procedure, or visitor, left his bedside.

But Nat had, on the third or fourth day, already died for Morris and me, when in keeping him pain-free, so much morphine was administered, that his eyes bulges, and he seemed not to be able to see, and then his eyes were covered with soft cotton pads, and so since he could by no other means convey his thoughts and feelings, or communicate in the spelling-mode we had employed since he was a little child, we were just able to grasp his hands and speak our love. We could only guess, amidst our barely controlled tears, what if anything he wanted to express. Even his hands could not press ours as we sat together, while I spoke love, or read to him from a favorite book, until a nurse or visitor claimed him.

This went on for another week, and Les came often, alone or with the children, who prayed over him and made their personal farewells. Nat's rabbi and his wife came several times. The ICU was wonderful in their affectionate attentions, and the doctors came and went.

Did Nat ever hear us?

Early one morning while seated in the lounge, our doctors emerged on their "rounds" from seeing Nat, and I bearded them in the hallway, and they recommended intubation for Nat's breathing…and I finally exploded into rage:

The Rags of Time

"Can you tell me that Nat will come out of the hospital at least as well as when he was admitted?"

"No, but…"

"You know that Nat has a Living Will. A copy is in your office, in the hospital records, and I want you to enforce it, and if you do not, I swear that I will break every window in this damned place, and create such a disturbance…," I screamed.

"LET HIM GO! IF I CAN LET HIM GO, I who have adored and nurtured him for the whole of his life, I order you to remove life-support systems, all the tubes, and LET HIM GO! Let him die with some dignity and control!"

They looked at each other, and did just that. Later that day I accompanied Nat's bed as it was taken out of ICU and down to another floor, the pulmonary section, which unfortunately knew us well. I called Morris, and he called Les who came up from New York the following morning. While Nat's aide remained at his bedside in the little curtained cubicle opposite the nursing station, Morris, Les and I went home where I had a much-needed shower, and reunion with Pepper, our Wolf-Dane, who, Morris told me later, went into Nat's room daily, slept on his floor nightly, and wandered the house between times looking for Nat, and who was always surprised at being left alone for such long periods.

I had just finished drying off, when Nat's companion called from the hospital with a terse and teary, "You'd better come at once please!"

It was a ride impossible to imagine, as impossible as this is to write. Les drove as Morris and I sat apart, anchorless, for almost the first time in our married lives. We jumped from the van while Les parked, and found Nat, still alive, but unresponsive, while we grasped his hands, crying, and articulated love amidst now unremembered phrases of sobbed-out endearments, kissing his face and hands, and suddenly his hands grew even more limp in ours, he grew cooler to the touch, the aide called for a nurse, and death was put at 10:15, Saturday, May 21, 1994.

The Rags of Time

Nat had been born on a Saturday morning at 10:30, just 35 years before!

Many ran to comfort Morris and me, who could not be comforted.

Les drove us from the hospital to the Byles-MacDougal Memorial Home in New London, and we arranged for Nat's body to be released to them for cremation, gave them a few salient fact about him, and a wallet-photo for the obituary in The Day newspaper. Then we drove home to do…nothing…still in shock, even though we had known the outcome in advance. Les went to his home in New York.

I asked Morris to take us somewhere, anywhere, just to shake off our darkness of soul, to give us another place to view through our unseeing eyes. Pepper accompanied us as we walked through one of Nat's favorite towns, the Stonington Borough, telling people we knew of Nat's death, just to hear the words, and thinking we might not break down, as we stunned them with the news, in that way perhaps to convince ourselves that "IT" had actually happened.

In this "best of all possible worlds," a child is NOT supposed to die before the parents.

It goes against nature!

Many people said, "Now Nat is walking and speaking as everyone else!"

Was this supposed to comfort us?

It did not!

That night, unaccountably, I told Morris that I wanted to go to the local cinema. We saw "Four Weddings and a Funeral," and I remember that at 8:25 PM, precisely, a poem is read attributed to W.H. Auden, and which deals with the death of the beloved partner of a homosexual man. We didn't recognize the poem, or find it in any of our Auden collections of poetry.

Later that night, we received a call from John Foley, an editor of The Day, who spoke with Morris and told him that the small obituary and photo had just passed his desk and was "too short, and doesn't say enough about your remarkable son!" Also, that he was going to add other "credits," and then, finally, Morris and I went to bed...or to be alone...to begin to be alone forever!

To be the remaining two points of a "triangle."

The following afternoon, we received a condolence visit from Rabbi and Mrs. Astor. When we explained that Nat was to be cremated, according to his wish, the rabbi told us that Conservative Judaism did not sanction cremation, "So, Nat's memorial, if there is to be one, will have to be held elsewhere, here at your home, perhaps?"

Rabbi Nager of Amsterdam, where are you when we need you?

I informed Rabbi Astor, that while his Synagogue was important to Nat, it was NOT important to us. We pointed out that the Young Men's Club of the Congregation had NEVER invited Nat to a single one of its functions, and despite Nat's hurt at this exclusion, his father and I had never, despite our rage, ever discussed this with Nat.

"You did not hesitate to ask Nat to write the occasional sermon, or to join your classes, and knowing his interest and background, since age five, in Judaism, why did you never intercede in his treatment by other members of your congregation?" His wife, seated at his side, nodded in agreement.

An old and marvelous Spanish proverb says,

"If I die, I forgive you.
If I recover, we shall see!"

But I, his mother, am alive, and unforgiving!

We informed the rabbi that he would be notified of the date and time of Nat's Memorial, and that he might, in Nat's memory, speak first, that I would speak next, then anyone who so desired, and that Morris would be the final speaker.

That Sunday night, at precisely 8:20, I asked for permission to enter the movie house, and in the dark, scribbled on the pad I had brought with me, the opening two lines of the poem. The next day, we went to our library to find their collections of Auden's works, but the poem we sought was not there, and a librarian kindly called the fine library at Connecticut College, explaining the reason for our search. They sent word that they would locate it. Could we come the next day? When we arrived, it was to find that they had already found the volume, opened it to the page, had made several copies for us, and asked if we wanted additional copies.

But then, book-lovers are wonderful people!

Auden wrote, in *Two Songs For Hedli Anderson*:

> *"Stop all the clocks, cut off the telephone,*
> *Prevent the dog from barking with a juicy bone,*
> *Silence the pianos and with muffled drum*
> *Bring out the coffin, let the mourners come.*
>
> *Let aeroplanes circle moaning overhead*
> *Scribbling on the sky the message He Is Dead,*
> *Put crepe bows round the white necks of the public doves,*
> *Let traffic policemen wear black cotton gloves.*
>
> *He was my North, my South, my East, and West,*
> *My working week and my Sunday rest,*
> *My noon, my midnight, my talk, my song;*
> *I thought that love would last for ever: I was wrong.*
>
> *The stars are not wanted now: put out every one;*
> *Pack up the moon and dismantle the sun;*
> *Pour away the ocean and sweep up the wood.*
> *For nothing now can ever come to any good."*

While all this was going on, we were contacted by our very dear Connecticut children, the Lloyd Bayreuther family, and Lloyd told us that whenever the tides and weather were in alignment (which sounded rather Astral to me), he would take us out in a boat so we might scatter Nat's ashes in Long Island Sound.

The Rags of Time

For years, I had teased Nat with the statement that after I was cremated, I wanted my ashes scattered on water, "I don't care what water, even flush them down the toilet, since ALL water eventually flows to all water!" Nat laughed, and expressed a similar preference, since he loved water and boating when given the opportunity by friends, but added that he DID object to the idea of the toilet, no matter the meandering of waterways!

Nat's ashes were delivered to us in a shoe-box-sized container.

Morris did me the kindness of taking charge of the box. He told me that he had an idea of how Nat's ashes were to be scattered. "Nat has always been our hero, so I have decided to give him a Hero's burial. I am going to build a miniature Viking ship which will contain his ashes, and we will send the vessel out to sea while it is aflame!"

Morris did just that. He disappeared into the "bowels of the earth" of our home, which is what I always called his shop in our basement, there to expiate, or try to, his sorrow during these first weeks after Nat's death. He did some research, and the local lumberyard became his daily destination, as he searched out the thinnest pieces of pine, cut into lengths, and which he bent into the peculiar ovoid shape in which these legendary ships had been constructed. He lined the exterior with pieces of tinfoil, and curved the interior so it might hold something, yet not be evident from the outside.

On a visit to my oldest friend, Dorothy Ross, in upstate New York, in New Paltz, with ever-present Pepper, in a small shop, we found a tiny, carved wooden dog, which would serve as the symbol of the earthly world. Some such symbol was always present on a Viking Death Ship, and Morris placed it in the vessel. He bought boxes of tiny birthday candles, and together with the shredded paper sold for Easter baskets, mixed this with Nat's ashes, and tinfoiled everything, but the top, which was destined to be set afire.

For days Morris worried about providing a foolproof system to ensure that the Viking vessel would burn once it was set in the water, and set aflame. Since Nat always wore a colorful kerchief around his neck when he ate in a restaurant, it being for him, more socially acceptable than a towel or a bib, and he owned dozens to match whatever shirt he chose to wear, I picked one which on a white background was speckled with a rainbow of confetti-sized dots. This Morris fashioned as a "sail," and which when attached to the mast he built, would both catch the wind, and burn.

It all seemed most fitting, and the vessel, when complete, measured about three feet in length.

On the chosen day, Morris and I met with Lloyd and his brother John, who actually owned the boat, and would "captain" it to the spot we picked, midway between Connecticut and the nearest New York landmark. Morris brought with him a can of lighter fluid, fireplace matches, and a very long, telescoping rod, which would be used to shove the Viking vessel, when lit, away from the boat carrying us all.

The day itself was Hollywood-Motion-Picture perfect. A blue sky, almost cloudless, a breeze. It was about 6 PM in June, when suddenly there appeared in the distance, and swept overhead, clouds, which ranged, like any rainbow, the entire spectrum of color, from yellow-orange to dark red-blue-purple.

As Morris stood poised to ignite the "sail," Lloyd asked, "Are you sure this will float?"

Good question!

Morris replied, in surprise, "I don't know. We haven't tried it!" and lit the masted sail, put the Viking ship into the water, pushed it away for the length of the pole, and, as we watched, the sail caught fire…then was aflame…and the breeze was strong enough to carry it off, the little concave waves surrounding it, and away it went until it was almost lost to view, the flames still a bit visible, then beginning to sink, the vessel was lost to view, but an echo of flame appeared now and then. Morris said, "Let's go home now!"

We wept a little, and a lot, all the four!

When the boat was again docked, Morris and I felt strangely comforted. Once home, we both, Morris and I, had a vodka, and again toasted our Viking, our Hero. We had not waited to see the vessel disappear beneath the waves…and Morris had performed his last bit of service, had fulfilled the promise made to Nat, and to himself…made it a reality.

The Rags of Time

Before Nat's final illness, Morris and I had planned another trip to England with him and with the woman who currently served as his aide. Hotel reservations, actually two flats, had been rented in our names in a new, very upscale apartment/hotel. We already had the tickets, our passports were in order, and we were set to go at the end of June for an early summer vacation. Naturally, when Nat died in mid-May, the trip was cancelled. Also cancelled were the hotel arrangements. Morris called the manager and explained the circumstances, and she was very understanding, and refunded our very large down-payment.

The English have ever been, and remain, a civilized people, kind and compassionate as always, to us. I think people there respond to the genuine and verbal and enthusiastic appreciation we have always evinced to them about their country.

Many people were invited to Nat's Memorial, which was held at our home...outdoors on the deck, and spilling over into the house. Even those neighbors who had NEVER graced our home by their presence, came bearing flowers, pastries, and condolences. There were 40 or more of us present.

This was June. Those of us on the deck stood or sat, the Rabbi mouthed platitudes of how Nat first came to his attention at the hospital many years before, and his confused impressions of someone unable to speak, who only made sounds, and of Nat's other physical disability, and then, finally, he realized Nat's solid knowledge of Torah and the tenets of Judaism, and on and on...and then he spoke the Kaddish, the prayer for the dead.

As I had earlier prepared the rabbi, I then spoke. I told the assemblage of Nat as a small boy, of his constant struggles for recognition, of his painful physical suffering, and of his grace under pain, and told them that I was going "to tell it as it was" to be the mother of a disabled child, his life day by day, and ended in a few minutes by reading Nat's own words from one of his poems, which spoke of his endless frustration of having a good mind, trapped in a useless body, and his rage at Society's indifference, and small cruelties. I was NOT going to assuage the gathering's conscience, by mouthing inanities, as did the mother of a small disabled child, who wrote a letter to a newspaper, calling her son, "my angel. Every day I thank God for him," and on, ad nauseum!

The Rags of Time

No, there was no solace in God, no solace in waking each morning with the ache, the fist in the heart, as you opened your eyes to a new day, and to the knowledge that YOUR son would never know the adventures, the loves, the passions, most able-bodied persons took for granted.

I never asked, "Why me? Why us?" Because I would not, could not, wish that kind of life on anyone. Enough it was that WE, we had the ability, the talent, the guts, the love, to deal with our, and Nat's life!

Each day was interminable, every successive day was spent in pain. I realized that Morris and I must deal with our grief alone. We did not so much comfort each other, or take comfort in our shared loss, but grieved alone, in separate fashion. Morris withdrew from me, from almost everyone.

In the same way that we had not leaned on, or tested each other during our early years together, during my adjustments to my failed pregnancies, which a woman cannot share with her husband, or closest friends, we were now alien to each other in our reactions to Nat's death.

We were almost too restless for grief!

I reentered my "bustling mode," compelled to listen to music, to talk, to devise plans for the spending of each day, and at first, thought to involve Morris in my way of grief.

But Morris met it more contemplatively; he read biographies, researched his hobby of compiling movie facts about silent, or early and sometimes remote films. He created crossword puzzles, made up other forms of them, over which he spent solitary hours, and watched mind-numbing television.

I spent hours roaming the streets, walking with Pepper, or alone, haunting antique shops for nothing in particular…not buying, just looking. For what?

For my life!

The Rags of Time

Chapter 17

By September we had had enough of our dance, of circling each other. We decided to go to England to either resume our "dance" …or to again become a twosome, who simply two-stepped our way to a life we could enjoy, could again walk hand-in-hand, laugh together at shared jokes, remembrances, try to build a life not always rooted in pain. Perhaps even to discover a happiness not based only on the struggle to reshape our world to meet the needs of our son.

Usually, in earlier times of travel, we drove to Les and his family the day before we went abroad, spent the night, and then Les or a member of his family drove us to Kennedy Airport, and on our return picked us up, and after hugs, kisses, the dispersal of gifts, we returned to Niantic.

This time, however, we refused their hospitality, and took a limousine from home directly to the airport. It was less painful, especially since the Jewish High Holy Days were a few days off, and the Ghosts of Holidays Past, and Nat's participation in the rituals of Les' home, only recalled pain to us.

It was difficult to remember that one of Nat's fondest wishes and dreams, was to be present at his "Godson, Noah's Bar Mitzvah." For this occasion, he had, years before the event, bought a special "Bar Mitzvah Bear," and asked that Noah be given other presents on his special day…all this being reminiscent of his grandfather's unfulfilled desire to be present at HIS!

As much as we didn't want to attend, just a week after Nat's death, we DID go to Les' home to spend the celebratory days with his family. When we arrived, Les told us that the speech Noah had written and memorized, Noah rewrote to also honor and express his love for Nat. Also, during the Bar Mitzvah, when a grandfather or a close male relative was to go to the Bimah and remove the

Torah from its accustomed place in the Ark, Noah requested that his grandfather give way, and allow Morris that honor.

This time however, we simply could not face the prospect and Nat's absence. When we arrived in London, and an Airbus took us to our hotel, we asked for a "cuppa" while our room was made ready for us. It was about 10 AM. Then we unpacked, took a walk to regain our "land legs," and while on that stroll noticed that a block away was a church on which was scaffolding, and roof repairs were in progress. We admired its stained-glass windows from the out-side, now almost blocked with metal scaffolds and tarpaulins, and went to what we assumed was the front door. It was locked, and so we went to an almost hidden side-door, and rang its bell, and to the man who answered, I asked if it were possible to gain admittance?

He sent us around to the side, and we followed a stone-pathway, which led back to the front door, which he opened for us. The interior, not very large, was beautiful, and there was a myriad of statuary scattered about, and on the walls were marble plaques. He explained that he was the Verger, what Nat called, a "sacred superintendent," and that he was responsible for all secular doings of this, the St. Stephen's Church, Church of England, in theological terms. Rather like the American Episcopal Church, and that it had NOT been built in Romanesque times, as I had thought from its architecture, but in the mid 1800's, though in a somewhat Romanesque style. He invited us to look around. We were the only visitors, it not being the time of day for services and masses.

As I walked about, admiring the windows and architecture, I had the thought that since the following day was but a day from the first day of the Jewish Holiday, rather than to attempt to light a memorial candle for Nat, and perhaps burn down the hotel, I might light one of the votive candles set in so many places in this church. I first asked Morris' permission, and at his acquiescence, went to the Verger who was again walking through the chapel and asked HIS permission:

"We are Jewish. Is it possible, permissible, to light a candle in memory of our son who died 5 months ago?"

"Yes, of course," he replied.

"Where might I light it?"

"Whatever speaks to you."

"Can you perhaps change a five pound note?"

He gave me five one-pound coins.

I looked again at the statuary, which were all marble depictions of a Jesus figure or of Mary holding an infant Jesus. There was one marble figure, a small Mary, holding the hand of a standing, small Christ-child. I looked toward Morris for his reaction, then at his nod of assent, I put the pound coin in the attached metal cup, below a sign which asked for 40 pence, lit a taper from another burning candle, then lit a glassed-in votive candle in front of the carved marble statue.

Only then did I look at the wall in back of the figure, to see that there, in a somewhat shield-shaped and engraved marble plaque, was incised:

"Of your charity
Pray for the repose of the soul of
THOMAS STEARNS ELIOT O.M.
Born St. Louis, Missouri
26 September 1888
Died London 4th January 1965
A Churchwarden of
this parish for 25 years
He worshipped here until his death"

Beshert!

I ran to Morris, seated a short distance away, his tears as evident as my own, and when he read the inscription, agreed! It WAS fated to be the place, because T.S. Eliot was Nat's favorite poet.

At this point, the Verger re-emerged, and wiping my eyes, I told him of Nat's study of and love for Eliot, and the Verger's surprise grew, as well as his enthusiasm, and he insisted on giving us some postcards sold by the Church, showing that particular plaque, and insisted we not pay for them, and invited us back whenever we wished and drew for us on the back of some Church papers he had with him, a map of where in London Eliot had lived. He told us that Eliot's wife still attended the Church (his second wife, since the first one had died while institutionalized). He asked to hear about Nat and his disability, and agreed that evidently Nat had made HIS choice as to where the candle was to be lit!

Despite this very kind man's insistence that we not, we did leave the other 4 pounds for the cards...and did not inform him that we already knew where Eliot had lived, having made the discovery several years earlier, by the round, blue enamel plaque affixed to the outside of the apartment house, similar to the many plaques around London, and all of England, which announced to tourists and residents, the former living quarters of their famous artists, writers, poets, musicians, scientists, statesmen.

In America, unfortunately, we are more apt to tear down historic buildings, than enshrine their famous occupants. The Grand Central Station building is a case in point, because use of "air space" was envisioned. If it were not for Jaqueline Kennedy's efforts to gain funds and public support, that, and many other historic and beautiful architectural marvels would be gone.

America tends to throw its history on the scrap heap!

On that trip to England, we decided to also memorialize Nat at synagogues as well. One day, soon after, in passing through Kensington Station, I saw a young man hunkered down on the tile floor of the tube station, reading some school text. Since he was wearing a yarmulke, I tapped him on his shoulder, and when he looked up, asked him what synagogue he attended? He must have thought me slightly insane, but Morris explained why we asked, and he told us that the Great Synagogue of London was not far, and we gave him thanks. The next morning we sought it by taxi. When we arrived, we saw a nondescript office-type building, also wreathed by scaffolding.

Was all of London readying itself, beautifying itself, for the Schwartzes?

Once in the building, we saw that the right side of the main floor was the synagogue, with bimah, stained-glass windows, pews...and absolutely empty!

The Rags of Time

An announcement posted by the elevator sent us to the rabbi's office on the third floor. Inside, the rabbi pointed us to some chairs as he completed some business with a congregant. When he acknowledged us, we told him of Nat's death, and that we wanted to make a donation to the synagogue in Nat's name and asked him to say the Kaddish for him.

"Of course. What is your Yiddish name, Sir?"
"Moishe," replied Morris.
"Your son?"
"Nussin Dovid."

The rabbi was uninterested in mine!

I presented the rabbi with a "double chai" in pounds, which added up to 36 pounds, but much more in American currency. This pleased the rabbi mightily, we gave our thanks, and did not mention the lighted candle in front of T.S. Eliot…or Mary and the Christ-child.

Still on our religious "pilgrimage," we ventured to Golder's Green, an upscale Jewish neighborhood, and on the tram, we passed many lovely gardens surrounding brick homes, very Long Islandish, I thought. We had the good fortune to sit at right angles to a woman who entertained us with gossip about the area, its good restaurants, and when she mentioned Bloom's, we knew where we were to lunch. Bloom's was originally located in London's East End, and was famous as the best "Cold Beef" restaurant, and we had gone there with Nat in years past. "Cold Beef" meant pastrami, corned beef, p'tcha (jellied veal bones), borscht, and other delectables.

When we left the tram, I stopped a young woman who wore a sheitl, a wig, long sleeves and hose and long skirt, which made me feel rather warm on this September day when the temperature was in the upper 70's, and also took me back to the days when Nat attended the Hebrew Academy. This young woman pushed a small boy, yarmulked, who smiled up at us as I stopped her.

"Excuse me, but can you tell me where the nearest Orthodox Synagogue is, in the area?"

"Why, please?" said she, looking startled.

The Rags of Time

"My son, who was a Hebrew scholar died recently and we want an Orthodox Rabbi to say Kaddish for him."

She pointed to the left where there was the synagogue we wanted. With thanks all around, we walked in the direction she indicated and passed some elegant shops, we came to Bloom's, and decided to lunch first. Borscht beckoned!

When we entered Bloom's, were seated, and gave our order, I saw a man wearing a cook's apron and a black hat, and who sported a lush beard, and decided that this was the person who would know exactly where the synagogue was located.

He was seated, eating his own lunch, and I asked the same question I had asked the young woman. Why did I want to know? I repeated the sad tale of Nat's death, and he told me that the synagogue was closed until evening services, but that HE would give the rabbi our request, and the double chai I gave him, and I decided to trust to his good offices after he took the information as to Nat's and Morris' Yiddish names.

Again, I was JUST the mother, hence, "relatively" unimportant, so no information was sought as to my Jewish/Hebrew background!

Finally, Morris and I decided that there were no other offerings we could make in Nat's memory, or for the repose of his soul. We, his parents, had made them for 35 years, and we hoped that his superb sense of humor would see him through to eternity.

Morris and I spent the remaining several weeks of our English journey with friends we met along the way. We seem to "pick up" people wherever we go. Some remained friends for years, some were useful for entertainment for the amount of time we assigned them.

Does that sound uncaring or cruel?

It's not meant to be, because we gave of ourselves in at least equal amount. We were, and I remain, fun to be with, if we, and I, are not bored, one of the three principle vices in our lexicon of modest expectations!

The Rags of Time

English Theatre remains a marvelous source of enjoyment, whether good or bad, because there is always SOMETHING outstanding, if not good acting in a mediocre play, perhaps the scenery, or an outstanding production of a well-loved Shakespearean play, to which we could silently mouth the words, and the speeches.

When we learned that the New Globe Theatre was under construction, and that guided tours were available in the unfinished theatre, we went to Bankside, Southwark, in London, and walked over the Southwark Bridge from the Mansion House tube stop. We passed wine bars in this commercial area of banks, investment houses, all this area being new to us, and once across the Southwark Bridge over the Thames on the St. Paul's side, we descended a steep metal stair, passed cobbled side streets, and there was a faithful copy of the famed "Wooden O," an almost completed replica of the Old Globe Theatre. When we entered for our tour, and saw what was being built, the first of many eerie chills of delight…and disbelief, hit us.

During the tour, we saw the not-yet-completed walls which are composed of horsehair mixed with plaster, as in Shakespeare's day, woodwork attached NOT with nails, but wooden pegs, saw the first rows of seats and the partitions separating them, and could imagine the "groundlings" space, the as-yet empty stage…and fell in love!

Morris and I bought paper "bricks" to help finance the building, and gave them to all the people we loved in America…and again mourned the loss, as we, oh so profoundly, missed our son for whom Shakespeare had been an almost "living presence," since he had read so extensively and had seen as many productions in America and England as possible.

We could identify with the American actor and director, Sam Wanamaker, in his single-minded dedication to the re-creation of The Globe. Story has it that when Wanamaker had visited London many years before, he asked fellow-actors to be shown the Globe, and reacted in shock and dismay when told that it had burned down 400 years earlier.

In his fervor to return this miracle of Elizabethan theatre to England, Wanamaker worked tirelessly to get donations, to research the architecture, spent years of time, and finally, sans any donations from the British government, it

327

was built. Of course, because the Schwartzes had made donations, Morris and I came away knowing that in small measure, Nat was again "remembered" in a concrete way.

When we read in an American newspaper that The Globe was to reopen with a production of "The Life of Henry the Fift," we sent for tickets before another scheduled trip to London. Of course, as Americans, we sent for the most expensive tickets, on the top floor of the center section, to make sure we saw everything. The tickets cost a hot 20 pounds, or almost $30.00 a seat.

As luck would have it, these seats were in full sun during the performance, and it was as warm in London as during any July or August in Connecticut. What we also didn't know was that the wood-plank seats under us, some eight or ten inches in depth, were as hard then, and as uncomfortable, as when Inigo Jones had installed them in the 1600's!

I ran down to the ground floor, where for about two pounds each, and I would have cheerfully paid twenty pounds, we rented pads for some small measure of comfort...very small! We then learned that there was a vendor who would have come upstairs to us, to make "seat calls." The theatre of Shakespeare's day was interactive. The "groundlings," and indeed anyone in the theatre, from any seat, felt free to call out his reactions to whatever was happening on stage. Suffice it to say that when the "French" soldiers (actors) spoke their lines, the audience booed lustily and frequently. The "English" soldiers won cheers, just as loud as the detractors of the French.

The "groundlings" proved to be the most favored after all. During the "interval," they were served tea, brought in on one of the teacarts in the lobby, but I decided it wasn't worth the effort, and so we went "dry!" Morris and I also stripped down to whatever clothing would not land us in Newgate Prison...and unfortunately, not enough clothes could be shed! When the scene arrived in "Henry The Fift," wherein the young standard-bearers were discovered massacred, there was not a dry eye in the house...certainly not in our row of seats. THERE, the sobbing was audible! The rage against the "French Army" who had perpetrated this evil was noisily evident.

This production was one of the most thrilling we had ever seen...and Morris and I had seen the play enacted many times on stage, and in film. Throughout, we, and the other members of our hip-to-hip row, could be heard softly murmuring the familiar speeches. Well, what did you expect? It WAS interactive theatre, after all!

Nat would have adored it…and were he with us, we would have enjoyed it even more, because we three would have been groundlings, and had the advantage of Nat's wheelchair next to the stage, AND we would all have had tea.

Because the "Wooden O" is open to the sky, and there is no heat or electricity, the audience chances change in the weather, but Morris and I, over the years, scheduled and schlepped many an English or newly-met tourist from wherever, to the New Globe and contributed money to this "Wooden Jewel." Sadly, Sam Wanamaker died before its completion and before the initial performance in 1997.

When first Morris, Nat and I moved to our home in Niantic, we were often asked, "Where will you spend your vacation?" This surprised me and I replied that as "city" folk, and this being as green and vast a piece of property, bordered on two sides by water, as we ever owned, we would vacation in this, our home. For some years we were very content with long daily walks through our town, our dogs leashed to us, entertaining the many friends and relatives from the "city" who were curious about our "country" life. We spent time in the minutia of our daily lives, each in his own way, took trips by car to places remembered by Morris from his boyhood years in Moodus, or my schoolmarm years in Madison.

We did make a few annual visits to Manhattan, calling this, "going for our New York fix," to revisit museums, concerts, ballets, theatres, to see the few remaining relatives still NOT retired to Florida. And of course, on every visit, we reunited with our beloved Herman Goustin. We went to restaurants formerly enjoyed, but sadly, New York City had altered…and not for the better. Each time it seemed seedier, dirtier, than the year before, many of "the old familiar places" had been torn down to make way for yet another store or skyscraper or business or apartment dwelling. The familiar skyline was no longer in place, and almost every mid-town street had enormous pits where buildings once stood, and either were fenced by lovely many-hued doors, or chicken wire, all plastered by signs, posters, or notices of future glories to sprout from the concrete.

The Rags of Time

Uglier and uglier, was our verdict, so trips to Manhattan became, oxymoronically, increasingly rare. We changed our destination to other states, other countries, to find some vestiges of our past.

When Morris and I returned from one such European trip after Nat's death, we decided that we would extend the "conspicuous consumption" of artifacts to add to our collections, to the accumulation of people. We tried to justify our restless urge to escape our newly-emptied lives, by searching for books we each collected, and so went to Hay-on-Wye in Wales, or to Scotland for some woolens and Georgian silver, to London and Bath for antique marionettes and puppets to flesh out our growing collection. These were Morris' bailiwick...and mine was Japanese Ukiyo-é, some pieces of Art Nouveau, and generally, we looked for whatever we deemed beautiful...and hopefully, affordable.

Morris and I worked as a team. If Morris spotted something he desired, or if we both did, he would approach the seller and ask, naively, "What is that?" or "What do you want for this?" and if neither approach was successful, I, the BIG GUN, would be sent in, and I countered with, "Give me your best price and I'll take it off your hands immediately!" This two-pronged approach was surprisingly effective, and often we carried the day...and carried off the object in question! Of course, we knew exactly WHAT the object was, as well as its probable value, and relied heavily on our combined wit and charm. Often, we made valuable friends among the dealers, who, if we did not buy anything that day, would keep in touch, and sometimes "find" what we wanted.

Morris and I very much enjoyed the friendly banter and good-will these antiquing expeditions afforded us.

Oh, we were a charming pair! And very often our charm paid off as we purchased genuine and lovely artifacts.

We made some wonderful friends, and assuaged our less-than-charming loneliness. Sometimes we corresponded with them, and entertained them if they came to the United States, and they enjoyed seeing us in our "native habitat" as we had seen them in theirs.

Except for gifts for special friends, we really didn't spend a great deal of money. I enjoyed "bargaining" with storekeepers, as I had learned to do in Mexico under the tutelage of Julio, our guide, but I knew that European tradesmen were a different sort all together. We were respectful, always, but were equally ready to admit, "I'm sorry, we absolutely LOOOOVE this, but just can't afford it!" Sometimes, even THAT worked, as the sellers were so taken by our good-naturedly rueful response, they actually lowered their prices, sometimes by quite a bit.

I guess they hated to see our disappointment!

I think that I also, in writing this, have tipped my hand. But since I no longer have the money, or space, to buy anything more, and have dispensed some of my treasures as gifts in lieu of being able to buy anything of comparable beauty or value, both I and the recipients are happy.

So Morris and I began "collecting" people and experiences instead. And with at least as much pleasure and satisfaction.

A number of years ago, Morris and I became acquainted with the young daughter of Niantic friends while at a concert in Niantic, and I was drawn to Marla as she enthused happily about a proposed trip to London. "I've always wanted to go to London," said this 12 or 13 year old. Since I am always delighted to meet another Anglophile, I told her that if she DID go, we would be happy to lend her books, maps, brochures of "must sees," give her some tips, and even help with an itinerary.

Some years later when Marla was 20 and a college junior, she DID go on a college student-exchange program, and remembering our tales of many trips to England, she visited our home, and we provided maps, booklets, and we hoped, some practical advice:

"Do not go to pubs alone. Always try to go with other students. Especially, go to London Theatre, and ALWAYS try to walk, walk, and see where the next street or turning leads you!"

When Marla returned to Niantic she gave us the news that she had met, and was interested in, some young man, and he, in her, to the extent that he visited her in college, and she made trips to visit him on her school holidays. A fairy-tale romance was unfolding evidently. Timothy, a dentist, very formally sued for her hand in a phone-call to her father, something probably NOT done in the Colonies since Miles Standish!

Morris and I decided to check this fellow out. When we were next in London, after receiving permission from Marla's family, we called Timothy Barnett, introduced ourselves and asked if we might meet him in Stockport? Since he assured us that he was in Surgery and busy during the week, we planned a weekend visit, and I told him, in my best Agatha Christie fashion, that I would carry a small shocking-pink brolly, and he was to wear a rose, to identify us to each other as we detrained in Stockport. Just as we left the train, Tim and his mother spotted us. Either our scent or our firm step gave us away!

On our return we gave a full and laudatory report to Marla's parents, Michelle and Harvey Snitkin. The following year we were told that the wedding was to be in England, but that Marla was upset at the thought that not many of her friends and family would be able to attend. Said I, "We'll be there! We'll simply arrange our trip so as to include the wedding!"

While at our Montana Hotel in London, I received a call from Marla asking if I would be the "first reader" at their wedding ceremony which was to be held at the historic and gorgeous Bramhall Hall in Cheshire. Bramhall dates back to the 13th century, and is set in unbelievably magnificent gardens. We had visited it when we met Timothy.

"What do you want me to read?"
"I thought something from Elizabeth Barrett Browning!"
Quoth I, "How do I love Thee? Let me count the ways!"
"That's the one!" said Marla.

The wedding was a lovely three-day Hoopla!

Morris and I very much enjoyed the VERY British experience, one we had never thought to witness. This was the happy outcome of what had begun in a very strange and unusual beginning of a trip, and one unique in all our years of travel.

A suitcase was lost! Missing when we deplaned at Heathrow Airport. It was

Morris' not mine, and he was very upset, and threatened all sorts of dire visitations of evil on the heads of the airline, because the valise contained ALL his gorgeous and carefully gathered "wedding clothes": his black silk tuxedo with cummerbund, quilted silk vest, his splendid tie, and his black velvet shoes.

You can imagine his anger and distress!

From the time Morris and I met, and then dated, he was very much the clothes-horse and dandy! His dress suits were formal and elegantly tailored, or made-to-order from fabric he chose, and he had NEVER owned, or worn, a pair of blue jeans.

The next few days we spent/wasted in Morris' attempts to locate similar clothes in London. To add insult to injury, each year I added to his collection of "braces," usually purchased at the Princes Arcade, and this year I had ordered, from a photo, a pair of suspenders based on Aubrey Beardsley's design, in black and white, of Oscar Wilde's "The Black Cape" from his "Salome." This same illustration was part of an Aubrey Beardsley Exhibition currently at the Victoria and Albert Museum.

The elegant shop of S. Conway, Shirtmakers, on Jermyn Street, London, catered to the likes of Princess Diana, who often bought vests for herself and others, and Mr. Conway was to call us if the braces arrived before the nuptials, when it would be added to my "dandy's" wardrobe. We had often made purchases there before.

Damn, it's only money, after all!

Morris stormed through Harrods where he was informed, "I'm sorry Sir, but we don't carry silk suits as you describe!" And so, Morris stormed out again, me in tow, and tried Harvey Nichols, in vain, and we went to one elegant haberdasher after another, all with similar results. Originally, when he complained to the Lost and Found Office at Heathrow, he was offered 75 pounds in lieu of the missing valise! Said my Hero, "THAT won't buy my wife and me a decent lunch!" There followed oaths which only I heard...I hope!

On day three after our arrival, we discovered the "missing" valise on the lounge floor of our hotel...and all was well. The mystery of its disappearance was cleared up because someone coveted the attractive cotton scarves I have always tied around the handle of our luggage, so as to distinguish them from others on the carousel. My bag was at first thought missing, but I located it by scanning the fabric, and looking for my identification tag. I was not so lucky as to spot my dandy's valise as it was black, like the many others in use. MY bag was of a printed fabric, it being well-known that outside the Avian World, the female of the species MAY be adorned in brighter plumage than the male. MY scarf had likewise vanished, but vanity had saved my valise.

My "Wedding" clothes, while attractive, would have been easier to replace, because my black linen dress and silk pumps were not unknown in London shops. My only regret would have been the loss of my elegant, large-brimmed straw Adolfo hat, which I had found by chance, in Connecticut in a small antiques shop, where it served as a "please do not sit" symbol on a couch. I had plunked it on my head as a joke, but to my surprise, it fit, looked good, said Morris in surprise, as he had rarely, if ever seen me in a head-covering, not a scarf or a cap!

I was reminded of the time I went with a close girl-friend with whom I had taught at the Grove School, to help her with her personal Easter shopping. While she sought out a bonnet, I flitted from one hat display to another, calling out to Maggie to see me in various "creations" I laughingly tried on. As I tried on an expensive "designer" creation, a saleswoman who had been watching my antics, raced over, and as though it were torn from her, yelled, "STOP! That's for a well-dressed woman!" Whereupon I collapsed in laughter, and the saleswoman realizing what she had said, apologized over and over again!

I reassured her that I was NOT insulted or upset, and that she was quite correct, although I WAS wearing a smart-enough Cashmere coat.

So ended my Millinery History!

It seemed as though Morris and I "collected" people wherever we traveled. One evening we arranged to meet with an English friend with whom we were going to the theatre, at a pub we liked. While awaiting his arrival, we managed to find in this very busy place, at the time when the people around us had stopped off before going home, the last remaining corner of a banquette, and we squeezed in next to the wall. While Morris went to the bar for his pint, and my 1/2 pint of lager, I overheard the conversation of my nearest neighbors, two young men, who discussed the "Pink Floyd" concert they were to see that night. When Morris returned with our drinks and some bar-nuts, he found me in conversation with the two, as I had read in an English newspaper, that the concert had been rescheduled from its earlier date due to the collapse of some seating.

I introduced Morris, and over our lagers, we spoke of the wedding we had attended, of one thing or another, of our enduring love for England, and of some past trips to the U.K.. Now who cannot feel pleasure at the praise of their country? We spoke of our fondness for the English theatre, and somehow the conversation turned to illusion, magic tricks, and Morris placed a pound coin on its end on the table, and told them that he would give the fellows 40 pence for every one of their coins that they upend in similar fashion.

Between them, they managed to find 3 pound coins, and placed them on end. Morris then took out 6, 20 pence coins and set them next to the pound coins, then picked up, and pocketed the pound coins!

The fellows looked at him with surprise, and a laughing Morris told them that they HAD agreed to the wager! Also, he cautioned them to not ever again be taken in by such a con! They relaxed, amused by the lesson/joke, as Morris returned the pound coins, and retrieved his 60 pence. Talk then turned to us, and to our trip, and then they told us about themselves, and when Morris went back to the bar for a refill, they arose, each of them kissed me, and left. When Morris came back, he told me that each of them had hugged him, saying, "You're a different kind of American. We don't often meet people like you and your wife!"

The statement had been made to us in almost every country or state in which we traveled. We decided that instead of writing our names and address for others, usually on bits of paper, that on our return to Niantic we would have made, what I called, "Ego Cards!" They contain our name, address, phone number, and at the bottom is printed, in Latin:

"Post Quem Matrix Fractus"

YOU figure it out!

It was on a return trip from Stockport to London that I "picked up" another man, one who has remained a friend through correspondence and visits, for a number of years. On that train ride, as we sat facing the doors dividing our coach from others, I noticed a young man whose back was to us. He sat reading and sipping his glass of wine from the bottle in front of him. Opposite him sat a young woman with a small child on the seat next to her. At one point she went to the toilet which was next to the dividing door. The man never lifted his face from his book.

I grew concerned when the child was by now off the seat and scooting around on the floor. I feared that he might try to leave the coach, or perhaps get hurt by someone's entry, so I went to the "father" and tapping him on the shoulder, expressed my concern, at which he looked up and said, "Oh, he doesn't belong to me!" At this, the mother returned and snatched up her child, and before I returned to Morris, I asked what poetry he was reading which so engrossed him? He obligingly turned the book to face me, and since we are also poetry-lovers, although this poet was unknown to me, we chatted a few minutes until I returned to my seat.

A bit later he left his seat and sat in one opposite us, and for the next two hours we spoke to Philip Lyon about literature, about the Globe Theatre, about him. He was bound for an acting school in London, there not being so good a school in Manchester. By the time we arrived in London, he seemed an old friend. We exchanged names, addresses, and as we separated on the platform, he "bussed" me on the cheek, hugged Morris, and we assumed that was that.

While in London, in Leicester Square, we boarded a bus to our hotel from an exhibition of paintings by Monet at the National Galleries, and it being crowded, I stood after locating a seat for Morris in the front section which is reserved for elderly or disabled passengers. I stood holding the overhead strap, on the opposite side of the bus, and noticed a young woman looking at a large book on Monet. When the seat next to her emptied, I sat down and told her we had also just come from the exhibit, and we talked "Art," and found out she was a collector also, and then Morris joined us, and we three spoke of his collections of puppets, my collecting Ukiyo-é, and for the next 45 minutes, spoke of all manner of things.

When Morris and I reached the stop where we were to get off and take a short ride in another direction, we invited her to join us in our favorite pub, "The Goat," which is the oldest pub in London, opened in the 1600's. She refused, saying she had to go to her office. I pointed out that this was Saturday, and why would she go to her office instead of spending time with two such charming people? She demurred, but gave us each a kiss before the reluctant parting, and we exchanged cards.

Once inside The Goat, drinks ordered, the only empty seats were at the front bowed windows. As we sat down, Morris pointed out the window saying, "Look!" Ever obedient, I looked out to see our new acquaintance, hurrying back to the pub. I waited at the front door, and she came in saying, "I thought about what you said! Why WAS I going to my office on a Saturday, and leaving two such charming people? So, I jumped out!"

Morris got her a "Shandy," a drink unfamiliar to me which consists of a lager and lemonade! Sounds horrible, but I tried a sip. Not too bad…but not good enough, I decided. And that was how we met our darling friend, Lindsay Cliff, who was a lawyer for "Yahoo!" a slim, very attractive, smiling woman, someone my parents would have called, "Sympatechnya." Over several years, we wrote to and spoke to Lindsay, but despite our many invitations to Connecticut, she was never able to visit until after Morris' death.

Some of the most interesting people we met just the day after Princess Diana's death. Since it was patently impossible to get out of London, we stayed put, and went nowhere we couldn't walk. Even the Tube trains and platforms were unsafe as they were so filled with mourners, most of whom got out of the station diagonally across from our hotel; one couldn't get on, or off, a train, or navigate one's way to the escalators or stairs, so many hundreds were there. We thought that we might leave London and go as planned to Bath and Rye after the funeral. On the day we COULD get on a bus to Piccadilly Square, we walked to Charing Cross Road, one of our favorite streets for bookstores, and while on that road, entered, at lunch time, a pub which had originally opened as a theatrical haven to hungry and thirsty actors from the many theatres in the area.

It was lunchtime and very crowded, and Morris and I were fortunate enough to find a small table next to the entrance. Almost as soon as we entered, another couple dashed in, and sat at the banquette at our right. Morris and I ate our favorite, a "Ploughman's Lunch," consisting of crusty bread and diverse chunks of English cheeses, including a huge wedge of Stilton, which I immediately halved for us. Also on the large plate was a salad of pickled vegetables, and of course, our pints of lager.

The couple began a conversation about the only subject on anybody's mind those days, Diana's death. They told us of how, getting the news while they were on a photographic safari in Kenya, they dashed back to London. We gave our version of how we learned the news and of how the tragedy had impacted us as we were unable to leave London, and compared the throngs of mourners who arrived daily, and spilled from trams and trains, everyone carrying white flowers, and children in strollers clutching Teddy bears and other stuffed animals, bound for Kensington Park which was just a few blocks from our hotel.

Every shop window was a shrine to the Princess. All were draped in black, and in each was her photo, and usually a vase in which was a white rose. Kensington Palace gates were hung with notes and cards, and flowers were heaped in front, each day more and more, attesting to the sorrow of the givers. We countered that we were never aware of public grief of this magnitude, even after John F. Kennedy's assassination, or of that of his brother, Robert, or of Martin Luther King.

This led to their story about the death of their eight-year-old son on a Christmas Eve, at the hands of a drunken driver, as the child and his friends were caroling. It was when the mother spoke of the inscription on his tombstone reading, "To our bravest little Viking," that Morris and I told them of the coincidence of our son Nat's "Viking burial at sea" and the vessel Morris had built to contain his ashes. We four pondered the coincidence of our finding each other in crowded London, and sharing a sorrow we all expressed in such a similar manner. Subsequently, they sent us a photo of their beautiful blond son, and we sent them a photo of Nat.

We obviously were NOT finished grieving, nor were they, and I admit we four hugged each other at parting, amid shared tears. Karma?

On a visit to London in 1997, while looking into the window of an antiques shop, I saw what appeared to be a carving in ivory of a rabbi's head. I went in, asked to see it, and found that what I thought to be a rabbi, was in fact, an elaborate umbrella top! Since we wanted to find a gift for Les and his family, I asked if the shop had any articles of Judaica available. The shopkeeper offered religious prints, pictures, embroideries, but No, said I, it must be something more interesting. What? I hadn't the faintest idea! Suddenly one of the women-owners went to a glass-fronted case at the rear of the shop, and produced what I immediately called "one of the ugliest, or strangest, artifacts I had even seen! What is it?"

"It's called the 'Breastplate of Aaron' and is set with 12 jewels into the gold, and with a gold chain, and it is French from about 1830, and used to be worn by the High Priests of the Jewish Temple!"

"It's Georgian!" said I.

"How did you know?"

"Because I know something of the Georgian Jewelry!" And I did, because our English antiques dealer friend, who specialized in Georgian Jewelry had taught me, in exchange for my lessons to him about Japanese Ukiyo-é…and I'm a quick study, I told myself.

"No, really, how do you know it's Georgian?"

"Because Georgian precious stones were not faceted, and the jewelers of the times backed them with pieces of crumpled foil so that they appeared to sparkle!"

"Quite right!"

"Okay, now how much is it?"

The price quoted was ridiculously high, so despite how intriguing I found this strange object to be, I fell back on my usual, "too high! Give me your best price, keeping in mind that if I don't buy it, it will probably sit in your case until the return of the Georgian Era!" I put it on the counter and made as though to move on, and she altered the price so that while still expensive, I told Morris who watched the exchange with amusement, this would be the LAST gift we would ever buy for Les, and it intrigued me, and he and I would have the fun of tracking its history.

And it did prove an exciting adventure, this peculiar artifact about which we, and the shopkeeper, knew so little, except its date! It was wrapped up, and I asked for, and received, a certificate of authenticity (I'm not so stupid as to be taken in by a shopkeeper!), and a statement as to its purported age, and so on, and the description of the Breastplate.

The following day, after wrapping this treasure (or not!) in my lingerie in the hotel room, (and why do women assume that jewelry is safe when hidden among underpants, brassieres, and slips?) Morris and I left to unearth some information about our "find."

I suggested that first we go to Charing Cross Road, and the first bookstore we entered had a section of books on Judaica. After looking through several, I saw an engraving of a Jewish High Priest wearing just such a jeweled breastplate! Since the book was printed by the Victoria and Albert Museum, we visited there first. At the entry hall information desk, I asked the location of the Judaica Art section, and we were referred to an area where were displayed ancient glassware, prints, silver cups and tankards, and other utensils used in Hebraic rituals, but NOTHING remotely resembling our Georgian treasure (I ALWAYS believe in the optimistic approach), and when back at the desk, we were NOW referred to the Book and Gift Shop, which yielded nothing, and when I spoke of the book I had seen in which I had seen it depicted, they informed me that it was out-of-print.

Back at the desk, I then asked to see the Department of Ancient Jewelry, but the very kind and patient woman asked, "Do you want to speak to someone in the Metal-work Department?"

"Yes please," and I realized that the descriptions of museum items might NOT be as in America. When the Metal-work Department was called, the patient desk clerk handed ME the telephone, saying I could better explain our mission.

I lied to the "voice" at the other end of the phone. I told the "voice" that I represented the Slater Museum in Norwich, Connecticut, and that they asked me to find out what I could about Aaron's Breastplate. Actually, Morris and I were members of that jewel of a museum which we always felt was not adequately recognized, as were others in the state. The "voice" at the other end took my description of the Breastplate, said she had never head of such an artifact, asked us to wait while she researched it, and she would contact us on the Lobby.

Morris and I sat on our stone bench and watched the crowds as they inspected one or another exhibit, and then, when our name was called, I was given the phone to hear, "Oh, I'm so excited! I have just found information about this Breastplate in the very last book I consulted, and if you will please come up to the — floor, and please get a Museum map to find me, I will have the pages copied for you of the information I gleaned!"

When we arrived and knocked at the door to her office, this dear and obliging young woman had already photocopied the 14 pages. She also told us that she intended to read the entire volume that had never been known to her. Her kindness made me wish I had not lied to her…almost…and in great and grateful excitement, we proffered thanks, and left.

…Then realized that neither Morris nor I had told anyone that the Breastplate was tucked into my scanties! And I also had a feeling akin to Sherlock Holmes and Dr. Watson when they successfully concluded a case…but I wasn't nearly as blasé!

I decided again that lying is not always such a bad thing…that it never does to reveal "all," if a fib will not cause harm to anyone…especially in a righteous cause!

On our return to the United States, we gave the Breastplate to Les, the only truly "religious" man, other than Nat we know, and in his later years, even Nat had some doubts. Les hung it by its gold chain in his living room. Back in Connecticut I xeroxed the pages to him, and made a copy for us, which contains a print of The High Priest wearing this, and its history.

During one trip to London, Morris and I went to dine at a restaurant owned and run by a friend, but when we arrived, it was not yet open for the evening, so we walked a few blocks further to streets facing the Embassy Road edge of Kensington Park. Kensington Palace was at the other end, nearest to where we stayed. As we passed a pub, and it being VERY warm for a September, we went in for a lager. The interior was so very crowded and smoky, that I felt unable to breathe, so told Morris that I would await him outside at one of the benches and tables used by patrons.

Since both were empty, I seated myself on a bench and faced the Park where I could watch some equestrians turning in, and was passed by crowds of pedestrians who spilled from the nearest tube station on their way home from work.

Suddenly I became aware of three young men who emerged from the pub and seated themselves opposite me, their backs against the pub wall. At first they sat quietly, drinking their lagers, and I, still waiting for Morris, turned to them, smiled, and turned back to watch the many horsemen who rode and turned into the Park.

The one glimpse I had of them led me to believe that they were gay, and very interestingly adorned. One man's head was completely shorn, and he sported in his ears at least six gold earrings. Another wore a colorful bandana over long, pony-tailed hair. The third was bejeweled, gold chains encircling his throat, and spilling down his shirt-front. All the three were young, late 20's or early 30's, I thought…and then understood, New York bred as I was, WHY they came out to sit at THIS bench, and not to the other. They thought that I, a woman, and probably old enough to be their mother, was offended by this pub for gays! As this went through my head, Morris appeared with our lagers and sat next to me.

"Thanks, darling. I thought I was going to gag, or faint, from all the smoke inside," I exclaimed, "and it wouldn't have helped your asthma either," I ended, with a smile at the men, who seemed then to relax their former somewhat pugnacious attitudes.

Morris understood my ploy immediately, and when the men asked if this were our first trip, he countered with, "Oh no, probably our twentieth! We love the U.K., England especially, our entire family does. You are so lucky to live here."

Then they told us that they were from Australia, that they, as video producers, had just completed some project in England, they were now on vacation and soon to return to Sidney. When they asked what we had been doing, we spoke of the New Globe, of all the wonderful theatre in England, the movies which had not yet come to America; of our collections of antiques and marionettes, our quest for certain first edition books. Then one of them asked if we had seen, "Priscilla, Queen of the Desert."

"We've seen it twice. It's wonderful and when it is released on video, we intend to buy it." Then Morris described the first time we had seen it, at a premiere at a movie-house on Kensington Avenue, at which, before the movie began, the lights went up on the short "stage" in front of the screen, and two men dressed in gold-lamé and feathers, walked onstage, and performed two of the film's songs, lip-synching the lyrics as in the film.

As we all laughed, I told them of the spate of dresses at Harrods, and indeed in almost every shop window, which were loosely based on the film's wonderfully outrageous costumes.

By this time, we five were having a gay and friendly conversation, with lots of shared laughter. Morris went inside to replenish drinks, "all 'round," and I took advantage of their friendly banter and good humor, to ask a question of my own.

"Please, will you tell me why, as good-looking as you are, you shaved your head completely bald?"

"Because in the morning, in front of my mirror I look at myself and I say, Damn I'm handsome…ALL of me!"

As good an explanation as I've ever heard, and inwardly, I applauded his healthy Ego!

And before we parted company, they said, in English laced with the charming Australian accent, what is printed on our Ego card!

Chapter 18

For the last eight years that Morris and I traveled, he carried portable nebulizers with him, to help when a spell of breathing difficulties beset him. Asthma can be very frightening when one feels oneself unable to draw a deep breath, and over time, the nebulizers and medications were a constant in his life, at home and abroad. When in Bath one year, we chanced on a nebulizer no larger than a small Coca-Cola bottle. We ordered it and had it sent to us in London.

Sometimes even the constant use of nebulizers was not helpful. We had several: one at home, one for the car, and a very small one that accompanied us when we traveled. This one had the advantage of being in a strapped case which could be hung around his shoulder and worn wherever we went. This last occasioned a strange/comical situation involving the London Constabulary! We had taken a tram to the theatre with friends, then we all went out for dinner, but when we returned to our hotel, the nebulizer was missing! Morris couldn't say when or where he first missed it, nor could I, but we immediately called the police to report its disappearance, then took a taxi to the theatre where a search was made. Nothing! Then to the restaurant. Also nothing! Then to the main bus terminal where it had not been turned in.

It was then that I recalled the constant written or voiced reminders on the tubes, on stations, and in all public venues, that, "Any object left unattended in a public place, will not be opened, but be SUMMARILY DESTROYED!" That is what must have happened, since London was always conscious of terrorist attacks by the I.R.A., or by other groups, due to the presence of so many embassies, and how often they had been targeted during the years of our travels.

Morris never located the nebulizer and it was reordered, when we made another trip to Bath where we first had seen one in a pharmacy. Now THAT was an expensive vacation! As in Mexico, when my basket-purse was picked and Morris forbade me to carry any pesos, I now commandeered his nebulizer and wore it over my shoulder when we left our hotel.

But there did come a time when even THAT, plus the medication didn't help. One very frightening night, Morris awoke gasping for breath, nothing helped, so I called for an ambulance and we went to the Westminster/Chelsea Hospital, to its emergency room, where he was put on oxygen, his blood gases checked, and where he was installed for three and a half days.

I stayed with Morris until he was given a room, and then expected to take a taxi back to the hotel, but was told that I could walk the short distance. I thought back to the ambulance trip which had taken so little time to arrive at the hospital, and seemed to arrive at the hotel within minutes of my call. After giving the beautiful Indian woman, Head of the Emergency Room, his history, I noted her sari and head covering. I think I was too worried to take note of anything more that night. By the time Morris was breathing more easily, and had fallen asleep, I left. It was about 9 AM.

Our friends at the hotel were very solicitous, and although I walked to and from the hospital daily, they insisted on driving me and visiting with Morris in the evenings when they returned from their jobs in various parts of London. I enjoyed the twice-daily walks in an area new to me, now that I was secure that Morris was well cared for. I discovered that this area was thick with clothing stores, antiques shops, cinemas, and on the way to the hospital I passed restaurants and bookstores, and lovely, gated communal gardens/parks, forbidden to passersby. Their delights were for the homeowners who lived in the houses ringing them.

I met the many doctors and nurses responsible for Morris' care, and heard from him in what ways the treatments he received, and other amenities, differed from our own fine local hospital. One difference was at mealtimes when instead of the plastic-trayed and covered dishes containing the "plastic" taste of the food, English patients who were mobile, were served HOT food directly from large vats which were brought up from kitchens in the nether regions, or were delivered to patients by the nurses. A menu described the dishes, and bed-patients made their choices.

The Rags of Time

While Morris ate, I took the opportunity to go down in the elevator to the balconied floor just above the ground floor lounge, where I ordered my Cappuccino and sandwich, and enjoyed watching the many doctors and nurses similarly engaged. If there was not an empty table, my request, "May I share?" always produced a smiling assent. In Europe, everyone "shares" table space, and so, having learned this civilized British custom, Morris and I made it our own.

One afternoon in walking through the corridors of this quite beautiful hospital, I saw that a re-decoration had graced its walls with excellent original paintings, with sculpture, and even in the tall space from a light-flooded ceiling, two or three stories high, hung Calder-like mobiles. It was an artistic treat.

Once, while I Cappuccinoed and chewed my muffin, I heard instruments playing sinuous-sounding music from the ground floor lounge, and as I looked over the balcony, saw a three-piece orchestra playing stringed instruments, and a tall, beautifully-costumed, young belly-dancer swaying provocatively before the sitting and standing visitors and staff, and in view of anyone else departing the elevators! I ran down the steps and stood behind the appreciative audience to see what was billed as "The First Saturday Concert of A Series." All the instrumentalists were in Turkish costumes. It was a most enjoyable break from illness.

When I rejoined Morris and told him of what I had seen, we realized that another country agreed with the Dutch that one might recuperate more quickly…and certainly more pleasurably, with and through the Arts. I tried to make our Connecticut hospital aware of what I had experienced, but obviously, sans wiggle and costume and revealed navel, my message didn't get across!

There occurred another welcome surprise before Morris was discharged. First, one of the physicians treating Morris handed me a personally hand-written letter for Morris' Niantic doctor, describing his admission diagnosis and treatment, and saying that he would be happy to give our doctor any further information he required, PLUS, he gave Morris a refill of his medication, large enough to "see him back to the United States!" The social worker who came to see to his discharge, presented me with the bill. The amount was such that I shook my head in disbelief.

In our local hospital, it would have cost more for just an hour of emergency treatment. The bill included charges for an MRI, and all tests and treatment procedures. When I asked whether they would accept a personal check or a credit card, I was told that if a credit card was possible, it would mean that payment was faster and easier for them. So, with our grateful thanks, our credit card was presented.

I would recommend to any travelers to whatever destination, to always pay a few more dollars in advance for medical insurance before leaving the United States. THAT fact, plus the socialized medical system in England, resulted in our payment of about 900 pounds, or $1400 American, in total. I wish we had been this intelligent before our trip to Holland, where every doctor who put his head in the door and greeted Nat, sent in a bill I honestly thought we had paid three times. Their system of socialized medicine is for the Dutch…and does NOT include visitors.

On our return to the United States, there began the slow decline of Morris' health…and of our marriage. I had long been aware that whatever anchor our son had supplied, instead of our being able to regroup, or follow some path through the remainder of our lives together, we would have to rethink our relationship, and rework our feelings towards each other, which now seemed not to have steady underpinnings.

We were now a Trapezoid, tied to each other in the center, but straining to separate at each end. To go our own ways…and make some changes.

The past years had led to an awareness on my part that I was slowly being ingested; digested; swallowed. It began when Morris' behaviour became more curmudgeon-like, and I had suddenly less and less ability to withstand his increasing criticism of me, and his almost complete negation as to the part I had played in Nat's life, and indeed, in our marriage. For a time I swallowed my resentment, and tried, as I had always done, to be the understanding and good wife, secondary to HIS utterances, never to disagree or contradict his version of some event, or an anecdote, or to voice what he perceived as a diminution of his contributions to Nat and to me, or to the "public" perception of our marriage.

We were liked. People enjoyed the anecdotes of our past, of our travels, and our hospitality, but bit by bit, my part in our lives, and my own talents, were not good or important enough, to be mentioned to anyone. Rather, and this hurt deeply, I was being returned to my status as "the good child" to my parents, as the proper "helpmeet" to my husband, with no recognition of my talents. My marriage was become like a piece of paper which was turning brown at the edges, and was slowly crumbling into dust and ashes.

I tried to halt my bitterness, and insisted on a talk with Morris, telling him of my hurt, my disappointment at the fact that he was now presenting himself as the chief and principal actor in our son's life and development.

I also made him understand that MY artistic talents were not to be dismissed so lightly. I think it made an impression, (it certainly made me smile inwardly) as he made a point of showing to friends and visitors those of my drawings and mono-prints, which hung in various spaces in our home. OR, of attributing to me some successful culinary triumphs. THIS, I admit, was of lesser importance to me. I was somewhat mollified, as I was now accorded some "separate but equal" status.

I found it the more amusing that for all the years we lived in Connecticut, I was aware that I must give my brilliant and creative husband a reputation for his many and true accomplishments.

He truly did not need access and ownership of mine. I had never taken anything away from him, and I told everyone of his talents in design and invention, and of his many talents in fields in which I could NEVER compete.

Morris was an innovator, an inventor, who had an enviable skill in meeting the needs of the disabled. All this I told everyone we met, now, I realize, rather in the same way I used to proclaim the talents and brilliance of my son, when HE could not yet make all HIS talents known. When we met, Morris told me I was "too independent," and proceeded through the years to strip me of my abilities and independence, until I was forced to confront his behaviour towards me, which evidently I had been too busy to do before…or even to recognize…or to make myself aware of my changing status.

I loved Morris. How could I NOT, with our interwoven lives which lasted forty-five years, and it pained me deeply to watch his disintegration through the years of his illness.

The Rags of Time

One year, on our return from abroad, when he complained of foot pain, of back pain, he saw our Dr. Thompson who, when he saw that on one foot, the large toe was discolored, sent Morris to a chiropodist. Of course Morris criticized her, tried for laughter in an anecdote involving her, but that was the same sort of denial on his part, as the denial when he suffered his heart attack years before.

He was sent to the hospital for tests, then hydrotherapy, and physical therapy, until the treating physician told him that he might lose that toe. Of course, as was his wont, Morris countered by brazenly telling the doctor to remove the toe, the sooner, the better, and that he was to amputate as high as was necessary to completely remove any signs of infection. It HAD been a shock to Morris and to me, when on a prior visit to our doctor, Morris asked if he had diabetes, and the doctor said, "Yes!"

It is ironic that 18 years of Prednisone, a steroid Morris was given to control his asthma, had resulted in diabetes. Yet, the word had never been said to him…or to me.

I chose to think what I have always thought, that our excellent doctor, out of fondness for us, always tried to be helpful, but he did not relish being the bearer of distasteful news. Indeed, on many occasions the doctor whispered to me, or signaled to me, to accompany Morris into his office. I was a buffer, I guess. I have always been a buffer.

Morris made a good recovery after the amputation, and when he quitted the hospital, enjoyed the challenge of constructing a false toe to replace the one he had lost.

For a while this pursuit occupied him, and then he began to research types of shoes, what was best for walking, and all through this, we planned trips abroad. And they were fun, and we "collected" more people. He handled his disability well, but increasingly, walking was a problem. We now used other forms of transportation to the theatre, to restaurants, and so, the pleasure of walking the cobbled streets, and lanes, was growing more and more limited.

The Rags of Time

In Amsterdam I prevailed upon our friends to encourage Morris to use a cane, and Morris actually bought one…which I carried, more than he used it, but we had it when needed.

Morris' diabetes and its influence on our lives grew apace. He had now to take regimens of medications…sometimes we traveled with 15 to 20 kinds of pills. Then he needed to test himself daily with pin-pricks, to keep a log of the numbers, and here I could not help him except as morale booster, to his increasingly foul moods, humors, depressions.

Our home is bordered on two sides by Dodge Pond, and until the severe drought which yearly plagued our area, the water even overswept 10 or 15 feet of our land. Years ago we had a deck built which overlooks the pond.

Our deck gave us much pleasure. We usually had our "preprandial" vodkas outside, and much conversation of plans for the future, of events and travels in the past. We focused through our binoculars at the large amounts of waterfowl on Dodge Pond, watched their mating habits and flight patterns each spring, their babies, and we kept count because there were also vultures and hawks and other predators flying above, and swimming or slithering below.

In time, having given all Nat's equipment away, the Chelsea Foundation of Connecticut lent us a wheelchair, and Betty Nazarko lent her recently deceased husband's commode and walker. Just as Morris had lent so much of Nat's computer equipment, with a Voice Synthesizer, to those we knew of with amyolateral Sclerosis, also known as Lou Gehrig's disease, we were now lent the things Morris came to need. Insofar as was possible, Morris still involved himself in the computer's use, ran interference, helped set up programs, while I served as listener and emotional-enabler to the disabled.

People contacted us through the years, even before Nat's death about the many disabilities suffered by their children, and we often referred them to Nat's wonderful neurologist, ever a friend, and interested in our family. What they reported after having seen him, was that Dr. Reuben referred to us as "Saints!"

This we discounted, as "Sainthood" was not in our plans for the future. Nor was it our desire.

The Rags of Time

As Morris' condition worsened, and he became dependent on glucose injections and special diets, we had a series of visiting nurses to check him daily, then when **he** could not, to bathe him, and with each added "indignity," his distemper and bellicosity grew. I tried hard to be sympathetic and helpful, but at my every effort to help him with any necessary therapy, I was met by yells of "Stop hovering!", "Stop trying to help!" and sometimes even, "Get out!"

So I got out! I walked the many bordering neighborhoods, tears streaming, then spoke to myself sternly, trying to pull myself together, to NOT feel sorry for myself, to remain positive, and finally told myself that I would do only what Morris asked me to do, no more. I tried not to do this with clenched teeth, or with sighs, or with condescension in my tone, and tried to come up with ideas for things to do that gave us both enjoyment, AND to regain my equanimity.

I did not want to feel guilty for being a bitch!

I also did not want to feel guilty at my increasing frustration at not being able to take his illness in stride. As I had not allowed his heart attack or Nat's constant demands to drain my energies, I now allowed Morris to try to pick himself up when he fell. When he screamed at me, I simply made myself scarce until he called for me.

But it was taking its toll, and wonderful friends were available when I realized that it was less and less advisable to let Morris drive, except in Niantic…and even then, I hesitated to drive with him after a few near-misses…and white-knuckle rides, not even in our town.

It was all I could do not to present to the public my feelings of rage that once again, I had no life that was not bounded by illness, and I cursed silently (and often, when alone, NOT so silently) as I again became a street-walker in attempting to walk away from the inevitable.

But if I walked, or jogged, or ran, it would make no difference to my future.

I tried for things in which I could lose to Morris, things he loved to do, and in which he could "save face." We played Scrabble…I lost. I messed up in puzzles he invented, I spoke of movies, and tried not to differ in my opinions. We sat on the deck and read poetry aloud to each other, discussed plays, Shakespeare, the music he most loved, and I read to him from whatever book I was currently enthusiastic about, and tried to defuse his rage and hurt over what I knew his wonderful intelligence presented him with: the knowledge of his approaching death.

Morris spoke more and more of where important papers dealing with insurance, bank accounts, and other financial assets were to be found, made sure I understood what HE wanted done with his puppets and marionettes, and those books especially dear to him.

And I made notes.

Once reassured that I understood, he seemed placated for another day.

This went on for over a year. We were evidently in another dance, a Trapezoidal Dance, yet circling each other. On several occasions when Morris went into the hospital, he evinced strange behaviour, and excoriated some nurses, and accused them of trying to kill him…and when I visited, he pulled me aside, and told me this in perfect and comprehensible French! The nurses excused his behaviour. The doctors explained that toxins were invading his brain, and that this was irreversible. I tried to reassure Morris, to joke with him, as he kept repeating his accusations against the staff, but somehow, the following day, his doctor told me that he had remembered his diatribe of the day before, and had insisted on apologizing to all attending him!

Once home, the Visiting Nurses kept hope alive by recommending certain treatment centers and dear Betty Nazarko, and other friends, drove us to these centers in other towns. Afterwards we went to Casinos…oh not to gamble, but for a noisy lunch! Morris even "quartered" his way to $2.00! To me, the best part of the Casino was the continuous self-dispensing toilet-seat covers. Now THAT, I told Betty and Morris, was a Goldbergian invention of merit!

While Morris still drove, we visited the Nazarkos who had been friends for some years, or went on "double dates" and shared many a laugh. Peter was a gentle man, a sweet man, and when he died, a year before Morris, and although Morris would NEVER attend a funeral, he insisted on going to Peter's wake, and the Church ceremony, because, as he put it, "There are not enough folks like the Nazarkos extant, who are not hypocritical, who are true friends! So remember that," he cautioned.

The Rags of Time

Betty and I supported each other's emotional needs. We still do. I remember meeting her one day before Peter's death, and of how desperate and broken she looked. For three years, she had taken Peter for his thrice-weekly blood transfusions for his type of cancer of the blood, and it was taking its toll. She held back tears as she confessed to me that HER strength was close to snapping by Peter's demands! She loved him, and in retrospect, I value her tearful candor, as I dealt with my own agony during Morris' last year.

Shall I flagellate myself for my truthfulness?

But, I wouldn't know how!

I have never asked for "quarter" for my faults and mistakes in judgment. Always have I tried to fight them with whatever weapons at my disposal…mainly, I suppose, a sense of the ridiculous, of humor at life's vagaries, has kept me from utter despair and hopelessness. My pugnacity had gotten me this far. My aim had been to never hurt anyone else in my sometimes fruitless efforts to protect MYSELF against hurt.

As Morris' last year brought more and more symptoms to the fore, and as he realized he could NOT tough it out despite his acts of bravado before others, his depression increased. Bit by bit, he became unable to handle the diabetes, to prick his fingers, to inject insulin into himself. He would not let me try to help. We had often to call upon the good services of the Bayreuthers, our Connecticut children, one of whose sons, had, since age six, childhood diabetes. They came whenever I called, hearing the desperation in my voice. Whichever of them arrived, or sometimes two or three, Morris was always appreciative and affectionate. He loved them all, Heidi, Lloyd, Jonathan, Peter, and I felt secure in their presence.

Finally there came the day when Morris had to enter a nursing facility. I again made lists and a personal calendar of the many friends who offered their service as chauffeurs. Often, a good friend took me, another came at day's end, to see me home.

For five weeks I went daily, spent almost the entire day, and sometimes Morris would scarcely acknowledge my presence, and some days he would be sitting at the nurses' station, either regaling them with stories, or giving them some of his recipes for a culinary treat, or playing card-tricks, and doing "magic" for them, and for the other patients. THOSE were the good days.

Then there were the days when some members of the medical and nursing staff complained of his incessant demands, and his outspoken criticism of them, …in French or English!

Mainly though, they liked him and his stories. About halfway through his stay, he had a birthday, and I decided that a party was called for. From a local bakery, I ordered a large, sheet-cake, specified the fresh fruit filling, the outside decoration, the message atop the cake. This was to be of a marionette, hearts, and an open book, inscribed, LUDWIG B., in honor of his favorite-but-one writer and artist, Ludwig Bemelmans, whose entire works Morris collected in the United States and abroad. My message on the cake was simply, "Happy Birthday, Darling." The bakery didn't have an image of a marionette, so I brought in an illustration from home, which they copied creditably, in the design and colors indicated. In addition to finger-foods and drinks, I brought in the original Bemelmans watercolor I had bought him so many years before, for my "engagement" gift to him.

As the guests sat near him, Morris appeared happy, and indeed this was the best day he spent in this rehabilitation facility. He seemed to pull himself together for this special occasion. Friends with cameras took pictures of him, of me perched on his lap, of us kissing, of him and his friends.

When Morris entered the facility, I informed the doctors, the entire nursing staff, of his Living Will, and that if his condition worsened, he was NOT to be resuscitated, but kept pain-free, the same conditions we imposed on our Lawrence and Memorial Hospital during Nat's final illness. The staff said that they understood, however I repeated this at frequent intervals during his stay, to anyone I deemed would listen.

Morris' condition and mental state deteriorated. All involved in his care kept repeating to me the phrase, "toxins are now in his blood, his brain, and these are what cause his erratic behaviour and outbursts!"

On days when the weather permitted, I insisted that we go in the gardens, and walk the paths around the buildings until he complained or insisted we go indoors. Sometimes I couldn't cajole him outside beyond the patio. When Morris complained of mouth pain, our dentist and good friend, Dr. David Primo, visited with his tools, actually treated his gums, made some adjustments to his partial denture. Privately, David Primo told me that the various medications were responsible for his irritated gums.

Friends were unfailingly kind and loving, to us both!

Les and his Wendy visited often, and Morris took comfort from their visits. When not able to come, they called and tried to comfort me as well, but each day I watched Morris disappear from me. The worst days were when he asked, "Where is Nat? Why doesn't he come to visit me?" At first I didn't say that Nat had died seven years earlier, but tried to deflect the question, to pretend to want to discuss something else. When I finally confronted him with the truth, his face crumpled and he wept, and then stopped asking further. I prefer to think he no longer asked as he read the agony on my face.

The last three days of his life, Morris lay curled in a fetal position in his lounge-type chair, and except for a very short period, when acknowledging my presence, or when I stroked his hair or gripped his hands, or kissed him through my tears before I finally left for the night, he was mainly far off, in some dream/ fantasy. And I sat reading, next to him, not wanting to see or speak with anyone.

I was awakened one morning at 6 AM, by a nurse, informing me that Morris had died about one-half hour earlier.

It was May 1, 2001.

What does one say to such an announcement? Nothing made sense, so I said, numbly, "Thanks, I'll be in later this morning." I called Les and a few local friends, scheduled my final "visit," and went to collect some of his clothes, give away others to their closet-supply area, and take a final leave. The staff was properly sympathetic.

And I was taken home to cry.

There is really nothing anyone can say at such a time that is of the LEAST comfort. Pain and grief are solitary pursuits. I walked a lot, people were very kind, sent flowers and cards, and all this blurred in my mind. Les and Wendy came up immediately.

The funeral company who handled Nat's cremation were called, I collected the necessary death certificates. The routine of shock and pain was reenacted. Neighbors and friends tried to surround me with their presence, but I found that I would rather be alone, to rehearse as it were, the loneliness, that would be my new constant companion.

When first told of Morris' death, I experienced a sense of relief that he would no longer have to bear his pain, or experience the frustration of his daily "dance of death," of no longer having to remember the past struggles and hurts and angers at a world which had short-changed him, as it had me! I tried to find solace in remembering his pleasure during the last birthday party. I recognized his Herculean efforts to keep his guests happy, and to see me smile, as though I were being rewarded.

The funeral director delivered to me the box containing Morris' ashes, which our dear Lloyd would help me to, once again, scatter in Niantic Bay, close to the spot where the Viking vessel had been set in the water. I couldn't do anything so spectacular as did Morris, so I contented myself in acting as "second in command" to Lloyd. I helped to set the small outboard motor-boat into the water, and on our return, tried to help him pull it ashore.

I didn't know what I was doing, so I concentrated on following Lloyd's orders in order not to submerge us, and silently mouthed my "Atheist's Prayer" which consisted of telling Morris how much I loved him, and silently recalling some of the more personal and peculiar and comical events in our joined lives. All this amid bitten-back sobs, as I told myself that the tide was already too high.

I informed whatever family and friends I still had outside of Connecticut and invited them to the Memorial I planned for Morris. Friends helped with the preparations, I ordered food from caterers, prepared some food at home, and accepted edible contributions from friends and neighbors. I made sure to have enough vodka! It is strange that even if "neighbors" are not quick to befriend, they DO know how to relate to, and party, in times of death.

The Rags of Time

Flowers, plants, sweets, cards, arrived in profusion. Shared foods seemed to mark these occasions. But NOT shared lives or social contacts.

Am I being too harsh?

Morris and I always thought that openness was a two-way street!

Lindsay came from London and her presence was a shared pleasure. She stayed with me for a week, my many friends invited her to lunches and dinners, or we dined out à deux. Everyone was as delighted with her company as was I, and she succeeded in driving me about, and for a bit, OUT of my doldrums and loneliness.

We went shopping in other towns, and one evening, after she had seen it in London, insisted on us going to see, "Bridget Jones' Diary," and it felt so "right" and was so delightful to me, considering my own feelings and experiences as a "singleton," that it showed me how other women sometimes resemble this, "my life in film" …but a better Ego, makes all the difference, I think.

Les and Wendy insisted on "gifting" me with a security system, which so frightened and intimidated me, that I never ventured to use it at all. Too much technology for a computer illiterate. Lindsay, owning exactly this system in London, put me through the paces, and I soon became proficient.

Many months later, when I failed to disengage it and walked out of the house to retrieve my daily paper, it caterwauled so loudly that I ran into the house, corrected it, just as the police arrived! I was embarrassed and met the officer, red-faced with many apologies! He kindly informed me that he had already phoned that "designated" friend, and was I all right? Not to worry, he said.

I am an unabashed supporter of our Police Department, and they have ever shown a helpful attitude.

Oh, yes, and my "designated" friend, a friend under ALL circumstances, drove up within the next few minutes! As I informed the Security Company which also called to check, "The system seems to work!"

The Rags of Time

At the Memorial for Morris, the food eaten, the drinks drunk, I informed the guests, about 45 or 50, that I would speak first, then anyone so inclined. I told of Morris as a young man, as few of those present knew him, NOT as the "curmudgeon" he was described as having become. I described how and when we met, our early shared lives, of his superlative "Fatherhood" and spoke off the cuff for about 45 minutes. Several guests wrote poems in his honor, and I was touched, as I think was Morris, from wherever he listened! Others asked questions, spoke prose, telling their memories of Morris, and a friend photographed us all.

Then everyone left, Lindsay drove off to Kennedy Airport, and my home was emptied of all but private grief, and pain, and memories which sometimes comforted, sometimes could not.

For the first few months, I dreamt of Morris almost nightly, in vivid color, and most dreams seemed to "speak" to me, or to remind me of love, long gone, of passion spent over the years. In the same way as in the past, after Nat's death, I awoke to tears and shock. When I finally turned to find the empty bed next to mine, it was with disbelief, but I arose and walked the rooms. Daily, I received and wrote notes to acknowledge the many expressions of sympathy I received.

I was not as yet to be permitted my own grief. Could I console myself, I wondered? And how does one do that?

In the public arena, I valued expressions of affection that Morris awoke in others. Morris was truly loved, by more people than I realized, as they related to me some amusing anecdote he told, or how they had been involved in some event with him. I tried to see him through their eyes. Having been so attached to him, physically and emotionally, I sometimes failed to see him as an individual entity. I was always conscious of the "WE" of our marriage. Still, today, people say to me, "I am so used to seeing you together, always, as a pair, doing so many things together." And I know exactly how they feel…and what they mean.

During the June after his death, I decided to travel to London to see to some business involving us both, and since we always preferred to travel in the autumn, I booked a flight for October 9th. I intended to go for just two weeks, and not travel out of London. One warm morning, just out of the shower, I called "our" Hotel Montana, and their first question was, "When would we arrive?" I told them of Morris' death, there was a stunned silence at the other end, then one after another of the hotel staff, and also some four or five others, guests who knew us, and were fond friends, spoke their shock and sympathy, until I, clutching the receiver and my towel, suggested I would explain when I arrived.

Then I cried.

The Rags of Time

Chapter 19

When I called Lindsay in London to tell her of my intended trip, she said she would meet me at Heathrow and drive me to my hotel. She asked what show, or concert, or opera I wanted to see, and I told her that since "Mamma Mia" had just opened, might we see that?

Then came 9/11, and the world as seen and known by the United States, again changed. Unfortunately, I who had lived through so many wars, and the tag-end of our Depression, and the many changes of public and private mores, was confronted by the possibility that travel to England would certainly not be the same as in the past. Many friends called to ask if I were still to travel, or to ask me NOT to travel! Other than to call my travel agent, and airline, to make sure my flight was still on, I was determined to go as planned.

The woman limousine driver whom Morris and I had used before drove me to Kennedy Airport, and since I had been told to arrive 2 1/2 to 3 hours before take-off, I pulled my bags-on-wheels into the Virgin Air terminal, to find several machine-gun toting National Guardsmen on patrol. This was not as off-putting as to find the area in which I was to relinquish my baggage, show my passport, answer questions, still closed to passengers. In truth, I was completely alone in the waiting area.

I damned myself for still, as always, following instructions to the letter!

There I sat in an empty terminal, clutching my two bags, my coat, my purse, and in possession of a full bladder. But I couldn't find anyone with whom to leave my possessions. And the ticket-takers and boarding pass and passport scrutinizers were STILL absent after more than one-half hour. I suppose I might have asked a strolling Guardsman to watch the stuff while I relieved myself, but

The Rags of Time

I remembered that always, the stern dictum of airline officials, was NEVER to leave one's luggage unguarded. None of the few people trickling in made themselves available, so I decided to disregard my inner discomfort, and to read my book.

Then appeared an older, well-dressed woman who limped and carried a cane. Ah, thought I, she isn't carrying luggage, and made room for her to sit next to me on my bench. We commiserated with each other for our "obedient-girl" promptness. She told me that we were on the same flight to London, that she had just come from upstate New York, having visited her son, her bags had been sent on ahead, that she lived in Plumstead, South Africa, and was en route to visit a daughter in London. Please believe that I did not ask for this information. I begin to think that there exists a placard somewhere on my body, unknown to me, that says, "Please tell me ALL, I'm a good listener!"

I didn't know if we were to be seated near each other on the plane, but in any case, I, who can NEVER sleep on a plane, and spend much time either reading, standing, or walking the aisles, told her that I would undoubtedly pay her a visit.

Finally, the counter for our airline opened, and I got on the line and made room for her with me. At the counter "window" manned by an older gentleman, before he opened his mouth, I handed him my passport, boarding pass, and with a smile said, "Sir, I travel alone. NO, no one other than I has packed, unpacked, or touched my luggage since I left home, and yes, I will need some young, strong man to lift my bag onto the shuttle…and here he is, behind me, and no, I don't know him, but he is handsome and strong! And please do this quickly before my bladder bursts!" I concluded.

The man behind the counter, smiled, then laughed, and said, "Susanna, you're a good one! A corker! And I will send your bag down to the hold, and have a marvelous time in London!"

That done, I high-tailed it to the women's toilet, rolling my small carry-on bag, coat and purse attached, after me.

It was a GREAT relief!

The Rags of Time

There was still some time before the plane could be boarded, so my new friend and I went for some food and a drink, and we exchanged stories of our widowhood. I was interested to find that despite her four children's invitations to make her home with them, she refused, preferring her own independent lifestyle in her home of many years.

We arrived in London after being delayed in both take-off and arrival. As I left the plane I said what I always say to airline personnel and crew who gather at the exit door, "Thank you for a completely uneventful flight!" My South African friend and I were whisked by, and off, and out, in even shorter time than usual, or perhaps than what I expected in these days after 9/11. My bag, and my traveling companion's were found at the same time on the carousel. We shlepped off together, dragging our luggage, and were spotted by Lindsay, and she, by her daughter. We made introductions all round, hugged each other, and voila, Lindsay walked me to her rather grand car, bags were tossed in, and off we drove to my hotel.

Once there, since it was still very early in the morning, I was greeted, hugged, kissed, fussed over, and we had a "cuppa." I left my bags, and we walked to my favorite museum, the Victoria and Albert, just a few streets away from the hotel.

Before leaving home, I had made a note to myself, that the great American glass-blower and glass sculptor Dale Chihuly, had just opened an exhibit there.

We walked into a magical stage! Glass in every shape and form, in every conceivable color, and in every display case, plus free-standing sculptures and shapes which seemed to drip from the ceilings. Even in the other galleries, and then extending to the out-of-doors, in the gardens, were fantasies in glass, too numerous to absorb at first sight. First, engorged with glass, Lindsay and I finally went to lunch on wine and edibles at the charming café in the Museum, then back to the hotel where Lindsay left me to unpack while she drove to her home. We were to meet later that day when she picked me up for a dinner at her house.

Lindsay had prepared me for her home and HER collections of antiques and more modern artifacts, in her letters to me, as I had prepared her for ours by sending photos as a "tour" of our home. Later she saw them for herself. My photographs presented room after room as though she were walking through.

363

The Rags of Time

Lindsay's home was three-storied, attached on one side, with a tiny front garden, and a larger one at the rear. It was an interesting mélange of styles and furnishings, and as in mine, filled with things she liked. Attached by love, not periods.

Before our dinner we had drinks, and because in America drinks are iced, she went to her basement and brought up an ice-cube tray. The kitchen refrigerators in European countries are usually miniscule compared to our "giant-sized," everything.

Morris and I were always fascinated to see the homes of European friends, and the uses to which these rooms were put, which often differed from those in America. The bathrooms, or toilets, were especially fascinating. I remember years ago when I asked our English hostess where was the bathroom, she replied, "Why, do you want to take a bath?" That began me on my non-euphemistic use of "toilet," if that was what was wanted! I have never taken a "bath" in the home of a friend in the States, or in Holland, or England!

I admit to using the "facilities" though, in Spain.

In Lindsay's home, in order to toilet, one had to go through her bedroom, and through tall French doors, usually kept open, to a very grand and large room in which sat a toilet, half-walled off from the tub, and across the room was a marble-counter in which sat a sink. Also present were chairs, delicate and elegant.

The bathtub was typically English: so narrow and deep, that were it mine, I would need assistance to get in, and most certainly, to get out! Morris always had my strict orders NOT to leave the premises in which there was no shower, just a tub, at one end of which was a shower which resembled an old-fashioned telephone hand-set. Usually when I yelled for help, Morris would inelegantly pull me up, and out, by grabbing me under my armpits, and lifting.

The furniture I most enjoyed in Lindsay's living room was an enormous ovoid-shaped mirror in a pewter frame which must have weighed a hundred pounds. Another was most fascinating. On a small table, in a glass-case, there was a shark's-tooth, inscribed to her when she left, with the names of co-workers, as a testament to the affectionate (I think!) description of her as a Shark in her business dealings.

Probably a pleasantry, but I did wonder how MY friends would refer to me…or in what animal form I would be sculpted? Or perhaps some other form in nature?

Oh well, if you can't take the heat…

When Lindsay and I saw "Mamma Mia," I think she dickered or "sharked" her way into the last two seats in the theatre, but I was not to complain since it was the number-one, sell-out show in London. Before the performance, came that most civilized custom of ordering our "interval" drinks. We were issued numbered chits in return for pre-payment, and went to our seats.

The story-line was as believable as any opera scenario, but who cared? The ABBA music was always a favorite for Nat, and of mine. At the interval, we retrieved our drinks from the bar where they stood on chits numbered as were those given us, and spoke happily with other imbibers.

At the end of the musical, no one in the audience would stop applauding, clapping in unison, or stomping and yelling, until the cast performed a 20 minute reprise of the show! In very un-English fashion, the audience sang along, even danced in the aisles, and would not leave until the curtain stayed down, and the lights came up!

During the week that followed, Lindsay and I shlepped to many museums and bookstores, to places Morris and I enjoyed so often. Then we parted, she to sell her London home and find another in Australia, and I, to continue my odyssey alone.

Once on my own, my many friends at the Montana took me out to dinners, out for drinks, and spoke of how they missed Morris, his intelligence and wit. They attempted to assuage my loneliness, but the wound was opened and reopened. I wanted to be alone.

Philip Lyon came from Stockport to spend a day with me. We went to dinner, and again, Morris was with me. I was kept busy, but I was not so insouciant as to always want company, to always be with these kind and caring people, to lean on, or to always be at the other end of these cords of sympathy, no matter how sincerely meant. In order to grieve, I still needed my "space," solitude, to weep, to curse my "oneness." That would not leave me so soon. That nonchalant, I was yet incapable of being!

I walked a great deal in London, sometimes for five or six miles rather than taking taxis or tubes. I wanted to savor the pleasure of the city. I had a mission, a purpose, rather than wandering aimlessly. I had two gifts to buy, one for the expected first grandchild of my dear and very close friends, Emily and George Mitchell of Niantic. Our lives intertwined in humor and friendship for over 20 years. I also wanted to buy a Victorian memorial brooch for Betty.

Both proved surprisingly difficult to locate. For Emily's grandchild, since the parents chose NOT to know the sex of the expected baby (an idea with which I concur!), I wanted something original…but what? Also, in years past, one would see memorial brooches almost in every antiques shop, but suddenly, they were not to be found.

In Chelsea's Antiquarius, a large antiques mall, in the first booth, I happened on a beauty! So, I had **that** gift. For the unborn child, I returned to the shop where Morris and I had stumbled on the Breastplate of Aaron. There I was shown something which puzzled me greatly: it was a copper plate, about 7 1/2 inches in length by 2 1/2 inches high, inscribed with an alphabet, each letter in a Heraldic Shield, but two letters were missing, "V" and "X." The storekeepers could offer no explanation, but I was so intrigued that I bought it. I did some research when I returned to Niantic, and on the copper plate itself, incised in tiny, almost unreadable letters, was:

Printed by
R. Alford, 10 Bridge St
Southwark

It was from 1820, but through the name and Heraldic designs, I opined that it was from a Celtic or Scottish alphabet. I very much enjoyed poring over books, and had the copper plate framed in colors suitable to either sex…and left the final work to the baby's father!

The Rags of Time

I didn't think of shopping for myself. The idea it presented was too final. Oh, I didn't think that superstition could ressurect Morris for me, No, just that I couldn't put him from me totally, so quickly.

I continue to wear my wedding rings.

I feel naked without them.

On a visit to one of my favorite museums, The National Portrait Gallery, just below Leicester Square, a new exhibit drew my interest. It was called, "Good King Charles and his Beautiful Ladies." On the walls of the various tube stations, usually going up or down the escalators, were posters announcing the exhibit.

I bought my ticket, and on walking through the many rooms of simply ENORMOUS paintings of Beauty after Beauty, all of whom were by a formerly well-known and admired artist, Sir Peter Lely, a Dutch-English painter, I concluded that the paintings must have been of clothes and jewels, because all the "Beauties" were fatuous-faced, with upturned eyes, and simpering, cupid's-bow lips! And not a jot of personality or character to set them apart. Perhaps in 1650, ideas of beauty in Holland were now changing? But what of Rembrandt, I asked myself? They were both artists at the same time!

I laughed my way through and past the guided tours, and the many visitors who crowded about this or that Beauty, and stepped happily into an almost empty room which boasted a glass-topped case, in which rested some historic tomes about Charles II, and came to a complete stop. There was a book held open by red ribbons which on one side gave the title:

IN GOOD KING CHARLES'S GOLDEN DAYS
A history lesson by
BERNARD SHAW

and added: illustrated by Feliks Topolski. On the facing page was a wonderful sepia-washed painting by Feliks Topolski!

As an art student, artist, designer, why had I never heard of Topolski...or come across any of his marvelously painted, caricaturish work? It reminded me of the wash drawings of Constantine Guys.

The Rags of Time

And was this MY George Bernard Shaw, the author of some of my, our, favorite plays? A history? I asked at the Exhibit, but no one was sure, although they seemed very sure that Lely was a great artist of the 1600's!

Next, I went to the Gift Shop for further information, but found nothing to help. I certainly did NOT want a book of Lely's Terrible Ladies, or his idea of vapid beauty.

Then began my crusade to find out, both about Topolski and Bernard Shaw. I haunted all my former bookstores, asked for a copy of the book, but was repeatedly told, "No, it must be out of print. We've no record of it." I kept on, going from Charing Cross Road, to the countless bookstores in the Kensington area, to the many small hidden-away shops, tucked away in side streets, several of them new to me. Finally, in Hatchards famous bookstore, celebrating its 100th anniversary, the elegantly-clad man at the front desk said, "Oh yes, Madame, we have it on the third floor, in the Play's section. Yes, it is the last play Bernard Shaw wrote. And it IS illustrated by Topolski!"

Well, I felt properly put in my place by this wonderful, older man, who seemed to have stepped out of the last century, with his black-tailed garb and haughty manner. I went to the designated area to find it empty, but then a young, slightly less well-tailored, but modishly-tweeded man, heard my request, and came back with another Shaw play, "Pygmalion." I was in no mood for substitutes. I told the young man that it was Charles II, or no one…and he left.

I was ever known for my singleness of purpose…and of men. During the last 45 years, anyway!

I left Hatchards, disappointed, but made it up to myself with an excellent lunch at an outdoor café of one of Sir Christopher Wren's churches, a few doors away. Wren was of the same era as "Good King Charles," although good mathematician, astronomer, architect, and genius that he was, also the husband and lover of just ONE, non-simpering Redhead!

My hunt continued. On the day before I was to depart London for home, I walked through a less-familiar neighborhood, in another direction, and saw a tiny but tall structure which housed an "Antique Books" shop. It was early in the day, and I rang the bell of this enchanting shop whose leather-bound volumes I

368

could see through the window. Down a tall, circular, winding stair, came the legs, followed by the rest of him, of a slim young man. He carefully unlocked the door, carefully relocked it as I stepped in, and welcomed me with, "Yes, Madame, How may I assist you?"

I do so love the courtesy which has always welcomed me everywhere in London, in the entire United Kingdom.

I explained my seemingly fruitless mission which had occupied so much of this week. He listened, smiling, nodding sympathy at my frustration, as all true booklovers understand the feeling. The thrill of the hunt! The exultation when an object sought is within one's grasp!

He said, "Please, Madame, will you follow me?" as he began to ascend the narrow, steep, curving metal stair which wound past other leather-bound "Beauties" on shelves along one wall, shelf after shelf, and the odor of leather, clean and polished, even if unread, permeated the shop.

At the very top floor, I found myself out of the past, and definitely in the 21st century. In the tiny open space allowed, was a desk, spread with books, and a computer, a large chair, and a small upright chair, undoubtedly meant for "visitors." My host immediately typed something, and on the computer screen appeared the information that yes, the book I sought, WAS out of print, that it was the last play Shaw wrote, BUT, if I wanted it, there was a very good, clean copy in Cambridge, and for about 18 pounds, it would be sent to me. Where did I live?

I told this more than charming young man that regrettably, I was to leave London very early the next morning for Heathrow, and could not bother the hotel or him, to receive and send the book on to me in Connecticut. Also, I told him that I was within walking distance to the largest, the best, new and used and antiques bookstore on the East Coast, and if the book I desired was not to be found in their acre of books, they would undoubtedly send for it. If not, then I would apply to Cambridge for it. Thank you, dear young man, my gratitude is boundless!

My book-host saw me downstairs, unlocked the door, and all but bowed me out. And I hadn't bought anything. Just made a request, and spent a delightful half-hour!

The Rags of Time

Back in Connecticut, after regaining my land-legs, over my jet-lag, I walked to The Book Barn in Niantic, its jewel, and my, our, "candy store," and put my request to them. A salesperson, Joy, by name, checked the shop and gave me the same information. No, they didn't have the book, but after punching it up on the computer, VOILA! I might have a copy sent to them from another English source, and for even less money than previously quoted. I paid for the book and was assured that on its arrival, they would deliver it to me.

Oh, Joy, the salesperson, and very much my feeling at the news! I received the volume in a plastic slip-jacket, and in excellent condition. I couldn't wait to turn the pages. Remember, I had no idea of what the book and other illustrations consisted. I was delighted to find Topolski on 12 of its 120 pages. When my "deliverers" departed, I poured myself a cuppa, and prepared to be delighted.

To my surprise and shock, no matter the wonderful illustrations, after about 25 pages of the play, I found myself unable to read further…so dreadfully bad, so dull, was the terrible prose. I could easily understand WHY it was Shaw's last play, also why I, and anyone with whom I had ever spoken of Shaw, especially with that other great reader, Morris, had never heard of it!

I found out through a booklet on G.B.S. which we owned, together with copies of ALL his plays, why we had never seen this play listed…or even referred to. It was performed (once, I ventured to guess), at the Malvern Theatre in 1939. Until his death in 1950, Shaw wrote several forgettable plays…and a play for puppets in 1949, called "Shakespeare VS Shaw." Now THAT, Morris and I might have enjoyed!

My volume, within its novelty of being, sits in my book-case not to be read again, but as an example of delightful illustration.

I was happy to be again in my "Museum" home, and tried to organize my days as well as I could, in midst of the loneliness I woke up to, and lived my life with. Friends are the one blessing I could count on, but one cannot lean on, or disturb the lives of friends, so I tried to be as self-sufficient as I could, thinking of my advice to Nat when HE sought friends, and was disappointed when their lives took them, perforce, in other directions, and away from him.

The Rags of Time

Daily I walked to shops in town, or to my "Candy Store" and ate a solitary breakfast at home while reading our daily paper, or walked to markets to buy my bits and pieces of food. For cooking, I had no patience, and now understood my mother's reluctance to cook anything. I threw away much food, which seemed to accumulate in my refrigerator and freezer, and my appetite decreased. It is hard to cook for one. Solitary dining is even worse.

It became my new credo to NEVER refuse an invitation, and I tried to even the debt by bringing the wine or dessert, or some gift, especially if there were children, and there was usually some friend with whom I could exchange a very simple meal…or go out to dinner with.

But no matter how good I thought was my adjustment, and how I tried to fill my time, my "Skin Hunger" grew.

Now there was no hand to clasp, no cheek to rub against, no body to enfold mine, whether sexually or not, so I thought of what Helen Gurley Brown once espoused in the Cosmopolitan Magazine: use your men friends, visitors, the man next door. All men, young or old, seemed to understand the need we all have for human/tactile contact. So, when people came to my home, they hugged me, or soothed with pretty speeches, and took to cautioning me against climbing ladders, or stools, to replace a light bulb, to retrieve things from difficult-to-reach places. I learned that I had indeed shortened two inches, and my hands, hitherto reliable, were slow to turn a knob, to open a jar.

I became a proficient "profaner in the wind!"

But I learned to ask for help to replace screens, or in its season, to replace storm windows and doors, to retrieve errant table-umbrellas which blew, and flew off, in high winds; to hire a gardener to do what Morris and I had done so capably and enjoyably through the years. I had the good Ego (and with some charm and wit, I must admit) to ASK for help when I needed it.

In the past seven or eight years, I have become allergic to the sting of the Recluse Spider, usually unseen, so tiny are they, but so potentially deadly, that as soon as I see an area of tiny blisters on very peculiar portions of my anatomy, I hie to doctors, or to the hospital for some medication to chase the symptoms.

The Rags of Time

Even Nature objects to my Reclusivity!

When my doctor sees an unusual blister, he says that something in my nature must attract the insects to me. Since I always listen to my physician, I keep my face away from the low foliage in which they hide, and I try to convince him that Nature, MY Nature, attracts the pests.

When a warm spring arrives, all perfume is prohibited to me, and I am as completely covered as any Chassidic or Muslim female, no matter the heat, when I am in my garden. I don long-sleeves, socks over my slacks, a Bee-Keepers hat over my straw bonnet, and much insect-spray of any exposed parts. If I present a startling and comical sight to any passersby, tant pis!

The first anniversary of Morris' death brought me, no, not to my knees, but to resolution.

I was finally going to have a life!

Mine own, I mean!

My first comical misstep was my decision that I was certainly intelligent enough to learn to use a computer. As though intelligence had anything to do with it.

Jonathan Bayreuther, with whom I consulted, thought a particular computer was just the thing for me. I trusted his judgment, not recalling that this same dear and very bright fellow had, when he was a good deal younger, ten perhaps, not only used and understood a computer (I think that by now, usage of computers is embedded in a strand of Watson's Double Helix), but that on one occasion when Morris and I took Jonathan and his younger brother, Peter, to see an art exhibition, and some antiques shops, and to lunch in another town, we passed and entered a shop filled with very upscale and elegant toys and games.

Inside, near the entrance, on the floor, sat a child's computer, and I bent down and attempted to probe its mysteries by typing something. No matter what picture or letter I tapped on the keyboard, NOTHING occurred on the screen! When I turned to Jonathan to ruefully complain, he sweetly pointed out that I had not as yet turned it on!

The Rags of Time

Then it worked, for him, that is!

Jonathan was already in college when I made my brave and fateful decision. He ordered the computer for me, plus a printer and disks, and whatever else went with this new and exciting toy I was ready to conquer.

This warrior-like frenzy proceeded from the decision I had made, to write a book, THIS book!

I bought a computer table, and goose-neck lamp, and a special chair, removed my antiquities from one corner of the family room. With great excitement, my Bayreuthers came to help me set up the table, then to install my black screen and all other alien components.

It certainly looked impressive. I was very impressed with it all, even with myself, as I pored over the completely Non-Informational Booklet, and received my first lesson from the Bayreuthers:

How to turn it on!

THEN how to read and translate the catalogue of possibilities it contained in its intestines!

In all confidence I began, under the tutelage of my friends. I kept on stressing to all, that I was to be treated as an Electronic Incompetent and Idiot! "Don't expect me to do anything at first," I said, in full confidence of my ability to bring this Monster to heel! After all, had I not trained my marvelous hundred and fifty-pound Wolf-Dane, Pepper?

According to the facile and good instructions given by my Computer-Tutors, I began…and began…and began, the next day, and for all the days after! I started that way, and was stymied by errors I made, and daily phoned, frantically, for help from anyone I knew who owned a computer, and people were kind. What they thought after my second, fourth, fifth call, I hesitate to think. (That I was an incompetent idiot, most likely. Hell, even **I** thought I was an idiot!) Daily there was a glitch, and the harder I tried to check my non-informational booklet, the more confused and frustrated I became…and the more panicky and hysterical when I was unable to access the computer even to come up with the name of my book.

373

The Rags of Time

One dog-loving friend came from another town to "teach" me, and punched in, with frightening speed, various information I hadn't even heard of, and there appeared on the screen the most confusing printouts and symbols, while she explained, "Oh, don't worry. This is just for ME. It will be all right, you'll see!" But "all right" was NOT what it was!

What it was, was so damned confusing, that I finally tried to raise a human employee of the computer company. After 45 fruitless minutes I accomplished what I considered the "raising of the dead," after planning vengeance on the television commercial and author of the non-informational booklet, which aired countless times during the day to extol the helpfulness of the company. What the man on the other end of the phone actually said was, "Mrs. Schwartz, according to our records, you have had the computer for 33 days, and so from now on, we will have to charge you $29 for information and help."

I blew! What I said was, "That's it! Come and pick up this unsatisfactory piece of trash, this lemon! I'll repack it today," but I left unsaid, showing GREAT forbearance, my opinion of this stupid and annoying and miserable piece of technology, which will soon reduce Man to his lowest level of ignorance and capability!

If, indeed, Man had not already reached the nadir of human accomplishment, considering the present state of this, which we call, The Best of All Possible Worlds.

Have I said this before? I'd rather be a dog!

And my blood-pressure which had risen alarmingly in the preceding month, went down 45 points to its former level. That is, as soon as the dratted machine was boxed and picked up for return.

Life went back to its former reliable unreliability.

A friend gifted me with an electric typewriter, one which she found no longer technologically advanced enough for her needs. I would have much preferred my W.W. II Correspondent's manual typer which I had bought years before at a flea market for $5.00. We were perfectly suited to each other, but ribbons are no longer to be found, SO, I make do with this, which is supposed to

The Rags of Time

correct errors, but just succeeds in frustrating me with its lack of response to old fingers, and in not hitting the key for which I aimed, in my haste to set down trenchant and challenging thoughts.

This has been a fascinating six months journey, punctuated by tears, angers, frustrations, and the shock that at the start of this journey has been my ready outpouring of emotions and disappointments…but all true, insofar as I can tell MY story and not cause hurt to those who may have different memories of the experiences we shared.

The photographs are self-defensive!

This is definitely NOT a novel masquerading as a Memoir! It is ultimately, the story of ME, in search of My Life.

I want.................

I want............

The Rags of Time

An Epilogue, in the words of my favorite writer:

"Follies and nonsense, Whims and inconsistencies
do divert me, I own, and I laugh at them
Whenever I can."

Jane Austen